Praise for *House of Outrageous Fortune*

"Michael Gross, America's answer to Robin Leach, takes another gossip-laden bite out of the upper crust in his dishy *House of Outrageous Fortune*. What's remarkable is the degree of access Mr. Gross was granted or finagled, a reflection that ego has no bounds."

—*The New York Times*

"If anyone needs convincing that the richest of the rich have continued to get richer, unaffected by the financial crash of 2008 and the subsequently misfiring economy, here is the proof. . . . Still [Gross] demonstrates conclusively the abiding truth of Clare Boothe Luce's observation, 'Money can't buy happiness, but it can make you awfully comfortable while you're being miserable.'"

—*The Economist*

"Michael Gross . . . rules the school of literature you might call Books about Buildings Where Lots of Rich People Live."

—Paul Goldberger, *Vanity Fair*

"All the glittery details [on] the Downton Abbey of Manhattan."

—*Refinery29*

"Michael Gross . . . has made the privacy-mad 1 percent of New York crazy because he investigates and tells their many secrets. This is called a scandal in some sections; journalistic excellence in others. Outrageous . . . fun."

—Liz Smith, *The Huffington Post*

"A steamy tell-all."

—*Radar Online*

"A lot of fun, and definitely worth a read."

—*Curbed New York*

"Gross takes a building, Fifteen Central Park West, and uses it to describe the face-off between exclusive co-ops and democratic condos, and between the old families of the Upper East Side and upstarts moving into the Upper West Side. . . . Well told . . . full of both contempt and admiration . . . overindulgence . . . irony."

—*Publishers Weekly*

"*House of Outrageous Fortune* pulls back the limestone curtain of 15 Central Park West to reveal seismic shifts in New York society and the astonishing lifestyle-without-limits of the new global elite. It's a dishy—but not trashy—page-turner."

—Barbara Corcoran, founder of the Corcoran Group
and star of ABC's *Shark Tank*

"Michael Gross has done it again! In intricate and revelatory detail, he shows how Fifteen Central Park West became the most famous and talked-about building in Manhattan: it's the people who live there, of course, and Gross gives us a front-row seat on their passions, their antics, and why they want the very best money can buy."

—William D. Cohan, author of *Money and Power:
How Goldman Sachs Came to Rule the World*

"Both an incisive social commentary on our modern Gilded Age and an irresistible peek behind the walls of Fifteen Central Park West, otherwise known as 'Limestone Jesus.' With characteristic audacity and wit, Michael Gross has deftly chronicled the immense egos (and bank accounts) of the nouveau riche who reside at Manhattan's most coveted address."

—Karen Abbott, author of *Sin in the Second City* and *American Rose*

"Want to understand what Occupy Wall Street was about? In *House of Outrageous Fortune*, Michael Gross explains it—and then some. With a rollicking, informative history of New York City, tales of mega real estate fortunes made and lost, and dizzying examples of the superwealthy's greed and ostentation, Gross deftly traces the arc of America both socially and financially and proves that the top two percent most certainly do not live like you or I."

—Dana Thomas, author of *Deluxe: How Luxury Lost Its Luster*

"Michael Gross captures the phenomenon that is Fifteen Central Park West, where creative talent, towering ambition, and unimaginable wealth instill a magical aura of glamour and romance not seen in a Gotham apartment house since the Gatsby era."

—Peter Pennoyer, architect, author, and chairman of the Institute of Classical Architecture and Art

"Michael Gross's *House of Outrageous Fortune* is a book about a building the way *Moby-Dick* is a book about a fish. History, real estate wheeling and dealing, the economics of the buccaneer class, the arcane realpolitik of condos and co-ops, even floor plans: it's all here. If you want to find out why Manhattan's skyline looks the way it currently does, this is the book to read."

—Amanda Vaill, author of *Hotel Florida* and *Everybody Was So Young*

HOUSE OF OUTRAGEOUS FORTUNE

Fifteen Central Park West,
the World's Most Powerful Address

MICHAEL GROSS

ATRIA PAPERBACK

NEW YORK · LONDON · TORONTO
SYDNEY · NEW DELHI

ATRIA PAPERBACK

A Division of Simon & Schuster, Inc.
1230 Avenue of the Americas
New York, NY 10020

First Atria Paperback edition March 2015

ATRIA PAPERBACK and colophon are trademarks of Simon & Schuster, Inc.

Brief passages in this book have previously been published in the *New York Observer*, *Newsweek*, and *Avenue*.

For information about special discounts for bulk purchases, please contact Simon & Schuster Special Sales at 1-866-506-1949 or business@simonandschuster.com.

The Simon & Schuster Speakers Bureau can bring authors to your live event. For more information or to book an event contact the Simon & Schuster Speakers Bureau at 1-866-248-3049 or visit our website at www.simonspeakers.com.

Text designed by Paul Dippolito

10 9 8 7 6 5 4 3

The Library of Congress has cataloged the hardcover edition as follows:

Gross, Michael, date.
House of Outrageous Fortune: Fifteen Central Park West, the World's Most Powerful Address/Michael Gross.
    pages cm
    1. Real Estate Development—New York (State)—New York. 2. Real Estate Developers—New York (State)—New York. 3. Apartment Houses—New York (State)—New York. I. Title.
HD268.N5 G83 2014
333.33/8   2013017367

ISBN 978-1-4516-6619-9 (hc)
ISBN 978-1-4516-6620-5 (pbk)
ISBN 978-1-4516-6621-2 (ebook)

To Ophelia

"Architecture keeps no secrets. It is the great communicator. It tells us everything we need to know, and more, about those who conceive and build the structures that define our cities and our time. We sense instantly whether their vision was mean or grand: whether they felt responsible only to themselves and the bottom line or to a larger idea of society and the world."

—ADA LOUISE HUXTABLE,
"THE CLASH OF SYMBOLS" (1997)

CONTENTS

CONTENTS

Preface

CLASH OF THE TITANS

> *Our hopes, like towering falcons, aim*
> *At objects in an airy height;*
> *The little pleasure of the game*
> *Is from afar to view the flight.*
>
> —MATTHEW PRIOR, "TO THE
> HONORABLE CHARLES MONTAGUE"

"Complete *bullshit*!" barks Carl Icahn.

The fourth-richest resident of New York City, Icahn, seventy-seven, is typically described as a corporate raider by detractors, an activist investor by admirers. All acknowledge that he strikes fear in the hearts of his prey. And he was cursing a blue streak at me.

He'd started almost as soon as I began telling him a story I'd just heard about an attempt he'd made, in fall 2005, to buy a new Manhattan apartment. And not just any apartment. It was one of a baker's dozen of penthouses atop Fifteen Central Park West, a two-tower luxury condominium then under construction at the southwest corner of Central Park. Or rather, two of its penthouses, which Icahn, who already owned one about ten blocks away, hoped to combine into something Brobdingnagian, the kind of home only a man like him might be able to afford, and more important, to fill, not just with possessions but with personality, a presence as awesome as the building's location.

But I'd also heard that this lion of finance had tried to haggle with 15CPW's developers, demanding a price cut, which certainly seemed in character for someone who'd picked fights with Phillips Petroleum, USX, Texaco, TWA, and Time Warner. But that had turned out to be a tactical error, because the developers, Arthur William Zeckendorf and William Lie Zeckendorf, the third generation of a New York real estate dynasty, weren't inclined to bargain.

Instead, the Zeckendorfs sold the double penthouse to the bidder behind door number two, Daniel Loeb, an equally prominent and pugnacious hedge-fund runner, another activist investor cut from the same cloth as King Carl. Only Loeb was a quarter century younger and willing to pay the full asking price. Which caused Icahn, on learning that he'd been outbid, to launch an epically profane tirade at Will Zeckendorf.

"'Fuck this, fuck that.' He said 'fuck' five or six times in thirty seconds, then slammed the phone down," says Will. "Dan was in there early. He was a fabulous buyer."

They didn't really know Loeb when he'd called them up just as they'd begun selling apartments at 15CPW. Icahn had gotten to them first, introduced by one of the Zeckendorf brothers' two partners, an Israeli-born billionaire named Eyal Ofer, who had invested with Icahn. Earlier that year, Ofer had pointed to 15CPW out the window of Icahn's office at Fifty-Ninth Street and Fifth Avenue and said, "Look at that." His new building, rising above the tree line on the opposite side of the expanse of Central Park, was an impressive sight.

It was also an impressive site: Fifteen Central Park West occupies the first full-block lot on the periphery of the park to be developed in decades—and likely the last for years. Its position is equivalent to oceanfront property in California, an Eiffel Tower view in Paris. Besides its immediate proximity to that 843-acre masterpiece of urban landscape design, 15CPW is also walking distance from Lincoln Center, Carnegie Hall, and the city's best stores and restaurants.

Not long after Ofer pointed the building out to him, Icahn was invited to a small cocktail party in a temporary sales office near the 15CPW construction site, where the Zeckendorfs themselves showed him and his wife, Gail, a model of the Robert A. M. Stern–designed, limestone-clad building and floor plans of some of those penthouses. One had already been reserved for Ofer, another for Will Zeckendorf. But the rest were still available, and Icahn focused on the building's thirty-ninth floor, with two apartments that, so early in construction, could easily be combined into the largest in the building, with 10,643 square feet of interior space, two terraces of 677 square feet, fourteen-foot ceilings, eight bedrooms, ten bathrooms, and 360-degree views of Manhattan and beyond. And it would cost a mere $45 million (plus $28,607.34 in monthly charges).

"We saw it, we liked it, I told them I was interested," Icahn says. "I wasn't *that* excited by it. I don't invest in apartments." But Gail Icahn liked it, and Gail wanted to move; a new building was planned right next to their current one, a few blocks to the southeast, and it was going to block the sunset from their fifty-second-floor terrace.

"I love the terraces," Icahn says dreamily. Even billionaires dream. But the risk of losing his view was real and Icahn understands risk and value in his bones. "We talked about price at the cocktail party," he continues. "I said it seemed high."

Zeckendorf recalls that Icahn offered him only half the asking price. Icahn remembers it differently: he wanted only one of the two apartments. "There was no hondling," he insists. "Bullshit."

Eyal Ofer laughs often and loudly when telling his version of the story. "Icahn has got a problem. He refuses to pay. I said, 'Carl, listen to me. This is not business. This is lifestyle. You will not find another ten thousand square feet in Manhattan. And it's within walking distance from your office because you don't like to take a car, it's too expensive.' And he said to me, 'But you want too much money!' I said, 'Carl, this apartment will be worth double. Close your eyes and buy it.' And then Will came and said, 'Eyal, you brought in Carl, but I have Loeb, who wants it.' He said Loeb wants to pay more than Carl. So I said, 'Be fair to Carl. Tell him that you've got somebody who is prepared to pay more, but we are prepared to sell it to you, if you'll confirm it now.'"

"I called Zeckendorf back," Icahn says. "He said, 'Hey, I sold it.' I said okay. I was almost glad. I didn't want to move anyway. I don't remember arguing with him. The fact that he didn't call me back was off-putting. It's not like he's a bad guy. That's what they do. He probably said, 'Icahn's looking at it, Dan, hurry up.' We didn't hear. Then I called or Gail called and he said it was gone. 'Loeb's got it.' People love this shit. I love the terraces I got."

After their phone call, Will reported back to Eyal Ofer. "He said that he had never been treated so poorly in his life," Ofer recalls. "Now, every time I see Carl, he says, 'You owe me an apartment!' But he could not bring himself to pay the full amount. And he lives to regret it."

<hr />

Like every New Yorker, Carl Icahn is fascinated by the ins and outs of local real estate. He loves to talk about it and, deep in his heart, likely knows that, after turning his back on 15CPW, he became one of the outs, which is evident as he rambles on, "Look, in retrospect, the building made sense."

The reason is that prime Fifth and Park Avenue buildings, the ones the writer Tom Wolfe called "the good buildings," are all cooperatives, not condominiums; in a nutshell, they operate like private clubs and have for years excluded people like Icahn and Loeb, the sort of rough-and-tumble, loudmouthed, first-generation rich guys—many, but not all of them, Jewish—who don't care whom they offend, guys whose hard edges have yet to be smoothed by a desire to fit in. Co-op owners are the kind of people who reject, not the ones who get rejected.

Icahn doesn't reject the rejection argument, but says what's really great are 15CPW's resale values. At $10,000-plus per square foot for its best spaces, the condos at 15CPW have defied conventional wisdom, the stagnating world economy, and, to some, common sense, too. In 2013, Sanford I. "Sandy" Weill, the financier who created Citigroup, sold his 15CPW penthouse—the second largest after Loeb's—for $88 million, twice what it cost him six years earlier and the highest price ever paid for a Manhattan apartment. "Big trophies are running high," Icahn says. "But I don't look at apartments or New York real estate as investments relative to what we do. Since 1968, when I started Icahn and Company, our annual returns have been thirty-one percent. No real estate comes close to that."

Will Zeckendorf admits that Icahn is right about what happened. "Carl just could never hit the number," Will says, "and Dan [Loeb] to his credit, when we said, 'Listen, we're talking with someone else,' he said, 'I'm there.'" Loeb had called the Zeckendorfs himself, without a broker as an intermediary. He'd heard about 15CPW from someone at Goldman Sachs, the renowned but wildly controversial investment bank, which was the third partner in developing the building. Theirs is a small world in which people want big homes high in the sky.

Normally loquacious, even loudmouthed (his pugnacious open letters to companies he feels are mismanaged are famous), Loeb won't discuss his purchase. But the Zeckendorfs are full of praise for him. "He completely flattened [Icahn] . . . destroyed him," says Will. "Full price, no flinching, no bad, naughty words."

"Then," Arthur adds, "I ran into a friend of Dan's in Paris, telling me how nervous he was. But he didn't show it to us. He played his cards like a true poker player."

Icahn played like a bad sport, they believe, bad-mouthing the building. Eleven days after Loeb signed a contract, the *New York Post* reported that Icahn was "taking a pass on his reserved $43 million condo." Sales "appear to have slowed" at the "ultra-pricey" condo, the paper reported, apparently unaware of Loeb's purchase. Quoting an anonymous source, it said other unnamed billionaires were also "giving up their places on the reserved list." That part was true. There are regrets to go around.

Though there was no direct contact between Icahn and Loeb, and Icahn says they are friends, their contest over Penthouse 39 at Fifteen Central Park West was a watershed. The clash of the titans was the first indication that 15CPW would become an apartment building like no other, a new colossus both literally and figuratively, a status signifier nonpareil, a towering symbol of its time.

It is a sign of a generational shift in the makeup of the 0.1 percent who dance on the head of the pin of American wealth, evidence of the torch passing from the aging financial lions of the mid-twentieth century to a brash new twenty-first-century crop of cats. It is also a signal of other paradigm shifts, too.

Over the months and years that followed that brief whose-is-bigger contest over that penthouse, it would become clear that 15CPW symbolized upheaval, both in New York real estate and in the upper echelons of international society.

First, the sums spent on apartments show just how much wealthier today's wealthy have become. The numbers are astonishing.

Second, the range of 15CPW buyers (and renters), Loeb's neighbors, who hail from all around the globe and are as likely to settle in London or Dubai or Hong Kong as New York, shows the new mobility and spread of great wealth; no longer is it just the product of Western European aristocracy or of American industry.

Third, 15CPW spotlights the new economic sectors that have

generated the new new money. Far more of the fortunes at 15CPW come from newly ascendant hedge funds than from traditional commercial, investment, or merchant banks. Many others were forged in emerging markets, and in the information, entertainment, and technology industries. These are not your grandfather's moguls and entrepreneurs.

Though it was designed consciously to echo the East Side co-ops that, for the most part, still won't let 15CPW types in, this West Side condo, which ten years ago would have been considered hopelessly déclassé, has redefined what first class is in New York, in America, and in the world.

Introduction

UP ON THE ROOF

> *There being no fixed caste in America, as in the foreign*
> *states, we have established a certain style of living and*
> *expenditure, as a distinctive mark of social position.*
>
> —SARAH GILMAN YOUNG, *EUROPEAN MODES*
> *OF LIVING; OR, THE QUESTION OF APARTMENT*
> *HOUSES (FRENCH FLATS)* (1881)

Fifteen Central Park West is more than an apartment building. It is the most outrageously successful, insanely expensive, titanically tycoon-stuffed real estate development of the twenty-first century. Nicknamed Limestone Jesus by the shelter porn merchants at the real estate blog *Curbed*, it represents the resurrection and the life of our era's aristocracy of wealth.

This is the story of the property-lust-making building and the cohort that calls it their tower of power. They are the newest of new money, the men and women of today's societal elite who are defining what it means to be rich. To some, they are the latest cyclical iteration of Society; to others, the latest nail in Society's coffin. No longer dignified, unified, wellborn, or even well-bred, they enjoy unheard-of incomes and the most extraordinary standard of living in history because they control the engines of today's unprecedented wealth: finance, technology, information, and entertainment. Today's cutting-edge rich profit from ideas more than products.

Sometimes they are people you barely know about. You don't see them in public or read about them in the press. But whether they are figures of wide, popular renown such as Denzel Washington, NASCAR's Jeff Gordon, and Sting—all 15CPW apartment owners—or the many lesser-known yet arguably more influential financiers, the residents of 15CPW are our latter-day priesthood of power, even as we worry what effect their use and abuse of that power is having on our world. For this moment, this house of outrageous fortune, 15CPW, is the high altar of their secular religion.

Fifteen's public story began in fall 2005, when Daniel Loeb, who once described himself and his hedge-fund cronies to an old-school moneyman as "a bunch of scrappy guys . . . who enjoy outwitting pompous asses like yourself," set an earlier Manhattan real estate record by dropping $45 million for his penthouse in what was then still a big hole in the ground. Approaching the apogee of the first financial bubble of the twenty-first century, Loeb's purchase of a still-imaginary home was an apt symbol of a new-money culture unrestrained by any sense of limits, propriety, or recognizable reality, its wealth outweighing its lack of elegance and subtlety.

As it rose out of that hole over the next year and a half, Fifteen—it's spelled out in the building's custom-designed logo—was something completely different from the buildings before it. Like its logo, the neoclassical über-condo was a throwback to the golden age of Manhattan apartment houses, which are called prewars though they were mostly built between 1912 and 1930, as well as a gauntlet before the remains of what, for half a century, had passed as American Society. The success of 15CPW consecrated a new, somewhat suspect Global Super-Society. Like them or not, these are individuals who have only one thing in common, staggering net worth, and have become the world's new ruling class. Typically in their first generation of wealth, they've made huge money in new ways. They organize their lives differently, have different standards, spend differently, and give back differently.

Just as apartments were offered for sale in September 2005, a Citigroup global-equity strategist, Ajay Kapur, coined the term *plutonomy* to describe nations and geopolitical blocs "where economic growth is powered by and largely consumed by the wealthy few." Sixteenth-century Spain, seventeenth-century Holland, the Gilded Age, and the Roaring Twenties were prior plutonomies driven by huge, interconnected economic, political, and commercial changes: disruptive technologies, financial innovation, capitalist-friendly governments operating under the rule of law, and "an international dimension" of ambitious immigrants or overseas adventurers. "Often these wealth waves involve great complexity, exploited best by the rich and educated of the time," Kapur wrote.

Kapur's plutonomists are defined by wealth, not nationality. But in the current day, the newest of the new rich come from emerging markets such as the so-called BRIC nations of Brazil, Russia, India, and China. All are well represented at 15CPW, where apartment owners include the operator of Moscow's Domodedovo International Airport, the biggest developer in Beijing, and an associate of the Indian industrialist known as the richest man in Britain. Central and South Americans at 15CPW run industries ranging from banking to airports to natural cosmetics. Israel is particularly well represented, starting with the country's richest brothers, Idan and Eyal Ofer, who come from the international shipping business, as do fellow owners from Greece, Norway, China, and Monaco.

Some owners come from countries with stable governments and economies, but many do not, and for them, 15CPW serves as an insurance policy against the possibility that in their native lands their luck might turn or their connections fail them. Far better to have assets in a country where the rule of law is secure and property rights respected. "If you buy here, it's yours," says an Indian-born banker who lives in 15CPW. "There are only two places that are safe havens like that, London and New York. The rest of the world is scary, unstable."

But those emerging nations are hardly the only sources of today's outrageous wealth. The reinterpretation and loosening of many Depression-era laws that restricted the activities of financial institutions beginning in the 1960s, and the deregulation of financial markets in the early 1980s, led in 1999 to the repeal of Glass-Steagall, the 1933 law separating investment and commercial banks, unleashing what Kapur calls a "massive premium," a torrent of raw gains for a small few that inflated bankers' wages, bonuses, and egos and led to the creation of too-big-to-fail financial institutions such as Citigroup, AIG, Bank of New York Mellon, Barclays, Credit Suisse, Deutsche Bank, Goldman Sachs, ING, JPMorgan Chase, Morgan Stanley, and the Royal Bank of Scotland. Each is represented at 15CPW. Former executives of the defunct Lehman Brothers round out its financial cast.

An even larger cohort of 15CPW residents comes from the alternative-investment universe, where they've earned disproportionate incomes both by betting on markets and backing the entrepreneurs whose innovations drove the economy of the last three decades. The contours of alternative investments are often indistinct, as they are typically complex, hard to define, illiquid, and lightly regulated, if at all. But to generalize, they are investment products designed for institutions and high-net-worth individuals that are *not* traditional cash, stocks, or bonds. Hedge funds such as Daniel Loeb's Third Point are alternatives, and so are private-equity, real estate, commodities, troubled-asset, biotech, and emerging-market funds.

Adding up the aggregate assets managed by the hedge funds and boutique investment firms whose executives own or rent 15CPW apartments is an inexact business, but combining their boasts with reported guesstimates yields a staggering number: about $437 billion. No wonder residents refer to it as Hedgie Hive.*

That's just the beginning.

These investment executives' neighbors at 15CPW include executives and alumni of our era's great innovators: tech giants such as Google (Omid Kordestani, a sales and marketing executive, paid about $30 million for a duplex next door to Sting's), Garmin (Min Kao, the founder, has a half-floor penthouse), Intuit, and Yahoo! (Roberta Campbell, the ex-wife of the chairman of the accounting software company, lives next door to the search giant's cofounder, Jerry Yang), and smaller, but still massively profitable enterprises engaged in hardware and software, advanced medicine, biotech, and biopharma.

By merging ideas and the means to communicate them, technology has also geometrically increased the audience for the information and entertainment industries. Thanks to the "audience magnification" brought about by globalization and instant distribution, Kapur says, "the monetization of talent is a lot bigger now, and talent creators get to keep a lot of that." Thus, international celebrities such as Sting, Denzel, NASCAR's Gordon, and NBC sportscaster Bob Costas, and renters Mark Wahlberg, Kelsey Grammer, and New York Yankee Alex Rodriguez, live at 15CPW alongside their titular bosses, infotainment moguls such as the writer-producer

---

*Among them are Titan Capital, Canyon Capital, SAC Capital, CCMP Capital, Duquesne Capital, Joho Capital, Kingdon Capital, Knighthead Capital, Millennium Capital, Point State Capital, Vedanta Capital, Kilmer Capital Partners, Meridian Capital Partners, Arts Capital Management, Goffe Capital Management, Davidson Kempner Capital Management, Och Ziff Capital Management, Capital Research and Management, Brevan Howard Asset Management, Citadel Asset Management, Marble Bar Asset Management, Visium Asset Management, Marathon Asset Management, Deerfield Management, RBC Wealth Management, Aurora Investment Management, Area Partners, Jana Partners, OpusPoint Partners, Realm Partners, D. E. Shaw, J. Goldman & Co., Urdang Real Estate Investment Advisors, Perella Weinberg, and JGP Gestão de Recursos of Rio de Janeiro.

Norman Lear, Disney chairman Alan Horn, NASCAR chairman Brian France, and Comcast's Brian Roberts, Stephen Burke, and Edward Snider. They don't need big names; their control of the pipes through which content is pumped ensures their fortunes.

There have also been more traditional wealthy types at Fifteen, including executives of the pharmaceutical giant Merck, MetLife, Princeton Information, Hearst Newspapers, and the big-four auditor Deloitte & Touche; the chairmen of legal giants such as Cadwalader, Wickersham & Taft and Case & White; energy-company executives; brick-and-mortar retailers such as The Limited's Leslie Wexner, Eric Smidt of Harbor Freight Tools, and Eugene Kahn, a former chairman of May Department Stores; doctors, surgeons, and health-care executives ranging from a vice president of corporate affairs at Pfizer to the owner of a small but thriving chain of dental clinics; and a raft of real estate developers, operators, investors, and brokers.

Apartments at 15CPW initially sold for as little as $2 million, so the building also attracted comparatively small-change types: a TV writer, an editorial cartoonist, and myriad small businessmen and women. Entrepreneurs-in-residence have included the owners of jewelry stores, Chinatown funeral homes and florists, a luxury travel agency, a metal framing and trucking group, several human resources companies, and two nutritional-supplement dealers, but also Beny Alagem, a onetime Israeli tank commander who bought the name Packard Bell out of bankruptcy and turned it into a thriving computer company before segueing into the hotel business with his purchase of the Beverly Hilton; Gerardo Capo, a Cuban émigré who became a controversial Miami developer; Marvin Shanken, the former investment banker who created *Wine Spectator* and *Cigar Aficionado* magazines; and Jesse Itzler, who started his professional life as a Jewish rapper but segued into private aviation as a founder of Marquis Jets.

Compared to those "good buildings" of the East Side, precious little inherited wealth is at 15CPW. What there has been tends toward the untraditional, at least by the standards of Manhattan trophy apartment houses. James Kohlberg, whose father was a founder of Kohlberg Kravis Roberts, the private-equity firm, and Andrea Kerzner, whose father, Sol, a Russian Jew from Johannesburg, developed Sun City, Africa's most famous resort complex, count as old money at 15CPW. Other heirs-in-residence have included Tyler Alexandra Gallagher Ellis, daughter of the late fashion designer Perry Ellis; Deborah Simon, daughter of a co-owner of shopping centers and the Indiana Pacers; Sultan Ahmed al-Qasimi, a crown prince of one of the United Arab Emirates; Caroline Lieberman, an heiress from a fashion and real estate fortune built by a Holocaust survivor in Sydney, Australia; and Ekaterina Rybolovleva, the elder daughter of the Russian potash oligarch Dmitry Rybolovlev, who bought that $88 million apartment for her out of the goodness of his heart or, as his estranged wife has charged in their divorce, in order to shelter some of his multibillion-dollar fortune.

As the Rybolovlev example shows, 15CPW apartments aren't only homes; they're "very expensive toys for plutonomists," says Kapur. "We underestimate how rich the very rich are. For them, the fraction they are spending is not that large. You and I show off our cars. Global plutonomists need that apartment, the fine wine, the gold, the Degas" to demonstrate who they are. Their toys also serve as banks, or what Kapur calls "a store of value." Apartments at 15CPW are often second, third, or fifth homes, and they are not rented out to pay expenses; they sit empty for months at a time. When banks and politicians dilute currencies such as the dollar and the euro, hard assets "tend to do quite well," says Kapur. "They hold their value in times of financial debasement." And at 15CPW they appreciate.

Arthur and William Zeckendorf, 15CPW's lead developers, are grandsons of the real estate legend William "Big Bill" Zeckendorf and learned invaluable lessons at his knee. Big Bill was an energetic dynamo who owned the Chrysler Building and a vast swath of western Los Angeles. He developed Roosevelt Field on Long Island, the first giant suburban shopping mall; southwest Washington, DC; Century City in Los Angeles; the Mile High Center in Denver, Colorado; Place Ville Marie in Montreal, Canada; the Society Hill towers in Philadelphia; University Towers in Chicago; and Kips Bay, Lincoln Towers, and Park West Village in New York.

But he was disdained by the very people who owned the buildings he managed and who occupied those he owned. They considered Zeckendorf a crude operator who should be kept, to use their phrase, below the salt. His attempt to move into 740 Park Avenue was rebuffed—while he owned it!—by the building's snootier occupants. Fifty years later, his grandsons saw the new Global Super-Society rising and looking to New York as one of the few true world stages on which to strut their stuff—as well as a safe place to stash their fortunes. Like their grandfather had been, this new society's members were often disdained as crass. The Zeckendorf brothers, who knew the type well, decided to build them a home. They made a fortune of their own in the process.

Outwardly at least, the new society has no cohesiveness or any guiding principle aside from the accumulation of almost unbelievable sums of money, which gives its leaders unprecedented clout in a world that now, to twist the well-worn phrase, cares more about the price of everything than it does the value of anything. Like F. Scott Fitzgerald's Gatsby, the members of this ultramoneyed class want not just homes but the consoling mirror image of other freshly minted sultans. They won't submit to being judged by snooty sorts with smaller bank balances but lofty self-regard.

The Zeckendorfs replaced the exclusionary principle that had long defined New York's so-called good buildings: the co-op–versus–condo distinction so basic to New York real estate yet mysterious elsewhere. Condos gave customers the ability to *buy* what would once have required them to *belong* to a selective cooperative, the bedrock of a society that like its doyenne, the last Mrs. Astor, is dead and buried.

In the process, Big Bill's grandsons turned a drab nonneighborhood into the center of a magnetic community for the upper strata of society. They linked what had once been the mixed-use West Side—a neighborhood considered middle-class, ethnic, and *deuxième*, despite a fringe of mansions, a smattering of architecturally significant buildings, and the culture hub of Lincoln Center—to the international condo corridor along Central Park South and the patrician Upper East Side. They changed the city's center of residential gravity, dragging it west with the brute force of filthy lucre.

Fifteen represents a massive paradigm shift in the lifestyle of New York's rich and famous. For centuries, they had followed a well-worn path when choosing where to lay their heads, and the city's aristocratic district moved with them, rising steadily northward from Trinity Church and St. Paul's Chapel in lower Manhattan to the crossroads of Lafayette and Bond Streets in today's NoHo to the town houses surrounding Washington Square, and then up the center of the island until the first famous Mrs. Astor, who'd created a list of the city's four hundred worthies, built her last house, a limestone château, at Fifth and Sixty-Fifth Street in 1893. By the time she died, the city's elite had taken their first tentative steps out of private mansions and into the shared ones originally known (and disdained) as French flats, though flats (or living quarters occupying a single floor of a larger building) were already common in London, Edinburgh, and Vienna. Vulgar as they were, French flats were considered far superior to the shared lodgings known as tenements, a common-law term that, in New York in the 1830s, came to refer to housing for the lower classes.

The first luxury apartment house, designed by the eminent architect Richard Morris Hunt, had been erected in 1869 just below

Gramercy Park. "Young people of the highest genealogical merit," as the writer Lloyd Morris put it, soon filled the place, but that still didn't lift the stigma attached to apartments, and most proper New Yorkers wouldn't think of living in one; they were barely less disreputable than the hotels that had begun appearing downtown in the 1830s. Not until the first decade of the twentieth century did the city's elite gravitate to apartments bounding the east side of Central Park. The completion of 998 Fifth Avenue in 1912, a luxury apartment building by the architects McKim, Mead & White, marked a turning point. The neighborhood—Fifth to Lexington Avenues between Fifty-Ninth and Ninety-Sixth Streets—became Manhattan's Gold Coast. And so it would remain for a hundred years.

<hr />

Fifteen Central Park West sits on a cartographic and sociological hinge. To its south are the business district of midtown and the cacophony of Times Square. To the southeast is the Central Park South corridor, historically lined with tony hotels. To the north is the wealthy eastern edge of Manhattan's West Side, where blue bloods once never tread. Central Park West and environs attracted a raffish, ethnically diverse aristocracy—artists, "show" people, wealthy Bohemians, even criminals—housed in palatial apartment houses, beginning with the Dakota, and later the Majestic, the Beresford, the San Remo, and the Century. Most of its older buildings are cooperatives, which represent a lifestyle and a phenomenon distinct if not unique to Manhattan.

Condominiums, where purchasers buy real property—their apartments, the walls, the floors, the space—and then pay taxes on them and common charges to keep up the building wrapped around them, are familiar to most Americans. Cooperatives are corporations and their occupants collectively own them as shareholders. Their shares give them the right to occupy the space they've "bought," which is actually secured for their individual use by a document called a proprietary lease. The shares associated with each lease are apportioned by apartment size and amenities, so a penthouse tenant will generally have more shares than the "owner" of a same-size ground-floor unit. Condominiums are generally loose with their rules. Owners can freely alter and sublet their apartments and sell them to whomever they wish. The co-ops of Fifth and Park Avenues (and the rest of Manhattan) are very different creatures, restricting their cooperators in myriad ways. Thus they typically cost less than condos. But condo monthly carrying costs are usually higher since co-ops generally carry mortgages and condos may not.

Co-ops first appeared in the 1880s, conceived as clublike residences for the like-minded—artists, initially—who chose to live together, holding their building and all its apartments in common. This bohemian ideal evolved into something altogether different by the 1920s, symbolizing exclusivity, allowing the wellborn, the wealthy, and the well-connected, until then used to their own homes, to share their collective living quarters, secure in the knowledge that they were among their own kind and could easily exclude anyone they felt would not fit in. Some co-ops were conceived and functioned like private clubs. The offspring of Henry Phipps, Andrew Carnegie's partner in the steel business, for instance, built One Sutton Place South for themselves and their friends.

Though other co-ops weren't quite such inbred affairs, they nonetheless had a social dimension. Executives of the Chase bank led by James T. Lee, Jacqueline Bouvier Kennedy's grandfather, were behind 740 Park, and they and their nouveau riche friends were among its first occupants. But they built 740 on property owned by the Brewster family, which had come to America on the *Mayflower* and was given the building's best apartment in exchange for its land.

"Developers offered [co-ops] to a simpatico group of people," says architectural historian Andrew Alpern. "Such buyers didn't want to mingle with those with whom they did not feel comfortable. Just as they wouldn't invite people outside their own circles into their own homes for a party, they wouldn't want to live next to those people, either. It was the sort of thing you didn't talk about. Everyone knew. You would invite these people but not those people. It was never voiced except perhaps when you explained to your children who was NOSD—not our sort, dear. They were the ones who didn't know how to behave, how to dress; they didn't belong to the right clubs."

Even today, woe and rejection meet any attempt by an Arab sheikh, Latin potentate, or Russian oligarch who tries to buy a home in one of the traditional "good buildings." The resistance of cooperatives and their owners to change made today's luxury condominiums inevitable.

A Roman Law of Condominium was established in the sixth century BC, allowing for individual ownership of a portion of a structure, joint ownership of the land it sat on, and communal responsibility for its maintenance. Condos were also known in Latin America and Europe, but the American condo is a relatively modern phenomenon. In 1961, a new law empowered the Federal Housing Administration to provide mortgage insurance on condos. They remained illegal in New York, however, until March 1964, when mortgage lenders and builders who hoped to encourage development won the day and New York became the forty-first state to allow them.

The first was the St. Tropez, completed in January 1965 at First Avenue and Sixty-Fourth Street. The dark brown building boasted a courtyard driveway, underground garage, and a forty-four-foot-long outdoor swimming pool on a setback rooftop—and appealed to the habitués of the surrounding singles' bar strip on First Avenue. The first truly luxurious condo followed. Early in 1970, along with other developers, Aristotle Onassis, the Greek shipping tycoon who owned Olympic Airways and had married Jacqueline Kennedy two years earlier, undertook a fifty-story office tower called Olympic Tower that would morph into an office-residential hybrid with 225 condos on its top twenty-nine floors. The age of the luxury condo had arrived.

Olympic Tower and the other pricey condos that followed it were clustered on and around the chic shopping corridor of Fifth Avenue between Rockefeller Center and Grand Army Plaza, the gateway to Central Park. But in heavily trafficked midtown, they appealed more to singles than to families, more to transients and wealthy foreigners seeking pieds-à-terre than to dyed-in-the-wool New Yorkers who cared about a location's quality of life as much as its centrality.

Well into the nineties, co-ops still attracted old and grounded buyers, while condos appealed to newer, faster money, and those with what one broker calls a "Swiss banking mentality" who wouldn't reveal their finances to their wives, let alone a co-op board. But the tide turned as the twentieth century ended. Despite their awesome self-regard, co-op dwellers began to seem not just embattled but impoverished, insular, and increasingly irrelevant next to the brainy, brassy, free-floating, once "suspect" sorts who were redefining not only what it means to be nouveau riche, but altering the axis of the whole world social order. The new breed, whether they were rappers or Russians, bought condos, not co-ops.

Suddenly, "the idea that you need a fancy co-op to be socially acceptable is gone with the wind," says Elizabeth Stribling, founder of an eponymous brokerage. "New York has become much more of a moneyed town, and buildings are now being created for them. Money trumped the club."

Today's individuals of great wealth don't want to be known as members of a set. Unlike their immediate predecessors in the Forbes 400, they profess no desire to assimilate into anything other than the floating crap game of wealth. Society was once defined by geography; even if you belonged to the jet set, you came from Rome or Paris or London or New York. Today, what matters seems to be continued accumulation, which makes rootlessness a virtue, and belonging, cohesiveness, and obligation vestigial. There's no need to assimilate when your money, not your country, your family, or old friends, is what defines you. "It's a different kind of club," says a 15CPW apartment owner. "You just need a big checkbook."

Buildings such as Fifteen have been called redoubts of the .01 percent, symbols of a self-perpetuating conspiracy designed to protect its wealth and privilege while denying them to the 99.99 percent outside its walls. The presence of Goldman Sachs, the much-reviled investment bank, among the investors in the building, and of numerous Goldman Sachs bankers and friends among its residents seems to support such a theory. But where cooperatives have actually functioned like secret societies over the last century, the rootlessness that defines those attracted to today's luxury condos argues against such a notion. Fifteen people are guilty of cosmopolitanism, but not conspiracy.

Yes, they sit on the same boards, attend the same conferences, share the same investment bankers, golf clubs, and schools for their children. They can, if they choose, hobnob with others occupying the same socioeconomic stratum, but "this is global as opposed to local connectivity," says Ajay Kapur. "You can't have both astronomical prices and local buyers." The local elite, at least in world cities, has become an endangered species.

The new global super-elite, though it enjoys the benefits of life in New York, adopted some of its predecessor's superficial trappings, and has developed a taste for unique experience, extreme quality, and personalized service, is still new to the territory and unsure of its footing. In its first generation of wealth, this new society remains tentative and resistant to the sort of assimilation that would make it a cohesive force with shared socioeconomic interests. Living under the same roof is one thing. Living under collective rules is precisely what these people have chosen to avoid by living in condominiums. For the atomistic cohort that cohabits at 15CPW, it's still every man for himself.

Part One

THE OTHER GOLD COAST

*He who considers things in their first growth
and origin, whether a state or anything else,
will obtain the clearest view of them.*

—ARISTOTLE

New York is not always kind to those who seek to leave their mark on it. Some names persist, sticking to streets and alleyways like gum to a shoe, even after the people behind them are forgotten. Names disappear, washed away in sudden storms or slowly eroded until nothing is left save a shadow of a memory.

John Somerindyck's name, for instance.

On October 19, 1784, Somerindyck bought two hundred acres on the west side of Manhattan from the new New York State's Commissioners of Forfeiture, who'd taken it away from the Tory de Lancey family after the American Revolution. The de Lanceys were the namesakes of today's Delancey Street, a Lower East Side thoroughfare commemorating a colonial-era chief justice of New York, a descendant of a French Protestant who came to New York to escape religious persecution in 1686.

That first de Lancey married a Van Cortlandt (later namesakes of a Bronx park), became a merchant, and rose in politics to membership on His Majesty's Council of the British Province of New York. He acquired what later became Somerindyck's farm in the early eighteenth century. Left to his children, it came to be owned by James, a grandchild whose service as a lieutenant governor of the British province during the Revolution led, after the war, to a charge of treason and the forfeiture of his land.

John Somerindyck died without a will in 1790, and his children divided up the farm and over the years sold it off. The block where Fifteen Central Park West now stands belonged to Abigail Somerindyck Thorn, a widow. With a later husband, William Cock, she occupied a rambling, one-story Dutch-gabled house with an attic in a dense forest about nine blocks north and west of today's Amsterdam Avenue. In 1826, their land was sold. In the meantime, the onetime Indian trail called Bloomingdale Road when it first opened in 1703—today's Broadway—was narrowed and widened again, and in 1867, it was rebuilt as a grandiose roadway called the Boulevard. Bloomingdale Road was and remains the spine of Manhattan.

Bloomingdale was an anglicized version of Bloemen Daal, or "valley of flowers"; it was a beautiful wilderness named for a flower-growing region of Holland. Manhattan's earliest European settlers called the island New Amsterdam, until it was seized by the British in 1664 and renamed. The closest thing to a community in the vicinity of today's 15CPW was Harsenville, centered on today's Seventy-Seventh Street, the southernmost of a string of hamlets off Bloomingdale Road. The local gentry clustered uptown on the elevated banks of the North (now Hudson) River. Their string of river-view estates "was the Newport of New York in the olden time," between the 1750s and the 1890s, said a 1901 real estate promotion brochure, "the watering place of the wealthy, the resort of distinguished strangers, and the place, above all others near the city, where social delights were the study and business of summer life." But the presence of swells notwithstanding, the two square miles of land on the West Side was not seen as swell.

In 1811, an official commission created a plan for the undeveloped part of Manhattan Island, most of the island, a rectangular grid, detailed down to streets and property lines, all the way north to Washington Heights, with wide, numbered north-south avenues and narrower cross streets intersecting them at regular intervals. Thirty years later, developers focused on and rapidly consumed the available land on the East Side—mostly level, it was easy to build on. The craggy, inhospitable West Side plateau was home only to what local historian Peter Salwen called "humbler settlements," those hamlets off Bloomingdale Road as well as lesser ones populated by the poor, including one in what is now Central Park, then the site of a reservoir, the city's first man-made source of water.

Just inside the future park at Eighty-Fifth Street, several free African-American laborers had bought small parcels from an English family, and on the steep, rocky land a squatters' community of about 250 sprang up with dozens of homes and shanties built of boxes, timbers, flattened tin cans, and other found material. Immigrants, freed or escaped slaves, and displaced American Indians occupied those structures, and even nearby caves. "A suburb more filthy, squalid and disgusting can hardly be imagined," observed a contemporary quoted by Salwen in his book *Upper West Side Story*. Dubbed Seneca Village, it lasted until the mid-1850s, when a civic experiment—the creation of a public park—caused its eviction and set the stage for the development of the West Side.

New York's population had exploded, pushing its boundaries ever northward. The city's outer limits were settled by the working and the criminal poor, some of whom squatted on whatever open land they could find on the rough, ravine-crossed western plateau. Some large estates were converted to inns in the 1840s, when a day in the country meant a trip to the West Side. But a cholera epidemic in 1849 caused wealthy residents to flee, and the arrival of a railroad on the riverbank in 1851 sealed the doom of the great riverside estates. The whole district was given up to squatters and wandering goats.

Before the Civil War, an American gentleman returned from a grand tour of Europe with the notion that his city, to be world-class, needed a great public park. He and some like-minded men of wealth and influence focused on a large piece of land on the East River, but as so often happens in New York, bitter argument followed. The board of the Croton Aqueduct floated the notion that a "central" park would better serve the city and could include a new water reservoir. They pointed out that a swath of craggy, uneven, swampy land to the west would be much cheaper to acquire. The 778 acres in question were, like the rest of the West Side, "rocky and precipitous," with ninety-foot outcrops, ledges, huge boulders, ridges, furrows, ravines, irregular plateaus, and watery spots that could turn into swampy breeding grounds for cholera, malaria, and even yellow fever.

In 1854, the New York State legislature approved that "central" park after "wealthy New Yorkers—motivated by a combination of private greed, class interest and a sense of duty as the city's 'leading' citizens . . . carried the day," Roy Rosenzweig and Elizabeth Blackmar wrote in *The Park and the People*, their history of Central Park. That the mayor then, Fernando Wood, owned land alongside the proposed park was likely not a coincidence. Two decades later, he would buy still more property adjacent to the park. For a time, he even owned a lot on the block where Fifteen Central Park West now stands.

Four years after the park was authorized, the land was bought and its residents cleared. That was both good and bad for the West Side. It would soon profit from proximity to the future Central Park, but first it faced an immediate problem. Dislodged from their squats in the underconstruction oasis, the poor—many of them honest laborers, but some of them vagrants and criminals—migrated west to Bloomingdale Road. Their shabby villages, where dog packs and bands of thugs roamed freely, set a bad image for the West Side, one that worsened after the financial Panic of 1873.

Central Park was finished that year. Frederick Law Olmsted, a progressive journalist and landscape designer, and his partner, an English architect, Calvert Vaux, had won the competition to design it with a plan later hailed as one of the world's greatest works of landscape architecture. The public was so eager for it that as early as winter 1858, a lake at West Seventy-Third Street filled with ice-skaters. By 1861, the southern end of the park was nearly complete, and its effect on the streets to the west was immediate.

Public transportation, like wealthy tastes, had long veered toward the east side of Manhattan. Only a stagecoach on Bloomingdale Road had served West Siders, but in 1852, construction of a horse-drawn streetcar line was approved and then slowly built and opened as far as Eighty-Fourth Street, setting off a speculative bubble in the late 1860s. Land prices tripled until the Panic, when many speculators went broke. So many who lost their shirts in that collapse were German Jewish immigrants that the West Side was briefly nicknamed the Hebrew Graveyard. "Jews couldn't own property in Europe," says architectural historian Andrew Alpern, "but they could here. Land was cheaper, so they ended up on the West Side."

In 1867, the city's administration had commissioned a West Side master plan that reinvented Bloomingdale Road as a European-style, tree-lined boulevard, beginning at a new traffic circle, dubbed the Grand Circle, at its intersection with Fifty-Ninth Street (*its* name wouldn't be changed to Central Park South until 1896). Officials predicted that a gracious new bedroom community would spring up beside it. That didn't happen, but a sewage system was nonetheless built, streets were cut, and water and gas lines were laid. Though still mostly empty, the West Side had state-of-the-art infrastructure.

Finally, an elevated railroad, popularly known as the El, opened

on Ninth Avenue,* up to Eighty-First Street in 1879, and a significant psychological barrier was overcome. At the same time, the
economy improved. Development of the West Side became a serious
possibility—but still, it wasn't realized. On Fifty-Ninth Street, right
at the gateway to the West Side, a stockyard and abattoir, when winds
blew wrong, served as a repellent. The predictions that the Boulevard would soon be lined with mansions like those on the Champs-
Élysées in Paris proved overly optimistic, too. Landowners on what
was touted as soon to become "the finest residence boulevard in the
world" held out for unreasonable prices. When West Side development finally did begin, it happened almost everywhere but along the
Boulevard. In 1878, *Real Estate Record and Building Guide*, which had
earlier deemed the west end "the cheap side of the city," flatly declared that Central Park had "failed as a device for attracting fashionable residence."

⚬⚬⚬⚬

Today, Edward Clark is remembered as a visionary, but in the 1880s,
many thought the president of the Singer Sewing Machine Company a damned fool. Clark paid $280,000 for a block along Eighth
Avenue from Seventy-Second to Seventy-Third Streets—close
to the Ninth Avenue el stop—and began erecting an eighty-five-
apartment, eight-story apartment house on about twenty lots there.
He'd decided to promote the West Side as a new upper-middle-class
neighborhood and wanted to give its streets and buildings names
inspired by the American West: he proposed that Eighth through
Eleventh Avenues be renamed for Montana, Wyoming, Arizona, and
Idaho. In the same vein, he named his yellow-brick apartment château—a riot of turrets, gables, cupolas, dormers, finials, and iron-

---

*In 1890, Eighth, Ninth, and Tenth Avenues would be respectively renamed Cen-
tral Park West, Columbus Avenue, and Amsterdam Avenue.

work mythological beasts designed by Henry Hardenbergh, later the architect of the Plaza Hotel—the Dakota.

Clark conceived of the Dakota as a palace to be shared by people who lacked the money but not the ambition to own one. The Dakota had a dry moat, gated archway entrance, and internal carriage courtyard just like a real European castle. Inside was a huge, princely dining room and vast wine cellar for use by residents only. Stephen Birmingham wrote in *Life at the Dakota* that Clark "was designing a building for a new class of New Yorkers of means." One hundred twenty-three years later, 15CPW, with its own gated carriage courtyard and restaurant, would prove the wisdom of Clark's vision, but at the time, his building's location was considered so far from civilized society that it was compared to the Dakota Territory. Nonetheless, by the time the building opened in 1884 (the same year electric streetlights first lit up Eighth Avenue), renters had already filled its apartments, which had between four and twenty rooms.

Most famous, perhaps, for its starring role in Roman Polanski's film of the satanic horror novel *Rosemary's Baby* and as the site of the murder of John Lennon, the Dakota has been defined since its opening by "vaguely intellectual and artistic" residents who "were choosing a social life independent of the rules and rituals of the Four Hundred," as Birmingham wrote. Over the years, they've included original renters Gustav Schirmer, a music publisher, and Theodore Steinway of the piano family, and later Boris Karloff, Leonard Bernstein, Judy Holliday, Judy Garland, Lauren Bacall, and Roberta Flack.

What the Dakota lacked—and still does—were the sort of wealthy, social residents who traditionally banded together on the East Side. "It couldn't have been more removed from Fifth and Park Avenues," says Wilbur Ross, a prominent investor who moved into the Dakota with his young family in the early 1960s. "People [on the East Side] did make fun of us. Parents wouldn't let their kids come play."

After the Dakota, the pace of building slowly picked up around the el stations at Seventy-Second and Eighty-First Streets, though it was concentrated on the side streets since speculators had bought up every vacant lot on Central Park West and were asking far too much money for their land to justify building private houses. Shanties, empty lots, and old frame houses still dominated, but they were being squeezed by the single-family houses that multiplied in the 1870s and '80s; like the Dakota, they were designed for the city's burgeoning upper middle class, who would come to define the West Side. "The houses sold readily to Jewish buyers," wrote architectural historian Sarah Bradford Landau.

The Boulevard was paved with asphalt, and the southern end of the neighborhood filled in with cheap-to-build tenements for blue-collar workers, clerks, salesmen, and civil servants, and with modest "flats" for white-collar professionals, doctors, engineers, merchants, and successful salesmen. None of them could afford the private houses that were occupying the numbered east-west streets. The riot of styles of the new buildings contrasted starkly with the monotonous rows of uniform brownstones and sober mansions of the East Side, where empty lots traded for twice the price. New mansions eventually rose on the West Side, too, built by and for members of the urban bourgeoisie, the professional and mercantile class.

The West Side building boom continued unabated until the turn of the century. Streets were graded and paved, more row houses sprang up, and luxurious multifamily dwellings finally justified the high prices speculators expected to get for land around Central Park. Tragically, Clark died in 1882, before the Dakota was finished, so he was never able to experience the flowering of his remarkable vision.

In 1913, Edith Wharton published *Custom of the Country*, a novel about a beautiful young social climber named Undine Spragg, whose ambition was matched only by her clueless obstinacy. Cultural markers in the novel set the time of Undine's move to New York with her parents from a fictional Midwestern city called Apex at about 1902. She quickly convinced her father to give up a house he'd bought on West End Avenue and rent rooms instead at a West Side "family" hotel called the Stentorian, which would be the base from which Undine would begin her conquest of first New York and then international society.

Apartment hotels were marketed to young families, bachelors, and widows—people who couldn't afford private homes but wanted self-contained, relatively private residences and wouldn't move into tenements. So they took suites of rooms, but generally had no kitchens and ate in a common dining hall, served by building staff who also handled housekeeping for all, spreading out the cost of servants and obviating the need to buy furnishings. Residential hotels had first sprung up before the Civil War and afterward became quite popular—in a sense, the condominiums of their day. Lavish, expensively furnished, and expensive to live in, they were the first sign that Central Park West had burst to life as an alternative to Fifth Avenue, complete with the requisite "teas, receptions, theater parties, [and] balls," a local paper reported.

"Undine had early decided that they could not hope to get on while they 'kept house,'" Wharton wrote, because "all the fashionable people she knew either boarded or lived in hotels." As she unlocked the city's social codes, she realized that her launchpad was a world away from Fifth Avenue, the home of "New York's golden aristocracy." The West Side was disdained by the city's better sorts. Undine found herself in exile, suffering "the incessant pin-pricks inflicted by the incongruity between her social and geographical station . . . and the deeper irritation of hearing her friends say: 'Do let me give you a lift home, dear—Oh, I'd forgotten! I'm afraid I haven't the time to go so far—'"

Still, the Dakota wasn't alone for long and was first joined by the Beresford, a six-story family hotel across from Manhattan Square, the four-block-long extension of Central Park occupied by the American Museum. It proved so popular that it was enlarged in 1892 to take up the whole block between Eighty-First and Eighty-Second Streets. Next came the Hotel San Remo at Seventy-Fifth Street in 1890 and the Hotel Majestic, with a grand restaurant, dancing salon, and roof garden. Erected by developer Jacob Rothschild, a German-born milliner-turned-developer, and his German-educated architect Alfred Zucker on an empty lot directly across Seventy-Second Street from the Dakota in 1894, it was known to its neighbors as "the Jewish place."

Although those hotels occupied the same corners and bear the same names, they were not today's grand Beresford, Majestic, and San Remo apartment houses. But the earlier edifices, along with a series of institutional buildings—the American Museum of Natural History, schools and hospitals, churches and a synagogue—and a few lesser apartment houses filled in all the empty spaces along the west bank of extrawide Central Park West and combined to give the street a special character that set it apart from the other avenues of the West Side.

In 1895, just as the frenzy of row-house building subsided, the *New York Times* consecrated the entire western district as "Itself a Great City" in the headline over a boosterish story that sprawled over three pages of the newspaper, touting the new neighborhood as a "model community" with "pure air and perfect sanitary conditions surrounded by pleasure grounds, crossed by fine boulevards and wide streets lined with artistic buildings." In the years since the opening of the Dakota, $200 million worth of buildings had been erected in a burst of progressive development. The new residents of the area were, the *Times* continued, cultured and refined. The announcement that Columbia College would soon build a campus near the West Side's northern end seemed to ensure that the young and the intelligentsia would become a permanent part of the new community. Businesses from banks to yacht clubs moved in, and the price of row houses rose steeply, from an average $15,000 in 1890 to $64,000 a dozen years later. By then, row houses were so expensive they would rarely be built again.

Even the Boulevard came alive at last with apartment houses, hotels, an armory, and many churches. Briefly, at the turn of the century, when its name was changed again, it even appeared that this new, uptown extension of Broadway would become the long-promised grand boulevard. The arrival of the first New York subway had proved a watershed. Underground rapid transit had first become a reality in London in 1863. An underground rail line running up Broadway was approved in the last years of the nineteenth century, with its first section opening in 1904 and the whole finished in 1908. Subways spread throughout the city, and the new Broadway was finally connected to the downtown business district.

In 1897, building laws changed, allowing apartment houses to rise to twelve stories and 150 feet, and in 1901, changed again; multi-unit residential buildings of those heights were henceforth *only* allowed on broad avenues such as Broadway and Central Park West. The Dorilton, a twelve-story rental apartment house that was, depending on one's taste, either garish or exuberant in its overdesigned beaux arts ornamentation, opened on Broadway in 1902. The next year, at Broadway and Seventy-Third Street, the eighteen-story Ansonia Hotel, another extravagant beaux-arts-style building, began accepting guests and was an instant hit with the culturati, attracting the likes of Enrico Caruso, Florenz Ziegfeld, and Fyodor Chaliapin.

By that time, Central Park West above Sixty-Seventh Street was almost entirely built-up. The American Museum finished its stately new façade along Seventy-Seventh Street in 1900. A few years later, the New-York Historical Society would erect the central section of its library and museum facing the park. The next residential building on the avenue, the El Dorado (a name alternately rendered, sometimes in a single document, as Eldorado), filled the block between Ninetieth and Ninety-First Streets and was touted by the *Times* as "the most notable apartment house on Central Park" when it opened in 1902. "Central Park West is given over to them that live in apartment houses," the architecture critic Montgomery Schuyler observed in 1902. "For the two miles, almost, from Seventy-second to One Hundred and Tenth, the frontage of the park is an almost continuous row of apartment houses."

Soon after, the last two empty lots above Sixty-Sixth Street were filled by the only buildings large enough to bear comparison to the Dakota for years to follow, the Langham, a 1905 rental a block to the north, with an ornate lobby, a conveyor system to deliver mail, and a built-in vacuum-cleaning system; and the St. Urban, on the south corner of Eighty-Ninth Street, its French Second Empire design and mansard roof over dormer windows reflecting the lingering notion that apartment living was a little foreign and outré, if now certifiably chic. At Sixty-Fifth Street, the Prasada, another mansard-roofed Second Empire–style confection, opened in 1907 with a Palm Room topped by a barrel-vaulted skylight in its lobby. The main rooms in the Prasada's apartments were designed to be opened and combined for entertaining—an innovation that other architects would soon follow.

When grand apartment houses finally came to the East Side a few years later (at 998 Fifth), they reflected the luxurious style of pioneering West Side builders from the Dakota's Edward Clark to the St. Urban's tragic Peter Banner, who defaulted on his mortgage and was paralyzed before going bankrupt in 1906. Banner had, for instance, separated public from private rooms and added such luxurious accoutrements as parquet floors, custom hardware, paneled walls, built-in safes, in-apartment ice makers, and private basement storage rooms. But East Side buildings tended to be restrained in design and, instead of the colorful names given to apartment houses across town, were typically known only by their street address. A good part of 15CPW's success can be attributed to its adoption of these elements of East Side style on its more offbeat side of town.

Between 1903 and 1919, six studio buildings were erected on Sixty-Seventh Street off Central Park West, the grandest of which was the Hotel des Artistes in 1914. Not actually a hotel, but rather a cooperative with hotel services, it harkened back to the original nineteenth-century co-op concept and was created by and for artists (albeit prosperous ones), who wanted to combine double-height studios that had northern light with spaces suitable for living and entertaining. The seventeen-story Gothic building attracted buyers with a central kitchen, restaurant, full staff of housekeepers, squash courts, a basement swimming pool, rooftop skating rink, theater, and ballroom (the last two are now part of the ABC Television studio complex next door). Over the years, it became home to artists Howard Chandler Christy and Norman Rockwell, the dancer Isadora Duncan, screen star Rudolph Valentino, the writer Alexander Woollcott, and the virtuoso polymath Noël Coward.

Following his 1901 success with the Graham Court Apartments at Seventh Avenue and 116th Street, a palazzo with a lavish interior courtyard like the Dakota's, William Waldorf Astor, the expatriate son of John Jacob Astor III, erected another, far larger courtyard-equipped apartment house in 1908 on land acquired almost fifty years earlier by his uncle William Backhouse Astor. The Apthorp, as he called it, bore the name of one of the neighborhood's colonial-era residents and occupied an entire block at Broadway and Seventy-Ninth Street. A year later, another developer erected the Belnord at Eighty-Sixth and Broadway, boasting an interior courtyard touted as the world's largest. Both would inspire Robert A. M. Stern's design for the gated motor court at 15CPW.

In 1909, the architectural team of Herbert Spencer Harde and R. Thomas Short (fresh from their triumph creating the most expensive rental building in Manhattan, Alwyn Court, a François I–style fantasia totally covered in terra-cotta ornamentation and boasting two fourteen-room apartments per floor), announced plans for 44 West Seventy-Seventh Street. Across the street from the south side of the Museum of Natural History, their cooperative packaged food service (as at the Dakota, but supplied by a restaurant next door) and double-height studios like the Hotel des Artistes in a hybrid Gothic-Tudor-style wrapping.

Early in 1915, the wryly named Ye Olde Settlers Association of Ye West Side held its fifth-annual dinner at the Hotel Majestic. Homeowners whose local roots dated back to the era of gentlemen's farms, river-view mansions, and horse-drawn trolleys gathered to indulge in nostalgia and celebrate the changes that had raised the West Side's profile and the profits that flowed from its development. Their dinner menus traditionally featured before-and-after neighborhood photos, and that year's contrasted the onetime home of Mayor Fernando Wood on Broadway at Seventy-Sixth Street with its replacement, another apartment block built and owned by Astor. A reporter covering the dinner drew the obvious conclusion: "Not only the west side, but every section of the city, has virtually been made over within a startlingly short period." But then, America entered the World War and the building boom that had remade the city was over. There would be no more steel to build skyscrapers until the war ended.

❦

The intersection where Eighth Avenue and the Bloomingdale Road crossed Fifty-Ninth Street was formally laid out and named the Grand Circle in 1869, according to Frederick Law Olmsted's plan for a significant circular gateway to Central Park. It was renamed Columbus Circle in 1892 after Italian Americans donated an eighty-foot column of Carrera marble to be placed at its center and, two years later, Gaetano Russo's statue of Christopher Columbus was placed atop the column. But it and the blocks just above it were not beneficiaries of the extreme residential makeover of the West Side in the early 1900s.

Directly above Columbus Circle were the lots on which 15CPW now stands, all of which changed hands repeatedly in the late nineteenth and early twentieth centuries. Until 1902, there was nothing at all on the Broadway side of the block and just a small, one-story, wooden structure on Sixty-Second Street. It was otherwise vacant. The corner of Broadway and Sixty-First Street had long belonged to the Methodist Church, then passed to Jeremiah Campion, a merchant turned mortgage banker and real estate investor. On his death in 1916, it was left to his children, who held on to it for two more decades. Campion also owned an adjacent lot on Sixty-First Street, which he sold in 1889 to Amos Eno, who also bought another lot on the block.

Born poor, Eno had gone from store clerk to store owner to real estate investor just before the Civil War. He built the Fifth Avenue Hotel on a block he owned that faced Madison Square. He also owned the narrow triangle of land nearby now occupied by the iconic Flatiron Building and accumulated a fortune of $25 million, the equivalent of $641 million today, before he died in 1898 and his properties were auctioned off.

Eno's midblock lot was sold to Ella Virginia von Echtzel Wendell, a recluse with a family fortune inherited from a fur trader who decreed on his deathbed that his descendants should "buy, but never sell, New York real estate." Three generations later, Ella was one of six sisters and a brother dedicated to preserving a $100 million fortune. Dominated by their brother, who was obsessed with the family legacy, only one of the sisters ever married. When another briefly escaped, at age fifty, for a rare night on the town, her brother had her committed and declared insane. Sister Mary married late in life, but all the Wendells lived in a mansion at Fifth Avenue and Thirty-Ninth Street, and its rooms were slowly closed up as the siblings died, until it became a spooky tourist attraction known as "the house of mystery." When Ella, the last of the Wendells, died in 1931, it was still illuminated with gaslights. A telephone had been installed only when Ella was on her deathbed.

Her lot on Sixty-First Street was transferred, according to that ancestral injunction, to the Wendell Foundation. Meantime, another building next door was sold several times before it was rented in 1924 to Selznick Distributing, a movie-distribution firm formed by Myron Selznick just after the bankruptcy of Select Pictures, the studio he'd run for a decade with his brothers Louis and David. David O. Selznick had left for Hollywood, where he became a legendary movie producer. In 1929, their building was sold to Trebuhs Realty. Trebuhs, which is *Shubert* spelled backward, was owned by the family of producers that established Times Square and Broadway as the American theater's center of gravity. In 1970, the Shuberts would also acquire 1880 Broadway at Sixty-Second Street, once briefly owned by Mayor Fernando Wood and later by the Wendell Foundation, which transferred it to the Jewish Guild for the Blind in 1943.

Before World War I, ground-floor space in most of the buildings around Broadway south of Fifty-Seventh Street were leased out to automobile dealers such as Cadillac, Stutz, Cutting Larson, and DeSoto. After the war, that "automobile row" stretched north into and past Columbus Circle. Car culture would define the district's street-level image for years to come. It displaced a smaller version of the restaurant and theater district in today's Times Square just north of Fifty-Seventh Street.

With the June 1887 opening of the New Central Park Garden, a summertime concert space on the triangular block where Broadway and Central Park West diverge, Columbus Circle had briefly come alive as an entertainment zone. Orchestras entertained and drinks were served on what had been an outdoor ice-skating rink. A review of the Garden's opening noted that the land was still thought "isolated." By November, the Garden was kaput and plans were filed to turn it into a riding ring with stables on Sixty-First Street. Durland's Riding Academy opened in February 1887, with a party attended by three thousand guests and three hundred horses.

Durland's was still operating a decade later when the *New York Tribune* reported rumors that a syndicate was considering leasing the block for a circus. Even after that plan fell through, attempts continued to turn the Grand Circle into an entertainment hub to rival Longacre Square. Columbus Circle was a natural link in the chain of uptown growth that had led from Union Square to Madison, Herald, Longacre (now Times), and Greeley Squares and would eventually end, decades later, at Lincoln Center.

William Randolph Hearst, the newspaper baron, was the next up to bat. He already owned a small piece of land at the circle's southern end, purchased in 1895 as a home for his first New York newspaper, the *New York Journal*. But it proved too small and he'd simply held it. In 1903, he headed a group that opened a theater on the west side of Columbus Circle as a legitimate theater. Called the Majestic, it was unrelated to the hotel a dozen blocks uptown and was the site of the debuts of *The Wizard of Oz* and *Babes in Toyland*. But by 1908, it had failed and become a movie theater. Wags dismissed its location as the Arctic Circle, a far-off place where legitimate theater was guaranteed a cold reception.

Still, in the years after it and Pabst's Grand Circle Palm Garden joined Faust's beer hall and Reisenweber's restaurant and cabaret (home of Sophie Tucker, the Red Hot Mama) on that block, the circle finally became a destination, luring others in show business to the north—and East Side swells to the west. Renamed the Park, the theater hosted the American premiere of George Bernard Shaw's *Pygmalion* in 1914. In "May Day," his first novelette, published in

1920, F. Scott Fitzgerald described the scene at 4:00 a.m. at Childs', a Columbus Circle cafeteria filled with "a noisy medley of chorus girls, college boys, debutantes, rakes, *filles de joie*—a not unrepresentative mixture of the gayest of Broadway, and even of Fifth Avenue."

Fifth Avenue types had by then been eyeing the circle for some time. In 1905, a theatrical impresario, Heinrich Conrad, announced the formation of a syndicate of wealthy men to back his plan to build a National Theater, as he called it, on Central Park West between Sixty-Second and Sixty-Third Streets, where he planned to produce both opera and theater. For $100,000, subscribers would each get perpetual rights to one of thirty boxes in an elite social horseshoe overlooking the stage. Rechristened the New Theater, Conrad's building, designed by Carrère and Hastings, opened in 1908. Despite backing from Otto Kahn, J. Pierpont Morgan, John Jacob Astor III, Harry Payne Whitney, August Belmont, and several Vanderbilts, it lost $400,000 in its first two seasons; bad acoustics, high operating expenses, and the unfashionable location were all blamed for its failure.

Finally, it was leased to other theater managers, who rechristened it the Century Theater. But not even Diaghilev's Ballets Russes, Stravinsky's American debut of *Firebird*, a basement nightclub run by the speakeasy queen Texas Guinan, or a *Midnight Frolic* review mounted in a rooftop cabaret by the famous showman Florenz Ziegfeld (and briefly, George Gershwin as rehearsal pianist) could save it. Prohibition would finally force the closure of the Century's roof garden, as well as Reisenweber's, with its Paradise Room and Viennese Four Hundred Club, all run by the same owner. Though the Century held on under the ownership of the Shuberts, by 1929 it was well past the prime it had never really had.

So, too, the former Majestic theater. In 1922, the Minsky brothers turned it into a burlesque house, then it was renamed the Cosmopolitan and run in turn by Ziegfeld and the Shuberts. During the

Depression, it would again become the Park, then be renamed the International before NBC took it over as a television studio in 1949.

W. R. Hearst was the one man who stayed true to the circle; he dreamed of renaming it Hearst Plaza. In 1911, he'd bought the Durland's block for about $2 million. The riding academy had moved a few blocks uptown in 1902 after its former home was condemned when blasting for the new subway weakened its foundations; it later burned to the ground in a fire that sent eight firemen to the hospital.* It was assumed Hearst was planning a new skyscraper for his *American* and *Journal* newspapers. But two years later, he announced he would build his newspaper offices just south of the circle and was planning a low Gothic building to the north, though its foundation would be strong enough to support a tower if and when he decided to add one. Hearst also spearheaded the public subscription campaign that paid for the massive Maine Monument, erected in 1913 at the southwest entrance to Central Park, commemorating the lives lost when the battleship *Maine* was blown up in Havana Harbor in 1898, setting off (to cheers from Hearst's newspapers) the Spanish-American War.

In 1921, another Hearst skyscraper south of the circle was announced but never built, although in 1923 he renovated a theater on Fifty-Eighth Street that fronted on the circle, for his mistress, the actress Marion Davies. In 1928, he finished an office building for his papers a few blocks to the south, and his building on the Durland's lot remained until the mid-1960s, known primarily for a giant neon sign on its roof that gave the temperature and weather forecast and advertised Coca-Cola.

Central Park West from Sixty-Second to Seventy-First Streets

---

* The Edison Company made a famous film of the fire that can still be seen today on YouTube. That film was later marketed as *Firemen Fighting the Flames at Paterson*, a much bigger and more famous fire in New Jersey that wasn't actually filmed.

had been vacant in 1891, but by 1902, two owners and three buildings shared the strip across the street from the park now occupied
by 15CPW. The half of the block nearer to Sixty-First Street belonged to the children of a businessman named George Poillon; in
1894, his son Winfield put up two near-identical seven-story apartment buildings there, and his wife, Winifred, later inherited them.
The other two lots (on the Sixty-Second Street corner) held what
had once been a private home, separated from the Poillon property
by a forty-five-foot-wide driveway leading to a brick stable in the
rear. Rented to a religious school for girls, it belonged to Marie Louise Morgan, granddaughter of a Matthew Morgan, who established
the Morgan & Sons bank in New York in the 1830s and made a tidy
but not large fortune.

In 1883, Marie was married in what was then her father William
R. Morgan's house. A generation earlier, their family had resided in
far more fashionable Murray Hill. William's move to a lesser part of
town may be explained by his checkered past. Thirty years earlier,
he and his younger brother went on trial for the savage beating of
a man in Newport, Rhode Island, where the family spent summers.
The victim had accused William of beating and imprisoning his own
wife, who separately filed for divorce and asked a judge to let her return to her maiden name. The wealthy brothers were released from
jail ten days later and returned to New York. Fifty quiet years later,
the Morgans were back in the public eye as speculation grew in real
estate circles that those otherwise empty blocks just above Columbus Circle were "in play."

In 1910, ground was broken for Harperley Hall, the first cooperative apartment house on lower Central Park West. When completed, it occupied six previously empty lots at Sixty-Fourth Street.
The building, which boasted its own guardhouse and an open entrance court facing the Ethical Culture Society's new auditorium
across the street, would gain fame many decades later when the

pop star Madonna bought an apartment there. Harperley Hall was nearly finished when another cooperative syndicate bought the former Marie Morgan house.

Plans were soon announced for a thirteen-story co-op on the Morgan site. But a year later, the family foreclosed on the syndicate's loan and bought the property back at auction for $325,000, $35,000 less than the outstanding mortgage. A year after that, Marie Morgan's estate was sued by one of her heirs, seeking to partition the property, which ended up in the hands of another family member, who built a taxpayer—a low building constructed to generate rents that cover taxes while the owner of land waits to decide what to do with the property. The Electric Vehicle Association, which sold, stored, and cared for cars that ran on electricity, rented it as a salesroom and garage.

In 1919, the Morgan lots were optioned by an athletic club that planned an eighteen-story clubhouse complete with swimming pool and indoor track, but two years later, the district attorney revealed he was investigating the club's promoter, who had disappeared after he lost his option to buy the land and was suspected of stealing the initiation fees paid by a thousand prospective members. He later surfaced in Syracuse, where he claimed he'd been forced out by a faction of those members—and disappeared again.

Central Park West became the next frontier after the 1923 announcement that a new subway line would run up its length into northern Manhattan. Ground was broken for the new line in 1925, and a fresh wave of land speculation along its route accompanied its construction. At the same time, the city widened Central Park West from forty-eight to sixty-three feet.

Back in the hands of the Morgan heir who'd sued his relatives for it, the Central Park West property, occupied by a two-story auto showroom, was leased in 1923 to one developer who planned an eighteen-story building, then sold to another who'd already purchased Winifred Poillon's apartment houses and begun demolishing them, planning a hotel for the southern corner. With the Morgan lots in hand, he decided to build another on the opposite end of the block.

Designed and built separately—but immediately if awkwardly joined together—the almost identical fifteen-story Mayflower and Plymouth Hotels (renamed the Mayflower-Plymouth) rose in 1926. By that August, model apartments were ready for inspection. Despite their two separate marquees and entrances, the buildings were connected on the lobby level. (Because the floor heights didn't match, the corridors upstairs were never joined.) The hotels shared a five-hundred-seat dining room and smaller rooms for private parties.

The architect of the Mayflower-Plymouth was more important than its developers to the creation of today's Central Park West. Emery Roth came to America from his native Hungary in 1884, age thirteen, and was working in a New York drugstore when the owner's brother, an architect, admired his artistic skills and made him an unpaid apprentice. A job as a draftsman on the architectural staff of the World's Columbian Exposition, held in Chicago in 1893, followed. There, he met Richard M. Hunt, the designer of what may have been New York's first apartment house, who gave him a job. By 1898, Roth was able to buy into an architecture practice and shortly set out on his own.

Roth's second big job was a Broadway apartment hotel, the Belleclaire. A flamboyant structure, influenced by art nouveau and the Vienna Secession movement, it impressed Leo and Alexander Bing, brothers and lawyers who'd become developers after making a fortune forming syndicates to buy and sell land near Broadway subway stops. Roth went to work for them in 1905 and pushed them to make their buildings architectural statements. Initially, their buildings on West End Avenue were restrained and sober, as was Roth's Hotel Alden, which he also built for the Bings; it opened at Central Park West and Eighty-Second Street just after the Mayflower-Plymouth and featured one of Roth's signatures, a water tank hidden in masonry designed to be an architectural finishing touch to the building. Diverse rooflines would eventually give Central Park West its singular visual identity.

Like his contemporary Rosario Candela, Roth worked on both sides of town, but where Candela and the slightly older J. E. R. Carpenter established the look of the East Side with their restrained designs, Roth indelibly stamped the West. The Mayflower-Plymouth, with its bands of terra-cotta ornamentation near the roof and at the third and fourth floors, was a handsome addition to the streetscape. Likely only because it was constructed as two hotels did Roth put two differently shaped towers on its roof—one a classic, boxy penthouse, the other resembling a campanile with a pyramidal top—above the unified cornice line that linked the buildings. Nonetheless, that accident made the Mayflower (as it would soon be known) the first of the avenue's visually defining twin-towered buildings. Roth, "the unquestioned master of the luxury residential skyscraper," according to Robert A. M. Stern, would soon be responsible for several others.

During the early 1920s, New York State and City governments decided to encourage building by granting tax exemptions to developers and allowing life insurance companies to invest in housing. At the same time, in Manhattan, apartment hotels enjoyed their second coming thanks, ironically, to the exigencies of zoning laws. First enacted in 1916 and then revised in 1929, the laws restricted the height and allowable lot coverage of apartment towers, but hotels, which were deemed commercial enterprises, were much less restricted. Because of rising land costs, developers needed to build higher to increase their returns, and in the roaring climate of the twenties, more people moved around and were more than happy to sacrifice kitchens for freedom from housekeeping and cooking.

In 1924, Roth designed Park Avenue's Ritz Tower, which, at forty-one stories, was, for a time, the world's tallest residential building. It was also one of the first of the slender, imaginative, sky-piercing towers that would soon define the proudly vertical uptown skyline of the Jazz Age. "Manhattan became an island of glittering pinnacles," Lloyd Morris wrote in *Incredible New York*. Roth called the Ritz Tower a "skyscratcher," as it resembled a spear sticking up into the air. A number of equally awe-inspiring apartment hotels around the southeast corner of Central Park followed. The spire-topped Sherry-Netherland (1926), McKim, Mead & White's Savoy-Plaza of 1927 (since demolished), Roth's Hotel St. Moritz and the mansard-roofed Pierre in 1930 joined the Plaza Hotel, which had opened in 1907 and was designed by the Dakota's architect, Henry Hardenbergh. Central Park South extended the new hotel zone to the west with the near-simultaneous addition of the towering, sign-topped Essex House and the Barbizon Plaza.

The trend petered out the next year as the stock market crash of 1929 led to the Great Depression, which gripped the nation throughout the 1930s. Work on the thirty-seven-floor Hampshire House, begun in January 1931, stopped only six months later when the developer defaulted on its mortgage before the building had even been enclosed. It would sit unfinished for six years.

After his triumph with the Ritz, Roth built another hotel, the Oliver Cromwell on Seventy-Second Street, just off Central Park West, across the street from the Dakota. Rising to thirty-two stories, it was the first West Side skyscraper. Towers were "not only possible, but also desirable," both visually and commercially, wrote Steven Ruttenbaum in *Mansions in the Clouds*, his biography of Emery Roth, since they allowed for private apartments with dramatic views.

Luxurious apartment houses—buildings with sixteen-room apartments, duplexes, triplexes, and ceilings up to twelve feet high—soon replaced what had by then come to seem stunted turn-of-the-century hotels. The first, by Roth, was a new Beresford, which opened in September 1929 and was the largest apartment house of its time. Though not quite a skyscraper at twenty-two stories, it has a "monumental presence," according to Robert A. M. Stern, with its Italian Renaissance and baroque elements, three separate entrances detailed in marble and bronze, elevators serving just one or two apartments per floor, and three corner turrets. Fully rented from the moment it opened, its 172 apartments have, over the years, been home to Beverly Sills, Isaac Stern, Tony Randall, Helen Gurley and David Brown, Adam Clayton of U2, Diana Ross, Jerry Seinfeld, and John McEnroe.

The next year, Roth's Italian-baroque, twenty-seven-story San Remo opened, with two colonnade towers topped with copper finials above a U-shaped base around a large light court reminiscent of the Dakota, the Apthorp, and the Belnord. Its 122 apartments have been home to entertainers from Eddie Cantor to Dustin Hoffman and Diane Keaton. A year after its completion, Roth codesigned a replacement for the old Hotel Eldorado, a more modern take on the San Remo's two-tower concept, though he concentrated on the floor plans while another architectural firm designed the art deco exterior of what became, again briefly, the tallest West Side apartment house. Sinclair Lewis once lived there, as did Faye Dunaway, Tuesday Weld, Mary Tyler Moore, Alec Baldwin, Michael J. Fox, and Apple's Steve Jobs.

It was also the home of the fictional actress Marjorie Morningstar, née Marjorie Morgenstern, Herman Wouk's update of Undine Spragg, whose father, a Jewish-immigrant businessman, moved there from the Bronx in the 1930s in the hope that her new address would help her marry her way "up" in the world. "Marjorie loved everything about the El Dorado, even the name," Wouk wrote. "It had a fine foreign sound to it . . . low foreign, like her parents. By moving to the El Dorado on Central Park West her parents had done much, Marjorie believed, to make up for their immigrant origin. She was grateful to them for this, and proud of them. The west side, her mother told her, was where the good families lived."

The two finest towers on Central Park West were also replacements for earlier buildings that bore the same names. They shared Emery Roth's twin-tower motif, though neither was designed by him, but were more au courant, reflecting the latest European design trends. Both the Majestic, a streamlined art moderne building that replaced the apartment hotel at Seventy-Second Street in 1931, and the art deco Century, which replaced Carrère and Hastings's star-crossed theater at Sixty-Second and opened early the next year, were designed by Jacques Delamarre for the builder Irwin S. Chanin. A steel frame for the former was already being erected when the market crashed, and Chanin quickly had the building redesigned to reflect the new legal and economic reality. So a forty-five-story hotel with a single tower became a twenty-nine-story apartment house with two towers offering more corners and more open views, though its eleven- to twenty-four-room apartments had shrunk to four to fourteen rooms. Among its most prominent residents over the years were the gangsters Lucky Luciano, Meyer Lansky, and Frank Costello, who would be shot and wounded in the lobby in 1957, Milton Berle, Zero Mostel, the gossip columnist Walter Winchell, and more recently Conan O'Brien.

In 1928, the Century Theater, still controlled by the Shuberts, and an adjacent midblock building they owned that ran from Sixty-Second to Sixty-Third Streets, were rumored to have been sold first as a new site for the Metropolitan Opera and then to Bing & Bing. Instead, Chanin acquired the old Century in exchange for his interest in a group of theaters near Times Square. He'd bought the

entire ninety-thousand-square-foot block, including a second theater and several other buildings, in order to build a sixty-five-story
office building. Two months before the stock market crashed, Chanin revealed that it would be called the Palais de France, a center to
showcase French industry and art, and would include an apartment
hotel, a restaurant, and something called the Académie des Beaux
Arts. But on October 23, 1929, the day before Black Thursday, just as
demolition of the Century began, Chanin's plans changed, a circumstance he blamed on both French politics and the American economy. France had dropped out, but the Metropolitan Life Insurance
Co. had agreed to finance an apartment house half the size of the
abandoned Palais de France and a separate office building on Broadway. Chanin framed his decision to proceed as an act of patriotism.

Plans for a *new* Century, a thirty-story apartment house, emerged
the following fall. It would be marketed to people who were downsizing from larger apartments; its sunken living rooms, one-room
studio apartments with terraces, and one-bedroom duplexes were
designed to cushion their fall from larger spaces. Like the Majestic,
the Beresford, and the San Remo, it was to be topped with a pair of
stunning towers and would eventually be home to Chanin, Lee Shubert, William Morris, Leo Lindemann, whose Lindy's delicatessen
was famous for its cheesecake, Fay Wray, Ray Bolger, Ethel Mer-
man, and Robert Goulet.

The Majestic and the Century were the last great buildings
erected on Central Park West in the twentieth century, both products of the frenzied economic atmosphere that led to the stock market crash and the Depression that followed, even though they didn't
open until well after the black days of October 1929. By mid-1932,
with stock values down almost 90 percent, the romance, glamour, and
optimism made manifest in their architecture had been pulverized.

A year after it opened, the San Remo was still about one-third
vacant, and the Bank of the United States, which had financed it and

many of the other Central Park West buildings, collapsed,* while across the street a so-called Hooverville (named for President Herbert Hoover, who promised that recovery was "just around the corner") brought shanties of paper and scrap metal back to Central Park. Rents at the San Remo were reduced, its large apartments were cut up into smaller ones, and the building became a financial sinkhole. In 1940, it and the Beresford, which had also had its troubles, were sold together for a mere $25,000 above their existing mortgages. Similarly, the Mayflower-Plymouth's owners were sued in 1934 after they stopped paying their mortgage. The hotel was finally auctioned off in 1939 and bought by its lender, which took a $1.5 million loss and held it until it could be sold again in 1946 (when it was assessed at a mere $2.45 million, about half a million dollars less than it had cost to build).

Emery Roth's biographer, Steven Ruttenbaum, considers the buildings that Roth and others erected on Central Park West between 1925 and 1932 the architectural apex of the era's Great Prosperity. Their unique, inspiring silhouettes, combined into a "spectacular linear skyline," were an attempt by both Roth and the ultimate consumers of his Central Park West apartments (whom Ruttenbaum describes as "rich Jews and successful artists, musicians and performers") to compensate for the street's failure to attain "the social desirability of Fifth Avenue" by reflecting their own status on their own turf. Ironically, then, the palisade-like street wall is best

---

*Despite pleas from regulators, the Chase, Chemical, J. P. Morgan, First National, and National City banks, among others, refused to help save the Bank of the United States, which had on its board of directors many of the leading Russian-Jewish developers of the time, including Irwin Chanin, David Tishman, and Joseph Durst. "Many people whispered that the Protestant bankers had deliberately withheld help from the biggest Jewish bank in the country," Tom Schactman wrote in *Skyscraper Dreams*, his book about the city's real estate dynasties dating back to the Astors, Goelets, and Beekmans. "The extent of the damage to the Jewish immigrant builder fraternity was considerable."

viewed from the apartments of Fifth Avenue, while the view from Central Park West is of the comparatively dull apartment buildings on Fifth, which Ruttenbaum deems "the center of the city's elite."

Somehow, despite its spectacular street wall, East Siders still managed to look down on the buildings they viewed across the park. Christopher Gray, the New York real estate historian, parodies their attitude while describing it. "I can't look at the San Remo as anything other than a Central Park West building," he says, "a little tacky, a little showy, a different sort of animal." And the people who lived in those buildings? "I don't see them as signatories to cotillion agreements. Schirmer? Steinway? A little thin. None of them are in the clubs. Just saying. Sorry!"

Nonetheless, by 1930, the West Side had developed its own alternate society. "Many Jewish immigrants . . . had achieved prosperity in New York by the late 1920s, and looked from the Lower east side to the Upper west side as a cultural and architectural haven," Nancy Goeschel wrote in a New York City Landmarks Preservation Commission report on the Beresford. "By the mid-1930s, more than half the residents of the Upper west side from 72nd to 96th Streets were Jewish, and more than a third of these families were headed by a parent born in Europe."

The crescendo of building that attracted them provided "a brilliant climax to the last great surge of development activity on the avenue," the commission said in its report on the Central Park West Historic District. It had truly been a remarkable fifty-two years, from 1879, when Edward Clark dreamed up the Dakota, to the Century in 1931. A great new neighborhood had been created, a real alternative, if perhaps not really a rival, to Fifth Avenue and its younger sibling Park. Instead of denying the primacy of the East Side, Jewish developers and architects such as Roth, outsiders building homes for other outsiders, first affirmed it and then ignored it by creating their own Gold Coast.

During this last spasm of building, "today's Central Park West curtain wall developed," says Andrew Alpern, "but then it stopped dead" as the Depression paralyzed the world economy. From 1931 to 1937 only seventeen new buildings rose in the West Side historic district, compared with thirty-three in the two years just before the stock market crash. Thereafter, development remained depressed. Though one last big apartment house was built just off Columbus Circle, the modernist 240 Central Park South, completed in 1941 just before civilian construction was halted by World War II, it was an exception that proved the rule that residential development after the Depression was mostly limited to the conversion of existing single-family houses into apartments.

Only two new buildings would rise on Central Park West in the next twenty-five years. So everything stayed the same, including the neighborhood's reputation as a place for those who were somehow "other" than the East Side's white, gentile elite. Jewish immigrants, now fleeing Hitler instead of pogroms, continued to arrive, along with intellectuals, the artistic, and the cultured. But in years to come, the denizens of the Gilded Ghetto of the West Side, who mostly clustered on its fringes on Central Park West, West End Avenue, and Riverside Drive, and in a few apartment houses on Broadway and a few blocks of brownstones in between, would no longer set their neighborhood's tone. The West Side would soon become far more like the Wild West than Edward Clark and his Dakota detractors imagined it to be.

Part Two

OUT OF ARIZONA

There has been no trader in real estate remotely comparable to Bill Zeckendorf. As a showman, he makes P. T. Barnum look like a piker.

—ROBERT MOSES

"I remember a little bit, during the glory days," says Arthur Zeckendorf about visiting his grandfather Big Bill. "Going to White Plains, seeing the DC-3, probably one of the first private propeller planes. The Greenwich estate, seventy acres on Long Island Sound. There were peacocks, monkeys. He had a 1955 convertible Cadillac he would drive us around in. We'd stop at the oyster pond and go in and get oysters. It was Disneyland."

Arthur William Zeckendorf and William Lie Zeckendorf were hardly the first people to see their grandfather William Zeckendorf Sr. as larger-than-life. An avid self-promoter, "Big Bill" was also hugely accomplished. He left his mark on cities across North America, creating an empire with assets in excess of $200 million controlling real estate estimated to be worth $450 million. He then failed as spectacularly as he had once succeeded.

In real estate circles, the Zeckendorf saga starts with him, passes through his son and namesake, Bill Jr., whose rise and fall runs eerily parallel to his father's, before reaching the third Zeckendorf generation, the one that conceived and built Fifteen Central Park West.

But the Zeckendorf story is a longer one. It is longer, too, than that of most of the other Jewish real estate dynasties of New York—the Dursts, LeFraks, Milsteins, Roses, Rudins, and Tishmans—all products of the Jewish ghettoes of eastern Europe.

The family's story starts earlier, long before 15CPW opened its doors, when Arthur and Will's great-great-grandfather, another William Zeckendorf, journeyed from Missouri to what was then the Arizona Territory along the Santa Fe Trail, at the head of a train of twelve of the covered wagons known as prairie schooners, filled with supplies for a trading post serving the miners who'd made Tucson a boomtown.

The Zeckendorfs had come from Hanover, Germany, where many Jews, legally barred from owning land or practicing professions, became merchants to make a living. In the 1850s, the first Zeckendorf came to America, one of the thousands of Jews who began crossing the Atlantic in search of freedom and opportunity. But unlike those who would work their way up and shortly populate New York's West Side, Aaron Zeckendorf, one of that first William's six siblings, made his way to Santa Fe to clerk in a store and then opened his own in Albuquerque and Santa Fe, as his brothers slowly emigrated from Germany to join him. William was fourteen when he reached New York in 1856 and, after a few months, joined that wagon train through Apache and Comanche country.

At nineteen, William joined the Union Army as a lieutenant and fought in the Civil War under Kit Carson. Once he returned from the fighting, his brothers put him in charge of their Tucson outpost. He often had to arrange military escorts to protect their goods from Indian raids. A natural promoter, he publicized a shoot-out with robbers at his store and celebrated the arrival of his supply wagons, as well as weddings, birthdays, and holidays, with fireworks and orations that made him a local character. He was nicknamed Z by the *Weekly Arizonan* newspaper, which regularly covered his antics. His grandson and namesake would inherit his promotional skills and then pass them on to *his* grandsons.

By 1870, William was rich, worth about $125,000 (the equivalent of almost $2 million today), and had added mining and politics to his résumé. His family grew, too. That same year, he had a son, Arthur William, who later gave one of his names to each of his great-grandsons. In 1885 William declared bankruptcy, but that didn't stop him. He rebuilt his life as one of Tucson's leading citizens. But his wife longed to return to New York, and in 1887 she and their children did, leaving William behind. After a four-year tug-of-war, William finally sold off all his stock and followed, settling his family in Far Rockaway on Long Island, where William died in 1906, when Arthur was twenty-six years old. William lived long enough to meet his grandson, the future Big Bill, who'd just been born.

Arthur William Zeckendorf and his family were among the original residents of the Belnord, the building with a courtyard at Broadway and Eighty-Sixth Street. But as he became a successful shoe manufacturer, he moved his family into a brand-new house in Cedarhurst, a bucolic suburb of New York. Seven years later, in 1917, the Zeckendorfs moved again, into the Dorilton at Broadway and West Seventy-First Street.

"This was a section of town to which many Jewish families were then moving," Big Bill, then twelve, later wrote. "The apartments were new, and there was a bake shop or candy store and a fancy delicatessen on every block. . . . An amazing number of people knew each other. On the Jewish New Year it was the custom for the gentlemen and their ladies, in their furs, to walk up and down that part of Broadway greeting their friends." Though the Zeckendorfs wouldn't always stay in the neighborhood, neither would they leave it behind.

Big Bill, six feet tall and nearing his adult weight of 250 pounds, played football after entering New York University in 1922, but dropped out at age twenty to go to work for an uncle who'd become a millionaire in the real estate business. Young Zeckendorf initially managed properties, but wanted to be a real estate salesman and badgered his uncle into letting him rent out an office building he'd bought on lower Broadway near Wall Street. When Big Bill succeeded and his uncle proved unappreciative, he quit and got another job.

In 1927, Big Bill, just twenty-two, met Otto Kahn, an investment banker, through Big Bill's new wife, who came from a good Jewish family. Like William Randolph Hearst, Kahn had believed that Columbus Circle would be the next great entertainment hub of Manhattan, and he'd bought most of the block bounded by Fifty-Sixth and Fifty-Seventh Streets between Eighth and Ninth Avenues, just below the circle, hoping to donate it to the Metropolitan Opera for a new opera house. When his offer was refused due to opposition from older families who didn't think the neighborhood was suitable, Big Bill suggested Kahn sell the plot to a developer who later erected the Parc Vendome, a large apartment house, there. Big Bill made $30,000, "the last big money I would see for some time," Zeckendorf would later recall. "The Depression had arrived."

Zeckendorf and his wife lived in a full-floor apartment on Park Avenue, though he didn't pay market rent for it; it was subsidized by another wealthy friend he'd helped out in business. The Zeckendorfs' first child, William Jr., had been born the week the stock market crashed in 1929, and their daughter, Susan, followed in 1931. Through the long economic slump, Zeckendorf made a living as a middleman, renegotiating mortgages, selling off foreclosed properties, and assembling sites for development once the economy improved. But he also liked to live above his means and, as a result, was, as the author Cary Reich once put it, "chronically overextended." Or as Zeckendorf himself put it, somewhat more colorfully, by the standards of the 1930s "we were affluent, even if often broke."

A few years later, Big Bill got his big break. Webb & Knapp, a real estate company, had been founded in 1922 to manage and develop property owned by the New York Central Railroad. Its patrician principals, a Vanderbilt heir named Webb, a real estate broker named Knapp, and the architects John and Eliot Cross, managed some of the best sites in Manhattan. But by 1936, Knapp, Webb, and one of the Cross brothers had died and the company needed new leadership. Zeckendorf had recently sold the firm an office building that needed tenants, and in 1938 it hired him for $9,000 a year to recruit some, and when he was successful, he was asked to become a partner. A lucky thing, since his taste for high living and gambling was costing him $20,000 a year. Then, in 1940, a cousin of the Crosses' stepped in, too, bringing with him $400,000 in fresh capital, and Webb & Knapp quietly began buying buildings.

During one such transaction, Zeckendorf had an epiphany: many of the best New York properties were owned by people who, battered by the Depression, were cash poor and would sell valuable real estate at low prices. Banks and insurance companies were simultaneously flush with cash they'd been afraid to invest and were desperate to find safe investments. By ferreting out buyers for cut-rate properties, Zeckendorf could make all three of the parties to transactions very happy.

Still, the company lacked the funds needed to do big deals. That changed in 1942 when Vincent Astor, heir to the Astor fortune, was going off to war and looking for a company to reorganize his family's $50 million worth of Manhattan real estate. Old school ties led him to Webb & Knapp, where Zeckendorf, the only partner who was too old to be drafted, was working alone. His proposals for reorganizing Astor's holdings won Webb & Knapp the job.

"Overnight," Zeckendorf observed, it became "the most important real estate firm in America . . . and we immediately, and with a purpose, began moving and dealing in a dozen directions at once." Three years later, the firm had done twenty-two big-money property deals, buying and selling airports, bus terminals, wharves, oil wells, railroads, golf courses, post offices, retail stores, movie theaters, the municipal jail in Boise, Idaho, and three-quarters of a mile of waterfront and piers in Hoboken, New Jersey. Its net assets climbed from less than zero to more than $2 million.

By the time his partners came back from the war, Zeckendorf was firmly in charge. "We did it with mirrors," Zeckendorf admitted, "contacts in proper places, lots of travel as well as travail, a pinch of ingenuity, careful study of the tax laws—and a crystal ball." Webb & Knapp's purchases were mostly outside the Manhattan market, which had been overbuilt in the 1920s. But Zeckendorf's most famous deal of the postwar era sanctified the island's new position as the capital of the world.

In 1945, Big Bill was offered eight acres on the East River that had been occupied by a string of slaughterhouses since the nineteenth century. Due to the odors wafting from those cattle pens and meatpacking plants, the value of land around them was almost nil. But the meatpacking companies that owned the properties had banded together and were demanding three to four times the going price for nearby lots. Zeckendorf realized that if he quickly and quietly tied up the slaughterhouse properties, he could then buy up the surrounding real estate for a song, bringing down the average cost per square foot of the whole transaction.* He hopped a plane to South America and stayed there for a month while his minions secretly snapped up seventy-five properties on eight additional acres stretching from Forty-Second to Forty-Ninth Streets, from Second Avenue to the East River.

As the secret land purchases were being made, Zeckendorf con-

---

* Zeckendorf's gambit had a precedent. A similar maneuver, twenty years earlier, had resulted in the development of Tudor City on slaughterhouse acreage assembled by the builder Fred F. French. Zeckendorf had worked for the broker who helped assemble the property.

jured up an extraordinary vision for the property. Inspired by the
platform the New York Central had built over its tracks running
up Park Avenue, which created not only a new residential zone, but
also vast real estate fortunes, he envisioned a two-block-wide, seven-
block-long platform upon which he would develop what he called
X City. It would have office buildings, an airline terminal with a
heliport on the roof, a six-thousand-room hotel, a series of apartment buildings, parking for five thousand cars and new homes for
the Metropolitan Opera and Carnegie Hall, all suspended above a
floating marina and nightclub and entertainment zone, connected
with moving sidewalks and ringed with gardens. It was a quixotic
notion, to say the least, but it got him the attention he obviously
craved. Soon, *Life* magazine would describe him as a Falstaffian figure, exuding the scent of the Sen-Sen licorice he gobbled to avoid
the big black cigars he preferred, "a big brash man of 41 with a baro-
nial paunch and a temperamental disinclination to do business in
amounts less than seven digits" and "a building program that makes
Napoleon II seem niggardly and threatens to change the face of
New York."

Just as Zeckendorf finished his assemblage, he learned the
United Nations, then based in temporary quarters on Long Island,
was looking for a permanent home and threatening to decamp to
Philadelphia or, worse, San Francisco, if it couldn't find land in New
York City. Zeckendorf, knowing in his heart that his X City plan
was a publicity stunt, saw a way to pull off the greatest of his inter-
connection tricks. "Marion," he told his second wife, an actress, "I'm
going to put those bastards on the platform," and profit greatly from
his ownership of all that surrounding land. He immediately offered
to sell seventeen acres to the nascent UN. But it lacked the funds to
pay for it—even at cost.

Meantime, across town, John D. Rockefeller Jr., the Standard Oil
heir, was sitting down for dinner at his home in the luxe apartment

house 740 Park Avenue with one of his neighbors and a houseguest, a Belgian diplomat who was the UN's treasurer. The diplomat told his wealthy dinner companion that if the UN couldn't raise funds to buy Zeckendorf's land in two days, it would surely leave town. Conveniently, the Rockefeller family's favorite architect, Wallace Harrison, had done preliminary drawings of X City for Zeckendorf and was an admirer. So Junior surely knew about X City and that, if built, it would compete with his family's Rockefeller Center office and entertainment complex in midtown Manhattan. And he objected to an alternative that had been proposed by his son Nelson (who was serving along with Harrison on the city's UN site committee) to give the UN Pocantico Hills, his own family's weekend property in Westchester. So Junior enlisted Harrison and Nelson to go to see Zeckendorf.

A few nights later, in a nightclub owned by Webb & Knapp that Big Bill used as his evening office, the trio made a deal to give the UN an option on about two-thirds of the X City land for $8.5 million. The next morning, Rockefeller Jr. agreed to donate that sum, and within a week the General Assembly accepted. Zeckendorf walked away a hero with a $2 million profit for Webb & Knapp and control of four-plus surrounding acres.

The deal made Big Bill the most talked-about real estate operator in America. In 1951, the *New Yorker*'s E. J. Kahn Jr. sanctified his new status in a two-part profile that described him as "unusually imaginative, venturesome, unpredictable, ambitious, and resourceful," as well as volatile, sentimental, and, understating significantly, "fond of publicity."

A few years later, in 1956, Bill Zeckendorf Jr. would forge another family tie with the UN when he married Guri Lie, the daughter of Trygve Lie, the Norwegian foreign minister who was serving as its first secretary-general. William Lie and Arthur Zeckendorf are the products of that union.

Though he'd spent part of his childhood at the Dorilton, Big Bill was no fan of Manhattan's West Side. In 1946, he and Marion were living in a four-room, seventeenth-floor penthouse in a Webb & Knapp building on Seventy-Second Street near Madison Avenue when he dreamed up a scheme to cover the entire West Side from Twenty-Fourth to Seventy-First Streets west of Ninth Avenue with another platform, this one of nine hundred acres and twelve stories tall, covering 144 square blocks (about the area of Central Park), on which he proposed to build an airport with three parallel runways. He figured the cost at $3 billion, or about $33 billion today.

At the same time, he was offered the chance to buy a group of buildings off Central Park West, including the last home of Durland's Riding Academy. Initially, he declined. He wasn't interested in residential real estate, "and the west side was déclassé," he wrote. "We would rather buy land at higher prices and get a better long-term deal on Park Avenue." But a few weeks later, stuck in traffic on that very block, he wandered into the equestrian center and, eyeing its dimensions (two hundred feet long and a hundred feet wide with a forty-five-foot vaulted ceiling), had a vision of selling it to one of the then-new television networks for a studio. But neither NBC nor CBS wanted it. Finally, the founder of the Life Savers candy empire called. He'd just bought a radio network and wanted the riding academy as a television production facility. It eventually became the home of the ABC network, which years later would sell a piece of land nearby and give Big Bill's grandsons their first opportunity to sell luxury apartments to New York's wealthiest.

After the UN deal, Zeckendorf had become a Rockefeller family real estate consultant and grown particularly close to Nelson, whose taste in modern art mirrored Zeckendorf's own predilections. He believed in modern architecture and had already worked with a number of talented practitioners, including Le Corbusier and William Lescaze, when, in 1948, Webb & Knapp began spreading its wings as a developer. So Big Bill decided he needed an in-house architect, and not just a hack or a wellborn dilettante, but an innovator. Nelson Rockefeller introduced him to a Museum of Modern Art staffer who spent the next year scouting talent before the eminent architect Philip Johnson recommended an assistant professor at Harvard, a young Chinese named Ieoh Ming Pei, who impressed Big Bill not just with his imagination and intelligence but also because they were both gourmets and oenophiles. It didn't hurt that, like Zeckendorf, both Pei and his father had been born in Chinese astrology's year of the snake, which supposedly confers wisdom, charm, and intuition.

Pei's first job as in-house architect was the redesign of Webb & Knapp's shabby two-story corporate office atop an office building on Madison Avenue. The centerpiece of its top-floor lobby became Zeckendorf's own office, a vertical, teak-paneled, windowless cylinder twenty feet in diameter with colored lights, which Zeckendorf could change according to his mood, set into a ring of skylights around the top. A private, stainless-steel elevator dubbed the Bullet sat inside its own cylinder-within-the-cylinder and rose to a larger, turretlike, glass-walled penthouse executive dining room, bathroom, and kitchen. Members of Pei's staff, which immediately began to grow, even designed custom furniture for their employer-patron.

At the time, Nelson's father was renting a huge duplex apartment that sprawled over thirty-plus rooms at 740 Park, but he was bedeviled by his upstairs neighbor, Clarence Shearn, a lawyer, former judge, and longtime associate of William Randolph Hearst, and Shearn's second wife, Dorothea, a fortune hunter.* Before she

---

*In 1938, at age seventy-five and in deep financial distress, Hearst named Shearn his trustee, tasked with managing the gradual liquidation of his nonpublishing holdings, which included art, mines, ranches, and other real estate.

entered Shearn's life, Junior had made inquiries about taking over Shearn's apartment. Shearn and later Dorothea would regularly tease their immensely wealthy upstairs neighbor with that enticing prospect.

After buying out his remaining Webb & Knapp partners in 1947 for a reported $6 million in cash and collateral, Zeckendorf bought the shell of a public company controlled by another of Rockefeller's 740 Park neighbors, taking Webb & Knapp public in what was called a reverse merger. Nearly simultaneously, Thelma Chrysler Foy, an heiress to the Chrysler automobile fortune, thought she'd made a deal with Clarence Shearn to buy the lease on his apartment. Shearn was elderly and becoming senile; his wife's behavior was erratic, too. And at the time, the owner of 740 Park, James T. Lee, was teetering on the brink of insolvency, causing his tenants, Rockefeller first among them, no end of anxiety. Then, seemingly out of nowhere, Webb & Knapp bought 740 Park from Lee and the iconic Chrysler Building skyscraper from the Chryslers. It wasn't long before Foy's two Chrysler brothers moved into 740 Park. Cryptic comments by Zeckendorf to a reporter indicated there was a connection—details unknown—between these deals.

Rockefeller Jr., typically portrayed as straitlaced and pious, was also crafty and capable of duplicity—and it's apparent he was operating behind the scenes, paying close attention to, if not overtly manipulating, his sometime ally Zeckendorf. He still wanted the Shearn apartment; getting rid of his wacky neighbors would be an added benefit. But he had a greater objective: late the same year, he bought 740 Park from Zeckendorf, made it a cooperative, and sold apartments to most of his neighbors.

Just before Rockefeller bought the building, Shearn, in decline and near death, had stopped paying his rent and was facing eviction as Thelma Foy hovered just offstage. But Rockefeller wanted the apartment, too, and suddenly, or so Dorothea Shearn claimed, so did Zeckendorf, though it is possible he wanted it for Foy and not for himself and his wife. All three were circling the apartment when Shearn died and Dorothea's slender grasp on sanity loosened. She was forced out, Rockefeller sold the apartment to Foy (though Rockefeller would later buy it from her, intending to combine it with his, but ultimately using it only for storage). Zeckendorf continued trying to buy an apartment in the building, making a serious play for another not long afterward, but cryptic letters between Rockefeller and the building's manager indicate that Big Bill had somehow been deemed unsuitable for the polished crowd in the new cooperative. That wouldn't be the last time a Zeckendorf circled 740 Park, but Big Bill would be long dead before the next chapter of *that* story would play out.*

The 1951 acquisition of that publicly traded company launched the third stage of Big Bill Zeckendorf's real estate career, which would play out over the next decade. Immediately, it elevated him from merely rich to seriously so. To celebrate, he bought his limousine, his DC-3 airplane, and his estate in Greenwich, which began as thirty-five acres (formerly owned by the reclusive "Witch of Wall Street," Hetty Green), but after a Zeckendorf-size redevelopment project, he more than doubled his acreage by filling in marshes. He also added a twenty-four-thousand-bottle wine cellar—said to be the largest in the country—beneath a new swimming pool.

A devotee of the telephone, he kept a battery of them in his office, was on them all day, and eventually owned not one but two of the very first car phones, actually ship-to-shore instruments adapted for his purposes. He also owned fifty handmade suits. But he was generous, not stingy, with his wealth and would make bad deals simply so old friends could make money. One associate said

_____

*Readers interested in the full story of the Shearn-Rockefeller-Foy-Zeckendorf quadrille should refer to pages 216–63 of *740 Park*.

he had "the memory of a bull elephant, the heart of a baby and the guts of a brass monkey."

⸎

With frequent backing from his new friends the Rockefellers, Big Bill could not only throw off an idea a minute but could also make some of them real. Despite having been frustrated in his attempt to join "Junior" Rockefeller as a resident of 740 Park, Zeckendorf continued to work with his family, even embarking on a five-year operation in concert with Junior's youngest son, David, who had recently joined the Chase National Bank, which was effectively run by his family, to relocate its headquarters and those of several of New York's other large financial institutions. Their grand purpose? Ensuring the permanence of Manhattan's downtown financial district, centered around Wall Street. They did such a good job—relocating not only Chase but Chemical, Morgan, and Hanover banks—that not even the September 11, 2001, terrorist attack on the neighborhood could alter Wall Street's identity.*

In the late 1950s, Zeckendorf also reinvented Webb & Knapp's airport, the same one Charles Lindbergh had flown out of on his pioneering first transatlantic flight to Paris in 1927, as Roosevelt Field, the largest suburban shopping mall in America, and entered the field of urban redevelopment with a five-hundred-acre project in Washington, DC. At the time, Zeckendorf recalled, "It was obvious that the central core of every one of our major cities was falling in on itself," with no new construction to replace older, often-

---

*The Rockefeller family would eventually overrule Nelson, who was Zeckendorf's champion, and disengage from most business dealings with him. But according to Cary Reich's *Rockefeller: The Life of Nelson A. Rockefeller*, it was Zeckendorf, along with Tex McCrary, a debonair PR man, who first put the idea of running for governor of New York in Nelson's head in 1954. He declined, but four years later, ran for the office and won. He was governor from 1959 to 1973.

decaying buildings. After World War II, many urban dwellers, back from fighting and starting families, fled those cities for new suburbs, and new businesses followed them, supercharging the phenomenon known as white flight, though in fact the whites who fled the cities were replaced not only by the descendants of Southern slaves, but also by less skilled, less educated whites who "had for several decades been leaving the farm country for work in the cities," Zeckendorf observed. "Because they were poor, they crowded together, which of itself tends to create a degree of urban blight."

The so-called urban renewal movement, designed to eliminate and replace slums, was codified just after the war in the Title I of the Housing Act of 1949. It allowed cities to use the legal doctrine of eminent domain to buy up slums, clear them, and offer the land at cut-rate prices to developers. In exchange, they promised to build low- and middle-income housing intended both for veterans returning from World War II and the nation's poor.

Urban renewal would ultimately be a mixed blessing and a political football. It was blamed for a host of dehumanizing urban ills—destroying businesses, disrupting lives, displacing communities, increasing racial segregation, and creating breeding grounds for crime and social malaise in the dreadful housing projects that, far too often, replaced the slums. "The buildings were not the problems," says Roberta Gratz, author of *The Battle for Gotham* and a journalist, neighborhood activist, and longtime resident of the Century on Central Park West. "The problems were social and economic. Urban renewal was not a response to problems. It was a means of taking property and stimulating development that profited a lot of people. The displacement of a million people did nothing for people with problems. In fact, it only exacerbated them." But it also had undeniable economic and cultural benefits, though at the time they were only promises of a better future.

Eventually, urban renewal changed much of the neighborhood

once called Bloomingdale, which had long since turned from a valley of flowers into a pit of despond. Romanticized in the iconic Broadway musical *West Side Story*, based on its street life—with the Irish and Puerto Rican street gangs called the Jets and the Sharks battling for power, respect, and love—the West Side's reality was somewhat different. "Except for West End Avenue, Riverside Drive, and Central Park West," James Trager wrote in his book *West of Fifth: The Rise and Fall and Rise of Manhattan's West Side*, the neighborhood "remained the depressed area it had been even before the Depression, a jumble of brownstone walkups, many of them rooming houses. . . . Hispanics were an ever-growing part of the population mix. . . . Blacks from the south were flooding into New York . . . where they found themselves in competition with Puerto Ricans, often in violent confrontations, for jobs and welfare payments. The resulting fear, combined with the impact of black and Puerto Rican children on public schools, persuaded some eight hundred thousand middle class whites to flee New York for the suburbs."

Urban renewal was designed to change all that, and Zeckendorf and Webb & Knapp played a significant role in it, in Denver, Colorado, Washington, DC, Montreal, and finally three notable Manhattan projects conceived of by the city's omnipresent and controversial master planner, Robert Moses. The first was Kips Bay Plaza, two monumental, reinforced-concrete slabs of apartments designed by I. M. Pei. Next came Park West Village, the redevelopment of six blocks of tenements on the upper end of Central Park West. Finally, he built Lincoln Towers, eight twenty-eight-story, middle-class apartment towers at the northern end of Lincoln Square, just above today's Lincoln Center.

The last was part of Moses's grand scheme for what he called "a reborn west side . . . marching north from Columbus Circle and eventually spreading over the entire dismal and decayed west side."

But Zeckendorf wasn't proud of Lincoln Towers. A financial partner, the Lazard Frères investment bank, removed Pei from that job in an effort to keep costs down. "I am ashamed of it," Big Bill said bluntly.

Zeckendorf stumbled again in 1953, when Webb & Knapp, by then allegedly worth a quarter of a billion dollars, tried to go into the hotel business by buying the national Statler chain, which did business in eight cities. He was outmaneuvered by the hotelier Conrad Hilton, who snatched them away, but could console himself with other accomplishments.

In January 1958, Twentieth Century-Fox announced plans to develop its huge studio property just west of Beverly Hills into a city-within-a-city. Zeckendorf was sure he was the only man who could build it, even though Webb & Knapp was, Zeckendorf admitted, "spread thin across America." Lazard Frères once again signed on as a financial backer with the right to walk away and demand its money back. Zeckendorf began planning what would eventually become Century City, the largest privately financed development in American history.

Then, likely still smarting from being outsmarted by Conrad Hilton, Zeckendorf bought a ninety-thousand-square-foot piece of land between Fifty-First and Fifty-Second Streets on Sixth Avenue, leased or bought most of the two blocks to the north, and committed to build a two-thousand-room New York hotel—the first big one in New York since the Waldorf-Astoria in 1931—which was going to require all the cash Webb & Knapp had on hand. So he made a deal to sell his contract to develop Century City to another developer. But then, the buyer backed out, and simultaneously Lazard asked for its money back. It was the first sign that Zeckendorf's wheeling and dealing might have a downside. "If we get hit by a depression, or make some bad mistakes, we could be selling hot dogs around here," worried his twenty-nine-year-old son and namesake, Bill Jr. "We live on borrowed money."

Big Bill's boy had started out working summers at Webb & Knapp while a student. After realizing he was "a terrible actor," the stage-struck Bill Jr. studied theatrical production while in college in Arizona, but then he went back to work for his dad until he enlisted and became an Army Intelligence corporal during the Korean War in the early 1950s.

When he came back home, his father put him in charge of renting out a three-quarters-empty apartment complex in San Diego. Working with the navy, he filled it with servicemen and their families and was a year later named a vice president and his father's "companion and adviser of all new developments," or so Big Bill later wrote. "I would say that's an exaggeration," says Bill Jr. now. "He kept me informed of everything he was doing." Bill Jr. worked on urban renewal and Canadian projects at first, but eventually began doing deals and working on building projects all over North America. On a trip to Europe, a mutual friend introduced him to Guri Lie; they married early in 1956 and eventually moved into the same East Seventy-Second Street building where Big Bill and his wife had lived. Later, they moved into 30 Beekman Place, a rental building bought in the name of Marion Zeckendorf in 1952, where they eventually took over Big Bill's I. M. Pei–designed nine-room penthouse. Pei and his family lived there, too. Bill Jr. and Guri stayed until their second son, Arthur, was born. Shortly afterward, they split up, and Guri and the children moved to 1100 Park Avenue, a 1930 cooperative on Carnegie Hill, where she raised the boys.

A big man like his father, two hundred pounds and five foot eleven, Bill Jr. found a way to combine the two passions that were also his inheritance, real estate and showmanship, in a new company, Zeckendorf Hotels. "The nearest thing to a combination of real estate and the theater is a hotel," he said. As that subsidiary's president, he presided over six hotels his father bought in Manhattan, then announced plans to build the Zeckendorf on Sixth Avenue.

"I like to say it was my project," says Bill. "It wasn't. It was my father's. I worked on it, but he always did the financing." Just as Bill Jr. was getting settled into his new jobs, his father's penchant for dreaming, scheming, borrowing, and stretching himself and his equity thin began to threaten both the business he'd built and the image of success he'd cultivated since joining Webb & Knapp. Early in February 1959, a front-page story in the *Wall Street Journal*, though couched in admiration of an entrepreneur apparently at the peak of his power, revealed that Webb & Knapp had taken on a nine-figure debt and was losing money for the first time since going public.

No longer able to borrow freely, the *Journal* reported, Zeckendorf had begun using his own money to fund ongoing construction projects worth half a billion dollars. His dire need for cash, and the layers of complications in his deals, led him to take in a financial partner under onerous terms, and to borrow from investment banks and private investors at short-term interest rates that would eventually run as high as 24 percent. So young Bill added overhead reduction to his portfolio of responsibilities; Webb & Knapp then had a staff of four hundred and spent about $8 million a year on operations and had seven offices across the country and three corporate airplanes.

"I would rather be alive at eighteen percent than dead at the prime rate," Big Bill once famously said. Within months, though, he was forced to stop spending and start selling as building costs rose and his accumulated debt threatened to overwhelm Webb & Knapp. At one point in 1960, he had to pay back $100 million in three months and still owed another $400 million. He was juggling these debts even as Webb & Knapp was gearing up for $150 million in slum-clearance development and starting to build Century City. There and elsewhere, cost projections proved overly optimistic and would soon force him to come up with even more cash.

So Zeckendorf sold skyscrapers, including the Chrysler Building, and his huge empty tract in the Santa Monica Mountains. Then, in July 1960, he abandoned the already-under-construction Hotel Zeckendorf and parted ways with I. M. Pei, who'd created his own firm in 1955 but continued to work exclusively for Webb & Knapp. Worried about Zeckendorf's finances, Pei cut that tie, too.

In 1961, Zeckendorf sold his Chicago hotels, lost control of his Denver development to his financial partner, but nonetheless bought Yonkers Raceway, a Westchester horse track, and three new hotels, including the famous Beverly Wilshire in Beverly Hills, and put his son in charge of a new project, Freedomland, an attempt to duplicate California's Disneyland in the Bronx. "Talk of his impending downfall became common," *Life* magazine would later say.

At the end of that year, Zeckendorf grabbed a lifeline, $44 million to cover his short-term debts, from a group of British investors in exchange for half of his thirteen ongoing Title I projects. But a month later, when his Yonkers Raceway deal fell through after he failed to get it financed, his new partners grew restive. "William Sr. could not live with oversight," says Will Zeckendorf. "He just couldn't stomach the idea of not being his own boss any longer."

That's when real estate values reversed a long run-up and began to decline. Zeckendorf was no longer able to piggyback one new project on the last, financing development with dealmaking. He stopped selling properties as their prices dropped, but still continued buying, even after his latest partners objected. In December 1962, the representatives of the British investors resigned from the Webb & Knapp board and began an effort to oust him. By mid-1963, they'd succeeded in taking over those big projects. Bill sold his remaining interest in Century City to what had until then been his minority partner in the project, Alcoa, aka the Aluminum Company of America.

Webb & Knapp was still alive, but it was staggering. Zeckendorf's desperation was an open secret; friendly competitors who'd once bought and sold buildings with him on a handshake now offered him less than the properties' worth because they knew he couldn't say no. "How can they say I'm broke?" he asked developer Alan Tishman, a childhood friend from the West Side, one night as they stood at side-by-side urinals during a black-tie benefit. "I owe a *billion* dollars!"

For the next two years, crisis after crisis, all attributable to the debts rung up by his frantic dealmaking, kept Zeckendorf off-balance. Freedomland started sinking, literally (it was built on marshland) and economically, and he sold his share in it in summer 1964, shortly before it went bankrupt. More mass liquidations of property were followed by more carefully choreographed sales, but all they succeeded in doing was keeping the terminally ill patient on life support. His wife even sold 30 Beekman Place, but kept a twenty-five-year lease on their penthouse at $10,000 a year. She denied that the sale had anything to do with her husband's troubles, calling the decision purely personal.

In early 1965, *Life* magazine revisited Zeckendorf. "A Big Man on the Thin Edge," its headline read, over a photo of him in one of his signature homburgs. But his other signature, a great big grin, had been replaced by a worried frown. "It's terrible, terrible pain," he told the magazine. "Agony. It's mortifying and humiliating." In its final paragraphs, *Life* noted that Bill Jr. had refused to be photographed with his father and was considering going out on his own. "Webb and Knapp has been too much of a one-man show," Bill Jr. said. "We should take a hell of a lot harder look at things." Today, Bill Zeckendorf's opinion remains pretty much the same: "My father owned the company, ran the company, and did all the financing. I worked project by project. Of course I was concerned. But there was absolutely no way I could affect it."

Soon, the Securities and Exchange Commission barred all trading in Webb & Knapp shares. A few days later, Marine Midland Trust asked a judge to declare the firm insolvent and put it into involuntary bankruptcy. "We just ran out of gas," Big Bill admitted, just before a trustee was appointed to take over. He was fifty-nine years old. "There was an almost welcome stillness," he recalled in his autobiography. "I became, in effect, a bystander at the wake." Zeckendorf resigned from his firm in July 1965. His son and son-in-law had quit a month earlier, vowing to open their own company. In fact, they bought back the furniture in a bankruptcy sale and almost immediately started again even as Webb & Knapp's remaining assets were sold. Its stock was delisted by the American Stock Exchange, an investigation found that its liabilities exceeded its assets by $39 million, and in 1967 the bankruptcy trustee sued Big Bill and others for $50 million for waste and mismanagement. People wondered if he would kill himself. Stories about an affair he'd had suddenly leaked to the newspapers. And still, the worst was yet to come.

In May 1968, Marion Zeckendorf was killed in a plane crash on the island of Guadeloupe, en route to a vacation with Big Bill, who was waiting at the airport. But the tragedy had an upside. He inherited enough money from Marion's estate to return to buying, selling, and trading real estate. He still lived in the penthouse at 30 Beekman, thanks to that lease Marion had arranged when she sold it. He also kept his I. M. Pei–designed office. His landlord was General Property Corporation, which employed him as a consultant. His bosses were his son and his son-in-law. It's unknown who paid the salary of Eugene, his private chef, who stayed on, too.

Big Bill celebrated his sixty-third birthday that summer by giving an interview to the newly launched *New York* magazine. He detailed his recent deals, many done on commission for others, but at least he was dealing: assembling a site for a department store; planning a Lower West Side artists' community and an upstate urban renewal project; buying and developing the *Queen Mary* as an attraction for the city of Long Beach, California, with Diners Club, the credit-card company; disassembling London Bridge and moving it to Arizona, the wellspring of the Zeckendorf fortune, as a tourist attraction. "They were doing deals left and right," says Arthur Zeckendorf. Big Bill was still "dreaming huge dreams," adds Will. "He wanted to convert the Staten Island ferry for gambling. He had ideas for nuclear power." But he was running on empty—and would soon have to admit it. Crushed by judgments and facing the imminent seizure of his personal property, Big Bill declared bankruptcy, listing assets of under $2 million and debts exceeding $79 million. The court took away his Greenwich estate, his wine, his Cadillac with its custom WZ-1 plate, and his airplane.

They couldn't take away his story or his accomplishments, though, so he took some time to write his autobiography, which, naturally, grew out of a bigger deal. Webb & Knapp had sold Metropolitan Life the underlying lease on its Madison Avenue office building, and MetLife agreed to sell it to Bill Jr.'s new General Property with financing from Equitable Life, but only if the Zeckendorfs could convince some existing tenants to renew their leases for twenty-one years. All agreed but one, the book publisher Holt, Rinehart and Winston, which would only sign a new lease if Zeckendorf wrote an autobiography for them. He did, preempting an unauthorized biography that was in the works, so everybody won . . . again.

Two years later, the bankruptcy trustee's mismanagement suit against the Zeckendorfs was finally settled with the payment of $86,000 in cash, and the issuance of two promissory notes, one from Bill Jr. for $275,000, secured by Philadelphia real estate, and the second, for $499,000, unsecured, from Big Bill. That settlement finally freed Bill Jr., then forty-two, to start his own career in earnest. His ties to his father were still too strong to break, though. In fall 1972, he bought the Kips Bay Plaza project from Alcoa, got back Lincoln Towers, too, and was soon making real money again.

General Property, with seventeen employees (and no airplanes), was much smaller than Webb & Knapp. It, too, did development deals and relied on financing from entities that had once backed his father, but like most of New York's builders, faced with rapidly rising costs and inflation in the midsixties, Bill Jr. was cautious. He stuck to "merchant" building, using other people's money on projects and selling out of them quickly.

Bill Jr. had seen what overreaching could do and openly admitted that his ambitions weren't as large as his father's. That would eventually change, but not until after Big Bill had left the stage. For the moment, he still had some living to do. Just after the Lincoln Square buyback, the elder Zeckendorf got married for the third time, to Alice Bache, widow of the founder of Bache & Co. stock brokerage, whom he'd been seeing since Marion died. They'd been constant companions and best friends, but marriage proved a mistake. The couple separated after three months. Zeckendorf would marry one more time, in 1975, but by then he'd been diminished by a series of strokes that culminated in his death a year later in his last apartment at the Mayfair House, a residential hotel on Sixty-Fifth Street and Park Avenue.

His landlord was his son.

⎯⎯⎯⎯⎯⎯

General Properties had bought the Mayfair in 1972 in partnership with a savings bank. It was an early move in Bill Jr.'s campaign to restore the family name and fortunes.* Shortly after his father died, Bill, who looked like him but was a man of few words, diffident, calm, remote, and stern where his father was voluble, excitable, engaging, and boldly optimistic, dropped the *Jr.* from his name—an act that symbolized his ascension. Newspapers continued using the suffix anyway.

---

* A few years later, Zeckendorf would reestablish the tradition of fine dining in residential hotels when he lured Sirio Maccioni, the maître d' of the Colony, a high-society watering hole, to the Mayfair House, to open the first of his famous Le Cirque restaurants.

Three years before his father's death, Zeckendorf had found the business partner of his dreams when his second wife, Nancy, a former ballerina, introduced him to Justin Colin, a lawyer-turned-arbitrageur, partner in a Wall Street brokerage, and head of the Ballet Theater Foundation, the parent of the American Ballet Theater. Nancy Zeckendorf sat on the foundation's board. When the foundation bought a new home for its ballet company, Bill Jr. was named its adviser.

Colin was the son-in-law of a Wall Street financier whose investments included the Grand Union supermarket chain. After it was sold in 1973, Colin began investing the family's fortune. Bill Jr.'s brother-in-law had left his wife and walked out of General Properties the next day. Zeckendorf brought in Colin and kept going. Though his primary interest was airlines, Colin also became a partner in a new Zeckendorf Co. in the early eighties.

In 1975, Zeckendorf and Colin bought the Hotel Delmonico, a few blocks south of the Mayfair on Park Avenue, and announced plans to convert it to condominiums. A year later, as that project neared completion (with the first American outpost of the Paris discotheque Régine set to open in its basement), they and a construction company bought the run-down McAlpin Hotel on Herald Square out of bankruptcy for a dollar. In the next three years, Zeckendorf and Colin added the Hotel Navarro on Central Park South, the Statler Hilton near Pennsylvania Station, and the Shoreham Hotel in Washington, DC, where they planned to add a new building full of condominiums.

Zeckendorf "was keeping it low-key," says his son Will, "building up a net worth. He did a great job buying and flipping hotels" such as the Mayfair, sold to a big hotel group. In the process, he amused his teenage sons. One summer, the Who stayed at the Navarro, and Will remembers his father's accountant presenting the bill after the group's drummer, Keith Moon, destroyed his room. "And Bruce Springsteen lived there," Arthur says. "That was cool for us."

Bill's sons remember Colin fondly as the best partner their father ever had. Again, though, in 1981, fate and finance conspired against Zeckendorf. Justin Colin's airlines began to lose money and abruptly closed, and in August 1982 he declared bankruptcy. Left hanging was their purchase, financed by two banks, of a large property at Broadway and Ninety-Sixth Street on the Upper West Side, where they'd just begun Zeckendorf's first new construction project since the collapse of Webb & Knapp, a three-hundred-apartment condominium tower called the Columbia. Zeckendorf's dream of stable backing evaporated, but still "he had an itch for development," says son Arthur. "Development is a lot of fun."

"I remember him saying, 'Hotels are great, but you're leaving no imprint,'" adds Will. And Bill knew where he wanted to build. "The Upper West Side was desperate," says Arthur. "This is when you couldn't walk on Eighth Avenue or in Central Park. He knew Ninety-Sixth and Broadway would change the entire West Side. He had a vision. He had the stage. He took the gamble." And took the Columbia project alone.

His dreams were even larger than the West Side. He saw decay up and down the chain of circles, squares, and plazas that had marked Manhattan's growth from Union Square up Broadway. Since the end of World War II, when New York solidified its place as America's financial heart, developers had been more interested in building offices than homes. Zeckendorf wanted to build the latter in a kind of one-man urban renewal program. "His vision was changing horrendous neighborhoods," says Arthur. It was a vision worthy of Bill's father. "Yeah," Arthur says, "all of a sudden, he goes from buying hotels to doing development. Boom."

<hr>

The end of Zeckendorf-Colin coincided with the arrival of the third generation of Zeckendorfs in real estate. Will, the elder brother, had gone to work for their father in 1980 at age twenty-two, after graduating from Tufts. Arthur, also a graduate of Tufts, had joined full-time a year later at twenty-one, just before Will left to get an MBA at Harvard Business School. At twenty-three, Arthur got to work on the Columbia, which was then something rare in Manhattan, new construction built on a vacant lot bought in 1981 near an express subway stop. Bill Jr. bet the area could be gentrified despite neighborhood skepticism. Arthur worked on the floor plans, oversaw construction, chose finishes such as paint, stone, and appliances, and oversaw marketing. "I'm manager for this gigantic project," he says. "We have nobody else. My father had three people working for him." Yet they succeeded, selling out the building at an average $200 per square foot after it opened in 1983. Within eighteen months, prices there had risen by 50 percent.

Zeckendorf wasn't just a West Side evangelist; he took his opportunities where he found them. In 1982, he'd started building Delmonico Plaza, a midtown office condo, and another apartment condo at Sixty-Eighth and Broadway, when Justin Colin went bust. "Of course it was a bad moment," says Bill Jr. But he knew fresh financing could be arranged—and where to get it. So though Colin's collapse stung him, it didn't stop him from undertaking even more new projects. As the economy began improving in the early eighties, new wealth poured into the city, and the building revival that had begun in 1978, fueled by government-sponsored bonuses and tax incentives, showed no signs of abating.*

Henceforth, he would always work with multiple partners, was far more comfortable (in contrast to his father) when spreading the risk widely, even at the cost of his own equity. His new backers were

---

*The boom was kicked off by a ten-year tax exemption put in place in 1975. It applied to any buildings that were begun prior to December 1985. Zoning regulations on the West Side had also been loosened in 1982 to nudge development pressure away from the East Side.

World Wide Holdings, a company originally formed to trade in surplus goods left around the world after World War II; Kumagai Gumi, a Japanese construction company; and Arthur Cohen, one of the local developers then dreaming with Aristotle Onassis of building the Olympic Tower. In exchange for their money, Bill Jr. assembled sites, handled the regulatory process, and designed buildings. Construction was generally left to others, though still supervised by the Zeckendorfs. And with partners, they spun off a separate company, Manhattan Marketing, to handle on-site sales; it paid Arthur and Will salaries and bonuses. "It was a very lucrative business to be in," says Arthur.

Will returned from business school in 1984 to a very different company, still tiny and headquartered at the Delmonico (Zeckendorf and Nancy lived in a four-room penthouse above the store), but building all over the city. In 1985, *Institutional Investor* found the Zeckendorf Co. development "pipeline quite full" and wondered, "Might Zeckendorf Jr. turn out to be a late-blooming Zeckendorf Sr. after all?"

Two years later the *New York Times* would describe Bill as Manhattan's most prolific developer. It found him at work on Zeckendorf Towers, a huge mixed-use project on Union Square named to honor his father, with commercial space alongside 670 condos. He was also selling six other condo projects that would put three thousand apartments on line within two years, plus a Times Square hotel billed (like the phantom Hotel Zeckendorf) as New York's tallest.

If his ambition was beginning to look a lot like his father's, so was his taste for the finer things. He'd been named a grand officer of the Confrérie des Chevaliers du Tastevin, an elite group of gourmets, served on the board of governors of the oenophile Commanderie de Bordeaux, and kept a wine cellar at Spilling Pond, his big weekend home in Bedford, New York. "I was left with nothing but the name Zeckendorf," he told a writer, "but that turned out to be a lot."

He worked hard for his money. A graphic with the *Times* story showed his projects as a string of condos running up the East Side from Union Square, a small bunch at the south end of Manhattan, and a swoosh of nine buildings across the West Side, including Central Park Place, a three-hundred-unit, fifty-six-story condo tower just south of Columbus Circle, where prices had hit $600 a square foot and a penthouse with terraces cost $4.1 million. It was distinguished by a green-glass-and-aluminum façade and larger apartments than in typical condos—and would eventually attract name-brand celebrity residents such as Goldie Hawn and Kurt Russell, Gene Hackman, and Al Pacino.

Bill Jr.'s bet on Columbus Circle was the first of significance since William Randolph Hearst's in the twenties. The circle is the point from which distances to and from Manhattan are measured. Could development move west and finally make it a focal point within the city, too? Zeckendorf saw it as a vital link between upper Broadway and west midtown. "We were a little bit early," he allows, "but we had Japanese partners doing marketing in Japan, which made it much safer." Nonetheless, that was the moment when Bill, whom the papers still called Jr., proved to be a little too much like his dad.

At the time "the boys," as they are still often called, each had his own turf. Will, the business school grad, handled finance, and Arthur, the shyer and apparently more diffident of the brothers, design and marketing. Balding, with a slight lisp but a tenacious grasp on all it takes to develop a building, Arthur is the inside man of their team. His brother, who has a silver tongue, a full head of hair, and an uncanny knack for marketing apartments, is Mr. Outside. "Will was very smart, a very smart talker, very analytical, very nice," says a banker who worked with them. "Arthur was much quieter." As time went on, they would overlap and share most jobs, but Will admits that Arthur had a particular knack for visualizing floor plans in three dimensions, while he was more involved with lobbies and other public spaces of the buildings. But both managed projects, and both lived at the Park Belvedere, built by Bill in 1984 on Seventy-Ninth Street, across the street from the American Museum of Natural History. Its architect, Frank Williams, would work with the family for years, and Bill was particularly proud of its good looks and the way it fit into a neighborhood where there'd been almost no new construction since the 1930s. The market agreed. Bill got an average $400 per square foot for apartments there, and their value quickly doubled.

The Park Belvedere had been Arthur's project. He would also eventually claim some credit for the Columbia, and two East Side condos. Will ran herd over three Hudson Towers buildings at Battery Park City and the Copley. Both boys worked on Central Park Place and Zeckendorf Towers. "There was never any doubt in my mind that I would go into real estate with my father," Will said at the time. Bill said his goal was "an ongoing family company that will have staying power."

Zeckendorf's focus that year was on the city block bounded by Forty-Ninth and Fiftieth Streets and Eighth and Ninth Avenues. It had been the site of Madison Square Garden until the arena was demolished in 1968 and replaced by a parking lot. But attempts to develop the block had hit the shoals of community opposition while its owner, the Gulf & Western conglomerate, was stuck paying about $1 million in taxes a year—so they sold it. In fall 1986, Zeckendorf was assiduously pursuing the zoning variances he'd need to achieve his dream of erecting three buildings there with offices, condominiums, and retail stores surrounding an open plaza in the middle of the block. The complex would eventually be named Worldwide Plaza after Zeckendorf's financial partner. Construction began that November and would take two years. "Our view is that Eighth Avenue will be one of the great streets in five to ten years," Zeckendorf said.

No one doubted it. Zeckendorf's track record of twenty completed projects worth a billion dollars made Worldwide Plaza seem like a sure thing from the moment the Zeckendorf-led syndicate bought the block for $100 million. The ad agency Ogilvy & Mather signed on as a partner and anchor tenant, sharing the building costs: $550 million. In July 1986, Zeckendorf won final approval to build it on the same day he won the right to redevelop South Ferry Plaza, the Staten Island ferry terminal at the bottom of Manhattan. *That* project was budgeted at $334 million. The *New York Post's* story on his coup was headlined "Zeckendorf's $884M Day." Unfortunately, the photo illustrating the piece was of Big Bill, not his son.

It was a critical moment. The company went from one or two projects a year to as many as a dozen at a time. "Massive projects," says Arthur. "He's hot and the market's strong and the banks are throwing money, Japanese banks, American banks, Canadian banks, and he buys all this land." "He pretty much said yes to every deal that came his way," adds Will. "He made a conscious decision to ramp it up. It was wild. Managing growth is tough under any circumstance, and managing the takeoff we had then was a Herculean challenge."

Negotiations to rent the remaining office space at Worldwide Plaza proceeded through 1987, with Cravath, Swaine & Moore, a stuffy white-shoe law firm, N. W. Ayer, another ad agency, and Polygram, the record company, all circling, but not committing, and the entertainment conglomerate Viacom making a handshake deal to rent space there. Just after, Ayer agreed to rent four hundred thousand square feet, but then it lost the US Army account (it had created the slogan "Be all that you can be") and backed out. Then, in October, the stock market crashed and the building craze that had lasted nine years abruptly ended.

Wall Street payrolls and profits contracted, and all over the city real estate suffered. In the late eighties, developers had rushed projects in order to collect government incentives and tax abatements that were set to expire, raising construction costs and glutting the market with condos. Suddenly, lenders grew wary. Leases weren't renewed. Apartment prices fell. More than 60 million square feet of office space sat vacant.

At Worldwide Plaza, still a construction site, Viacom suddenly lost interest in leasing a new headquarters. To hook Cravath (which wanted thirteen floors) and keep Ayer interested, Zeckendorf had had to put more bait on his hook: equity in the building plus bargain-basement rents. Polygram and, later, lesser tenants got sweetheart deals, too. Making matters worse, well into the midnineties the blocks surrounding Worldwide Plaza that Zeckendorf had believed would radically improve after he started building did not. A quarter of the condos, which were sold for an average $380 per square foot, would still be vacant in 1990. More than a quarter of the retail space in the development stayed stubbornly empty, too, the *New York Times* would later note, because the area "sometimes feels threatening to tenants and visitors alike."

By then, Bill Zeckendorf was in worse trouble than the neighborhood—thanks to his itch for development. "Go from '83 when he had one project, the Park Belvedere, to 1990 when he had eight or nine massive projects under way," says son Will. "You can't manage that. Developing a major building takes four years, and once the process begins, it rarely stops, even if the market slows down." Arthur was uncomfortable and voiced his concerns. "You're stuck," he recalls grimly. Asked if his ambitions had grown too large, their father sounds impatient. "The market had turned," he says now. "You're always ambitious, but you go with the market."

Zeckendorf Co., Bill Jr.'s post-Colin company, had grown to 150 employees with half a dozen executives overseeing separate departments dedicated to specialized areas such as construction and retail leasing. Things still seemed like business as usual—even to Will. "It was a very late-eighties capital structure," he says. "Highly, highly, highly leveraged." But that was normal. Or so Will himself thought until fall 1989, when his father suddenly blurted out,

"I think I'm broke." "I don't know," Will answered. "I think things are going pretty great." But father knew best. The Zeckendorfs had made commitments and had to keep going, straight into a financial abyss.

Even though Wall Street was frozen and represented 40 percent of the condo market, keep going they did. In 1990, Will was the project manager on the Alexandria, a new condo at Broadway and Seventy-Second with a vaguely Egyptian design and apartments conceived to fill the gap between the sprawling units popular in the late 1920s and the studios and one-bedrooms in undistinguished brick buildings that represented the pinnacle of residential urban architecture after World War II.

Each of their buildings had improved on the last. "Bigger apartments, higher ceilings, more generous amenities, better design," says Arthur. At the Alexandria, Will targeted baby boomers with children who wanted larger apartments but were willing to trade old-style amenities such as dining rooms for the building's setback balconies and its basement health spa complete with a pool. To counter the still-lingering memories of what had been known just a few years earlier as Needle Park, a gathering place for drug addicts just across Broadway, the Zeckendorfs paid to fence, plant, and light it. Though it was clearly in their economic interest to do that, the Alexandria also evidenced the family's belief in the West Side. Their target price for sales of about $425 per square foot was a bet that the neighborhood was on the upswing. Their father kept making deals south of Columbus Circle, too. "It's a natural area for new development," he told David W. Dunlap, a real estate reporter at the *Times*, simultaneously revealing his plans and his unabated self-delusion.

Zeckendorf must have known that, in 1989, the real estate market had hit a speed bump. Sales slowed, credit tightened, real estate values flattened and declined across the country, and inflation jumped just as troubled savings and loan associations across the country started dumping their real estate assets at fire-sale prices. By the following year, when Zeckendorf gave Dunlap that optimistic quote, he was already in serious trouble. "The music stops and he has six or seven projects in midstream," says son Will. Adds a wistful Arthur, "If the dance had continued, it would have been great."

More dominoes fell. Integrated Resources, a financial-services company that specialized in tax shelters, collapsed and went bankrupt shortly after signing a lease for three hundred thousand square feet at Zeckendorf Towers. Bill's hotel on Times Square had another two hundred thousand square feet of unrented office space. Five of his condo projects had unsold units, too. Zeckendorf was renegotiating loans on two other deals that were both suffering from cost overruns, redeveloping the Herald Square and Upper East Side sites that had been home to Gimbels department stores. Zeckendorf sold a big assemblage on Fifty-Seventh Street between Park and Madison to the same hotel group that years before had bought the Mayfair. Most significant of all, he was negotiating the sale of a majority of his company to Tobishima, a Tokyo-based construction company. The dollar was falling against the yen, and Japanese had started snapping up real estate all over America, from condos at Central Park Place to troubled trophy properties, Rockefeller Center among them.*

In September 1990, the *Wall Street Journal* ran an exposé of Zeckendorf that "effectively ended his career because, when the banks saw it, they flipped," says Will. He thinks a banker leaked the story. His brother blames an attorney. Regardless, the piece, headlined "New York's Realty Woes Hit Zeckendorf, Who May Sell Stake in Firm to Japanese," was devastating. "Bill Jr. was a risk-taker," says

---

* That transaction "signaled the complete end of Rockefeller dominance in New York real estate," Tom Shachtman wrote in *Skyscraper Dreams*. "What family or families would now be dominant?"

one of his bankers. "I wouldn't say gambler, but he was willing to sign guarantees. He had an unusual personality. He was very 'Don't bother me with details.' He'd listen to a fine-tuned analysis and half-way through he'd say, 'How much per square foot?' That was all he was interested in. He just liked to do deals."

Luckily, he was also well liked, so his creditors were inclined to help him work things out. He was hardly alone. "There's a lot of wreckage in that cycle," says Will. A number of other major developers, including Donald Trump and Larry Silverstein (who was one of Zeckendorf's partners on the Gimbels deals), had gotten caught in the collapse of realty values and restructured at that time. Bill Jr. finally admitted to the *Washington Post*, "Things are as bad as I have ever seen them—for everybody."

At the time, a broker he'd worked with predicted that Zeckendorf would be back when the market improved, but five years later he was still shrinking. He'd lost control of Zeckendorf Towers and his Columbus Circle office building. The former "was his undoing," said *Crain's New York Business*. He'd paid out millions to brokers and to build out Integrated Resources' space, which sat empty until Zeckendorf could no longer service his loans. The Times Square hotel was so delayed that Zeckendorf, who'd sold the place but was still responsible for finishing it, ended up in litigation with its builder over costs that ate up all his profits. Falling condo prices hurt as well. He was being nibbled to death. Worst of all, Zeckendorf Co. was no longer Bill Jr.'s business. *Crain's* also revealed that his sons had quietly taken it over a few years earlier.

———

For Will and Arthur Zeckendorf, the early nineties were a nightmare. "From '90 to '92, it's all hands on deck with fire hoses, trying to save the ship," says Will. "By the middle of '91, I know it's an utterly hopeless situation." During those years, though formally still employed by their father, "we worked for banks," says Arthur. Within the small circle of Bill Jr.'s close associates, it was said that the boys "more or less threw him out of the office," according to an architect the Zeckendorfs worked with.

"It was my decision," Bill Jr. insists. "At that point, there was much less to do and I decided I should give the boys every opportunity." Regardless of whether he was physically in the room, he remained a tangible presence as they helped his lenders understand his deals and, as projects were foreclosed or restructured, worked out rescue plans based on intimate knowledge that let them map the road to ultimate success. When a Japanese bank took over the Gotham, for instance, the Zeckendorfs convinced the bankers to make it a rental for the moment and wait for better times to sell the apartments. "Why sell for ten cents on the dollar when we can recover all your assets?" Arthur asked them. They did the same at Worldwide Plaza, which was taken over by the Blackstone investment bank, "who, as a thank-you note, kept us on as asset managers for three or four years," Will says.

"We were on a risk diet," he continues. "We don't want to take risk. And we're trying to earn enough income to support ourselves and the employees and their families. There's not much left of the old Zeckendorf Co. at that point. I don't want to say 'lights out,' but it was close to lights out. The company is basically Arthur, myself, and a secretary. I'd say '91, '92 were the lean years. My worst two years." But in 1992, they started their own business, Zeckendorf Realty, and began offering their services to others. "They had to go into the fee business to use their knowledge and skill set as opposed to risking capital because you have to have capital to risk it," says a banker who met them at the time.

The hotelier who'd bought Bill Jr.'s Fifty-Seventh Street project hired them to help develop what became I. M. Pei's and Frank Williams's Four Seasons Hotel. They were hired by banks that had foreclosed on other developers, too. "We said, 'We have no debt. We have no problems with banks. We're clean. Do you want an experienced developer to work the property out for you?'" Will recalls. "They hired us to finish construction, do marketing and sales and asset management. By '93, it was a new kind of life. It was kind of liberating, actually."

Though Bill Zeckendorf "packed his bags and moved" to New Mexico in 1992, in Arthur's words, and was no longer involved in the business in any way by 1995, it took the rest of the decade before he let the world know that he'd left the arena and created a new life in Santa Fe. At age seventy, Bill gave his last interview to the *Wall Street Journal.* Sitting on a pillow designed to cushion a back so bad that he'd had a pump surgically implanted in his body to give him constant doses of painkillers, he blamed a lifetime of horseback riding not just for ruining his back but for hastening the professional downfall kicked off when the market cratered in 1987. But he also acknowledged other crushing problems: "Millions of dollars in court-ordered judgments for failing to pay debts," the *Journal* said.

A few months earlier, a longtime business associate had even hired a safecracker to enter Bill's Park Avenue penthouse and appropriate valuables to pay off a $4.8 million loan guarantee on a condo project in the Bronx that had failed in the eighties. It was, in Yogi Berra's phrase, déjà vu all over again. He was accused of hiding assets while living large, just as his father had done. Thus, a collection agency, a city marshal, two cops in uniforms, and a locksmith had arrived at the Delmonico in February 1999. Escorted to Bill Jr.'s penthouse by a manager, they broke in, videotaped a Modigliani and a Degas sculpture, but found no safe and took nothing with them. Will and Arthur later swore in court that the artworks were theirs and on loan to their father.*

---

* They'd inherited money from their grandmother. "It wasn't a Rockefeller inheritance," Arthur says, "but it was a respectable sum."

"Mr. Zeckendorf lacked the toughness frequently required in development's sharp-elbowed world," the *Journal* said in its scathing indictment. "He often lost sight of the day-to-day details . . . was too eager to please outside investors," and finally, worst of all, cared more for building than making money. Thus he'd given personal guarantees against business loans and ended up destroyed by debts. Refusing to declare bankruptcy out of respect for his family name, or to ask his sons for help, he'd ruined himself.

He'd since worked out a settlement with one former partner and would do the same with others. When he could (as when he sold the former Adonis Theater block he'd assembled just north of Worldwide Plaza to fellow developer Harry Macklowe early in 1997), he paid down his debts. When he couldn't, he stopped. Sometimes, he ended up back in court. Eventually, his sons say, he was left in peace.

In a brief conversation, Zeckendorf, now eighty-three and ailing, rejects the idea that he grew too ambitious and too like his father. But he also rejects the notion that he was merely another casualty of inevitable market cycles in real estate. He acknowledges that after the stock market crash of 1987, his fortunes turned downward, "but it affects you on a building-by-building basis," he continues, adding that it's fair to say he was putting out one fire at a time.

"I took certain risks," he admits, "maybe too many, but I got most of the projects built, and I'm very pleased my boys have had the successes they've had. I have tremendous respect for what they've been able to do. They deserve everything that's come their way."

Asked, finally, how he would describe his own accomplishments, he replies briskly, "What I accomplished can be seen. The buildings are there."

Part Three

CONDOMANIA

"Keep, ancient lands, your storied pomp!" cries she
With silent lips. "Give me your tired, your poor,
Your huddled masses yearning to breathe free,
The wretched refuse of your teeming shore.
Send these, the homeless, tempest-tost to me,
I lift my lamp beside the golden door!"
—EMMA LAZARUS, "THE NEW COLOSSUS," 1883

We ought to change the sign on the
Statue of Liberty to read, "This time around,
send us your rich."
—FELIX ROHATYN, 1977

Just when Bill Zeckendorf Jr. stepped out of the big shadow cast by his father, a rival for the crown of New York's next "Big Bill" crossed the East River and crowned himself the brash new king of Manhattan real estate. He, too, was a "son of," only his name was Trump and his father, Fred Trump, got his start building small homes in New York City's "outer boroughs"—only unlike Big Bill Zeckendorf, he never lost his fortune. As a boy, his son Donald began dreaming of crossing the river to Manhattan; like many ambitious young men, he wanted to outdo his successful father. And just like Bill Zeckendorf Jr., he was his father's opposite, only in Trump's case, the son was the boisterous, cocky, self-promoting dynamo and the father was quiet, careful, and undemonstrative. At age twenty-seven, in 1974, Trump started looking for the sort of bargains that are often available in a troubled economy—and New York's, at that point, was catastrophic.

His smartest early move was hiring Louise Sunshine, a former fund-raiser for New York's governor Hugh Carey, as his in-house lob-byist. Sunshine recalls meeting Trump when he asked for help get-ting a Big Bill–Style license plate for his Cadillac limousine bearing his initials, DJT, from New York's motor vehicle department. With Sunshine's help, Trump next won the right to develop two freight yards (nine acres in midtown and seventy-six more on the West Side) owned by the bankrupt Penn Central railroad. He also briefly took over a bankrupt hotel Penn Central owned next to Grand Central Terminal. Those Zeckendorf-size deals put him on the map.

Sunshine recalls driving down Fifth Avenue with Trump in 1975 when he pointed at the Bonwit Teller department store on the cor-ner of Fifty-Sixth Street and asked her to find out who owned it. "That's the site of our first residential building," he declared. It be-longed to Genesco, a conglomerate; in financial trouble, it was willing to sell Bonwit Teller. Genesco also owned the lease on the ground beneath the store, which had twenty-nine years left to run, and the air rights—the right to build higher than zoning would nor-mally allow—attached to Tiffany & Co.'s next-door headquarters on the corner of Fifty-Seventh Street. Equitable Life Assurance Society, which had helped finance Trump's Penn Central properties, owned the land beneath Bonwit Teller and was willing to sell it—and pro-vide financing for a new building, too—but only if it could find a partner with a compelling vision of what could be built there.

"Donald was perceived as a brash young kid with a lot of nerve and boldness but little substance," says Sunshine. "I thought he was brilliant, a marketing genius, the best teacher I ever had." Once the deal to buy Bonwit was made, she continues, "we were out to make

Trump a brand and begin an empire; we were not just building a building. We were about getting more per square foot than the guy next door." Or rather, the guy six blocks south. The model for the glitzy condominium he would call Trump Tower was the Greek ship-owner Aristotle Onassis's Olympic Tower, itself built on the grave of a dowager department store.

Olympic Tower and Trump Tower were both products of a special zoning district created in 1971 to keep the famous Fifth Avenue shopping strip from becoming another Avenue of the Americas, lined with boring, boxy office blocks. The new rules allowed developers to build higher if they included ground-floor retail spaces and pedestrian arcades and to cover a larger percentage of their plots if they included residences above. The technical term for the latter calculation was FAR (floor area ratio), the ratio of the size of a buildable lot—its footprint—to the amount of floor space a developer could erect there. Air rights like Tiffany's and those of other low, small buildings could be bought and added to the allowable FAR on a neighboring lot. The higher the FAR, the bigger a developer could build and then sell or rent for the greatest return on his (for developers were and are generally men) investment in land and construction.

Onassis and his partners used the new FAR incentives to put up the first building in New York ever to combine homes, stores, and offices under one roof: twenty-nine floors of condos atop two levels of retail spaces with nineteen floors of offices in between. But more important, it was the city's first luxury condominium. Even before their formal offering plan was approved by New York State, Olympic was expected to contain the most expensive apartments in the city.

In mid-1974, Olympic Tower apartments went on sale. Among their unusual amenities were a staff of three dozen multilingual security people, intrusion alarms linked to a central monitoring system, concierges lured from the world's best hotels capable of booking yachts and jets on a moment's notice, a business center with telex service and news and stock tickers, when-you-need-it secretarial services, a health club, an international newsstand, twenty-four-hour valet and dry cleaning, a barbershop, short-term office rentals, a three-story-high waterfall in the atrium, and then-uncommon bidets in most bathrooms. With all these tricks up its sleeve, Olympic Tower and the luxury condos that sprang up in its wake were throwbacks to the residential hotels of the late nineteenth century, service-rich establishments where transients might well outnumber full-time residents. Something old had been made new again.

Prices ranged from $40,000 for a one-room studio to $650,000 for a nine-room duplex penthouse, and many of the most expensive apartments were snapped up before the building was even topped off and formally dedicated that September. The buyers were three-quarters foreign, which was what Onassis wanted. He'd launched the sales effort with a multilingual marketing campaign. But combining luxe condos, high prices, and foreign buyers was a risky new idea, and the global economic crisis set off by rising oil prices in late 1973 slowed Olympic sales considerably. It didn't stop them, though. Foreign corporations had already bought a third of the apartments sold; one had taken three. Corporate ownership was generally barred in co-ops. Brokers were agog. They "had no idea what condominiums were," admits Elizabeth Stribling, then a vice president of a carriage-trade brokerage. "I thought, this rich Greek is crazy. But he thought he could sell them to his jet-set, moneyed international friends, Greeks, Swiss, and South Americans."

It turned out he could. All it took was patience. In December 1974, five of six penthouse duplexes had already been sold, four of them for $1.8 million to Adnan Khashoggi, a Saudi middleman often described as an arms dealer. Khashoggi had the designer Adam Tihany cut them up into a master duplex and several guest apartments. The $2 million decorating budget included the installation of a sky-high swimming pool in Khashoggi's own pad. "It is a palace in glazed walnut fit for Kubla Khan, lush with vegetation including orchids and roses with no thorns, littered with silver, gold and marble knick-knacks, with ivory tusks, dragons, statues and bronzes, tables inlaid with lapis lazuli," gushed England's *Observer.* The building beneath it was similarly described as a "pleasure dome" and compared to the hanging gardens of Babylon. The Olympic message was finally getting across.

Not even Onassis's death in March 1975 could slow the Olympic juggernaut once it gained momentum. A week after the tycoon died, his local partners reassured the market when they revealed that an American conglomerate, a law firm, a Dutch oil-trading company, and two Onassis-family companies had together leased two hundred thousand square feet of the office space in the nearly finished tower. The smaller, remaining spaces were sold or rented to tenants as diverse as a South American bank and the glam-rock star David Bowie.

When it opened in summer 1975, Olympic Tower was a mini–United Nations with twenty-seven different nationalities represented among its owners; 180 apartments had been sold, a quarter to Latin Americans and only a fifth to Americans. Olympic was considered so successful it had already spawned an imitation, the Galleria on East Fifty-Seventh Street, where a General Motors heir, Stewart Mott, was designing a quadriplex penthouse for himself high above the Europeans who were buying the lower-floor apartments—only 10 percent of its 253 apartments were owned by Americans. What they all had in common was wealth. "People threw money around," says a former Olympic concierge. "They had astronomical parties. There were no rules. Nobody cared. Look the other way. The rich were in total control." At least in Manhattan condos.

Beirut had collapsed, British taxes were rising, Swiss banks were failing, France was unstable, and kidnappings of the wealthy were a growing trend in Italy and Latin America. America beckoned. "To capitalize on the movement to New York," the *Los Angeles Times* said, developers had begun "catering to multinationals" leading to the "conspicuous success" of Olympic Tower.

Donald Trump was one of the few American residents at Olympic. "I lived there for three years," he says, between 1980 and 1983, in an apartment rented from a foreign investor. "I liked it. It opened my eyes." One night, he went to a party at Adnan Khashoggi's apartment and afterward revised his plans for Trump Tower.

In 1980, Trump had opened the Grand Hyatt Hotel on the site near Grand Central Terminal formerly owned by Penn Central and started demolishing Bonwit Teller. The Grand Hyatt's style, conceived by his wife, Ivana, was disdained by one critic as overstated opulence. But it was just a dry run for the sixty-eight-story Trump Tower. Architect Der Scutt of Swanke Hayden Connell came up with a design of bronze-colored reflective glass with stepped setbacks starting on low floors near the building's base, giving its southwestern corner a saw-toothed, ziggurat look. It was an immediate hit, if something jarringly new to New Yorkers, with its eighty-foot-high atrium containing a vertical shopping mall lined with pink marble, brass, and mirrors, filled with music from a piano player and strolling violinists, and guarded by uniformed doormen who resembled the offspring of Buckingham Palace beefeaters and the Wicked Witch's Winkie Guards from *The Wizard of Oz*. To the grandees of upper Fifth and Park, Trump Tower was a house of horrors. Little did they know Trump had seen the future, and it wasn't a Fifth Avenue co-op.

Appropriately enough, Steven Spielberg, the movie director, was one of the first to move into Trump Tower when it opened in April 1983. His apartment was owned by Universal Pictures. Within three years, all but a few of the 268 condos had been sold for $277 million, more than enough to pay off Trump's construction loans and generate the estimated $100 million profit he shared with Equitable. Their partnership was also expected to collect almost $30 million a year on rentals of the tower's office and retail spaces. He'd achieved the highest new-construction prices ever in America: an average $700 per square foot.

Then and since, the tower has attracted high-profile names: Michael Jackson and Lisa Marie Presley, Elton John, Andrew Lloyd Webber, Johnny Carson, Bruce Willis, Paul Anka, Liberace, Sophia Loren, Dick Clark, and Martina Navratilova. But Trump Tower had more than celebrity firepower. Beginning with the sultan of Brunei, Trump Tower has also housed the powerful, including the Greek billionaires Sokratis Kokkalis and Dakis Joannou; James Dolan, the chairman of Cablevision; the art dealers and collectors Jose Mugrabi and Hillel Nahmad (who owns four apartments); Sid Sheinberg, the former president of Universal Pictures; and banking, chemical, asset-management, and oil-and-gas moguls from the former Soviet Union, Canada, Germany, India, and Iran.

Trump Tower was nonetheless considered the urban-planning equivalent of the maroon suit with matching shoes Donald had worn when he'd first crossed the river from Queens. Architecture critic Paul Goldberger called Olympic Tower "a huge, banal slab" in order to damn Trump Tower with the faint praise "better, but not by enough." Both, he wrote, offered only "the glitter of the new." But none of it bothered Donald. Disdain was already nothing more than confetti in the wind to him. At thirty-six years, his biggest worry was that he'd already peaked. Despite its distaste for his taste, even the *New York Times* was forced to admit that he'd pushed his way to the front of Manhattan's sharp-elbowed real estate crowd and earned legitimate comparison to Big Bill Zeckendorf.

Others soon jumped into the game of building luxury condos for the then-rare sort who wanted to own Manhattan real estate but wouldn't play the co-op board game. As the Galleria had followed Olympic Tower, so Museum Tower followed Trump Tower. Foreigners "only knew condo living," says Marilyn Kaye, who worked for her husband's LBKaye brokerage. "It goes back to Christ." But New York's appeal was a large part of the equation, too. It was the post–Studio 54 era, and young Europeans were among the first to see that New York was undergoing a revival but was still inexpensive. Soon enough, locals would follow their lead into the condo market. "A lot of New Yorkers couldn't get into co-ops," says Lewis B. Kaye. Adds his wife, "As you got into the more expensive buildings, it got even harder to get in. Women always got turned down. Blacks got turned down. Intermarried couples got turned down. People would say, 'Don't even apply.' It was pointless."

The lure of lucre and the success of Olympic Tower were surely behind the Museum of Modern Art's decision, early in 1976, to erect a condo atop its building on West Fifty-Third Street, two blocks away from its inspiration. It hoped to generate income to erase its annual operating deficits and double its exhibition space. The Argentine-born architect César Pelli was selected to design the new tower, and in mid-1979, the $60 million, fifty-two-story project got a green light. Three years later, construction was ongoing when Museum Tower apartments were finally offered at prices ranging from $225,000 to $4.4 million for a penthouse.

Before Museum Tower opened, apartments had been sold to buyers from twenty countries. "Foreigners above all want to be in the center of town," observed Brewster Ives, an old-line broker. "They have no interest in going uptown to what you'd call a family neighborhood." That Museum Tower apartments were relatively small compared to sprawling thirteen-room Park Avenue co-ops proved to be as much a selling point as the $250,000 in art that decorated its minimal marble lobby. These were grand apartments boiled down to essentials for wealthy transients passing through town. But Museum

Tower never achieved the glitzy cachet or the high prices of Trump Tower. Initially, apartments there sold for only $450 a square foot.

That was chump change to Donald Trump, who was doubling down all over Manhattan. When he started demolishing the site of Trump Plaza on Sixty-First Street and Third Avenue in 1981 while Trump Tower was still under construction, it was his first collaboration with the man who would emerge as the philosopher-king of condos, Constantine "Costas" Andrew Kondylis, the most prolific architect of his era in New York, with eighty-six city skyscrapers to his credit.

Kondylis was born in the former Belgian Congo and studied architecture in Geneva and urban planning at New York's Columbia University before spending ten years as a designer of housing projects. He emerged in the 1980s as the new fortunes generated by Wall Street during Ronald Reagan's presidency washed away the last remains of the malaise of the seventies. "It used to be, if people came to the city, they rented apartments to see how they would do," Kondylis says. If they were successful and started families, they would often move away to the suburbs and be replaced by other young people just starting out. "But suddenly, wealth was being created," he continues, "the economy grew stronger and stronger, and people returned to the city from the suburbs and decided to buy apartments. They didn't want to throw money away by renting. And to own a piece of Manhattan was an achievement. There was pent-up demand." It wasn't being satisfied by co-ops, which were still desirable but tended to reinforce the idea that Manhattan was a closed society or, as Kondylis puts it, "a WASP city.

"The demography started changing. New York was conquered by outside people like myself. The city became more international, more cosmopolitan." Kondylis simultaneously became a senior partner in the firm of Philip Birnbaum, the successful but undistinguished architect of the Galleria, where his first job was Madison

Green, a banal condo on Madison Square Park. But with his next commissions, Manhattan Place on the East River and Trump Plaza (both completed in 1984), Kondylis came into his own. He'd decided that to be successful, condos had to be iconic. "The black building, the pink building, the building with the balconies," he says. Manhattan Place occupied "a whole city block on the waterfront and had great views and was sunbathed because of its bay windows in contrast to prewar buildings with small windows and dark rooms." It also had a health club, a jogging track on its roof, a swimming pool with a retractable ceiling, and a restaurant and party room. It caught Trump's attention, which changed Kondylis's life.

His Trump Plaza was distinguished by its Y-shaped design, which created extra corner apartments boasting magnificent views, as well as a health club, garage, and sundeck. It was not "distinguished," Paul Goldberger wrote in the *New York Times*, "but it surely glitters amid the banality of the rest of Third Avenue." Other critics of Kondylis and Trump, who would continue working together for twenty-five years, scorn the model they championed: flashy, eye-catching façades and lobbies leading to undistinguished, boxy apartments with staggering views. But their commercial appeal was inarguable. Unlike co-ops, condos could be traded, just like stocks. "People started to look at apartments the way they look at cars and labels," Kondylis says. "Apartments became commodities, proof of success. The market caught on fire. Everyone had to have a brand name, an architect and great kitchens and bathrooms, to justify the cost and satisfy the ego. The idea of buildings as lifestyle had come to Manhattan."

⎯⎯⎯⎯⎯⎯

Two more mixed-use, luxury-lifestyle condo towers—both near Carnegie Hall—sprang from Manhattan's schist in the mid-1980s. Harry Macklowe, a broker-turned-developer, had started planning what became Metropolitan Tower two doors down from the concert hall on Fifty-Seventh Street in 1983. Bruce Eichner, a prosecutor-turned-developer, hired the German architect Helmut Jahn to design CitySpire, just to the south, across Fifty-Sixth Street, in 1985. Nearby blocks were already home to a number of sophisticated luxury co-ops such as the Osborne and Alwyn Court, but they were more than a century old. The sparkling new condos were a welcome addition. Metropolitan Tower was completed at the end of 1986, CitySpire the following year. For a moment each held claim to the title of New York's tallest residential building, but height alone would make neither one iconic, nor would it turn the busy streets around them into a sought-after residential neighborhood. But they were vital links in the chain that would eventually connect Olympic Tower to Fifteen Central Park West.

Metropolitan Tower, architect Peter Claman's $165 million, forty-six-story triangle rising from a twenty-story rectangle, and clad in a ruthless, reflective black-glass curtain wall, came on the market with apartment asking prices as high as $5 million. Macklowe set its condos apart from the nineteen thousand others already in the development pipeline by promoting them as better-than-luxury homes. A reporter described the building's promotional video as "an everyday story of rich folk who give up their stately homes in England, their yachts in the Aegean, and their ranches in Texas to come to New York to take advantage of the lavish facilities in Metropolitan Tower."

Macklowe hoped to get a mind-boggling $1,300 per square foot for a penthouse duplex with views in all directions—and an average price of $500 per square foot. To attract that kind of money, he offered 1920s frills such as a full floor of separate staff quarters, a waiting room for chauffeurs, a private dining club with a catering kitchen for parties, health club and pool, and valet and limousine service. "Apartment kitchens have been purposefully minimized because the majority of tenants at this profile level are not interested in preparing food," Macklowe said.

Despite all that and the Léger tapestries in the building's lobby, critics still said his apartments were overpriced with odd corners that made them hard to decorate, minuscule kitchens, and too-small closets, and detractors mocked his claim to have sold half of them before the building opened. Initially, a significant number of apartments were sold to Japanese and Italian investors who swooped in and bought America on the cheap in those years, picking up as many as a dozen apartments at a clip and renting them out. Not until mid-1991 did Macklowe finally sell the 7.5-room penthouse for $4,328,000, about a million less than he'd hoped for.

But Metropolitan Tower quietly attracted a brace of celebrities over the years, such as Miles Davis, Diana Ross, Michael Jackson, Martin Scorsese, Jackie Mason, Patrick Swayze, Marc Anthony and Jennifer Lopez, and O. J. Simpson attorney Johnnie Cochran. The daughter of the late shah of Iran, and the late Norio Ohga, former chairman of Sony Corp., who owned the penthouse, also lived there. The big black building was definitely not just for white people.

Helmut Jahn's CitySpire, a seventy-two-story office-condominium tower, benefited from twenty-six stories of air rights bought from the city-owned landmark City Center theater and a bonus of twelve more floors that Eichner earned by paying to renovate the theater. His lender, European American Bank, and several other companies had already leased office space on its bottom twenty-two floors when the apartments above went on sale in March 1987 at prices ranging from $190,000 for a studio to more than $1 million for a three-bedroom duplex penthouse. Eichner promised purchasers private conference and billiards rooms, a fitness center, and such novel perks as priority reservations in "exclusive" restaurants and a branded "SpireCard" credit card. Ads for the building showed Jahn's slender stone-and-glass tower topped by a Moorish-style copper dome in silhouette over the slogan "Above it all."

Alas, that wasn't quite true. That June, it emerged that, due to a miscalculation, the tower had been built eleven feet higher than the design approved by the city. After almost a year of wrangling, Eichner agreed to cut down some setback parapets, eliminate sixteen spires that were part of the original design, drop a lawsuit against the city, and add three finished floors of rehearsal space above a pedestrian arcade that connected to the adjacent City Center—and give that to the city gratis in exchange for not having to lop off the top of his tower. Until the space was finished, the two top floors of CitySpire—where its most expensive residences were located—could not be offered for sale. Even after the agreement, arguments continued, and at one point the steel ribs erected to hold the dome were removed.

But that wasn't CitySpire's only problem. Shoddy finishes, an inappropriate granite base, and cramped apartments (more than two-thirds of CitySpire's condos were one-bedroom units or studios) symbolized a miscalculation of the market. Nonetheless, after a year, foreign money rode to the rescue, and by the time closings began, 200 of the 340 units were spoken for, with about a third sold to offshore beneficiaries of a decline of the dollar against other currencies.

CitySpire's bad luck continued, however. In mid-1989, a fire broke out in one of the still-unfinished penthouse duplexes. Then, in December 1990, after the building was ostensibly completed (though neither its pedestrian arcade nor the promised rehearsal space had yet been built), it started to whistle—a high-pitched noise that generated hundreds of complaints and fines and was blamed on louvers in the copper dome. By then, Eichner was in money trouble, too.

In 1993, the bank that had foreclosed on CitySpire turned to Will and Arthur Zeckendorf to market the seventy-five apartments left unsold—the first project of their new company, Zeckendorf Realty. Fourteen months after they'd signed on, the Zeckendorfs had disposed of the last of them. But even twenty years later, in 2012, when the owner of the penthouse there put it on the market, asking $100 million in a bid to top Sandy Weill's $88 million sale of his penthouse at Fifteen Central Park West, the reputation-challenged CitySpire was and remained an also-ran. Appropriately enough, the building that finally topped CitySpire was Donald Trump's 861-foot Trump World Tower near the United Nations, Costas Kondylis's elongated tribute to the iconic Seagram Building. Completed in 2001, it would hold the title of New York's tallest apartment tower until 2014.

As the Zeckendorfs already knew, Manhattan real estate is a feast-or-famine business, and by the late 1980s Donald Trump was in big trouble. He was stuck paying millions in annual taxes for the hundred acres of the former Penn Central yards stretching from Fifty-Ninth to Seventy-Second Streets along the Hudson River, where he'd envisioned a development called Trump City. But the project had been put on indefinite hold. Big Bill Zeckendorf had once "had the same city-sized dream," for his Television City, Tom Shachtman wrote in his book *Skyscraper Dreams*, "and had been bled dry by holding the area."

Only six years earlier, Trump had acknowledged his debt to Big Bill, but drew a key distinction. "I used him as a model," Trump said. "He was a great visionary but he wasn't fiscally conservative. Having seen the way he went down taught me to be overly so." Now, though, Trump's overreaching was making headlines. The *Wall Street Journal* would soon conclude that his personal guarantees on loans might exceed $600 million.

But Trump was not one to go down without a fight. In 1993, contracts were out on 81 percent of the apartments at his latest condo, Trump Palace, averaging $634 per square foot. And despite the collapse of the real estate market, Trump Tower, by then a decade old, was commanding resale prices of $1,000 per square foot. "That was a barrier," recalls Marilyn Kaye, one of the first condo specialist-brokers in New York. "Donald always said he'd get more. People said it would never happen." But it did. Like his signature tower, Trump himself would survive, prosper—and continue to drive his detractors to distraction—for years to come. But it would be the end of the century before he completed his comeback. Meantime, Arthur and Will Zeckendorf were setting the stage for their own.

∽∾∽

In July 1992, excavation began on a block bounded by Broadway, Columbus Avenue, and Sixty-Seventh to Sixty-Eighth Streets for what was touted as the most significant mixed-use condominium project in New York City history. Lincoln Square was set to include a multiscreen movie theater, a sports club, a post office, retail stores, and rental and condo apartments for both the middle class and the wealthy. This was the first of three connected projects near Lincoln Center that would stir up intense controversy, but would also set the stage for the construction of Fifteen Central Park West—and define its architecture. But it wasn't the first building project in the neighborhood with the name Lincoln Square. Given their family history, it is not surprising that all three generations of real estate Zeckendorfs would have played a part in its story, which stretched back almost forty years.

In 1955, a Slum Clearance Committee headed by Robert Moses, who'd been a planner working for the city and the state since the 1920s, first used the name Lincoln Square when it proposed razing about thirty acres north of Lincoln Center between Broadway and West End Avenue—a decaying working-class neighborhood sometimes called San Juan Hill—so that Bronx-based Fordham University could consolidate the four separate schools it ran in Manhattan. The plan was expected to cost more than $75 million.

A year later, Moses presented a revised plan that would cost twice as much and had been expanded to fifty-three acres and eighteen city blocks, in which 595 parcels would be cleared and only half a dozen buildings would survive the slum-clearance project. Not only Fordham but also a new music and arts center sited on a so-called superblock three blocks long would be its beneficiaries. They were to be joined by new municipal buildings, a housing development, stores, hotels, and office buildings. In June 1956, the cultural center was incorporated as a nonprofit called the Lincoln Center for the Performing Arts. John D. Rockefeller III was chairman (and his father was one of the backers) of the group that had brought the Metropolitan Opera, the New York Philharmonic Symphony, and the New York City Ballet together as partners in the project. A month later, plans were announced by Wallace K. Harrison, the Rockefeller architect who'd also designed X City for Big Bill: Lincoln Center's style was to be "monumental modern."

Big Bill and Webb & Knapp soon signed on to build the Lincoln Towers portion of the project, and he became one of its spokesmen when, inevitably, critics began tearing into the plan, which delayed implementation until mid-1958, when the first of more than five thousand families were evicted and relocated after the US Supreme Court refused to stop the redevelopment. Construction of Lincoln Center began in 1959, Philharmonic Hall (later renamed for the audio pioneer Avery Fisher) opened in 1962, the New York State Theater in 1964, the Library and Museum of the Performing Arts in 1965, the Metropolitan Opera finally moved north in 1966, and in 1969 the Juilliard School and its Alice Tully Hall joined them. Eventually, the center would be home to more than two dozen indoor and outdoor performance venues and would host everything from the New York Film Festival to fashion shows.

New apartment towers followed in Lincoln Center's wake. Paul and Seymour Milstein, whose father had made a fortune from a flooring company, bought an entire block of Broadway three blocks north of the theater complex in 1961. Dorchester Towers, sold as a luxury rental building "with virtually all the accouterments of east side apartment living," according to the *New York Times*, opened there in 1965 and took three years to fill. A white brick building typical of the era, it really had none of the virtues of old apartment houses, east or west.

The Milsteins struck again in 1968 when they began demolishing a plot on Broadway across from Lincoln Center for Lincoln Plaza, but the city's planning department filed suit to stop the forty-two-story tower, claiming that it threatened a proposed special zoning district to take effect the next year. It ran from Sixtieth to Sixty-Eighth Streets between Amsterdam Avenue to the west and an eastern boundary running between Broadway and Central Park West. The new zoning gave developers the right to build high-density towers like Lincoln Plaza if they provided street-level plazas and arcades. The Milsteins won the right to exceed the prevailing FAR by more than 30 percent and finished Lincoln Plaza in 1971.

The Milsteins also owned the blockfront just to the south, and three years later they were still fighting with the city and community groups over their desire to erect a forty-three-story tower there. They finally won permission to build a shorter, thirty-four-story tower with arcades and a plaza. The Lincoln Plaza district was "a deadly failure," says Roberta Gratz, the journalist and neighborhood activist. "They thought they'd get Bologna, with arcades. It was not Bologna. Then came the next one and the next one and the next one. Every year there was a zoning fight." Thankfully, in the economically disastrous late 1970s, she concludes, "new construction ground to a halt."*

---

*Among the rare exceptions were another Milstein rental building at 30 Lincoln Plaza and a tower on Sixty-Second Street west of Broadway. It replaced a 1904 movie house that was later the site of Walter Winchell's radio broadcasts and was then converted into a troubled dance venue by Rebekah Harkness, the widow of a Standard Oil heir. Guri Lie Zeckendorf would spend the last years of her life living on its top floor.

In April 1990, the owners of the American Broadcasting Company decided to sell two full blocks along Broadway between Sixty-Eighth and Sixty-Ninth Streets. A syndicate made up of Bill Zeckendorf Jr., Martin J. Raynes, another second-generation real estate operator, the American subsidiary of a Japanese conglomerate that had invested in Bill Jr.'s Central Park Place and Zeckendorf Towers, and the Goldman Sachs investment bank, which was playing matchmaker as well as investing its own money in the deal, won an option to buy the land.

General Atlantic Realty, a branch of a private investment firm specializing in low-income housing, wanted a piece of it, too. It had pioneered a procedure that allowed the transfer of tax abatements and incentives to developers of luxury apartment towers, giving them the right to erect taller buildings, and made a deal with the Zeckendorf-Goldman-Sumitomo-Raynes consortium for a piece of the project. General Atlantic Realty's principals were thrilled to hook up with "masters of the real estate universe," says its then-president Philip Aarons. "But no sooner was the ink dry on the deal," and a $10 million deposit paid, "than the world collapsed."

Raynes fell victim to the real estate downturn and would soon be driven out of business. Zeckendorf fell out next. Will Zeckendorf well remembers the day he accompanied his father to Goldman Sachs "to break the news that he was fundamentally unable to make his capital call on the project," Will says. They told Bill Jr. politely but firmly, "You're out as a partner." But Goldman was out, too. "The market nose-dived, we couldn't raise the rest of the money and we lost the deposit," says a party to the transaction. "But then, Chris came in and saved the deal."

Christopher Jeffries, a lawyer-turned-developer who worked alongside Aarons at General Atlantic, was an ambitious man who'd recently married Princess Yasmin Aga Khan, the daughter of Rita Hayworth and Prince Aly Khan. Jeffries wanted to try to take over the project, but General Atlantic balked. "Everyone thought it was valueless," says Aarons. "There was nothing nearby you would call high-end other than a few nice blocks" of brownstones. So they decided to go it alone and, as "a departure gift," General Atlantic gave Aarons and Jeffries the right to proceed, and they left to form their own company, Millennium Partners.

Jeffries and Aarons won Goldman Sachs's backing, and eager to keep the deal alive, the corporation that owned ABC agreed to a $13 million reduction in the original $105 million purchase price for its land and lenient terms on the second payment in exchange for equity in whatever was eventually built. Jeffries personally came up with $1 million to secure the arrangement. After bargaining for free office space from ABC, and fee-deferral agreements from their lawyers and architects, the Millennium team faced their biggest problem: finding the remaining $81 million in a market where the credit cupboard was bare. Jeffries came up with a compelling and creative way to finance the project. They would presell segments of the multiuse building, just as developers sell condos, only in this case, separate buyers would purchase blocks of rental and condominium apartments, the retail stores, the theaters, and a sports club facility. To differentiate those uses, the commercial entrances would face Broadway and Columbus Avenue, and the residences, Sixty-Seventh Street.

By summer 1991, they had commitments from the Gap, Loews Theaters, and an LA-based chain of health clubs. They subsequently sold the J. P. Morgan bank a piece of the building as a training center and traded a building that Morgan owned on Madison Avenue for six floors of apartments to house its trainees and visiting executives. Eight more floors with fifty-six apartments were sold to a group of Saudi investors, and Millennium kept thirteen floors as rentals. The partners even induced the US Postal Service, which had a post office on the property, to move out temporarily and then return as the owner of its own new condo post office. "It all took years," Aarons says. "It was groundbreaking." And it was successful enough that Millennium was eventually able to develop three more buildings on the northern end of the bow-tie-shaped intersection of Broadway and Columbus Avenue.

Will and Arthur Zeckendorf would eventually adapt aspects of Millennium's mixed-use formula at Fifteen Central Park West. They knew that formula well because they'd helped sell it as they transitioned from working for their father to working for themselves. After Marty Raynes and Bill Jr. both wiped out of the deal, the Japanese and Goldman (who had joined forces with the Saudis who owned the floors below) agreed to buy the top eleven floors in order to develop and sell eighty-eight luxury condos, complete with their own entrance, lobby, and elevators; it would be called Millennium Tower to differentiate it from the Park Millennium on the floors below.

Arthur and Will approached Dan Neidich, the number two man in Goldman's real estate investment department and offered their services to Millennium Tower, "and [Dan] kept us on to do development management and sales," says Will. "A little messy but it was nice of Dan to keep us." That partnership would eventually lead to Fifteen Central Park West.

Jerry Karr was a senior member of the Goldman real estate team and its overseer on the project. The son of a homebuilder, Karr had worked on his father's jobs as a teenager and looks like a construction foreman. He speaks with visible delight about the intricacies of construction and knew the kind of condos the Zeckendorfs had built until then. "Fairly standard product," he says, "a step up from rentals." The Millennium Tower units—two-bedroom apartments larger, grander, and better appointed than those beneath them— were a step up from that. By the time they'd all sold in 1995, "we'd gotten the highest prices in the city," says Arthur—bringing in an average $675 per square foot, with the best apartments commanding $890, which nudged the prices of better two-bedroom units over $1 million.

Neighbors screamed that Millennium had committed fraud on its applications and was insensitive to the environment, and that the building would create traffic jams of both cars and pedestrians on the Broadway side of the building, where a nine-screen theater (including an IMAX auditorium) would open in 1994 along with the rest of the building, followed hard by Millennium's One Lincoln Square (nearby on Columbus Avenue) the next year and the Grand Millennium on Broadway in 1996. The protests led to revisions of the Special Lincoln Square Zoning District. New, post-Millennium rules and restrictions on height would shortly define what could be built a few blocks south, in the oddest corner of the Special Lincoln Square District, a single block at its southeastern end that extended like a notch all the way to Central Park West: the future site of 15CPW.

But the truth was, in a city where new construction had essentially stopped, the Millennium Tower and its siblings were heaven-sent. Celebrity tenants such as Howard Stern, Liam Neeson, Jon Bon Jovi, and Regis Philbin made them magnets even if NIMBY neighbors didn't agree. The West Side renaissance was at last under way. And thanks to Millennium Tower, Goldman and the Zeckendorfs had taken their first steps into business together and were set to embark on bigger things. First, though, the brothers made an acquisition that nudged them even higher up the luxury-residential food chain.

Brown Harris Stevens was a carriage-trade real estate brokerage that had seen better days. Early in 1995, the Zeckendorfs and several partners bought it from Harry Helmsley, an elderly developer. Helmsley had been trying to sell BHS ever since he'd been found mentally incompetent to stand trial for income tax fraud and his wife, Leona, had been found guilty and sent to jail for thirty months for income tax evasion. Seventeen Brown Harris Stevens employees had also been implicated in a conspiracy by city managing agents to extort kickbacks from building contractors and suppliers, and the firm was forced to pay a $1 million civil settlement.

Brown Harris, its new owners pledged, would strengthen its hand as the city's premier management firm for exclusive cooperative buildings and also expand its existing brokerage business. They immediately invested $1 million, bought a new building to house the company, and upgraded its computers. Part of that investment went to developing software to track data and trends in Manhattan real estate. Brown Harris Stevens was, the Zeckendorfs figured, a life preserver that might keep them from the fate of their father. "It was 'How do we survive?'" Arthur recalls thinking. "Developers have four good years and then four bad years." With a steady stream of income from a well-run brokerage and management businesses, their future would be far more secure.

Goldman Sachs were impressed by the Zeckendorfs' strategic maneuver. Developers could outsource the creation of a building: they could hire architects, contractors, and salespeople. But the trick to selling condos, especially in a depressed market, was getting the deal right, knowing how to size and design apartments to create the right mix to make the biggest possible profit. Residential developers need to know what customers want, and there was no better way to get that real-time knowledge than to own a management and brokerage company.

The more they talked to Will and Arthur, the more confident in them the Goldman real estate executives became. Goldman had just launched a fund called Whitehall to attract outsiders to invest in real estate alongside the bank. Dan Neidich was chairman of its investment committee; while he ran them, the Whitehall funds would raise $12 billion and buy $50 billion in real estate worldwide. Whitehall money would regularly fuel the third Zeckendorf generation's projects as they segued from sales and marketing and followed their grandfather and father into development.

Goldman's next investment in the Zeckendorfs was to buy Bill Jr.'s debt on the Gotham, which stood on the old Gimbels parcel on Third Avenue, where only 90 apartments had been sold and 150 were rented out as a holding action until the market improved. Within a year, as the rental tenants moved out, the Zeckendorfs sold them all.

Next, the Zeckendorfs took over another failed deal of their father's. In 1989, in partnership with a US subsidiary of Tobishima, the Japanese construction company that had invested in several of Bill Jr.'s projects (and ultimately bought him out of many of them), he had paid $38 million to buy 515 Park Avenue, a vacant twelve-story apartment house built in 1912 at the southeast corner of Park Avenue and Sixtieth Street. Just outside the Upper East Side Historic District, it had an odd but intriguing location, on the border of the midtown business district, close to residential Park Avenue, yet just far enough away that a developer would be allowed to put up something quite tall there.

But their father's deal was, Will Zeckendorf says, "underwater," due to the declining value of the land, which was encumbered by a $60 million mortgage held by yet another Japanese company, Mitsubishi. And as their father had failed to meet his obligations on that mortgage and taxes, Tobishima had paid his bills for him, diluting his share.

Will and Arthur owned one-fifth of their father's rapidly declining half share in the deal, and all through the nineties they'd kept tabs on the loans. "It was a complicated, delicate relationship with the Japanese," says Arthur. The trick was to stay involved and keep the Japanese from torpedoing the deal by writing it off and bailing out, instead convincing them to extend the loan throughout the economic downturn with the notion that eventually the value of the property would be restored. "It was a ten-year effort, pretending the loan still had face value," Arthur continues. "Will and I took them out every month. Ten years of whiskey bars—we'd spend a hundred dollars on whiskey and these Japanese girls would come talk to you. They would speak English to us and Japanese to the Japanese. That relationship kept bad things from happening to the property."

"It was fun," says Will, chuckling, but it was business, too, and after years of watching helplessly as their father tried to sell the project to third parties, and then as Tobishima went into receivership, Will had a revelation when he heard that Mitsubishi had given up and was going to foreclose and schedule a live auction to sell the mortgage. "Why don't we just buy it?" he asked.

Arthur agreed, and they made a deal with their father, who still controlled the land; he said that if they could find a way to recapitalize the project, they could have it.* They then approached Goldman Sachs, "and thank goodness we did," continues Will. Neidich and his team put them off at first, worried about the location. "They didn't take us seriously," Arthur says. "It was no, no, no, but then eventually, yes." Finally, even though deferred interest of $12 million had by then increased the technical indebtedness, which also included about $47 million in principal, the bank's executives came around.

"Their father opened the door; they walked through it," says Ralph Rosenberg, a younger member of the Whitehall team who arranged for one of Goldman's bond traders, who had a relationship with Mitsubishi, to buy the loan at auction at a steep discount. Whitehall was reported to have paid about $20 million, when, actually, to win the auction, it would have to bid much more than that. The

* Bill Zeckendorf Jr. doesn't entirely agree with his sons' description of the resurrection of 515 Park. "They saw an opportunity and we made the most of it," he clarifies. "They certainly worked it and became the developers," he adds, but "I got money out of it. I had an ongoing equity position."

numbers were so high, says a Goldman executive, "people thought we were fucking nuts." But they weren't as crazy as they sounded.

The customer base for condos had finally expanded beyond the international set. More and more people wanted to live in the cleaned-up Manhattan of the Giuliani years. Instead of moving away, young families were opting to stay, older people who'd spent years in the suburbs were opting to return, and even dyed-in-the-wool Manhattanites were getting restless in old-school co-op apartments they'd occupied for decades. Due to restrictions on renovations, they were often forced to move out for a year or two to upgrade them. "People had long been reluctant to buy condos because they were so inferior to the great old buildings," says Robert A. M. Stern. But the latest crop of luxury condos offered an alternative. "Just sell and move into a new place." The city's rising demand for large apartments had altered the equation.

The night of the auction, Will says, Rosenberg called them at 8:00 p.m. The bidding for the mortgage had passed their maximum bid of $38.5 million and hit $40 million, he told them. Although that was the number the Zeckendorfs felt the property was worth, Rosenberg said Goldman would likely have to go to $43 million to win the $60 million note. To do that, he wanted them to agree to lower their development fee by $1 million and told them he needed an immediate answer as he was on a plane that was about to take off.

"I don't care," Will remembers Rosenberg saying. "It's going into the dead-deal file. Tomorrow morning you can read that Donald Trump owns the mortgage. What's your decision? The phone is going off and the dead-deal file is open." Will describes it as "tough love, Goldman Sachs style." On the spot, they agreed to cut their fee. Goldman won and Whitehall tore up the note because, Rosenberg says, by then "we knew Will and Arthur as partners and we'd made a deal." Will is more effusive. "I'll say this: Goldman Sachs was utterly brilliant, fabulous."

Goldman was taking a leap of faith, but judged the risk acceptable. "Will and Arthur were just beginning to develop a track record," says Dan Neidich, "but the site was unique—the last buildable site with height on Park Avenue and protected views to the north and west. It was more about the site than their track record. We bought it cheaply enough to make it worthwhile." Goldman's involvement also encouraged banks to issue the loans that covered some of the mortgage as well as construction costs. "It was a very difficult time and the banks had a lot of comfort based on our involvement," says Neidich.

Finally, it was Will and Arthur's turn to show what they could do, and their father had prepared things well. Sitting on the northern border of the midtown commercial zoning district, the hundred-by-sixty-foot property could only be redeveloped as a big residential tower if a portion of the building had a commercial or community use. Next door on East Sixtieth Street were two brownstones, but just past them was the headquarters of Lighthouse International, which was just the kind of community facility Zeckendorf needed. So he'd reached understandings to buy the air rights from the Lighthouse and one of the town houses. Immediately after closing their new deal with Goldman, his sons bought air rights to the other town house just to the east of their property; conveniently, Goldman had a relationship with its owner. The Zeckendorfs then combined the four properties into one zoning lot and transferred the air rights from all three neighboring buildings to 515 Park, enabling them to add eleven stories to the thirty-two that existing zoning allowed on the site.

"Will and Arthur drove that," says Rosenberg. "We were copilot, but day-to-day they did it." But still, the bankers didn't let the young developers stray far off the leash. "We said we'd give them a shot because they controlled an intriguing asset," says Rosenberg, "but we'd have close interaction with them" through Jerry Karr, who "was as important as Will and Arthur on that project. We didn't give them the keys to the car."

Investment bankers are, to a great extent, gamblers. But they generally try to know the odds before they make a bet. "We happened to hit at a great time," says Rosenberg. "I remember saying all you need is forty rich people. It wasn't that complicated a bet to make."

Since Olympic Tower, the rich had shown not just a willingness but an eagerness to invest in condominiums in midtown Manhattan towers. As Trump Tower begat Museum Tower, Metropolitan Tower, CitySpire, Central Park Place, and the Millennium Tower, the prices realized had continued to climb, and now they'd neared the magic number of $1,000 per square foot. All it would take was a little nudge—perhaps apartments designed to appeal to both domestic and foreign buyers—and that figure would look quaint.

Part Four

CIRCLE GAME

*What I like to do is recognize a great piece of land
and conceive a suitable edifice for it.*

—WILLIAM "BIG BILL" ZECKENDORF

In the late 1980s, when Bill Zeckendorf Jr. was building standard-issue condominiums on the West Side, his son Will, then in his late twenties, would regularly walk up and down Broadway, looking for potential development sites and stopping, *"of course,"* he says, to notice the "big, huge, empty square block" between Sixty-First and Sixty-Second Streets.

It wasn't entirely empty. Emery Roth's Mayflower-Plymouth Hotel still stood on the Central Park West blockfront, but all the other buildings had been demolished, and a chain-link fence barred access to the rubble-strewn lot, an eyesore and an obvious opportunity. After sixty years, Columbus Circle, a block to the south, remained a promise unfulfilled. Since the pre–World War I days of William Randolph Hearst, the circle had consistently resisted upgrading. At the same time that Will Zeckendorf was taking his Broadway walks, David W. Dunlap, the *New York Times* reporter who lived at the Century and daily stared down at that empty lot, wrote a story about the fifty-five blocks on Broadway between Columbus Circle and Columbia University where ten new towers containing two thousand apartments had recently opened. But new construc-

tion had ground to a near halt after the eighties building boomlet
ended, leaving Broadway, Dunlap wrote, "more a hodge-podge than
ever, vibrant and schizophrenic."

Among those Dunlap interviewed was John J. Avlon, the owner
of that empty Broadway lot. "You're going to see exciting, eclectic,
daring architecture" there, Avlon predicted. But Dunlap seemed to
pooh-pooh him. "An enormous tower may rise one day on that parcel," he wrote. "But current plans envision only a parking lot for the
adjacent Mayflower Hotel." Long after the last automobile showroom had left the neighborhood, cars were still better served than
people in the environs of Columbus Circle.

A half dozen years later, the chain-link fence was still around
the lot, and something akin to a war zone had sprung up around it.
The economic slump that followed 1987's stock market debacle and
the end of the real estate boom had soured New York City on itself. Quality-of-life issues—the deterioration of public behavior and
the public life of a city that was, in large part, defined by its street
culture—loomed large. New York's legendary tolerance was being
stretched to its limit. Politicians seemed paralyzed; criminals felt
empowered; and all over the city, shantytowns reminiscent of both
the Great Depression and of the West Side in its earliest days sprang
up again, aural, visual, and olfactory symbols of apparent decline.

In 1991, David Dinkins, the only African-American ever elected
mayor of New York, drew a line at Columbus Circle. Early that
June, his administration had cleared a homeless encampment out of
Tompkins Square Park on Manhattan's Lower East Side. Five days
later, a homeless man killed a former Radio City Rockette who was
walking her dogs on Sixty-Ninth Street near Central Park, stabbing
her repeatedly and leaving an eleven-inch butcher knife in her back
as he fled into the park, where he was apprehended.

Twelve days after that, a public ceremony was held in Columbus Circle celebrating its restoration. Several foundations had raised

funds to refurbish the statue of the explorer and the fences that surrounded him, but demonstrators wanted to know why money was
being spent on a statue instead of the needy, some of whom were
right nearby, watching, smoking, and selling frayed old books off
the same blankets they slept beneath at night, tucked into the arches
and doorways of the semiderelict buildings around the circle. Unfortunately for those homeless souls, the ceremony rededicating the
ninety-eight-year-old monument cast a harsh light on their encampment, and over the next few nights, the occupants were encouraged
to leave. Those who refused the carrot of housing in shelters finally
met the stick of police in riot gear, who forcibly removed those who
remained. "They were symbols of a city out of control," a deputy
mayor told reporters, echoing the sentiments of Robert Moses some
forty years earlier.

⸺∞⸺

World War II was still raging when Mutual Life, which had taken over
William Randolph Hearst's property on the north end of the circle
seven months before Pearl Harbor, sold it to two investor-developers.
In 1946, it changed hands again, and the new owner, head of a
clothing-store chain, announced plans for a twenty-five-story tower.
Like Hearst, though, he planned in vain, and the American Circle
building, with its Coca-Cola weather sign (vintage 1938), remained
in place. After the war, Columbus Circle mostly served as an outdoor
advertising amphitheater until Madison Square Garden Corporation
announced that it would move to the circle and erect a new arena span-
ning two full city blocks. The city's coordinator of postwar planning,
Moses, who'd come to see himself as a latter-day Roman emperor, decided to call it the Coliseum. But by 1951, the Garden was out, and the
federal government was in, thanks to its new urban renewal legislation.

The Coliseum was to be the first act in Moses's remaking of
the West Side. To qualify for those federal funds, Moses added two

rental apartment buildings on Columbus Avenue to his plans. To build it all, he would have to clear out the five hundred families in the tenements there, as well as neighboring stores, a gas station, a clubhouse, the NBC theater, and a twenty-four-story commercial building, and condemn and demolish them. Two-plus years later, a wrecking crew moved in to begin demolition.* By spring 1954, when a groundbreaking ceremony was held, four more buildings were coming down, and Moses had discarded the idea of a semicircular façade on the building, made it rectangular, and added a large office tower to his Coliseum, now a convention center.

Hyman Burt Mack, co-owner of Wreckers & Excavators, Inc., carried out the demolition of a bank building north of Fifty-Ninth Street and the theater to the south. As teenagers, his sons, Earle and Bill, both visited the demolition site, where Moses was in such a hurry to start building that Mack was offered a bonus of about $50,000 if he finished the job ahead of schedule, but worried he'd have to pay a penalty if he was late. Bill Mack recalls his father telling him, "Son, this will be a good neighborhood one day." Looking around, Bill wasn't so sure. But he was never allowed to forget the site after his father got the job done and collected his bonus. "He talked about beating Moses for the rest of his life," says Mack. And almost fifty years later, the thirteen-year-old who'd watched his father clear the site would play a central role in making his father's prediction come true.

The new twenty-story tower attached to the Coliseum opened in April 1956. A month later, the Coliseum itself opened with simultaneous philately, auto, and photo shows. It was said to be the largest

---

*At the time, John Barrington Bayley, a classical architect, proposed a radical Roman-style remake of Columbus Circle, opening tunnels beneath it for traffic and surrounding the statue with a massive colonnaded portico and pedestrian forum evocative of Bernini's St. Peter's Square, only with the Vatican's big basilica replaced by a concert hall and opera house, public houses of worship of a different sort. Within, Bayley envisioned a great gallery inspired by the Hall of Mirrors at Versailles. But his dreams never made it past the sketch phase.

and most technologically advanced exhibition hall in the world, but it was also one of the dullest, with a glazed tan-brick façade decorated only with a small marquee and four medallions by the sculptor Paul Manship representing the seals of the United States, New York State, New York City, and the building's official owner, the Triborough Bridge and Tunnel Authority, which Moses ran and used as the vehicle for his civic-improvement schemes. Ground was broken that same week for the two apartment buildings that were the legal, if secondary, purpose of the urban renewal project.

⧟

In 1956, George Huntington Hartford bought the old five-story building on the tiny, odd-shaped lot on the south end of the circle for $1 million. One of the heirs to the Great Atlantic & Pacific Tea Company (better known as A&P) supermarket fortune, Hartford had about $500 million. An odd, directionless duck, he would go on to produce plays and films, buy a theater, develop Paradise Island in the Bahamas, and open at various times a nightclub, a magazine, a parking garage, a modeling agency, and an institute to study handwriting before spending his last years and the remains of his fortune on a debilitating drug habit. But he is arguably best remembered for the building he constructed for another $1.5 million on that irregular parcel.

Hartford abhorred modern art and thought it "thoroughly degenerate," but nonetheless called his building the Gallery of Modern Art and, in 1959, filed Edward Durell Stone's design for it with the city. Columbus Circle had no architectural landmarks aside from its City Beautiful Movement monuments, the Columbus column, and Hearst's *Maine* memorial. Hartford's museum would become an antilandmark, an object of derision for the next half century.

Clad in white Vermont marble with few windows, Hartford's building was made somewhat memorable by the lollipop-shaped colonnade at its base and arches forming loggia at the top of the sheath.

In a memorable takedown in the *New York Times*, critic Ada Louise Huxtable dismissed it as a "little seraglio . . . suggestive of houris . . . a provocatively misplaced pleasure pavilion transplanted from some Shalimar garden to a Manhattan traffic island." Hartford's gallery would soon be shut down and the building taken over by Fairleigh Dickinson University, which used it for exhibits and lectures.

Despite its failure to fit in, Hartford's building (and a dramatic new fountain surrounding Columbus on his column, donated to the city in 1965 by the publisher-philanthropist George Delacorte) contributed to the sense that, at last, something might be happening on Columbus Circle. With Lincoln Center's buildings opening a few blocks to the north, it looked like a turning point for the entire district. Once again, speculation was that a skyscraper would finally rise at the north end of the circle, and indeed, a forty-four-story office building was announced in 1967. It would be named for its principal tenant, Gulf & Western, a conglomerate that owned Paramount Pictures, but also more prosaic zinc-mining, sugar-refining, tomato-growing, cigar-making, and auto-parts-distributing concerns. The white marble and aluminum Gulf & Western Building tried to blend in with the bland, boxy Coliseum and Durell Stone's seraglio, but became the finishing touch on what would be remembered without fondness as an architectural bull's-eye in the center of Manhattan.

Yet as it rose, the Gulf & Western tower was hailed as a symbol of the circle's renaissance; it had inspired nearby property owners to upgrade buildings, such as 1860 Broadway, the seventeen-story office tower on the northeast corner of Sixty-First Street, with automobile showrooms in its base. It was then owned by Philip Lipton, who'd come to America from the Jewish ghetto of eastern Europe in 1897 at age fourteen. "He was the first off the boat," his daughter Barbara Agar says of the eager, self-educated teenager, who went into the underwear and uniform business and began buying stock on margin after the 1929 stock market crash. He made a fortune and became a financier and philanthropist.

Twelve years after buying 1860 Broadway, Lipton invested $100,000 to renovate the building. A pleasure-boat company leased all three of its storefronts on Broadway and offices above as a showroom because the Coliseum, the site of an annual boat show, made the location desirable. Other new tenants included a concert promoter; the local public television station, Channel 13; Arthur Penn, the film director; and Avis rent-a-car.

The Gulf & Western Building opened in April 1970, and for the second time in two years, a newspaper proclaimed a local renaissance, noting that land prices had risen from about $35 per square foot to $225 in the eight years since the first Lincoln Center theater had opened. Alas, both the Gulf & Western Building and the company that owned it were on shaky ground. Realty Equities, the owner, lost millions in the three years following the building's opening; its stock was delisted and it pled guilty to second-degree grand larceny for diverting money from government-subsidized projects it controlled to pay its parent company's debts. Around the same time, it became generally known that the tower, one of Realty's best assets, had a serious issue itself: because its steel frame was flexible and its glass exterior lightweight, it would twist and sway noticeably in high winds, causing workers on its higher floors to complain and its walls to crack. Guests invited to watch films in Paramount's sky-high screening room worried that they might find themselves stuck in a real, as opposed to a cinematic, disaster.

In truth, there was discomfort but no immediate danger in the tower's movement, and Gulf & Western's management was unconcerned. Indeed, in 1976, it bought Hartford's museum building, which Fairleigh Dickinson had turned over to its mortgage lender. Afraid it would be demolished or otherwise defaced, Gulf & Western gave it to New York City as a gift (along with a promise of $900,000 over four years to maintain it) to ensure it remained part of the view out its tower. Office-space lessees apparently liked it far more than contemporary architecture critics. The city eventually installed its Department of Cultural Affairs in the building. At almost the same time, the Gulf & Western tower itself was sold to an investment company owned by an insurance billionaire, John D. MacArthur, a cousin of the World War II general Douglas B. MacArthur's. The building remained the property of one of his companies until it was sold to a Boston-based real estate group five years later.

Why buy a building considered ugly and unsafe? Likely, the purchasers suspected that the Coliseum's days were numbered. Downtown, the Jacob Javits Convention Center was under construction, and once it opened it would, it was assumed, take much of the trade-show business away from the Coliseum. So it was that in 1984, the Metropolitan Transit Authority, which had since subsumed Moses's Triborough Bridge and Tunnel Authority, began to actively consider the future of its aging and ugly Columbus Circle exhibition hall— and whether funds from its sale might finance desperately needed improvements to mass transit in the city, including the chaotic subway station under the circle, where three lines converged to form one of the busiest transfer points in the system.

A contest to gain control of the site attracted bids from fifteen developers. Boston Properties, headed by Mortimer B. Zuckerman and Edward H. Linde, won. One bidder offered $22 million more than they did, but Zuckerman had a winning card up his sleeve: a partnership with Salomon Brothers, the Wall Street investment bank, which had committed to be the anchor tenant and agreed to give up any tax benefits from the deal. So Boston's bid of $455 million for the four acres—on which it proposed to build two towers with offices, condominium apartments, a hotel, and stores—prevailed.

Zuckerman made it clear that he hoped to sell his apartments for high prices—and at the announcement, New York's mayor then, Ed

Koch, had his back. "Hundreds of millions of dollars ultimately will come to the city of New York," Koch said, not just through the sale of the land, but also from taxes and the further development of the neighborhood, which was sure to follow. An immediate rise in property values after the Coliseum deal was announced seemed to portend a windfall for all concerned.

Many quickly voiced opposition to Zuckerman and Linde's plan and focused on the design by Moshe Safdie, who'd gained prominence as the master planner of the Montreal World's Fair Expo 67. Zuckerman, a naturalized American, had been born in Canada, attended Wharton and Harvard Law School, and taught urban planning for nine years before joining the Boston development company where he met Linde. In the years immediately preceding their bid for the Coliseum site, Zuckerman had expanded into journalism, buying first the Boston-based magazine *Atlantic*, then *U.S.News & World Report*.

Safdie's plan was fleshed out in mid-1986. He proposed two knifelike pink-granite towers, one sixty-nine stories tall (making it the sixth-tallest building in Manhattan), the other fifty-nine, with slanted roofs, chevronlike structural beams, and multiple diagonal setbacks, rising from a curving shopping arcade at the base, echoing the curve of Columbus Circle. It was too big, too tall, too dense, critics immediately howled. Despite a notch between the towers that would allow a sliver view of the western sky from Fifty-Ninth Street, they charged that the project's bulk—2.7 million square feet—would reduce the circle to insignificance, cast long afternoon shadows across Central Park, and add to traffic and pollution. And it was all the Koch administration's and the MTA's fault, since their stated priority, getting the highest-possible price for the land, had made it financially necessary to erect something gargantuan there. Not only that, one of Koch's chief deputies had intimate ties to Salomon Brothers, and Boston Properties had hired a former director of planning at the MTA as the project manager and liaison with the agency and the city. To the project's opponents, the concern was clear: Was the fix in?

Nonetheless, as long as interest rates stayed low and apartment sales chugged along, as they did early in 1987, the wind was at Zuckerman and Linde's back. Indeed, demand for the larger apartments that the Zeckendorfs had pioneered kept rising, increasing the chance that Boston Properties would make back its bet of nearly a half billion dollars on the site. Concerned nonetheless, Salomon Brothers threatened to withdraw from the project unless it was approved essentially as it was (Boston had made a half dozen design changes during the approval process) by the city's then-all-powerful Board of Estimate. And so it was.

In summer 1987, the Municipal Art Society, the city's Parks Council, and several community groups sued the MTA and the city to block the project and began recruiting celebrity opponents—an influential mélange ranging from Jacqueline Onassis (who called the building monstrous) and Norman Lear to Henry Kissinger, and even I. M. Pei—in an effort to influence public opinion. City officials' derided them as wealthy, clueless elitists unconcerned about the mass transit system, which was to benefit from what had been named Columbus Centre. Zuckerman, who'd already contracted to buy granite for the building, tried to be diplomatic, praising the protesters' values. "But there is another value called the democratic process," he told the *Wall Street Journal*. And to *New York* magazine, he added the blunt reminder that his Columbus Centre would "replace dead space."

In that same story, *New York*'s John Taylor pointed out that the southwest corner of the park "lacks the features, such as the zoo and the skating rink—not to mention the handsomely designed Grand Army Plaza—that draw people to the southeast corner. And Columbus Circle is a frantic, intimidating place. . . . Prostitutes have loitered at the corner of Broadway and 60th Street. Purse and chain snatchings are commonplace. And drug dealers lounge insolently in front of the Maine Monument." In other words, it was a typical public space in late-eighties Manhattan. The Koch administration's stance was also unsurprising. "Like most of its predecessors," Taylor wrote, the administration "likes big construction projects. They mean lasting memorials to the public servants that bring them to life. They also mean jobs for union members, patronage power, and campaign contributions from builders immeasurably enriched by the projects."

Taylor also revealed that Salomon Brothers had an out, the right to withdraw if it couldn't occupy its new quarters by 1990, and a reason to take it: even before the 1987 stock market crash (which was just a few weeks away), empty space around Wall Street was renting for a third less than Salomon had agreed to pay uptown. Zuckerman, still determined, said he intended to start demolition by the end of the year. But he kept taking punches. On October 12, Salomon announced it was cutting its workforce by 12 percent and reassessing its need for office space. So on the fourteenth, as stocks began a vertiginous fall, Zuckerman announced a sudden willingness to compromise and reduce the bulk of the buildings. Then, on the eighteenth, Goldberger of the *Times* chimed in to declare Safdie's design "ghastly" on the same morning a protest against it was set for Central Park. More than eight hundred people came, lining up from Columbus Circle to Fifth Avenue, and at 1:30 p.m., all opened umbrellas to symbolize the building's shadow. The next day the stock market crashed. The situation on Columbus Circle changed overnight.

Less than two months later, Salomon Brothers withdrew from its partnership with Boston Properties. Zuckerman remained unbowed. "It isn't over till it's over," he told the *Wall Street Journal*. In a sense he was right. There would be seven more years of redesigns, political arguments and lawsuits, and three mayors of New York before he left the field to others. But in retrospect it's clear that Boston's Columbus Centre was already a goner.

———&———

The luxury-condominium market was still alive and humming, though many builders were forced to the sidelines or out of business entirely in the years after the market crash. A much ballyhooed condo glut never materialized, thanks in large part to the same foreigners who'd kicked off the condo binge in the first place. Bill Zeckendorf never made it back into business, but while Zuckerman and his project twisted in the wind, rather like the Gulf & Western Building, the latter became the unexpected vehicle for Donald Trump's comeback, and the second high-profile condominium on Central Park West's Gold Coast. Irwin Chanin's Century had been converted to condos in 1989 after a seven-year battle between renters and its latest owners.

All through 1992, the Gulf & Western tower was in financial limbo after the bankruptcy of the real estate company that had bought it from the MacArthur Foundation. The following year, the General Electric subsidiary that held the building's mortgage foreclosed and faced two pressing issues: Paramount Communications, the successor to Gulf & Western, still rented 85 percent of the building, but its lease was set to run out in 1995 and it had no intention of renewing, and the building's swaying problem remained; inspectors had finally declared that it was unsafe and demanded the immediate realignment of façade panels that had been knocked loose and the strengthening of all the others.

Meantime, as Trump worked out his own financial issues, it emerged that one of his assets was untarnished: his name. When it came to selling luxury high-rise condos, Trump was "like no one else," said the Gulf & Western Building's managing agent. In 1993, fourteen Trump Palace condos were sold to a single buyer for $16.5

million—an average $634 per square foot. Trump Tower apartments were still changing hands at $1,000 per square foot.

So after a year spent mulling its alternatives, when General Electric rejected the idea of selling off the building and began soliciting bids from developers instead, Trump was one of those it approached, and eventually, G.E. asked him to team up with the Galbreath Company, an Ohio-based developer that had helped G.E. consider its alternatives. "I didn't know either one," says Dale Frey, then-chairman of the General Electric subsidiary that controlled the tower. "I liked Donald's proposals, but I didn't trust him. I knew I could fall back on Galbreath." Jack Welch, G.E.'s overall boss, was skeptical. "He said, 'I wouldn't, but go ahead,'" recalls John Myers, another G.E. executive.

Success has many fathers and many have claimed credit for the moves that followed, Trump primary among them. "It's hard to say who did what," Myers admits, though Frey is willing, crediting Trump and his right-hand woman, Sunshine, with finding a way to "get around the zoning" and maximize potential profits by grafting a condominium to a condo-luxury-hotel with a restaurant in its base, with "very good design ideas," and with what he brought in the first place, that name and the glitzy salesmanship that went with it, that made the project "take off." Trump claims he also came up with a way to stop the building's swaying, but Galbreath's point man on the job, Scott Coopchik, takes exception to that, crediting a structural engineer, Ysrael Seinuk, Galbreath hired early in the process. "We were a very quiet company," Coopchik says, adding that when it was sold in the middle of the process, "no one cared anymore, so fine, let Donald take all the credit."

All agree that Trump and Sunshine hired Philip Johnson, then the biggest name in architecture, to remake the tower in collaboration with Costas Kondylis. Johnson called their design a tribute to Ludwig Mies van der Rohe, with whom he'd collaborated on Park Avenue's landmark Seagram Building as young man. Though some quibbled with Johnson and Kondylis's choice of a dark bronze, pleated glass skin (called Trump-style gold by detractors), most agreed it was a vast improvement over what it replaced. "This is not a major work by Mr. Johnson," Herbert Muschamp wrote in the *Times*. "Still, he has introduced considerable refinement to an essentially crass idea." Johnson would later credit Kondylis for the job, telling the architecture critic Karrie Jacobs that Kondylis had done "the real plans" and he was "just the decorator." But Johnson's name on a building got attention.

It was Trump's name that really mattered, though. It "meant something to the Hong Kong Chinese," then facing the imminent turnover of their city to mainland China, says someone privy to the deal details. G.E. knew they would want safe havens for themselves and their money. At G.E.'s insistence, he announced he would buy himself a penthouse, a purchase G.E. financed. "The Chinese wanted to know that he was going to live there," says the source. Lots of apartments were sold to Hong Kong Chinese. The building's success was assured. And it was probably doubly sweet for Trump, who had no other equity in the deal. Trump eventually flipped his penthouse without moving in or putting down a penny.

Trump was also paid $75,000 a month and got a back-end share of sales profits above an agreed upon price per square foot. The observer adds a comic coda: "The building was going to be named the Trump International Tower until G.E.'s in-house lawyer noted that the acronym would have been unfortunate." Trump and G.E. kept doing deals together. Trump still manages the building and owns its commercial spaces.

Trump adds a coda of his own. He points out that he decided to relocate the entrance—complete with a new gold canopy—from 15 Columbus Circle to 1 Central Park West. And, of course, his name stayed on the finished product, the Trump International Hotel & Tower. His changes "immediately quadrupled the value of the asset," Trump asserts. "And it was successful from the first. I've been given a lot of credit for having created Columbus Circle because I was the first there, but despite what people have said, I didn't see it that way. I got rid of that address. I saw it as Central Park West."

Paramount's lease on the Gulf & Western tower expired in spring 1995, when Trump and Galbreath started taking it apart in order to put it together again. That fall, the Metropolitan Transit Authority hit the reset button and started the process of selling the New York Coliseum all over again. The MTA finally had luck and timing on its side.

In the intervening seven years, Boston Properties had hired a new architect, David Childs of Skidmore, Owings & Merrill (who'd designed Worldwide Plaza for Bill Zeckendorf), to scale back its plan; the city had dropped the price for the land; and Salomon Brothers had agreed to pay some of the preconstruction bills that had piled up in the meantime. But critics continued to pound on all concerned. Faced with shrinking demand and discounted real estate values, Mort Zuckerman and Ed Linde had downsized their dream again, and again won city and judicial approval to proceed, but a year later, with the project stalled by yet another lawsuit, the MTA hedged its bet and sought proposals to reopen the Coliseum until the situation could finally be resolved. Meantime, Zuckerman bought the *Daily News*, the city's largest-circulation tabloid newspaper, giving himself potential leverage at the same time he'd decided to press the city and the MTA into allowing him to keep the project on ice until the real estate market improved. For its part, the MTA wanted to force the issue, take Boston's $34 million guarantee, and run. And no wonder. In the meantime, the potential bounty from the deal had shrunk from $455 million to $100 million, with a fifth of that coming from the city. It seemed relevant that Zuckerman's *Daily News* had endorsed Rudolph Giuliani's candidacy to replace David Dinkins as mayor in 1993. Even the project's most vocal advocates were now wondering if what had first been presented as a windfall for the city had become just another corrupt political deal.

The deadline for closing Boston Properties' latest Coliseum contract came a few weeks after Trump's arrival on Columbus Circle, which had served as a reminder that even in a bad economy, there was money to be made in real estate development. That deadline passed, though, and the parties ended up back in court, with Zuckerman seeking further renegotiation. Just hours before the trial was set to begin in June 1994, Boston won yet another revision to its deal. It would build only an office tower to start, and its guarantee was cut in half to $17 million; in exchange, Zuckerman and Linde promised to quickly secure both a new anchor tenant and construction financing. But not six weeks later, that deal, too, collapsed after Zuckerman refused to sign the contract and threatened to sue the MTA again for the return of his $17 million.

Finally, Mayor Giuliani had had enough and pushed the MTA to seek a new developer rather than rent out the building, and in fall 1995, the agency agreed to make another formal request for proposals. A fresh crop of developers began circling the project.

In the meantime, Donald Trump upped the ante, announcing something that his partners at Galbreath had actually arranged, that Jean-Georges Vongerichten, the culinary equivalent of a starchitect, would open a new restaurant serving three meals a day in the Trump International. "A luxury building with a star chef?" says Louise Sunshine. "Nobody had done that." Vongerichten strikes a similar note as he recalls the day Philip Johnson dined at one of his earlier, more modest restaurants, spread the plans for the Trump International across his table, and "called me over and said, 'I have a perfect place for you to open a restaurant.' Everyone said we were crazy, going to Columbus Circle," Vongerichten continues. "There was nothing around. Bums! An empty lot! But I wanted to do a four-star restaurant."

Both Vongerichten and Sunshine exaggerate. Bill Zeckendorf Jr. had long since brought Le Cirque and its superstar owner Sirio Maccione to the Mayfair Hotel, and there were already two high-end restaurants within a block of the circle when Jean-Georges opened in 1997, but it did eventually earn that four-star review, and it was a key factor in the tower's immediate success. Even before that, *New York* magazine had noted that change was afoot on Central Park West. In September 1996, an article by Christopher Mason called "West of Eden" declared it "the glammiest address in town," using the prices at the Trump International and resale values approaching those on the East Side's Gold Coast as proof that it was suddenly competing with Fifth Avenue. Mason's story noted that show people—Sting, Kevin Bacon and Kyra Sedgwick, Barbra Streisand, Bruce Willis and Demi Moore, Steven Spielberg, Dustin Hoffman, Steve Martin, Madonna, and Jann Wenner—still lived there and quoted the film producer David Brown, who'd been in the Beresford for two decades, saying the street was "no longer déclassé."

Really, Central Park West was the same, but perceptions had changed. "At co-ops on Fifth and Park, new money is frowned upon," broker Linda Stein told Mason. "On Central Park West, it's *worshipped.*" Donald Trump was quoted, too, of course, declaring that his new building had "led to the resurgence." Around the same time, the *New York Times* ran a story calling Trump's comeback a fait accompli thanks to his newest namesake tower. The proof? More than half its condos had been sold, sight unseen, at an average $1,000 per square foot, even though the building wouldn't reopen for months.

Among the other reasons: Trump peddled what one of his salespeople called the Wow Factor. He offered condo owners a health club with a swimming pool, hotel services such as fresh flowers delivered to your apartment as your flight is landing in New York, room service from Jean-Georges, larger bedrooms, his-and-hers bathrooms, higher ceilings, and higher-quality finishes than he'd ever before installed in his buildings. And though he'd toned it down a bit, there was also Trump's signature glitz. "That's the way Donald prefers it," says Sunshine. "And in those days, the market was Asians,

Europeans, Middle Easterners, and people from California, Texas, and Florida who wanted pieds-à-terre. Those cultures like that." Trump played to those cultures with an international marketing effort that even included a feng shui ceremony.

Change doesn't happen overnight, and the one that had begun at Olympic Tower was only beginning to organize itself into something discernible. But one pundit saw what was happening at Columbus Circle and put it into a larger cultural perspective. In 1994, William J. Mitchell, dean of the architecture and planning school at the Massachusetts Institute of Technology, wrote an essay for *New York Newsday* titled "Will Manhattan Become a Bedroom Suburb of the Global Village?" Before most Americans had even heard of the Internet, Mitchell predicted that it would stimulate the market for high-end Manhattan apartments, "not because the jobs are there," he wrote, "but because [buyers] are attracted to the cultural, entertainment and social possibilities that only large, intensely concentrated, well-connected populations can provide. . . . It's nice to go out in the center of the universe."

Columbus Circle finally found itself at the center of that center.

∞

Fully aware that the moment was now, no matter what Mort Zuckerman thought, the MTA selected Eastdil Secured, a real estate investment bank, to "come up with a plan to select a group who would be capable of creating a workable plan for the redevelopment of the [Coliseum] site," recalls Eastdil's chairman, Ben Lambert.

Once the bidding was opened—this time with an all-cash requirement—it was rumored Trump would be among the applicants, along with the Zeckendorfs and the Related Companies. Eastdil selected nine groups to take part; the Zeckendorfs were not among them. Most of New York's other major developers were, including Trump, Related, and Millennium. Also in the mix were the Morgan

Stanley, Goldman Sachs, and Donaldson, Lufkin & Jenrette investment banks. All spent enormous amounts of time and money trying to win a deal, confirming the appeal of the strategically located property.

The mixed-use proposals they brought with them included the obvious—hotels, apartments, offices, and big and small retail—but also television studios, auction houses, museums, an aquarium, rooftop gardens, a pool, and something called Discovery Circle, an entertainment/education complex for children with Rollerblade boardwalks, a bodysurfing pool, restaurants, and stores all rolled up into one hyperactive environment.

Every starchitect on the planet wanted to follow Safdie and Childs into gladiatorial combat for the Coliseum site. Among the aspirants were Kohn Pederson Fox, Kevin Roche John Dinkeloo, César Pelli, Helmut Jahn, and, working for Trump, Robert A. M. Stern Architects, whose design placed a massive glass-and-masonry tower on the southern end of the site. In its rejection of a glass curtain wall, their proposal was a precursor to Stern's 15CPW.

Ben Lambert was still winnowing down the candidates when the Trump International opened early in 1997. "We eliminated all but three groups for various reasons," he says. He met personally with each developer to ensure "they understood all the sensitivities of the selection process," and that summer, with the MTA, chose Millennium Partners. "I called Chris Jeffries," who was at his beach house on Long Island, Lambert says, "and suggested he fly in by helicopter so we could discuss finalizing the transaction as soon as possible." But within hours, Mayor Giuliani threw a wrench into the gears, insisting that the winning design include a public performance space. Jeffries turned around and went home.

None of the principals knows (or is, perhaps, willing to say) why Giuliani called a halt to the sale, but there are several theories. In one, Giuliani hoped the Metropolitan Opera, which ranked with the

New York Yankees as his favorite cultural diversions, would open an annex, a "mini-Met," at Columbus Circle. But the opera had no interest. Several of those involved think the mayor heard that Related was talking to Time Warner, the infotainment conglomerate (possibly through its then-president Richard Parsons, a prominent Republican), to move its operations into the project and wanted to give them time to make it happen. "He *was*" favoring Related, says one interested party flatly. Regardless, "everyone was sent back to the drawing board," says Lambert. "It was a whole new process."

Millennium had been talking to Jazz at Lincoln Center, then a concert series without a home, to build it a performance space on Amsterdam Avenue, says Philip Aarons, but Giuliani's demand caused a year's delay, and in the interim Millennium lost its hotel partner and its deal with Sony and dropped out of the contest. Others did, too, and in April 1998, Related made a deal with Time Warner to rent almost all the planned office space. It also reeled in the Mandarin Oriental Hotel Group for a new hotel, and Jazz at Lincoln Center, and raised its bid.

Stephen Ross, Related's founder, a tax lawyer who, like Fred Trump, built subsidized housing and became a billionaire, "knew what he was doing," says Ben Lambert, who sat down with Ross and hammered out the last details. An ironclad financial guarantee to the city from Time Warner was the clincher. "Nobody questioned if they could come up with the money," says Lambert. So Giuliani's pause turned out to be profitable for the MTA and the city. In the end, Lambert estimates, the price paid for the Coliseum acreage was about $100 million higher than Millennium's earlier arrangement.

Though Related and Ross have taken much of the credit for what became the Time Warner Center in fall 2003, it wasn't all the developer's doing. Ninety percent of the $250 million purchase price was paid by a financial partner, Apollo Real Estate Advisors (now called AREA Property Partners), founded by Bill Mack, who decades earlier had watched his father's wrecking company prepare the Coliseum site. Related and Apollo had already collaborated on deals. A year earlier, they'd won a site a few blocks south on Broadway that would become the Park Imperial luxury condo and an office tower, another addition to the Columbus Circle district.

"We'd started marketing those [Park Imperial] apartments at eight hundred dollars per square foot," says Mack. "But we averaged eleven hundred dollars and at the end were making deals at thirteen hundred dollars, so we had specific knowledge of what the demand was. The neighborhood was being improved, there was a natural transportation network, there were the views. And the building Trump did gave us the indication that people would pay high-end numbers. Everything said Time Warner would be a success."

Related's plan for the site was created by David Childs, Mort Zuckerman's second architect, and retained elements of his Boston Properties design, notably a pair of towers that paid homage to the Century and Majestic on Central Park West. The trapezoidal, dark-glass columns rising from the city-mandated curved base were positioned to echo Broadway's diagonal slash through the otherwise regular street grid—a dash of jazz in an otherwise rational visual composition. The Rafael Viñoly–designed Jazz at Lincoln Center complex seemed to have been positioned atop that 150-foot-tall, glass-fronted base so its performances could be shared by strollers on Central Park South, drawing the eye toward that central retail atrium.

Seeing and raising Donald Trump, Related announced that the complex would have six restaurants, including a steak house by Jean-Georges Vongerichten, even though its building was still a hole in the ground. Though he would depart, as would others, two of the restaurants—Per Se by Thomas Keller and Masa Takayama's Masa—would gain renown as much for their exorbitant prices as their food.

The Coliseum started coming down early in 2000, and Time

Warner apartment sales began in summer 2001, with penthouses priced from $25 million to $36 million. Related's sales team touted a unique opportunity to buy new construction with park views, the advantages of hotel living, "and anonymity," says Susan DeFranca, who ran Related's sales effort.

There were two hundred apartments between One Central Park (which has the address 25 Columbus Circle though its entrance was on the decidedly less chic Fifty-Eighth Street), the south tower, and the Residences at Mandarin Oriental (at 80 Columbus Circle) in the north tower. Residents all have access to a private fitness center and pool, and a chauffeurs' lounge, a 1920s-style amenity. Floor-to-ceiling glass windows that are ten to twelve feet high offer spectacular views of the park and the city.

All the requisite top-of-the-line finishes and appliances were included, which was no longer remarkable. The odd geometry of some rooms proved challenging, but these were status symbols so their deficiencies as homes weren't much discussed. Another deficiency in the north tower didn't become obvious until fall 2003, when it opened. SEE, YOUR VIEWS AREN'T SO GOOD, ARE THEY? read a sign hung from the top of the Trump International, right out the window of the newer building. WE HAVE THE REAL CENTRAL PARK VIEWS AND ADDRESS. BEST WISHES, THE DONALD.

A dozen contracts to buy apartments in the south tower were signed in the first month; many more were said to have been issued. But then came the September 11, 2001, terrorist attack on another twin-towered New York building—and sales at Time Warner "stopped dead," says Louise Sunshine, who'd been hired to market the building. "It was an interesting time to be selling a high-rise," she adds, deadpan.

Only a dozen more contracts would be signed for south-tower apartments that year, and another four in the hotel, where residents would get Mandarin Oriental services. One of the penthouses in the latter tower quietly went into contract for $29 million in December, sold to the cofounder of Nu Skin Enterprises, a cosmetics company sometimes criticized as essentially a pyramid scheme. That sale set a new Manhattan condominium record, but it went unnoticed in the immediate aftermath of 9/11. Much noticed were improvements to the building's security—including strengthened steel and backup generators for all the elevators.

The next year, as the two towers approached their halfway point, sales picked up briefly. Twenty-seven south-tower contracts were signed between February and April, and the singer Ricky Martin, movie producer Arnold Kopelson, and Wynton Marsalis, the artistic director of Jazz, were reported among the buyers. But then sales dropped and stayed depressed until well into 2003, when apartments started selling at a regular clip again. "The international market went black in 2001," says DeFranca. "It opened up again in 2003—one of the biggest votes of confidence in the United States. But the truth is, we had fewer foreign than domestic buyers."

An unprecedented publicity and marketing campaign had begun with a June 2000 press conference in a tent erected over Columbus Circle, with CNN's anchor Bernard Shaw as master of ceremonies and a team of event planners behind the scenes. The terror attack slowed but didn't stop that campaign. Even during the postattack lull, Related had reason to be cheerful. The building was achieving prices just under $2,000 per square foot for small units and over $3,000 per square foot for larger trophy homes. There could no longer be any doubt: the fortunes of Columbus Circle had changed—and a threshold had been crossed.

The rebound in sales proved profitable for all concerned. Until it made back its initial investment, Apollo Real Estate Advisors took most of the proceeds, but as the apartments sold and other hurdles were crossed, Related's share of the profits increased until it got half of every incoming dollar. Some of the profits were returned to the neighborhood: Related paid $1 million to renovate and relandscape Columbus Circle with a new fountain and paving. It was all in service of drawing the public to Time Warner's commercial atrium, which by early 2003 had attracted a supermarket and more big brands, though not the sort of East Side luxury retailers the apartment owners upstairs might have preferred. Still, it was unprecedented, "the largest mixed-use development in Manhattan," says Alan Segan, Rubenstein Public Relations' front man on the project, "the first-ever combination of corporate, cultural, hotel, vertical retail, parking, and residential. The scale, 2.8 million square feet costing $2.1 billion, made it different."

More important, perhaps, in giving the complex cachet was the news in July 2003 that David Martinez, a reclusive Mexican-born sovereign-debt specialist, had purchased the largest home in the towers, or rather two homes he planned to combine into a twelve-thousand-square-foot duplex penthouse. It was reported that he'd spent $45 million (or $3,541 per square foot), setting a new record for a Manhattan apartment by topping Stephen Schwarzman's 2000 purchase of the Rockefeller duplex at 740 Park Avenue for just under $30 million. It was an epochal moment, the first time in recorded history that a condominium had become New York City's most expensive residence. Braden Keil, the *New York Post* real estate gossip columnist, who got the scoop, added that Martinez had bought raw space and would spend additional millions to finish it. In fact, he would buy another apartment as well, bringing his total paid to almost $54.8 million and giving him the entire seventy-sixth and seventy-seventh floors of the south tower.

In fall 2003, the Time Warner Center began its yearlong opening in stages. Even after the February 2004 black-tie gala opening, there were more heavily promoted events to ensure the last apartments would sell. In November, the *New York Times* ran a story about Time Warner called "Who's Who, and What They Paid," revealing that buyers included the widow of the owner of Harrah's Casino, bankers from Hong Kong and Kazakhstan, several medical entrepreneurs, a Colombian politician, the daughter of the richest man in Turkey, a Saudi royal, and the widow of the Atkins Diet doctor.

The success of first Trump International and then Time Warner had another epochal effect. "There is still a significant group of Fifth and Park people," says Pamela Liebman, CEO of Corcoran Group, a large real estate brokerage. "But there's a limited number of apartments, and not everyone who likes them can pass the boards, so by natural selection some people are forced away and others have opened their minds. Ten years ago, condos were not well thought of. It wasn't until those worldly towers that people took notice."

Sitting in a penthouse apartment at the Mayflower Hotel two blocks north of the Time Warner construction site and just across the street from Trump International, John J. Avlon, a courtly, preppy, horn-rimmed graduate of both Yale and Harvard, was watching the changes on Columbus Circle with particularly intense interest. A second-generation real estate man, he ran a company that bore his name, but a good portion of his and his father's business lives had been spent tending to the real estate interests of one of the richest families in the world, the Goulandrises. Through Avlon and thanks to him, they owned that entire block, bounded by Central Park West and Broadway, and Sixty-First and Sixty-Second Streets. They'd been sitting on it for years, waiting for just such a moment.

Born on the island of Corfu in Greece, Avlon's father, John Avlon, was orphaned in the Spanish flu epidemic after World War I and was a nine-year-old loading baggage onto ships on the island's docks in 1920, when an American suggested he should make his way to the United States. A few days later, according to his grandson, he stowed away on a ship and sailed to New York, where he was taken in by a Jewish family who ran an insurance agency. Nine years later, he founded a real estate firm, John Avlon, Inc. In 1943, he was the broker on a real estate deal that saw John P. Goulandris buy two buildings on Fifty-Seventh Street at (what was then still called) Sixth Avenue in midtown Manhattan, adjacent to another parcel he'd already purchased through Avlon. Today, the 1960s apartment building standing on that property is managed by the second John Avlon. John P. Goulandris was his godfather.

Goulandris came from the island of Andros, where his family had been shipowners since 1850. Their sailing vessels plied the Mediterranean and Black Sea routes, and in the nineteenth century they were among the earliest Greeks to operate tramp steamships. In 1940, John P. moved the family's operations to New York, where he founded more shipping lines and diversified into real estate. He was one of four cousins who had the same name and were differentiated by nicknames such as Strauss (that John loved music) and Hirohito (who had vaguely Japanese eyes).

John P., the one known as Megaleas, Greek for "the big one," was the eldest of his branch of the family and the founder of the Petros Goulandris Sons Group, which the *Chicago Tribune* once described as "the crown jewel of the Goulandris empire." In 1975, it controlled about 130 ships and other holdings valued at $2 billion (the equivalent of $8.7 billion today). The main subsidiary of Megaleas's company, Orion Shipping, owned almost half of those vessels. When he died of a heart attack in 1950 at age forty-three, his survivors included four brothers, a sister, who was married to another shipowner, and two children. His company is still going strong, run by two cousins, both named Peter, one a son of Megaleas.

Notoriously private, the large, complex family has cloaked most of its subsequent dealings in anonymity. So the family members who owned what would become the Fifteen Central Park West site are unknown. The business activities of large, wealthy families like theirs tend to be amorphous, with different individuals participating in different deals. Often, their managers and operating partners are themselves unaware of whose money is in play. All that's certain is that the Avlons have long represented the Goulandris real estate interests and done quite a remarkable job of it.

In 1969, Avlon went to work as a vice president at his father's company. New York was in a recession, the best time to buy distressed real estate, and he and his father were looking to do that. "I tend to look at real estate as a very long chess game, whereas most people see it as poker," Avlon says. "We were always walking around looking for property to acquire. The Mayflower block," where Fifteen now sits, "is a perfect example that attracted my attention at a very young age." The block was smaller than most and, due to Broadway's angle, not a perfect rectangle. And it was something rare, an entire block that fronted on Central Park. From property records, he'd learned that the land had only five parcels and four owners.

The block had obvious advantages as a potential development site. Standing on Columbus Circle, Avlon looked at the six roads that converged there and felt the rumble of the subway lines beneath his feet. Then he looked up at the statue of the explorer on his column and followed his eyes down Eighth Avenue. In a flash, he realized that Columbus Circle was "the least prosperous" link in the chain of great intersections up and down Broadway. At Harvard, he'd learned that it can take a decade to revitalize a neighborhood. Lincoln Center was approaching its tenth birthday, but the development of its perimeter was still incomplete.

"The Coliseum was vestigial, badly conceived, and clearly had a finite life," he says. "Columbus Circle's possibilities were so large, yet its present fact was so dismal." He stood there, staring, weighing the possibilities, "knowing it would be a *long* time" before that changed. "But if you got enough land to develop and you were not in a disadvantageous position, the only risk was that the neighborhood was not so good. So we went for it."

Across town at the East Side stockyards, Big Bill Zeckendorf had once done something similar, but there was no secrecy, no ostentatious trip abroad, for Avlon. Within a year, he'd gained control of three of the five parcels. Fortunately for him, the first two of them were in the hands of a single owner. And in 1972, that owner's world collapsed.

Seventy-two years after its founding, the Shubert family lost control of the world's largest theatrical-production company, the Shubert Organization, a collection of almost two dozen entities owned by the Shubert Foundation. It was handed over to three members of the foundation's board, two of them law partners who'd represented the Shuberts, the third a friend of the family's. Aside from its seventeen theaters, Shubert also owned a vast portfolio of real estate. But the company had lost money for the first time since the 1930s despite the profitability of that portfolio, and it had declined in value by more than 75 percent from its peak of $400 million.

In August 1973, Shubert sold both 3 West Sixty-First Street and 1880 Broadway to John Avlon. Four months later, Avlon acquired the Mayflower Hotel from its second owner, the Sherman-Taylor Corp., a consortium of wealthy real estate operators that had owned and operated it since 1946. That sale passed unnoticed, which was lucky for Avlon, as he still needed to buy two more buildings to own the whole lot.

Meantime, in fall 1977, he demolished 1880 Broadway. Next door, 3 West Sixty-First Street, a seven-story, block-through loft building, was home to Brooks Costume, which had rented theatrical costumes from there since 1952, the Tepper Auction Galleries, and the American Ballet Theater's school and rehearsal spaces, where the likes of Mikhail Baryshnikov and Gelsey Kirkland still danced. It was emptied in 1979 and demolished the next year. By then, Avlon had acquired 9 West Sixty-First Street, buying the corporation that owned it from three brothers who'd come out of the automobile business and owned vast amounts of West Side real estate. Avlon leased the building for five years before taking possession in 1979 at the request of the sellers; the arrangement helped them avoid taxes.

The final piece of the puzzle was 1860 Broadway, the big office building on the corner of Sixty-First Street, and it took seven years to get it. He'd been trying to buy it from Philip Lipton, the self-educated immigrant, for years, says Lipton's daughter Barbara Agar, "but my father wouldn't sell because at the time he would have had to pay a double tax on it." She ended up running the building, and her father left it to her when he died in 1976. "I was instructed to sell it to Mr. Avlon," she continues, "but I was having fun and I wasn't in any hurry to sell and the price went up."

Many meetings ensued as Agar drove a hard bargain, finally giving in when Avlon pointed out to her that if his block was developed without her property, whoever did it could build "right up to our lot-line windows, and no one would want to rent those offices," Agar says. Avlon was gentlemanly about it, "but he meant it. He backed me into a corner. I didn't want to sell. But I got him to assume the remaining mortgage and he paid not a lot, but for those days it was as good as it could be." The sale closed in November 1983, and Avlon finally owned the whole block. He left the Mayflower Hotel standing and operating because it remained a viable business and had tenants in residence who were protected by rent regulations. But in 1986, he took down the two other buildings on the block. He was a patient man with a patient family behind him, so despite the expense of holding on to idle properties, they would wait.

In 1979, Alexander Godunov had defected to the United States while staying at the Mayflower with the Bolshoi Ballet troupe. That same year, a piece of masonry fell from a building owned by Columbia University on upper Broadway and killed a student. The next,

Local Law 10 took effect, requiring that the owners of large, decorated buildings periodically inspect their façades and do so for the
first time within two years. Some owners quickly stripped ornamentation from their buildings, which allowed them to avoid that deadline
and the potential cost of repairs mandated by the inspections. John
Avlon seemed to be one of those. "He did a little cosmetic work on
the building," Arthur Zeckendorf believes. "He's a crafty, smart guy."

In fact, Avlon removed every bit of the terra-cotta ornamentation—pediments, pilasters, and angels—leading Paul Goldberger to
joke that the Mayflower should be renamed the De-Flower. Some
wondered if Avlon hadn't also stripped it to ensure that it would not
be included in the Upper West Side/Central Park West Historic
District, designated in spring 1990. Its southernmost boundary was
set at Sixty-Second Street, just north of the Mayflower. In response
to all the speculation, Avlon told the story of a red Volvo.

Local Law 10 was already in effect when a huge dagger-shaped
piece of terra-cotta fell from the Mayflower's façade, smashing the
window of the Volvo parked in front of the hotel. Avlon had the
building inspected and found that the ornamentation was "all loose."
Terra-cotta was crumbling and falling off, too. The building was, in
effect, exfoliating. So Avlon finished the job and predictable outrage
ensued. Then, also predictably, it died down. Regardless of Avlon's
intentions, he no longer had to worry about Landmarks Preservation Commission oversight.

Another potential hurdle to development was zoning. Under existing law, a new building on Central Park West would have had no
height limitation but would have been required to have multiple setbacks and look like "a wedding cake with the mass forced back to
Broadway," Avlon recalls. He thought the prevailing zoning made
a mockery of the Central Park West street wall—the harmonious
backdrop to city life that architecture provides. There was talk in the
real estate community about zoning changes; the first Millennium

tower was rising along with unhappiness about its bulk. Avlon got word that New York's City Planning Commission was considering wide-ranging changes to the prevailing zoning laws and brought the architect Rafael Pelli, César Pelli's son and partner, into the conversation, arranging for him to meet with the planners to discuss what might be built on Avlon's block. "He went into high gear to defend the parcel," says someone close to Avlon.

Pelli's challenge was to work with community groups, city planners, and Landmarks all at once and come up with a way to meet a new demand that 60 percent of any future development's floor area be located below the height of 150 feet. That was a direct response to Millennium's movie-theater complex, with its high ceilings but low square footage. "Square footage is worth more high up," where it is enhanced by views, says Pelli. So he suggested lowering the height of the portion of the building on Central Park "to preserve the ability to build taller on Broadway."

The architect came up with a number of solutions, all incorporating a low building facing Central Park and a tower behind it nearer to Broadway, both growing out of a podium base a few stories tall with retail all around. Pelli, lobbyists, attorneys, and specialists went back and forth with the city. Avlon avoided the meetings. For him it was just part of the chess game, a useful exercise or, as he puts it, "a rough massing response to a problematic spatial association." But when he realized that the City Planning Commission was focused on the rarity of a full-block development site, a lightbulb went off and he understood he might induce the city to enter into a quiet understanding of special treatment for his special block. The raw power of real estate in New York City cannot be overstated.

The Special Lincoln Square Zoning District was formally revised in February 1994, and city planners endowed Avlon's rare block with special zoning status. Formally speaking, the agreement limited the size of what could be built there, but it actually enhanced the development possibilities. The new rules mandated a 125-foot street wall on Central Park West and a lower one on Broadway. But Avlon successfully argued that the greater good was to protect the streetscape of Central Park West and reflect the block's importance as a transition point from high-rise midtown to sedate Central Park West.

"It was a critical site," says Joseph B. Rose, then the chairman of the planning commission. "The goal was to let them do something special there, to recognize the Central Park street wall but tie it in to Columbus Circle, which I saw as the gap tooth in Broadway's smile. The redevelopment of the Mayflower site was crucially important to making that part of town work. What evolved was not an accident. I find it quite gratifying, actually."

His success with the city aside, Avlon still didn't know whether he wanted to develop his block, net-lease it, sell part of it, sell it all, or enter into a joint development venture with others. But those who don't need money often make the most of it. So Avlon was content to sit back and watch, sometimes from that penthouse he kept atop the Mayflower. He held an annual holiday party there to which he invited all the city's top developers—as if they needed to be reminded that they were partying atop a gold mine.

Part Five

INHERITANCE

*Greatness of name in the father oft-times
overwhelms the son; they stand too near one another.
The shadow kills the growth: so much, that we see the
grandchild come more and oftener to be heir of the first.*

—BEN JONSON, *TIMBER; OR, DISCOVERIES
MADE UPON MEN AND MATTER*

Will Zeckendorf rejects the notion that he and his brother inherited their first ground-up development project from their father. "The simple fact of the matter is that, yes, our father bought 515 Park, and then he got, as usual with him, waylaid on six projects and was in financial difficulties," Will says. "We were always partners in 515, Arthur and I. From the get-go. And there came a time when Arthur and I wanted to go in a different direction and we flat bought him out. Period. End of the discussion. So at that point we had a hundred percent but we had nothing, because all we had was a mortgage that was worth thirty or forty million dollars more than the property and a Japanese firm that wanted to go back to Japan." Once their new partners at Goldman Sachs bought that mortgage and ripped it up, though, nothing turned to something. In 1998, the brothers Zeckendorf finally became developers on their own account.

"You cannot let a legacy tell you how to run your business life,"

Will continues. "I'm hugely proud of my grandfather. The B-word [bankruptcy] is just a footnote; I look at his accomplishments. But the experience with my father from 1989 to 1992 was not fun. We were young. We had no wealth to speak of. We were getting paid, but no more than that, and we were essentially unemployed in 1991. It was traumatic. The ship was underwater, and unquestionably those three years instilled some things in us: One building at a time. Keep debt down, cash high, and structure low-risk deals. We struggled and then things started to click. I think Arthur and I are fundamentally self-made. But we got an education that was unrivaled, a gold-plated education, the best education one could have gotten, from our father. Five or six years of massive responsibility."

That education, followed by graduate work at Millennium Tower, set the stage for 515 Park. They'd demolished the old building there and were laying a new foundation when they finally revealed plans for their $100 million building early in 1998. The news earned them a front-page story in the *New York Times* under a headline that made it clear that something significant had changed—both for the brothers and for luxury living in Manhattan: "A Haven for the Super-Rich with Room for the Servants."

Their part-ownership of Brown Harris Stevens had confirmed what they'd seen at Millennium.* Only two decades earlier, grand East Side apartments from the heyday of Candela and Carpenter had been white elephants. But in the years since, they'd become rare trophies, and since co-ops were hard to buy and sell, a pent-up demand existed for similarly grand domiciles. The Zeckendorfs decided to refresh the old template.

After studying floor plans and touring some of New York's best

---

*Early in 2001, the Zeckendorfs and their partners would strengthen their hand by buying Feathered Nest, a rental agency, and Halstead Property, a midmarket brokerage, passing the giant Corcoran Group to become the second-largest real estate brokerage in New York. Only Douglas Elliman was larger.

prewar buildings (many of them managed by Brown Harris Stevens), they wrote a business plan about "how to hark back" to the grandest buildings in Manhattan "and translate that into modern living," Arthur says. They studied 834 Fifth Avenue and 740 Park, seeking a way to build old-fashioned apartments for the newfangled rich. Obviously, they'd be condominiums, but what kind of condos would they be? "Prewars are great," says Arthur, "the best housing ever built. But with the exception of a few buildings—834 Fifth, 2 East Sixty-Sixth, 740 Park, and the San Remo—they're generally cookie-cutter. The same windows, the same brick. So you copy but you want to make it better."

In the larger narrative, 515 Park was a rehearsal, a training-wheels version of what would follow across town. The *Times* announcement notwithstanding, it was also a stealth condominium, particularly after the Sturm und Drang that had accompanied the Trump International and the Time Warner Center. But it revealed the brothers' ambition and their style, which had matured since their days marketing West Side condos. Now, they decided to offer not just standard-issue amenities—gym, concierges, setback terraces—but to revive such old co-op chestnuts as five-bedroom duplexes, twenty-by-thirty-foot parlors with ten-foot ceilings, fireplaces, stately baseboards and moldings, and a ground-floor restaurant with a catering kitchen for large parties. They'd also reinvent servants' quarters and individual wine cellars as new profit centers by moving them out of apartments and selling them (and storage spaces) separately. This was the sort of opulence that had, after the 1930s, disappeared. They added 150-square-foot marble bathrooms and state-of-the-art heating, air-conditioning, electrical, and technological systems as sweeteners. All in all, 515 Park was going to be, as the *Times* put it, a hot young thing "made to look like a gracious old dowager." Lamb dressed as mutton, you might say.

Convincing their backers at Goldman Sachs that this was a good idea wasn't easy. Though the bank's real estate professionals were on the Zeckendorfs' side, they had to get approval from an investment committee that included top Goldman hands, some of whom had their doubts about reviving 1929-style apartments. So the Zeckendorfs ferreted out where the skeptics lived, printed floor plans of their personal apartments, and explained why, in each instance, 515 Park would be better. "People really dug that," says someone who was in the meeting where they won approval of their plans.

The Goldman honchos weren't the only skeptics. Owners of the condos would "have no say about who their neighbors are," the *Times* warned in the last sentences of its page-one story. "The only guarantee would appear to be that they will all have a lot of money."

At the turn of the century, people with a lot of money were quite a bit different from those who'd long called the rarefied but hidebound East Side home. In May 1998, when the Zeckendorfs celebrated the start of the building at a caviar-and-champagne reception in the pit of the finished foundation, New York's economy was soaring, new money was sloshing around town, and the very notion of what constituted wealth was being redefined by the almost unfathomable fortunes being spun out of the ether of the Internet and high-tech-driven finance. Whether they'd made their money on Wall Street, as entrepreneurs, or had just inherited it, the new wealthy had a new set of expectations. Empty nesters and jet-setters who would once have settled for a tiny Manhattan pied-à-terre with a Pullman kitchen suddenly wanted mansions in the sky, even if they only planned to use them a few weeks a year.

Fueled by the money of the superrich, Manhattan real estate had been flying high for three years, with prices leaping an average 20 percent a year. So once the 515 Park condo plan was approved and the units went on the market in late spring 1998, the developers had high expectations for quick sales despite unprecedented prices. Their optimism was rewarded when 40 percent of the apartments were sold in the first two months. Before the year ended, they'd raised prices on the best remaining units to $3,000 per square foot, with penthouse duplexes exceeding $15 million, easily topping the record prices achieved a year earlier at the Trump International. "The building embodies the bull market," *USA Today* wrote in summer 1999. "515 Park Avenue is about as good as the good life gets."

Even the usually reticent Arthur Zeckendorf started boasting. "Breaking new records every week," he crowed, claiming to have signed contracts from Wall Streeters, entrepreneurs, and tech types. Demand for the maids' rooms was so high, he continued, that they'd removed and broken up an apartment to create more. By spring 1999, only six apartments were unsold, and at the end of that summer, only two remained. Names of buyers had begun to leak out, including record-company and fashion executives, and the theatrical producer James Nederlander Sr. Even Donald Trump was impressed. "They've done a really terrific job," he told the *New York Post*, which named 515 the city's new top condo.

The building had already opened and owners were moving in when it emerged that another purchaser was Jon Corzine, who'd been the chairman and CEO of Goldman Sachs when it agreed to finance the building, but had since been forced out of the investment bank and was running for a US Senate seat in New Jersey. He'd bought a duplex penthouse as an investment, as he intended to remain in his longtime home in New Jersey, but his purchase was one more indication of 515's instant cachet.* By that point, the Zeckendorfs were already on to their next project.

---

*In December 2002, the condo board would sue the developers for what it deemed faulty construction, and owners, including the French-luxury conglomerateur François Pinault, followed with their own suits. The litigation proceeded for years, but prices in the building were unaffected, and in January 2006, Pinault sold his duplex for $22 million.

Early in the year 2000, as 515 Park was selling out, Arthur and Will zeroed in on two more development sites. One was just down the street from 515. In March, they bought a six-story apartment house on East Sixtieth Street between Madison and Park. A Goldman Sachs client owned the adjacent property, and in 2001 the Whitehall team introduced Will and Arthur to him. It proved a fortuitous encounter.

Eyal Ofer was one of two sons of Sammy Ofer, a Romanian Jew whose grandfather arrived in the Mediterranean port of Haifa, then in Palestine, in 1924. "Foreign ships used to arrive at the port, and vendors would rush to the vessels and ask for captains' favors in accepting their supplies," says Eyal. "So this is how we started a shipping business." Shortly after Israel won its independence, Sammy Ofer became a shipowner, buying his first vessel on the day Eyal was born in 1950. "So he called me and the ship Eyal."

In the late 1960s, Sammy Ofer enrolled Eyal in a British school and, later, moved to London himself. Eyal went home to Israel for military service, but then returned to England to study maritime law while working for his father, who'd relocated their shipping interests to Monaco in the late 1970s. In 1980, when oil prices peaked, Sammy Ofer decided to diversify and sent Eyal, his wife, and children to New York to scout its real estate market. Over the next decade, Eyal "figured out New York ways," he says. "We did not know the name of a street. We had no clue. And we had to identify the good guys from the bad guys, and we had to take advice from people we had no familiarity with."

Ofer's first purchase was a brownstone on Forty-Second Street near Fifth Avenue. He paid $800,000 for it. His father told him he was crazy—"the Deuce," as it was known, was still a derelict corridor full of prostitutes and drug addicts. "Those people will move,"

Eyal promised his father, "but the building will stay." Sammy wouldn't listen—and ordered him to sell it immediately. "In less than a month, I called him back and I said we sold the building."

"How much you lost?" Sammy asked.

"I sold it for $1.8 million," Eyal replied—a million-dollar profit.

"So, you know what you're doing?" his father marveled. "Okay, go and find another one!"

"And the rest was history. In eighties Manhattan, you could not go wrong."

Though Ofer eventually returned to London and the shipping business, he continued to invest in real estate through the 1990s, expanding the family's interests around the world. Meantime, Sammy Ofer moved into the top rank of Israeli business when he acquired Israel Corp., the country's largest holding company, in 1999, adding chemicals, energy, raw materials, and semiconductors to the family portfolio.

That year, the family was said to control $3.5 billion in businesses, including three banks, several more financial firms, Judea Hotels, and the Royal Caribbean cruise lines. The Ofers were also in joint ventures with wealthy American counterparts such as the Pritzkers of Chicago and the Millers of Denver, as well as the handful of families who composed Israel's transnational commercial ruling class. That brought them into the orbit of Goldman Sachs.

Though domiciled in Monaco (Eyal Ofer holds dual citizenship in Israel and the European Union), the Ofers had ties with Israeli politicians and economists, some of whom moved freely between employment by Israel the corporation and Israel the country. That made the Ofers controversial. They sued to block the airing of a 2008 documentary that looked into a purported cozy relationship with the government. Ofer brushes it off, saying he was more upset by the family's first appearance, in 2007, on a newspaper list of the ten richest families in the United Kingdom. He admits, "Our hold-ings in Israel are the largest," but says he called the *Times* of London, which had published the list, to complain. "I managed to convince the editor that I don't belong there."

His brownstone on East Sixtieth Street attracted more welcome attention. "One day we get a call from Will [Zeckendorf]," Ofer re-calls, "and he said that he is interested to buy our brownstone. We told him the building is not for sale." Zeckendorf pushed to meet. "We knew then little about Will except that he was involved with Goldman in 515, and so we tried to get out from him what was his unique interest in the dilapidated, secondary brownstone, in a fine location, which we always esteemed for greatness but it took too long to achieve it."

Initially, Will refused to say, so Ofer refused to continue the conversation. Zeckendorf wanted "to fish without paying for the license," says Ofer. But soon, Will was back with "a guy from Goldman Sachs. 'Okay. Full disclosure. We own jointly with an-other party three other brownstones and we have an intention to develop a skyscraper there. And your building, to tell you the truth, is the key to the safe because without it [our] building is too narrow. With it, it is just the right size. Now, will you sell?'" Ofer said yes, but not for cash. He wanted part ownership of the skyscraper. "So we negotiated and we got the right proportions of ownership and we became friends. In the meantime, the land of the Mayflower Hotel was about to be auctioned. Everybody wanted to participate."*

No one concerned can now recall with precision when the Zeck-

---

*In 2005, the Zeckendorfs agreed to pay $430 per square foot, or $37 million, to the neighboring Grolier Club on Sixtieth Street and later made a deal with Christ Church, a Methodist congregation on the corner of Park Avenue, for their air rights—each transaction billed as the highest amount ever paid for such a purchase. Plans have been filed for a fifty-one-story building designed by Robert A. M. Stern.

endorf brothers first met John Avlon, another shipping heir and son of a man who started life doing manual labor in a port. But Will is sure that he encountered Basil Goulandris, one of John P.'s grandsons, at a dinner party. "He had a site he'd talked about for years," Will remembers, "and he said, 'Actually we're thinking of doing something.' And he set a meeting up for Arthur and me to go visit John Avlon at the Mayflower."

Avlon made a deep impression on the brothers. "John is American but with European manners," Will says. "He conducted meetings in a very formal way around the coffee table. A Mayflower maid would offer you coffee." Everyone had his designated seat. "We were told to sit in a specific location," says Arthur. "And his right-hand man, Bob Konopka, was always there." Konopka had worked for the Mayflower's owners and joined Avlon's company when it bought the hotel.

Their first meeting was "perfectly pleasant," says Will, and they continued to get together for the next seven years, always following a similar script. Avlon would tell them the block wasn't for sale, but the corporation that owned it might be. That meant any buyer would face significant exposure to taxes and various corporate liabilities, even unfunded pension liabilities for the hotel workers. Avlon also said that the remaining rent-regulated tenants in the building would be "your problem, not our problem"—and quoted "a very high price."

The property was, in fact, not yet for sale, and as they continued cultivating the block-teasing Avlon while he, in turn, studied them, the Zeckendorfs learned that they were only one of a number of parties circling it. "Everybody knows the property's there. It's not a secret," says Will. But who, exactly, was the competition? "John will never say."

Unbeknownst to Avlon, one tire-kicker had commissioned a study of the block by Michael Parley, New York's go-to zoning consultant, and his opinion turned out to be harsh. "He starts cursing under his breath," Will says. " 'It's terrible.' And he begins to send out the same sketches to everybody." The consultant's solution was a single-tower plan rising from a podium in the middle of the block. Other developers took his word for it. The Zeckendorfs weren't so sure, but they were certain that Avlon was "absolutely teasing everyone."

In Avlon's mind, he was just playing chess, waiting and watching as the neighborhood began, finally but inexorably, to improve. Something had to happen at the Coliseum site before he could make his move because, as he says, the Coliseum "controlled the tonality of the circle."

Time Warner proved to be the game-changer, breaking the existing record of $3,000 per square foot, set in 2000 by the Zeckendorfs at 515 Park. But not until 2004 did it become clear those high numbers would be achieved. Only then did Avlon set in motion the sale of the block he'd so carefully assembled over thirty-one long years. At last, his endgame had begun.

—∞—

"We don't do deals, we make investments," says John Avlon. "But chess sometimes turns into poker, and you have to be good at both." For years, he and Bob Konopka had been meeting with suitors seeking the Mayflower. "Arthur and Will were among the first and the most persistent over a long period of time," Avlon says. But the field wasn't theirs alone.

The Zeckendorfs heard rumors that Jerry Speyer, a builder who'd married into the Tishman real estate dynasty, and Millennium had both expressed interest. Still, though they knew the competition would be fierce, they began to suspect they had an edge. Avlon appeared to like and trust them. At one meeting, just as 515 Park was opening for business, he'd walked them out to his terrace and pointed to it. "You guys are the best, you're the greatest, you got five thousand dollars per square foot," Arthur recalls his saying. "He's also extremely nice to us and very complimentary. 'You guys hit the highest price ever in the history of New York City.' He had a lot of respect for Will and me. And our family."

As time went on, they learned Avlon was also talking to Related and to Donald Trump. "Everyone's there," says Will, "every person had the same meeting with him." And as the seemingly endless conversation continued, they noted a shift. "He actually begins to seem like a seller, as opposed to just a farmer," Will says. "A farmer wants his land. He really was acting like a seller. I think he was sensing the hold was coming to an end. He seemed like a different person."

The Zeckendorfs kept their ears to the ground and heard some potential bidders had dropped out because they couldn't play the game by Avlon's rules. "You have to go there and have dinner with him and have lunch with him and talk to him for two hours," says Arthur, "and he still wouldn't say whether he'd sell it to you for two hundred million dollars." And Avlon never wavered on his big condition—he was selling all the stock in the corporation that owned the land, and the buyer would have to shoulder the financial liabilities, as well as the problems of emptying the remaining tenants and terminating the hotel's staff—even though he knew that would likely mean a lower sale price. "It's a daunting exercise, mind you," Avlon says, though he doesn't entirely explain what made it so: The block was the sole asset of Park Summit, a corporation run by Avlon, but owned by Selborne Co., Inc., a Panamanian corporation, itself owned by Orville International Ltd. of the British Virgin Islands. "Real estate guys like to buy real estate, not stock," Will Zeckendorf explains, but they swallowed hard and kept coming.

The next challenge was deciding how much to bid for that stock. For years, the Zeckendorfs back-of-the-envelope calculations had made them wary, despite their lust to own the block. But by summer 2003 "this crazy number that he's always put out there—he always said to us, 'Give me a number with a three and a very high second digit'—was beginning to make sense because of 515, because of Time Warner," says Will. "And when Peter came up with a two-tower plan, that really changed the whole ball game."

Peter was Peter Claman of SLCE, a sixty-year-old architectural firm renowned for its technical prowess. That spring, taking nothing for granted, the Zeckendorfs had approached Claman to take a fresh look at the block and its zoning. He first consulted Michael Parley, the zoning expert, "but to his credit," Will says, Claman didn't accept the expert's conclusions. The term of art Claman uses for his brainstorm is "packing the bulk," placing the legally required percentage of floor space in the lower portion of the block, but altering Rafael Pelli's proposal by eliminating the full-block podium base, which Pelli had proposed be used for retail stores and recreational amenities. Instead, Claman proposed two separated buildings—"a *huge*, huge, huge breakthrough," says Will Zeckendorf.

Claman and his SLCE partner Jim Davidson, who grew up at 65 Central Park West, are more modest about their accomplishment. "The real author of the building is the zoning," says Davidson. "It mandated that the house [on Central Park West] be a certain shape and size with certain setbacks. But it's a split zone, so a tower was allowed on the west side of the site." SLCE had recently designed a building for a site similar to the Broadway end of the block, where an eighty-five-foot street wall was required, but there was no height limit after that setback. Because a Central Park West building was a given, the lower floors of any tower built behind it would effectively be void space lacking park views. But Claman realized that if they installed the mechanicals for the whole complex as well as the amenities for residents—neither of which are included in FAR calculations, but which take up a lot of space—and servants' apartments, too, in those floors, they could "get as much up in the air over Central Park West as possible to give views on the park." Parley "wasn't wrong," Claman says. "We just adjusted it slightly to give a better product. He didn't see that alternative. It was a gimmick that was available and approvable."

By hiring SLCE well before the auction to create that preliminary design for the building, the Zeckendorfs gained "a supersolid understanding of the project, the economics, the market studies," Will continues, "and that's going to become relevant in about six more months." Because by then, Claman had even proposed apartment layouts to demonstrate how many they would be able to build, and based on his drawings, they had a firm idea how many would have straight-on views of Central Park, and began to consider how much of a premium those views would command. Another key decision was the placement of two separate banks of stairs and elevators in each building, which meant that almost every apartment could be a floor-through.

All those decisions "raised the pro forma price per square foot we thought we could achieve," Will says, and allowed them to value the apartments higher and bid more to win the deal. Simultaneously, in collaboration with one of their executives, Judy Kessler, they'd begun writing a business plan that advanced what they'd done at 515 Park, "to hark back to the grand 834s, 740s, 960s, and translate that into modern living," Arthur repeats.

Only after all that was done did they call the executives at Goldman Sachs, tell them the block would soon be in play, and ask if they would serve as advisers on the deal, as well as their equity partner. They knew that buying a company rather than land and buildings would be complex, and that Goldman had the resources they needed to make it work. In late September 2003, Goldman signed on.

By year's end, Claman had calculated unit-by-unit square footage that allowed them to project apartment prices. Construction manager Bovis Lend Lease was poised to finalize a budget and project schedule. But early in 2004, there was a snag. "The deal was too big for Goldman," says Will. "We were not short of cash," clarifies Stuart Rothenberg, the Goldman partner then in charge of all its real estate investments. "It was just a judgment decision that we did not want to allocate any more dollars to that one deal. We said, bring in another partner."

So in April, the Zeckendorfs informed Avlon that Eastgate Realty, an affiliate of the Ofer family's real estate group, would be an investor, too. Ofer, it turned out, owned two investment buildings just across Broadway from the empty lot and had been watching it with interest, too. "Everybody in the city who had two dollars to knock together wanted to participate," he says. He also had more than deep pockets. His family and the Goulandrises had been friendly competitors for two generations and worked together in an insurance association for shipowners. "So we approached them and told them we are very interested to acquire the property and asked them what it would take," Ofer says.

Peter Goulandris, Ofer continues, explained that his family and the Avlons had "been doing for many many years the same type of acquisition of land and strategic locations, assembling them, zoning them, and then selling them, never wanting to be involved with any actual nitty-gritty of brick and mortar." Goulandris confirmed the price level they hoped to achieve and added that their intention was to decide quickly, likely on a first round of bids, but that beyond the price, they would also take into account the character and style of any buyer, which could eliminate a contender regardless of the size of the bid. "One of which they mentioned was Trump," Ofer says. Their Columbus Circle neighbor had somehow offended the ever-correct John Avlon—another participant describes "a massive blowup, a screaming match."

"I tried to get it," Trump admits. "But the number was so crazy, I said they must be kidding."

"So Avlon told him, don't even bother," Ofer says.

Everything had to be kept hush-hush. Though the Zeckendorfs were feeling out their brokers at Brown Harris Stevens and Halstead about what superluxury apartments needed to be, they had to keep their designs on the Mayflower a secret, so they gave the project a code name, Project W, for "West Side," and wouldn't divulge the location. "Supertight lid, everybody's sworn to secrecy," says Will. The same held true in Avlon's camp, where the project was code-named Beagle.

∼∞∞∼

In spring 2004, Beagle got real. "We narrowed it down to five finalists and notified each that the bidding would be closed, limited to the five. We sent them the terms of the contract and asked them to just fill in a price," in what's known as a first-price, sealed-bid auction, John Avlon says.* There would be no second round. "And I stuck to my word," Avlon adds. "I did hear through the grapevine that two bidders were stunned that we meant what we said. Nobody in New York real estate does that. But it was time for us to go and for someone else to come in."

The Zeckendorfs got that message at another Mayflower meeting, where Avlon laid out his rules and explained there would be no deviation from them. They brought Stuart Rothenberg, who'd replaced Dan Neidich as the head of Goldman Sachs's worldwide real

---

*Along with the Mayflower block, Avlon was going to sell two properties on West 102nd Street that would allow the winning developer what was called an inclusionary housing bonus. "By building a 36,000-square-foot building for us, they gained 183,000 square feet FAR for zoning," explains Carol Lamberg, executive director of the Settlement Housing Fund, a nonprofit that creates and maintains affordable housing. Ever since it opened in 2006, Semiperm, as the building would be called, has provided a home for twenty-three formerly homeless single-parent families, including thirty-five children, helping them learn to support themselves, seek education, care for their children, and become self-sufficient.

estate business; Justin Metz, a younger banker who'd been named Goldman's point man on the 15CPW deal; and Ofer and Samuel Kellner, the head of Ofer's Eastgate Realty. The Zeckendorfs wanted "to demonstrate the credibility of our team," says Will.

The meeting began, as sessions with Avlon often did, with a lengthy stretch of "shooting the breeze," as Kellner puts it, "talking niceties." But then Rothenberg, who thought he'd just been invited along to say hello but found himself mired in those niceties instead, took a cell phone call that seemed to go on forever. "Stuart was up and down and running around," says a party to the meeting. Frustrated, Avlon asked Kellner to step out to his terrace, where, in his quiet way, he went ballistic. "I don't like that," he whispered. "How do we overcome this?"

"You know Will," Kellner assured him, "and your [Goulandris] family knows the Ofers. Our word is our bond and we take responsibility." Avlon studied Kellner, then briefly turned back to the view before walking back inside, vowing, "I take you at face value."

Rothenberg can't recall that Kellner told him, "Get off the phone." Perhaps as a matter of discretion, Avlon professes to not remember it either, but allows that he would think it impolite if someone used his cell phone in a meeting. "The deal happened in spite of Rothenberg," Kellner says. "His attention was elsewhere. His aspiration was to build Whitehall in megasteps and this was not a megaproject." Henceforth, Rothenberg would have little direct involvement; Metz would handle the deal side, and Jerry Karr would watch over the development itself. But the moment signaled that relations with Goldman Sachs wouldn't always be smooth.

Shortly after that meeting, contracts arrived from Avlon with a request for their return with comments accompanied by a bid. On May 17, 2004, their deadline, Will personally delivered the marked-up contract to Avlon's lawyer. Their instruction to their own lawyers had been to "make as few changes as you humanly can, but don't let us make any big mistakes," Will says. "So we sent back a *very* clean contract." The partners had also decided to bid high, very high, even higher than the number beginning with a 3 that Avlon had long said he was seeking.

"Some credit is due to Goldman Sachs on this one," Will says. "Whitehall had lost a deal a month earlier, betting there would be a second round. Arthur and I were pushing like hell on 'em to get as high as possible. We'd also lost a lot of deals recently." They all understood that an auction conducted by a principal without brokers was unusual, as was John Avlon. So the Zeckendorfs were also sure he wouldn't shop their bid, seeking a better one from another developer, even though that was something they might do under similar circumstances. With Eyal Ofer's enthusiastic approval, they'd convinced the ever-skeptical Whitehall team that the block was worth $400 million.

"I was so bullish on this deal, you have no idea," says Will.

"We knew the market had popped by five hundred dollars a square foot," Arthur adds, thanks to their Brown Harris Stevens data. "And everybody else was six months behind."

"Eyal was bullish, too, like a cheerleader," says Will. "He completely got it and loved it. The other partner had more nerves going on." And that party, the Goldman group, would remain nervous. Goldman worried that the Zeckendorfs were being messianic, seeking to put their mark on the skyline and change New York forever. "We weren't perfectly aligned," admits a member of the Whitehall team.

Ofer and Kellner noticed the disconnect. Goldman was "involved with everything," says Kellner. "Their lawyers did all the contracts. They did the bulk of the finance with the banks. They were present at every meeting. But consensus needed to be arrived at, and we were the peacemakers between the Zeckendorfs and Goldman. It was not necessarily that Goldman was wrong, but sometimes they were too abrasive in the way they dealt with the Zeckendorfs."

But for the moment, the Goldman men agreed that they should

put a bullish bid on the table and not hold money back for a second round. They added an extra million dollars at Ofer's suggestion. The Zeckendorfs were all for it; they like odd numbers. They bid $401 million "and some change," Will says, actually $401,050,000, which would later be characterized as more than twice the going rate for Manhattan land. Why the extra $50,000? "We make numbers up for good luck," Will says. That kind of joking wasn't funny to the Goldman Sachs team. "The Zeckendorfs would have paid any number," says the Whitehall source. "It wasn't their money." Their backers were putting up about 90 percent of the initial outlay, even though the three partners would share equally in the profits.

Their basic bet was that they could sell apartments for an average $2,450 per square foot. "It was a winner, a perfect storm, the top of the market," says Ralph Rosenberg, who'd left Goldman but kept his eye on the deal. "And the beauty of the deal was, they had a high degree of conviction in their strategy." Or at least, so it now seems in hindsight. At the time, though, the bid took their breath away. "We all looked at each other and said, 'Omigosh,'" one participant recalls. "*Nobody* ever paid $400 million for an acre before."

Will and Arthur quickly learned that the other bidders were Related (run by Stephen Ross); Vornado, which was primarily an office developer, but had lately made forays into the residential arena; Edward J. Minskoff, who'd been one of the losing bidders for the New York Coliseum site in a consortium with Richard LeFrak and Donaldson, Lufkin & Jenrette; and Elad Holdings, a subsidiary of an Israeli conglomerate controlled by the gruff, self-made Isaac Tshuva. Like Eyal Ofer, Tshuva had a wide range of business interests with investments in energy, real estate development and construction, property rentals, tourism projects, insurance and finance, automotive, biochemical, and telecommunications. The Zeckendorfs knew Elad was bidding because Will had run into its president, Miki Naftali, when he dropped off his bid with Avlon's lawyer.

The Zeckendorfs worked their sources, trying to learn who else had bid and how much—and heard that they'd come in about $35 million above the next-highest bidder. Avlon isn't saying, but he allows that two of the underbidders made substantial offers, two did not, and a sixth party "tried to come in at the last minute and was advised the bidding was closed. They got rather upset. I found that behavior uncomfortable." That sixth party was SJP Properties, a New Jersey development outfit that had not been invited to the auction. Instead, SJP tried to crash the party at the last minute, and Allen Goldman, president of its residential-property division, is convinced that his arrival inspired the Zeckendorfs' winning bid. He even claims that Will later told him, "You cost me about fifty million dollars."

SJP's Goldman says he'd learned that the Zeckendorfs were going to bid just $350 million and increased their number only after SJP offered Avlon an even $400 million and named Costas Kondylis as its choice of architect. "We had people interceding on our behalf with the family," Goldman adds, admitting that might have backfired. "You never know. We did not have the prominence and the name, and the Zeckendorfs had sufficient leverage and they were determined to get it." Years later, Goldman is still angry. "I did not believe we got a fair shake." He suspects that his bid was leaked to the Zeckendorfs. "How do you think they came up with $401 million? We wouldn't have spent the time if we knew the Zeckendorfs would get the last look." John Avlon is blunt in response: "The Zeckendorfs did not receive special treatment." As a man of his word, he simply wouldn't countenance SJP's uninvited eleventh-hour appearance.

The rest of the welcome bids matched Avlon's initial request for a nine-figure number starting with a 3, with Related and Elad in the vicinity of $350 million and Vornado on the low end, around $320 million, or so the Zeckendorfs heard. Briefly, Will and Arthur worried that either Elad or Related might top their bid on a second round. At Goldman Sachs, they'd thought the deal was Related's to lose. So they waited to see what would happen next. They didn't dare call Avlon.

About a week later, John Avlon finally called. " 'Can you meet me tomorrow morning, nine a.m.?' " Will recalls. "Luckily Ofer was in town, and we got the Goldman people together and went over to John's law firm. John loved formal meetings, so it was a big formal meeting." Again, he told them where to sit. "With Will and me sitting next to him," Arthur adds. Also in the room were a clutch of lawyers and Samuel Kellner.

After they dickered over a few small issues, with Ofer leading the horse-trading, Avlon asked the Zeckendorfs to step into a side office, where he told them their offer would be accepted if they'd sign the contract and pay a deposit within twenty-four hours. "Clearly, the team, the ability to close, made a big difference to John," says Arthur. "He obviously likes Whitehall and Goldman Sachs, he knows the Ofers from shipping. And Will and I have been with him—"

"Seven years," Will adds, laughing. Back in the conference room, Will hastily scrawled on a legal pad and passed it around. *If we can conclude tomorrow, they will postpone "parallel bidding,"* it said. *They would like to end tomorrow w/us. They are prepared to call a vote of their group tonight.* Then, Will, Arthur, and Metz left the lawyers behind "to clean up the documents" and rushed off to arrange a wire transfer of that 10 percent deposit, $40 million. Ofer, who'd once lost a deal after leaving a negotiation to let the lawyers finish the job, was disinclined to make that mistake again and decided to order a Chinese take-out lunch and stay until every detail was dealt with. "So the next twenty-four hours is a nail-biter because you don't know what's gonna happen," Will continues. "But John's a man of his word, and so we reassembled the next morning, the wire had hit their account, and it was signed, that was it." Listening to his brother tell the story, Arthur Zeckendorf starts to giggle, for a moment a child recalling the moment he opened the best Christmas present ever.

The closing, delayed by summer vacations, took place in August 2004. Two days later, a small story about the record-breaking sale appeared in the *New York Times*—disappointing the Zeckendorfs both with its placement inside the local-news section and with how the deal was portrayed. Real estate reporter Charles Bagli had the price ("more than twice the going rate for land in Manhattan on a per-square-foot basis," he wrote) and identified the mysterious sellers as the Goulandris family, but he also intimated that the Zeckendorfs had overpaid, describing the price as risky and quoting Donald Trump's calling it crazy. "The story didn't say, 'The losing bidders said we overpaid,'" Arthur Zeckendorf notes wryly. "And Whitehall said, 'Who cares what losing bidders say.'"

Part Six

GROUNDBREAKING

The best luck of all is the luck you make for yourself.
—GENERAL DOUGLAS MACARTHUR

"The whole thing was just a horrendous nightmare," says Will Zeckendorf.

He isn't referring to the money that went out to pay the un-funded pension liabilities and severance for the remaining em-ployees of the Mayflower. Nor the liquidation sale of the hotel's furniture and fixtures—pedestal sinks, hotel art, chandeliers, and even the bronze mail-chute boxes and the swinging doors to the room-service pantry—that was held in November 2004, a month after the last of the guest rooms were shut down. The Zeckendorfs expected the auction would add $1 million to their war chest—but got about a fifth of that. "They come in and tell you you'll get all this money," Arthur recalls. "And you get nothing," Will says, com-pleting his brother's thought. "We really got ripped off. That was a complete waste. Idiotic."

Idiotic, but not a horrendous nightmare. Zeckendorf saves that description for the four rent-regulated tenants still in residence after the hotel stopped renting rooms. The Zeckendorfs would eventually be allowed to demolish the Mayflower, but first they were legally responsible for paying those tenants a stipend and moving expenses or even relocating them. In cases where tenants kick up a fuss, that can take a grinding five years. But initially, at least, the Zeckendorfs weren't worried; they had long-standing relationships with relocation experts, as well as profiles of the four compiled by the Mayflower's staff. They also had a plan in case any of them balked: all four lived in the north half of the building, and since the Mayflower and the Plymouth had originally been built separately, disconnecting them would require little more than slapping up a wall in the lobby. In the best version of that worst-case scenario, demolition of the south wing would then begin and add to the discomfort of the lingering tenants. That was more a joke than a serious contingency plan, but circumstances were about to make laughs hard to find.

The Zeckendorfs turned to Michael Grabow, a relocation lawyer, "to get the last four, four bachelors, out," he says. "They'd been there thirty to thirty-five years each, each in a tiny little room." Two were happy to take some money and run. One was ninety-eight and had relatives in Mexico. "After thirty-five years, he checks out with a single suitcase," says Will. "Plus a million-dollar check," Arthur adds, laughing grimly.

The second, an aging show-business agent, also in his nineties, accepted a similar sum and disappeared. Then, things got complicated. Negotiations with the third dragged out, and when a deal was finally made, the tenant's lawyer called to say that the tenant's check should be made out not to David Jordan, as the hotel knew him, but to Arthur MacArthur. The Zeckendorfs spent the next weekend "just going nuts," Will says, trying to confirm the mystery man's identity and ensure they were paying the right person. What they learned astonished them.

David Jordan's real name was Arthur MacArthur IV, and he was the son of the World War II general Douglas MacArthur. Arthur, in his late sixties, bore a tremendous burden: the name of the general's father, his brother, and an ancestor who had fought in the Civil

War. Born in Manila in 1938, Arthur IV appeared four years later on
the cover of *Life* magazine, while his father was running the Pacific
war theater; later, he ruled a defeated Japan. After that, Arthur lived
with his parents at the exclusive Waldorf Towers on Park Avenue,
but dropped from sight following his father's death in 1964.

MacArthur fans had tried without success to find him ever since,
while recalling a sensitive twelve-year-old with a mind of his own
who wanted to march to a different drummer. His father's biographer, William Manchester, observed that Arthur "lived for his music,
a fugitive from his father's relentless love." In these comments was a
hint of what the Zeckendorfs learned: Arthur MacArthur might be
gay and may have disappeared in order to lead his own life in a way
that would not reflect on his father's legacy. "He was extremely shy,
meek, quiet," says Grabow, noting that MacArthur avoided eye contact. "You knew right away he had social problems." Satisfied, the
Zeckendorfs cut him a check, which he used to buy a $650,000 con-
dominium a few blocks away.* It was the first and last time his name
appeared in public records as an adult.

Compared to the last tenant, MacArthur was easy. "Herbert
Sukenik's profile was a nightmare," says Will Zeckendorf. "Hugely
intelligent, a PhD, unmarried, embittered, a loner, disconnected
from society, and too smart for his own good. He was not a poor
man; he had independent means. And we knew all that up front."

Sukenik had lived for about thirty years atop the Mayflower, two
flights of fire stairs above its highest elevator landing. His tiny room
had "mold growing up the walls," says Will. At first, he sounded as if
he'd be easy to please. "I don't want money," he told the developers.
"I just want a new apartment with a park view, okay?" The Zecken-

---

*Grabow had first shown him a seventeenth-floor East Side apartment, but on
entering, he backed against the wall farthest from the window and confessed he
was afraid of heights. "He wouldn't go above the seventh floor," Grabow says. He
ended up in a fifth-floor unit.

dorfs assigned a Brown Harris Stevens broker to find one for him and hoped it would quickly be over. But then months went by.

Herbert J. Sukenik was born in the Bronx in 1930 to an American branch of a prominent Israeli family. His father's brother was the archaeologist who first recognized the importance of the Dead Sea Scrolls. His cousins were equally accomplished. Herbert's father, conversely, was a pharmacist who'd been arrested and found guilty in the 1950s for selling amphetamines without prescriptions.

Herbie, an academic whiz kid, breezed through Cornell University in just three years, earning a physics degree, made Phi Beta Kappa, and went on to get a master's in physics, a PhD in physics, and an MD. After a stint at the General Electric Research Laboratory, where he studied nuclear magnetic resonance, he was named chief of space medicine at Martin Company's Space Systems Division. Sukenik never married. His closest relationship seems to have been with Irwin Shapiro, now an astrophysicist at Harvard. They'd been frat brothers at Cornell. Shapiro called Sukenik annually. "He never called me," says Shapiro, who thinks his friend had issues. "His father was a strange, strange, very quiet man. A total mute. In another world."

Sukenik's career spiraled downward after his stint in space science. In the midsixties, he moved east to work at Massachusetts General Hospital, where he played a role in its earliest installation of computers. "He took a job that was far beneath him and he became more and more isolated and angry," Shapiro says. "He was angry at the world, but, I thought, angry at his father."

In August 1974, Sukenik moved to Manhattan and a room at the Mayflower Hotel. "He was very reclusive," says a younger relative, Herbert Chirlin, who recalls overhearing older relatives talk of Sukenik's bitterness at never living up to his potential. He sometimes worked as a school doctor, but, Shapiro thinks, he finally took to his room and rarely left.

Sukenik was seventy-three when he met Michael Grabow in that 350-square-foot room, which had a kitchenette, a bathroom, four exposures, and fabulous views of Central Park and both the East and Hudson Rivers. But its windows were so filthy, those views could barely be seen. He shared the place with thirty years of scientific journals. It was "a wreck, a mess," Grabow says. "Clothes everywhere. Papers, magazines, two computers. He had to clear chairs to sit on." Grabow settled in and tried to get to know the Mayflower's last holdout, who was short and balding, with a wild fringe of gray hair, kempt but not well dressed, with the "old-man smell" of someone who "didn't shower much," Grabow says. "He was clearly brilliant, but he didn't dwell on any topic very long."

"I wasted my life," the embittered Sukenik told Grabow in one of their many conversations over the next six months. His father had died while he was finishing his medical degree and left him just enough money that he didn't have to work. "I could have been at the heart of research into CAT scans and MRIs," Sukenik said. "I should have invented something like that. Instead, I've been up here thirty years doing crossword puzzles." Grabow asked around and learned Sukenik was universally disliked by the staff. He never let anyone into his room to clean, even though he was entitled to maid service. "He was a bitcher, a complainer, an old, grouchy guy," says a former Mayflower manager.

"But he had fun with me," Grabow continues. "He had a nice time beating me up." Sukenik was strange but not stupid, and his computer had taught him all about the block on which he lived. He knew its precise acreage and how much the Zeckendorfs had paid, and he'd calculated the taxes, insurance, and carrying costs of the empty properties and recited them all to Grabow. "He understood his value," the lawyer says. And he wouldn't begin negotiations until his three fellow tenants were gone. "He knew the last man standing was *very* valuable."

When he finally got around to stating demands, there were many. Where would he move? How? Would he have maid service? The only thing he didn't want was money. "He wanted to be pampered," says Grabow. He called Grabow several times a week, often raising the bar. "You want me out?" he'd tease. "This is what I want." Finally, an acceptable apartment was found.

His key demand had been a park view, so the broker took him to the Essex House on Central Park South, the old hotel that had been partly converted into a condominium, and showed him a twenty-two-hundred-square-foot, two-bedroom unit on the sixteenth floor. Sukenik loved it. "It looks like a bed of green," he rhapsodized, staring out at Central Park beneath him. Grabow sent Sukenik a letter spelling out their agreement: the Zeckendorfs would buy the condo and retain ownership, but he could have it for life, and they would even furnish it for him. The one demand they refused was free meals twice a week at the Essex House restaurant, then run by the world-renowned chef Alain Ducasse. Sukenik's response to the letter was silence. "Which was not like him," Grabow says.

Then, David Rozenholc, a noted tenants' attorney, called Grabow, and the moment he started talking, it was clear things had changed. Rozenholc told Grabow that Sukenik wanted more than the apartment and moving expenses. A lot more. Grabow hung up and called Sukenik. "I thought we had a deal," he said. "We didn't and now I have a lawyer," Sukenik replied. He went on to confirm that he did now want money—even though he had no use for it, no kids, no charitable impulse, and didn't want to leave it to his brother.

The negotiation "was a game" for Sukenik, Grabow decided, and the Zeckendorfs decided to play hardball. As they'd planned, they separated the two halves of the building lobby and began demolishing the southern end. Sukenik's response: "Oh, I love to watch construction." Jackhammers began pounding away for hours a day. "I love the noise," he said. The Zeckendorfs served Sukenik with papers setting in motion the multiyear demolition-related eviction process they'd hoped to avoid.

Finally, it had all come down to a simple question, " 'Where's the cash?'" Will recalls. "This is just a break-the-phone moment. We've got a fifty-two-thousand-square-foot property with one tenant." After two months of silence, the Zeckendorfs turned to an ambassador, a third lawyer who knew Rozenholc. "And finally, we get a number, which is big enough to break another phone." But at last, they had a deal.

Fortunately, during Sukenik's extended silence, they'd bought the Essex House condo "because we cannot wait six more months to find this guy another one," Will continues. That set them back $2 million. They won't reveal the additional sum they finally paid Sukenik, citing a confidentiality agreement. All the Zeckendorfs will say is that it was, in Will's words, "by far the highest price ever paid to [relocate] a single tenant in the city of New York." Another record, albeit one they wish they didn't hold. It was $17 million, according to someone with knowledge of the transaction. Rozenholc also forced them to pay for shelves in the new apartment to hold Sukenik's scientific journals. In return, Sukenik promised to pay the Zeckendorfs $1 a month in rent. "As a joke," Rozenholc, who got a third of the settlement, says he gave them a check for $120 for the first ten years and added a clause to the final agreement requiring them to return a prorated amount if Sukenik died in that time.

The first wrecking ball hit the walls of the Mayflower two days after Michael Grabow delivered Sukenik's check. "He walked out with Rozenholc's assistant carrying his belongings in a battered suitcase," says Grabow. He lived on as a shut-in in his new home right around the corner until his death at age eighty in January 2011. Despite his wishes, Sukenik's $9.8 million estate apparently went to his brother. When the Zeckendorfs recovered and sold Sukenik's condo, they made a profit of $362,500 before closing costs.

David Rozenholc can't recall if the Zeckendorfs ever returned the $48 overpayment on the rent for the Essex House condo. But he spoke to Herb Sukenik several times before he died. "He seemed . . . ," Rozenholc starts, then pauses. "He had no complaints, but he should have been happier. But some people who should be happy may not be."

For his part, Michael Grabow still bears a grudge: "He promised to take me for a drink, but he never called me again."

———∞———

In summer 1999, the architecture critic Paul Goldberger, who'd taken his byline to the *New Yorker* two years earlier, penned a review of 515 Park. Under the headline "A Touch of Crass: The retro look gone wrong," Goldberger castigated the building as "particularly ungainly . . . weirdly gangly . . . clunky" and "a pretentious muddle." Whether the Zeckendorfs took his barbs seriously or not, the design of 15CPW seems to address each and every one of them. But the Zeckendorfs and many, if not all, of the architects they worked with on the building say they didn't really create it. Its zoning did.

That is false modesty. Even before the Zeckendorfs bought the block, SLCE's Jim Davidson "personally built a little model just to show them" how he and Peter Claman had "jacked up the tower," Davidson recalls. In their original conception, the tower and base on the Broadway side both followed that wide boulevard's diagonal orientation. The developer-architect collaboration really began that day. Will Zeckendorf ripped the paper tower off the model and reoriented it parallel to Central Park West. "I understand why you want it that way," Will said, "but your views are looking northwest into the Century."

"So I dutifully cobbled it back together," Davidson continues; his client had a point. Meantime, Claman was at work on the interiors, a secret that would later cause bruised feelings at the firm. "Peter was responsible for the layouts, pre-Stern and prepurchase," says a senior figure at SLCE. "He [Robert A. M. Stern] added a diddle here and a nuance there." Davidson doesn't exactly contradict that, but he offers a more generous perspective: "I am not a starchitect. I just design a building and go on to the next one. They needed a signature architect to help move the product." So, as soon as they knew they owned their block, the Zeckendorfs set out to choose one.

Even before closing on the purchase that August, the Zeckendorfs had launched an architectural bake-off to decide who their signature architect would be. They interviewed five: Robert Arthur Morton Stern, of course; Rafael Pelli, who'd done the earliest work on the site, and his father, César, who'd just completed One Beacon Court, a mixed-use luxury condominium in east midtown that contained the latest iteration of Le Cirque; Daniel Libeskind, who'd just gained worldwide notice for his design to replace the destroyed World Trade Center; Hugh Hardy, architect of the restorations of Radio City Music Hall, Bryant Park, and several Times Square theaters; and finally, a sentimental choice. James Polshek's first job after graduating from Yale was working for I. M. Pei and Big Bill at Webb & Knapp. But Polshek suspects the Zeckendorfs included him only as a courtesy. At a meeting with Will and Arthur "it was obvious within ten minutes that the chemistry was no good," he says. All were given SLCE's massing design and told to stick to it, but elaborate upon it as they saw fit. And all were told "to be closer to classic," says Arthur Zeckendorf, "to the Dakota, the San Remo, residential."

The Zeckendorfs were disappointed by Hardy, a classical architect they had high hopes for, whose ideas they deemed indifferent and uninspiring. Libeskind proved "too out there," says Will, and it wasn't easy to communicate with the architect, who was then struggling with the fraught politics of the World Trade Center site. So Stern and the Pellis were asked to prepare more elaborate proposals, for which they were paid. Arthur, who calls himself both an admirer and a friend of César Pelli's, says his firm's design was beautiful, "in the I. M. Pei category. But he had too much modern in it. It was a little too Time Warner. But Stern came up with an amazing scheme. They probably put the most time in on the project. We had never really used Bob before and we were dazzled, just dazzled."

Stern shared Arthur Zeckendorf's passion for the great buildings of the golden age of New York apartments. "I've been studying New York apartment houses for a very long time," says Stern, including all the buildings that obsessed the Zeckendorfs. "They are houses in the sky," he says. "I like the term 'apartment house.' It gives it a more residential character."

But no one was building anything like the white-elephant co-ops of the golden age anymore. At least, not until the late 1990s when the Zeckendorfs were developing 515 Park and a competitor, Steve Ross of Related, hired Stern to do something similar, albeit at a less prominent address, Sixty-Fifth Street at Third Avenue. "It was not an important or desirable location," says Stern. "But it was a Park Avenue–type building." And, he says, it set a new price-per-square-foot record for apartments east of Park Avenue. Stern liked it so much, he bought and designed an apartment for himself there.

When the Zeckendorfs called, Stern was already familiar with their site and had spoken to Edward Minskoff about it. "I knew what Pelli would do," he says, "and I knew what I wanted to do—the kind of building it turned out to be. The Zeckendorfs wanted to do something exceptional. Their necks were stuck way out because they'd paid so much for the site." Stern knew that Pelli's office would offer serious competition, but he liked the direction in which the Zeckendorfs seemed to be going. "I've always argued you could go back to go forward," he says. Using what architects call punched windows in a masonry building instead of a sheer glass-curtain wall, for instance, would seem to be retrograde. "But we were able to convince all concerned that a wall with punched windows could still provide a sense of openness to the park *and* enliven the façade," Stern says.

Stern's presentation in the bake-off was close to the building that stands today, including its most notable features: the motor court to the south and the garden to the east between the two wings, the cupola atop the reception pavilion, and the asymmetrical roof line of the taller building. "Most buildings are remembered for their skyline features or their street-level features," he says. Stern also rejected a notion floated by SLCE and Will Zeckendorf in their preclosing concept drawings: three separate lobbies, one each for the house, the tower, and the small number of comparatively budget-priced apartments on the lower floors of the Broadway building. He replaced them with two lobbies connected by a long corridor with one concierge stationed at Central Park West and another off the motor court, and thus solved one of the biggest challenges the Zeckendorfs faced, making the tower apartments seem as valuable as those on Central Park West, by making them all Central Park West apartments.

Inadvertently, perhaps, this created something quite uncommon in luxury apartment houses. Most have a tightly defined population; they remain, to a great extent, the little clubs of the nineteenth-century creators of the first cooperatives. Unusually for one of the city's most desirable buildings, 15CPW approaches a democracy, and not only because it holds two hundred apartments, but because of the wide range of their value. Its richest residents ride the four main elevator lines but get to push buttons set apart from the others beneath the engraved word PENTHOUSE. The poorest, in those inexpensive apartments on the Broadway base that lack Central Park views, have a separate elevator bank that serves only the "back of the bus." But their segregation isn't absolute; their owners and occupants get to share the lobby, the restaurant, the health club, and the screening room with the gods above. At Millennium Tower, the richest rode their own elevators from their own lobby. Intentionally or not, Stern and the Zeckendorfs chose more inclusive symbolism.

Symbolism, too, was in the choice of material for 15CPW's skin. Its limestone exterior was a rejection of the preceding decade's paradigm of glass houses. Richard Meier's towers in Greenwich Village— with their floor-to-ceiling windows overlooking the much-traveled West Side Highway—suited a time when the rich and famous put themselves on display, saying, "Look up at me," from their mountaintops. Stern's 15CPW harkens back to the 1920s, when the wealthy lived in worlds of their own and developers built apartment towers on Manhattan's Gold Coast that resembled block after block of impenetrable fortresses. After the stock market cratered in 1929, those limestone châteaus seemed remarkably prescient, as if their architects had foreseen the need to protect those who'd created the crisis and exploited it for their own gain, and even the ones who merely survived it intact. The message sent by 15CPW's stony skin is "Look if you like, but you won't see much." Once again, the mountaintop is cloaked in a protective shroud.

After rejecting a precast-stone façade like the one at 515 Park and flirting with the idea of a brick exterior during the bake-off, Stern proposed that the two wings instead be dressed from street to roof in limestone. Arthur Zeckendorf was pushing for limestone and had even compiled a book of photographs of all the important stone buildings in New York. That told Stern they were of like minds, though he was not seeking to make a sociocultural point. He saw limestone as the solution to the challenge of the "transitional" block: ignore the buildings to the immediate south. Just as Donald Trump had rejected a Columbus Circle address, Stern was convinced the new building had to reject any architectural or visual association with the roundabout and identify north, instead. Time Warner and the Trump International were "the glass world," he says. "We were the stone world."

Although the Zeckendorfs had briefly considered a front building covered in masonry and a Broadway tower in glass, they couldn't help but agree and abandoned that schizophrenic notion. Stern's "design captured Will's and my vision for the site," says Arthur.

By September 2004, the Zeckendorfs were meeting with Stern's staff twice a week. "Monday and Friday or something like that, and if we left them on a Friday, they would do fifty versions of the cupola or the gate to the motor court by Monday," says Will. Stern's office would build and then rebuild models. Look-through models. Life-size models. "We'd walk through the lobby like it was Disneyland," says Arthur, "and see the wood and the columns and the texture. By March of '05, everything you now see was pretty well set. We didn't change our minds. We made no changes. For developers, the kiss of death is changing your mind." They were single-mindedly setting out to build the best building they could, one deserving of the site for which they'd spent a fortune.

Unassuming as they appear, the Zeckendorfs harbored a huge ambition: to build the consummate residence of its era. That wasn't the mind-set at Goldman Sachs, however. They wanted profit, that's all, profit, profit, and more profit, to turn Big Bill Zeckendorf's family phrase about real estate value: location, location, location. So Goldman wanted Will and Arthur to rethink the limestone, which was not only a symbol of the brothers' ambitions, but also of how their interests sometimes diverged from those of their partners.

Goldman's jitters were evident moments after the purchase of the block, when it quietly sold off about half of its share of the deal. "It was a big check," says Jerry Karr, "so we decided we would lay off part of the equity." Hotel companies had called immediately, expressing interest in the site, as did one of the "travel clubs" that rent luxury residences to tourists. Goldman rejected their overtures, but they helped convince the development team to add hotel-style services to their building.

Victor MacFarlane, the chairman and CEO of MacFarlane Partners, a real estate investment manager for institutional investors such as the California Public Employees' Retirement System (CalPERS), the largest pension fund in America, already had an interest in Columbus Circle, having bought just under half of the retail condo and a portion of the office section of the Time Warner Center from Related and Apollo Real Estate in 2003, when those developers were looking to reduce their postconstruction risk and refinance the property. "That was before everyone knew it would be a success," says MacFarlane, who invests in urban centers. MacFarlane had been a silent partner in Related's bid for the Mayflower block. "Steve [Ross] wouldn't go beyond" a certain number "and got outbid," MacFarlane says. "We provided most of the capital. We really liked the site, and in retrospect, we should have paid more."

Immediately after Avlon declared a winner, MacFarlane called Goldman Sachs. "I got the sense they'd always assumed they would sell down [their share of the deal]," he says. "They were prepared to go forward if no one showed up, but they were happy to sell it down." He says he "paid what they paid" and also tried to buy some of Eyal Ofer's share but was spurned. "Ofer proved to be right," he adds, laughing. "It wasn't like they needed us."

To Goldman's Stuart Rothenberg, it was all about risk management. Everything is a gamble, and there is always an argument for taking your chips off the table. "At the end of the day, we created the right balance," he says. He has no regrets. "I never regret anything that makes a profit." All concerned agreed that MacFarlane and his backers at CalPERS would have no operating input. There were already enough cooks in the kitchen. But Goldman wasn't finished with its sell-down.

Goldman's Justin Metz had approached Madison Capital, another real estate investment and operating company specializing in urban retail and mixed-use properties, before the sale and asked for an opinion on the retail component. In January 2005, in concert with one of its equity partners, Fortress Investment Group, Madison offered to buy the retail component, and Goldman sold them a 49.9 percent share for more than $50 million. Though the retail space was already effectively designed, Madison retained "major decision rights," according to a principal, and oversaw leasing with Will Zeckendorf.

Though they hoped to lease it all to a single entity and talked to both Nordstrom, the department store, and Topshop, the British fast-fashion chain, neither bit, so they quickly made a deal with Best Buy for a large store on the ground floor and two basement levels and slowly added other tenants, finally filling the majority of the retail spaces in late 2009. Despite the time it took to lease the retail stores, the Madison principal considers the decision by Goldman Sachs to downsize its risk "a smart strategic play." He says, "They wanted the Zeckendorfs focused on selling apartments, not retail." According to another party to those transactions, clauses in the deals with both MacFarlane and Madison gave Goldman Sachs a rising share of the realized profit if sales in the complex exceeded expectations. Profit, profit, profit.

Unfortunately for the Goldman team, the Zeckendorfs' laser focus on creating a building of great quality, aided and abetted by their chosen architect, meant still more, not less, investment. "An entire building of limestone?" asks Eyal Ofer. "Limestone is expensive, so the façade of the building [caused] great discussion. 'Why are you putting limestone on a forty-three-story building when the visual effect on the driver or the walker is only up to the second floor?' The limestone was adding a heavy toll."

With Ofer on their side, the Zeckendorfs "really pushed hard with the partners," says Arthur. "Goldman was not that enthusiastic about spending the money, but Eyal certainly was a major supporter of the limestone." Large buildings, they and Stern knew, are civic gestures as well as financial plays. When they occupy visible parcels and will be looked upon for decades by millions, the developers have a responsibility, albeit one rarely shouldered, to carefully consider the urban context. That is not easily quantified on a spreadsheet.

Nonetheless, an economic, not an aesthetic, argument finally won the argument over the use of limestone. The Zeckendorfs showed Goldman that by constructing the exterior of two-inch-thick limestone attached to precast, eight-inch-thick concrete panels, as opposed to using standard concrete blocks covered with brick (with a gap in between), the building's walls would be several inches thinner, so "you actually picked up square footage inside the apartments," says Arthur. The panel system also costs far less time and money than hand-laying stone one piece at a time.

Two quarries were capable of producing it. One was in Oolitic, Indiana, which most famously provided the stone used for the Empire State Building. The other, in Anamosa, Iowa, uses the local penitentiary as a sort of showroom ("the best-looking prison you've ever seen in your life," says Arthur), but is better known for the Disney Concert Hall in Los Angeles. The quarried stone would have to be shipped to Canada to be embedded in the precast panels before another truck ride to 15CPW. Still, it surely wasn't lost on Goldman Sachs that unionized New York City construction workers laying a block of stone at a time would be more expensive.

Nonetheless, Goldman did not simply acquiesce. "Some people write a check and say, 'Send returns,'" says Goldman's Jerry Karr. "We're involved day to day, in planning, in construction, and we do the financing. We're very hands-on investors." The limestone was "an eight-figure decision." Even after Goldman's two equity sell-downs, further expenditures required the approval of the bank's investment committee, which has a fiduciary responsibility to safeguard client money by keeping a close eye on costs. Fifteen's costs were setting records. So the tug-of-war over the limestone went on and on.

It didn't help that a faction on the investment committee hated the deal. "Nobody lived on the West Side," says another Goldman executive, Alan Kava. "Nobody got the West Side." They were convinced no one rich would want to live there. A London-based banker led the skeptics. "If you're not living and breathing in New York City, you don't get it," Kava continues. "I pounded the table, and at the end of the day, we went along. I'm convinced it added to the building's cachet." Jerry Karr says the Whitehall team also advocated eliminating five thousand salable square feet on the second floor to enlarge the lobby for the same reason. But limestone wouldn't be the last point of contention between Goldman and the Zeckendorfs.

Significant elements of Fifteen Central Park West's exterior are pastiche, borrowed from buildings that Bob Stern particularly admires in order to firmly place his creation in their midst despite their distance from Columbus Circle. The curved scoops just below the roof on the northern side of 15CPW call to mind a near-twin atop 1040 Fifth Avenue (long the home of Jacqueline Kennedy Onassis). The colonnade at the center of the roof line is an homage to the top of 10 Gracie Square, one of New York's most gracious co-ops. And the gated motor court, fountain, stacked bay windows, and decorative window surrounds all owe a large debt to River House, the formidable 1931 building on the East River at Fifty-Second Street that Stern calls "one of my favorite buildings."

Other inspirations are not as obvious. "The Dakota was very much on our minds," says Stern, who cited its original restaurant and courtyard skylights as the inspiration for their equivalents at 15CPW. Candela buildings inspired the floor plans, which were adapted for modern life. "Wealthy people live differently today," says Stern. "They have fewer servants, fewer live-in servants, they don't tend to eat in their apartments." Dining rooms are rarely used anymore except for formal entertaining. Restaurant culture barely existed in the 1930s. "We have many clients who have only a distant relationship to their kitchens," says Stern, "but people like to make breakfast for themselves." Closet space is far more important now. So are bathrooms. "Those 1920s and 1930s bathrooms are so tiny there's barely room to turn around."

But much of the design is new, and supervised by Stern, the team that did the heavy lifting was headed by one of his longtime partners, Paul L. Whalen, whose credits include the master plan for the revival of the theater block of West Forty-Second Street off Times Square, which turned a seedy, crime-ridden strip into a shiny tourist attraction. Whalen mostly stayed behind the scenes at 15CPW. Never mind the man behind the curtain.

Whalen ran the design process from the beginning of the bake-off, working closely with the Zeckendorfs, who, as much as he, loved getting lost in the weeds of apartment-house architecture. "They said they wanted a great New York building," Whalen recalls. "To us, that had to do with the fantasy. When people want to live in New York, what do they think of? We looked to buildings like the Century or the San Remo. Not just their character on the skyline but also the way they meet the ground. They're really great to walk along. At the same time, we looked to the Upper East Side—and buildings like 1040 Fifth and 740 Park—which was always thought of as the place with the most expensive, best apartments. They're much simpler, more sheer, all limestone, not brick and limestone. They tend to not have iconic tops, so in a sense, they're more discreet."

After settling on touchstones with Stern and the Zeckendorfs, Whalen weighed out a mound of clay that represented the allowable floor area ratio for the block. Clay is tactile and easy to manipulate. Whalen used it to "draw" and redraw the building in three dimensions. With the basic shape of 15CPW essentially predetermined by zoning, and the material for its skin chosen, windows were the next major factor in defining the look of the façade. Subtle arrangements of differently sized and shaped beveled windows gave them individual depth, lent variety and visual interest to the elevations, and would, along with the stone around them, affect the way light and shadow worked together to animate the building and enhance its residential character. Whalen tinkered with the SLCE floor plans, laying out wider living rooms and narrower bedrooms to see the effects of the arrangements on the building's face—an exercise the Zeckendorfs also greatly enjoyed. "We spent countless hours sketching them together," Whalen says. "Do you put the master bedroom and the living room on the front, or the dining room and the living room?" They decided, for example, to defy East Side convention and give the occupants of master bedrooms park views to wake up to.

Window size and windowsill height are also important considerations for those looking out of the building as well as those looking up at them. Sills and the spaces between windows can disrupt views from within. So Whalen ran computer simulations to help him maximize those views with larger windows and lower sills. Typically, living rooms are placed in corners to maximize views through huge windows on both sides. "We wanted a difference between the front and the sides," says Whalen, so he juggled big bay windows with smaller ones to create the illusion of vast open views.

"People want to hang pictures and place furniture," Whalen continues. Stern's office had worked in Time Warner Center and found they sometimes had to work around support columns and block windows to make spaces more habitable. The desire for larger windows as viewed from within also had to be balanced against their effect on the façade. "You can have too much of a good thing," Whalen says, chuckling. "There's a point where windows get so big, there's no wall left. It looks like a frame. It becomes totally unconvincing."

These decisions weren't made in a vacuum. As they'd consulted Brown Harris Stevens brokers while formulating their bid for the block, the Zeckendorfs convened focus groups with a wider cross section of Realtors, both their own and competitors', to help shape the final product. What would sell best? "In general, they gave us great tips," says Arthur Zeckendorf. " 'We want a family room.' 'We want heat in the kitchen.' 'We love double master bathrooms—his and hers or his and his or hers and hers.' "

John Burger, a top Brown Harris Stevens broker, felt it was a chance to improve on the Candela and Carpenter floor plans long considered the Gold Coast's gold standard. "In those days," he says, "architects were forced to provide windows in every room." But modern vent shafts allowed far more leeway in the layouts at 15CPW. So bathrooms could be bigger because they didn't need to be situated on an exterior wall. And those kitchens so many of the owners would never visit could be placed midbuilding, too. But with broker input, they were designed to allow long views through doorways into connecting rooms "so you don't feel you're in a windowless space," Burger says. "We asked the architects to give people the flexibility to use a library as a bedroom, too."

Throughout the process, those and other general principles emerged to guide the apartment designs. "We like to come in the front door and see the view right away," says Whalen. "We like to put the living room in the corner. We like a foyer that's a room, not a corridor. Libraries separate master bedrooms from living rooms so they can flip either way. Dining rooms can open to living rooms for flexibility, with kitchens behind and family rooms off the kitchens," where staff quarters were placed in old-school apartments. "Doors are carefully placed either clearly in the center of rooms or at the edge of the room, allowing you to use the wall for furnishing. There's nothing worse than a door that's slightly off center."

Another problem in the prewar-apartment inventory is the positioning of dining rooms and secondary bedrooms. In all but the largest apartments, second bedrooms are typically adjacent to masters.

"Their emphasis was to have the staff at one end and the bedrooms together," Burger says. But today's wealthy buyers often want to be sequestered from their children. And prewar formal dining rooms, usually evening-only rooms, were typically placed in the dark back of apartments. So the layouts for 15CPW were changed: secondary bedrooms got their own rear wings, and dining rooms, when possible, were given views so they could easily be repurposed.

The brokers had the Zeckendorfs' backs, too, on another point of contention with Goldman Sachs. They were absolutely certain that there should be larger, even massive, apartments at 15CPW, even if that meant there would be fewer—two per elevator bank as opposed to three. The brokers agreed with the data coming from Brown Harris Stevens and Halstead: there was an aching need for apartments on steroids in prime locations. But the Goldman Sachs team was aghast when the Zeckendorfs told them they wanted to build about forty apartments and penthouses with price tags at or above $10 million. "I remember meeting after meeting after meeting, they would drag us down there," Will recalls, "to explain to them how we were going to sell—"

Arthur interrupts, "—four-thousand-square-foot apartments! At three thousand dollars a foot! That's twelve million dollars!"

Goldman "was stuck in the mud," Will continues because of what the sales data *seemed* to show: that, in a recent year, only twenty trophy apartments had changed hands in Manhattan. Goldman was skeptical about their claim that they could sell twice that number of apartments over two years in a single building. "We said, 'You're asking the question backwards,'" says Will. "If there were more [apartments], there would be a lot more transactions. But it was tough to convince the Goldman guys." One concern was paramount: profit, profit, profit.

Despite the obvious misalignment, Goldman's Rothenberg considers those meetings more conversation than conflict and insists all were guided by cautious realism. "Obviously, you can look at demand over the previous twelve months," he says, "but predicting what will happen in three years? That's not so easy." Even if the Zeckendorfs could easily sell ten or twenty or thirty superluxury units, "the last ten are where your profit lies. Can you sell them?"

Finally, they reached a compromise. Lower floors might have as many as six apartments, but higher up, the apartment count would drop to four, two, and even one unit per floor. Even with that, the apartment-size conversation still wasn't over. But despite its annoying persistence, the Zeckendorfs would have the last laugh.

<hr />

The tower atop Paul Whalen's first model for the bake-off—when the building was still made of red brick—had a symmetrical top with swoops and columns at both north and south ends and made the architects nervous. "We thought it would be a pompous ass of a building," Whalen recalls. "We had to make the top looser and more casual. It's a slightly feminine gesture on what's otherwise a masculine building." Recalling an asymmetrical tower that Stern had once proposed for another building, they molded a new top with extra height to the north and a series of visually engaging stepdowns with terraces and bay windows to the south to maximize light in the upper apartments. Thanks to those setbacks, more apartments could be marketed as penthouses.

The next priority for the Stern office was the building's street-level appearance and entrances. The simple, sleek base is made of golden-granite stones chosen to be as close as possible in color to the limestone above, then individually hand-laid "so there are no seams on the first two or three floors," says Whalen.

Most modern buildings have enormous entrances that make them look like office towers. Stern and Whalen wanted to convey privacy and discretion, "like you're entering a house and it's not about the public looking into an atrium," Whalen says. Spindlelike metalwork, designed for the doors and flanking lanterns, created a visual leitmotif that was continued throughout the building, as well as in its logo and promotional materials, all of which were designed by Pentagram, an eminent graphic-design firm.

The lobby was conceived with two priorities. The first was inspired by a tour that the Zeckendorfs had arranged for their architects of lobbies along Fifth Avenue and Central Park West. "It gave us a series of precedents we could refer to, a common vocabulary," says Whalen. "Those building don't generally have enormous lobbies, though the best have high ceilings." The second must was ensuring that tower residents would feel they live on Central Park West, so a long back-to-front corridor allows a glimpse of the park as one steps from the tower elevators.

Flanking that corridor are the library (still barely stocked in 2013; the most represented author was Robert A. M. Stern) and the restaurant, both off the front lobby, with its English-oak paneling, red-, pink-, and purple-marble, fluted columns, two fireplaces, and seemingly floating ceiling with a central oval cutout that gives the illusion of sky above. The restaurant, which is small and low-ceilinged, was given translucent Veneziano-stucco walls as elegant compensation. The English-oak paneling was inspired by the work of Sir John Soane, the nineteenth-century neoclassical London architect and collector. The modern-classical furniture and rugs were custom-designed by Stern's interiors division. Arthur Zeckendorf, a collector of contemporary art, commissioned the lobby paintings, representing summer and winter in Central Park.

On the Broadway façade, double-height retail windows at street level were required by the zoning, as was an asymmetrical setback above, and an indentation in that long wall, to create the illusion of separate buildings. The glass storefronts raised an aesthetic issue because stone that appears to rest on glass can look peculiar. Inspired by early- and mid-twentieth-century buildings, Stern's architects designed storefronts that appear to be applied to the masonry rather than set into it. A Doric frieze motif was used to hide required vents. "There was a big concern that Broadway retail was not Fifth Avenue, but Central Park West was one of the fanciest addresses, so somehow they had to come together," says Whalen. "We brought them together by making the storefronts look like they belong to the building. We also stopped the storefronts so there's a transition of masonry before you get to the residential part of the building, which brings the two worlds together."

Between the two wings and the worlds of Broadway and Central Park West, they placed two courtyards. The northern one features a reflecting pool that doubles as a skylight on the seventy-five-foot, three-lane lap pool in the health club, directly beneath. The court around it would eventually be used as an outdoor dining terrace for the building's lobby restaurant and an outdoor event space for residents. The southern court had an unusual drive-in turnaround; an Edward Lutyens–style fountain made of a single piece of black granite in the middle; and an auto drop-off in front of an oval pavilion inspired by Frederick II's Sanssouci Palace.

"It needed to look great from above, so it got a copper roof," with a small stone cupola on top, says Whalen. "We asked for it, but we didn't think we'd get it. So few developers will stick their necks out like the Zeckendorfs did. They came into this project with a big vision and a notion. They weren't nickel-and-diming the project, which is typical." The result of that typical caution is value engineering, cutting corners where possible, usually where compromises are less visible, to save money. "We hate value engineering," says Whalen. "But they knew they had to shoot the moon, and that kept their architects happy and so we worked our butts off for them."

That fourteen-thousand-square-foot basement health club was designed to be both classical and more obviously high-tech than the rest of the building, though it also has a womblike feeling, with its glassed-in central pool surrounded by areas devoted to weights, cardiovascular machines, yoga, and workouts, as well as private massage rooms, two steam rooms, and a sauna. Stern's office even designed its walls, which they thought of as "glass artwork," Whalen says.

As 2005 began, Stern's office finalized the floor plans, but even then, they weren't quite alone. During the bake-off, Goldman Sachs had brought in Alan Wanzenberg, who'd started his architectural career with I. M. Pei, then formed a partnership with the interior designer (and intimate friend of Andy Warhol's) Jed Johnson. After Johnson's death in the explosion of TWA Flight 800 off Long Island in 1996, Wanzenberg went out on his own and developed a clientele among Goldman Sachs partners, including Dan Neidich, who'd brought him into the planning for 515 Park; he was responsible for its apartment layouts. Now, Wanzenberg set to work on the mix of sizes and shapes of 15CPW units, rejecting notions such as double-height lofts like those at the Hotel des Artistes. "We worked with Stern, though once he was on the scene, we knew we'd be ushered out," Wanzenberg says.

At the bottom of the "house" building, the final plans showed five and six apartments per floor, the smallest in the building. Whalen's great regret is not buying apartment 2B, a relatively affordable ($2.2 million) one-bedroom unit facing Central Park. Starting on the third floor, there were four corner units and two floor-throughs. "We always thought the best view was toward midtown," says Whalen, "where you get the tinkle of the lights on Central Park South. It's more interesting." Northern views were judged to be worth less, and because the Zeckendorfs considered the units on the northeast corner of the building less salable than their southern counterparts, an extra E-line, an extra apartment line, designated with the letter E, was added on two lower floors in the rear of the house to tease extra transactions out of the square footage.

The sixth floor of the house got five apartments instead of six.

On the seventh to eleventh floors, the unit number dropped to four, which would be the most common layout in both wings, with a pair of two-cornered units (the A and D lines) boasting three exposures and two floor-throughs between them. On the twelfth through fourteenth floors, above the first setback, the square footage shrinks ever so slightly, but on twelve, the units all have small terraces.

Already thinking about potential purchasers, the Zeckendorfs had decided to do whatever they could to attract a core of local families to the house. "They targeted a generation who had young families, were looking for family living, but were having a tough time finding co-ops," says former Whitehall executive Ralph Rosenberg. So four duplexes were planned for floors fifteen and sixteen, and three larger ones for floors seventeen and eighteen. Each of the seven two-floor units got a setback terrace on the lower floor that held its entertaining rooms, but only on eighteen would there be additional terraces off the master bedrooms and adjoining sitting rooms of the corner apartments. The upper duplexes also got his-and-hers bathrooms in their master suites, and libraries and family rooms on their upper floors to reinforce the notion that they had been designed for families. Those seven duplexes, though arguably not as spectacular as the full-floor penthouses in the tower, were designed to set the tone for 15CPW.

Finally, there would be a simplex penthouse atop the house, complete with a three-sided, wraparound terrace accessible from all its major rooms as well as its master-bedroom suite. Early on, a house architect in Stern's office was asked to draw up multiple floor plans for that apartment after a prominent banker expressed interest in it, "to show him how great it could be," Whalen says. "The idea was to have all the public rooms facing the park, and this spectacular enfilade going through all the rooms so you get a block-long view of the park. Very few people can say they have that. Even the entrance hall has views over the park, which is very unusual."

As the crowning touch, a simple formal garden, inspired by one on the rooftop of Rockefeller Center, was placed atop that penthouse for the sake of the residents of the tower above. It was "designed and engineered to support real plants," says Whalen. It would get an automatic watering system and roof drains to lessen the potential impact on the penthouse.

The tower, with its multiple uses, was a more complex jigsaw puzzle of floor plans. Directly over the retail stores Stern planned three floors (numbered six through eight) that would contain smallish apartments with views of either Broadway or the central courtyard; relatively spartan servants' quarters that could double as home offices; and the building's additional amenties: a twenty-seat modernist screening room designed by Theo Kalomirakis, the father of home theaters; a meeting center with two conference rooms; a billiards room; and a computer room. A north-facing terrace off those shared spaces (looking at the Century) would also be available to residents for events. The superintendent's apartment shared the amenities floor. Above it, the core of the succeeding floors, where apartments would only have had views of the courtyard and the back of the house, were reserved for mechanical equipment.

The ninth floor of the tower—actually the first floor of the physical tower—was designed to hold four corner apartments, all with terraces on the roof of the Broadway base; three of those terraces are enormous, larger than many entire Manhattan apartments. The two floors above that, both with high ceilings, are dedicated to more mechanicals, including the huge refrigeration plant and the hot-water heaters the massive building requires. For marketing purposes, there would be no unlucky thirteenth floor, and other physical floors would not be sequentially numbered, so floors eighteen, nineteen, twenty-one, and twenty-two in the tower would appear to not exist as well.

As in the house, the next nine residential floors of the tower (floors ten to sixteen and twenty-three to twenty-five) were designed with six apartments per floor, including two one-bedroom units with obstructed park views over the top of the house. The three floor-throughs on the upper three of those floors would have open western views to the Hudson River. The better the views, the larger the apartment.

The assumption was the tower apartments would sell to foreigners "who wanted helicopter views," says Brown Harris Stevens broker Kathy Sloane. So the next thirteen floors, starting at the twenty-sixth, each contain two huge corner units on the north and south ends and two floor-throughs in the center. Again, the south apartments got an extra room because, in the Zeckendorfs' eyes, their midtown and park views would make them more valuable.

The thirty-ninth floor, with two apartments and two central terraces facing the park and another over Broadway, would shortly be redesigned as hedge funder Daniel Loeb's floor-through simplex. The next floor up was also split into two penthouses, one served by each elevator core. As below, the southern-facing penthouse was slightly bigger. On the forty-first floor, the architects planned one huge penthouse with a three-sided terrace and a somewhat smaller unit with only a small terrace off its dining room. "But it's just so perfect," says Whalen, "and the height and shape of the living room are just amazing."

The forty-second floor penthouse, which boasts what Whalen calls "the incredible King of the World terrace" beneath the arches atop the building, isn't the largest, but is arguably the best residence at 15CPW. "It's only slightly smaller than the Weill apartment, but it has those arches you can see from an airplane, which to me is worth a lot," Whalen continues, "and a living room that's open on three sides and another incredible terrace facing the park. The master bedroom suite gets lovely, lovely views through Columbus Circle and down Broadway, one of the nicest in the building. It was a surprise view for us. We didn't expect it to be so spectacular." Other touches include a maid's room and a kitchenette off the master bedroom, presumably for late-night snacking and grabbing a morning espresso before having to face that maid.

Though substantially smaller than several of the other penthouses, the highest aerie at 15CPW was designed with a half-pentagon-shaped terrace with south, east, and western views, a second large terrace looking over the Hudson, and three French balconies on Central Park. And though its master suite only has a single bathroom, the architects planned adjoining his-and-hers dressing rooms, two secondary bedrooms, a study, a family room, a formal dining room, a library, a small bar, and a kitchen complex complete with a pantry and serving station.

Stern's office also designed the standard kitchen, master bathrooms, and secondary bathrooms that would come with each apartment (and boast requisite high-end brand names such as Dornbracht and Toto plumbing and Sub-Zero, Miele, and Wolf appliances), though it was always assumed that many buyers would rip them out and replace them. Despite that, in the final stages of the design, digital renderings showing how rooms might be furnished were created and walk-through prototypes of typical rooms were prepared for eventual use in sales. Just as they wanted to encourage families, the Zeckendorfs wanted to discourage purchasers from asking for customized apartments; only about a dozen would be sold as unfinished white boxes or, as the Zeckendorfs call them, "cold, dark shells," to the earliest buyers only. "We have a very firm rule," says Will. "We're not going to change for you. We'll delete. So if you want a bathroom with no marble in it, we won't put the marble in it for you. Like restaurants: you can take it the way we deliver it, or you can delete, but there's no in-between. 'I want orange marble'? Do it yourself."

The architects' enthusiasm for and pride in the project would shortly become one of the building's unique selling propositions and help raise the prices for its apartments to previously unheard-of levels. But as enthusiastic as he was, Robert A. M. Stern would tacitly admit, when pressed, that while they'd improved upon the classic Gold Coast co-ops in many respects, in others, they couldn't match them. Value engineering was not entirely anathema.

In the prospectus for 740 Park, for instance, developer James T. Lee had boasted that even hidden components such as the brass pipes and concrete were the finest available. Asked if the Zeckendorfs could make the same claim, Stern said, while the building was still under construction, "I'm not going to comment on that. I would say that aspects of our building are comparable in terms of high ceilings, high-quality window frames, fine-quality glass in the windows, nice molding profiles. We're building a reinforced-concrete building that meets every reasonably exacting standard. It's wired properly and all of that. I'm *not* saying that someone touring the Wrightsman rooms [at the Metropolitan Museum of Art] will immediately feel that we've done just the same job; there's a little more boiserie over at the Met."

The only part of the 15CPW plan that the public had a voice in was the Zeckendorfs' desire to build a garage beneath the building, which was left out of the original descriptions because it required a special permit that had not yet been approved. The need to get that permit also caused the delay of an announcement of their architectural plans.

"We held off as long as humanly possible," Will Zeckendorf explains. "Then we had to start making presentations [to win approval of the garage]. I kid you not: We go to make the first one to [officials and neighbors, including the local city council member who had been vocal in opposition to the Time Warner Center]. We swear them to secrecy. This is in connection with our garage, but we present the whole building." Within an hour of the meeting, David

Dunlap of the *Times* called Stern and the developers. Someone had described every detail of the project to him.

The Zeckendorfs had hoped to make a splashy announcement shortly thereafter, resulting in something like the front-page story in the *Times* about their smaller, less significant 515 Park. But Dunlap had readied another, longer story for the next day's paper on the city's latest redesign of Columbus Circle, which would soon be completed with a radical makeover of Huntington Hartford's museum by its latest owner, the Museum of Arts and Design. That story was set to run on the front page of the local news section. So Dunlap's editors rushed a brief—624 words—note about the new building into print, effectively burying their scoop on the seventh page of the same section.

But the Zeckendorfs didn't have time to dwell on the *Times*. It had been a year to the day since they had closed on the block. Demolition had begun in November 2004, but wasn't completed until the following June; demolition of the northern hotel building didn't begin until after Herb Sukenik finally took his leave in March 2005. Foundation work on the southern half of the site had already started by then. "The structure and composition of the rock outcroppings beneath the site slowed the foundation effort," reported *New York Construction*, a trade publication for builders. "Moving from west to east on the parcel, the rock transitioned from medium soft to hard. The team used excavators and blasting to remove it." The foundation for the tower was begun in the early days of January 2005. "On the Central Park side, the rock went to medium soft again but also dipped down so deep" that normal concrete footings were inadequate support, the construction magazine continued, so the rock was drilled and boxlike caissons inserted to support the building. Within nine months, the foundation work was complete.

Aboveground, 15CPW is made of reinforced concrete—forty-three thousand cubic yards of it, reinforced with fifty-five hundred tons of steel. The house was topped off—its skeleton completed—in July 2006 and the tower that September. As that happened, the Canadian contractor, working with the architects, developed technical drawings of the 2,832 limestone panels it would take to cover the 290,000-square-foot façade (which represented a small fraction of the eighty thousand stone elements in the building, fifty thousand of those uniquely cut). Indiana Limestone had won the job because it had recently opened a new area of the quarry that, in 1929, provided the stone for the Empire State Building. It had stockpiled what is called "full color blend material," stone that ran the gamut of available limestone color from buff to silverish gray. It also had the technical skills to cut it precisely to the dimensions required by Stern and Artex, the Canadian precaster, where pins were embedded in the stone with epoxy, and concrete was poured over each panel to form the backing. Only then were the panels shipped to New York.

"With construction, we make it sound easy," says Arthur Zeckendorf. Adds Will, "It's never easy." Even before the demolition began, the Zeckendorfs opened a construction office directly across the street at 1881 Broadway, one of Eyal Ofer's two adjacent buildings there; it had a view straight over their new property. From that office they visited the site "every day," Arthur continues, "meeting with the contractors, walking the building, watching the quality." Sometimes contractors didn't behave "and had to be disciplined," Arthur continues wryly. "We had two supers, three hundred pounds each."

The most exciting moment for the Zeckendorfs was when the two kangaroo cranes—which had the capability to grow taller along with the building—went up on the site. But that thrill was brief-lived. One of the two brand-new cranes "was a lemon," says Will, that "had a motor issue, so it would break down." Then, the concrete crew had to share a crane with the stone installers, "and the concrete guy would literally toss the poor Canadians out of their crane and take it over for himself." One day, things almost came to blows. "Ten Canadians versus two hundred big guys from Staten Island and Queens," Will reports. "It wasn't much of a fight." Adds Arthur, "Over in one minute."

Finally, a third crane arrived, and once the house was topped off, all three worked on the tower, lessening the tension. In 153 days, work on the concrete skeleton was completed. By the end of 2006, the construction managers and contractors were able to shift their attention to the interiors.

Nothing was taken for granted in the marketing of the apartments, either. The official Condominium Offering Plan, which had to be approved by New York State's attorney general, offered a description of every apartment and a price for it. Though those prices could—and did—change, the initial numbers were of vital importance. The Zeckendorfs are loath to discuss the secret process known as inventory control, but the general idea was to price the units as high as possible, so there would be a bedrock of support beneath the investments that Goldman, Ofer, and their lenders had made, yet appropriately enough to attract immediate interest and buyers who would, if all went well, lure even more, allowing prices to steadily rise. As it turned out, they rose meteorically, to the surprise (and profit) of the Goldman guys.

The initial pricing was done before the formal ground-raising, which took place after the foundation was laid and signified the start of aboveground construction. That meant the price of each unit had to be set by educated guesses off the plans, since no one could yet visit the physical space and see the views, which would have the most profound effect on value. It was off floor plans that the Zeckendorfs decided that A-line units would be the most valuable and the D-line slightly less so. ("A was labeled A for a reason," says one of their salespeople.) The apartments in between were essentially railroad flats, long lines of rooms with windows at the two ends, but they would bask in the glow of the limestone and the bigger residences beside them, so they would be priced for rich people, too. Just slightly less rich people, or ones with several homes who cared more about a chic address in New York than a windowed kitchen.

But how much could they charge? The Goldman team, Ofer, Kellner, and key members of the Zeckendorf Development staff were all given spreadsheets showing the two wings and all their apartments in the form of a grid that allowed them to value one in relation to the rest and fill in a price for each. The grids were prepared by the manager of the 15CPW project, Judith Kessler, who'd worked with real estate syndicates in the 1980s before joining Bill Zeckendorf Jr. as assistant project manager on Central Park Place.*

"It was fun," says a participant in the pricing process. "Where do different people see value? Where [at what floor] do you put price breaks? You're guessing where the market will see value versus where we saw value. Who's smarter? Do you make a hundred-thousand-dollar break here? A three-hundred-thousand-dollar break there?" Foreseeing the psychology of buyers and then controlling the release of the apartment inventory was key to maximizing the return on their considerable investment; they'd paid about $690 per buildable square foot for the land, then spent about $750 per square foot on their 886,000-square-foot two-tower behemoth.

The developers planned to work their respective networks and ensure that several penthouses would sell immediately—to the right sort of people—but what then? "Some apartments are so valuable, you don't want them to fly off," the participant continues. "You want to identify those with the most value and [keep them off the market initially and] price them high and be left with the most valuable units."

---

*It was also Kessler who'd figured out years before that the key to getting the US Postal Service to temporarily move out of its home on the future site of the Millennium Tower project and then buy it back was to show its executives how much money USPS was losing (about $24 million over the life of the lease) by being a tenant instead of an owner.

The lower-priced, smaller units, on the other hand, were of less concern and could be sold off without as much thought. Balancing those considerations, however, particularly for the money-conscious Goldman Sachs executives, were the terms of the construction loan. The interest rate on that hefty debt dropped as the developers collected deposits on apartments in contract, creating a financial incentive to sell more apartments sooner. If selling is done carefully enough, early contracts cover the building's costs and help drive down borrowing costs, while the prices of bigger and better units still in inventory keep rising, ensuring bigger profits, profits, profits.

The proposed prices varied wildly. Will and Arthur's numbers were the highest. Jerry Karr's were slightly lower, and Justin Metz was the least optimistic. Once again, Goldman's perspective, which valued quick returns over the highest possible profit, was obvious. "And we somehow merged them, averaged them, to create one pricing structure," says Arthur, who compares the process to butchering and pricing cuts of beef.

"There's only so much good product," he says, and it's "based on the location in the building. The corners, the penthouses." They also compared their numbers to asking prices at other nearby, comparable buildings. "You can't completely divorce yourself from the realities of where you are," says Will. Apartments facing Broadway would be worth less than those on the park.

Wealth, whether large or relatively small, would define their buyer pool. The lowest price for a unit in the initial offering was only $1.78 million—but that was still well above the $1.479 million average price of a Manhattan condo in 2005. Only 24 of the 201 apartments would be offered for less than $3 million. But as Arthur points out, "Three million dollars is still a lot of money, double the average price of an apartment in Manhattan."

The middle class at 15CPW would occupy the fifty-one apartments priced between $3 million and $5 million. The bulk of the rest, sixty-seven in all, carried asking prices between $5 million and

$9,999,999. The final fifty-two apartments were mostly priced be-
tween $10 million and $20 million. Those were the most desirable
A- and D-line units, but also some of the view-enhanced B- and
C-line apartments on high floors in the house, and the two forty-
first-floor penthouses. The real trophies were the seven house duplexes, which ranged from $22 million to $30 million, the simplex
penthouse above them, which would have a $41.25 million price tag,
and the tower penthouses, all priced between $21 million and $26
million (for the one with that King of the World terrace).

Ground-floor office suites, some with private street entrances,
cost between $1.2 million and $2.184 million, and servants' quarters were the real bargains, selling for between $650,000 and $1.74
million. But they could only be purchased along with an apartment,
as was the case with the seventy-three $35,000 storage units and the
thirty wine cellars; they ranged from $50,000 to $80,000.

The condominium plan was submitted to the state in April
2005 by its official sponsor, which bore the ungainly name
W2001Z/15CPW Realty, LLC. On September 8, a month and four
days after David Dunlap's article revealing their plans, the Offering
Plan was accepted. In the meantime, two construction loans of $360
million and $100 million were arranged, bringing the total financing
for the project to $900 million.

Meantime, the Zeckendorfs had begun putting together their
sales operation. Richard Wallgren, a former investment banker
who'd segued into a second career in real estate and had worked for
Louise Sunshine at Time Warner, was already on board as head of
sales. By summer, his team had been assembled and given floor plans
so they could begin memorizing the seventy-one different layouts in
the building. Letters of intent were already coming in, "from people
who knew," says one of the salespeople, Karen Duncan.

"You are selling dream apartments because they're not built yet,
so you create a vision of how someone will feel walking into 26B

even though they won't open their door with keys for two years," says Marlene Marcus, who joined in August. Marcus had known the Zeckendorfs since 1986, when she sold Central Park Place for their father, "the first time I can remember saying the word *millions*," she recalls. "The penthouses there were about one and a half million dollars. We thought they were so expensive." Marcus had also worked for Sunshine at the Trump International and Time Warner.

Even before the Fifteen plan was declared effective, the team was making presentations in the construction office on Broadway. They were also making calls. "I knew people at Time Warner who would follow me from building to building," says Marcus. "They're not attached. They want to be in the new best building." Damn the expense and the inconvenience. She also called clients "who'd passed up Time Warner and regretted it."

Meantime, the Zeckendorfs had already started making money through what might be termed insider sales. Six apartments collectively worth just over $100 million were immediately reserved—and blacked out on those Excel grids—for Arthur and Will; Eyal Ofer and his younger brother, Idan; Goldman Sachs executive Justin Metz; and Lloyd Blankfein, then the second in command at Goldman under its chairman and CEO Henry "Hank" Paulson.

Will chose the northern penthouse on the tower's forty-first floor, which had a $14 million price tag. "I wanted a private elevator landing," he says, and it was the least expensive unit that fit the bill.

Arthur went so far as to ride the hoist and walk the concrete slabs before there were walls, looking for the best view of the park when he was sitting down, before deciding on a D-line unit on the tenth floor of the house, listed at the same price as Will's. "I picked the one with the biggest window on the highest floor facing the park," Arthur says. He would later name the limited liability company he formed to buy the place Eight Forty Three LLC because he can see all 843 acres of the park from that window. "Up a few floors and you're looking down, not sitting with the park," says his interior designer, Kevin Gray.

Ofer claimed the top penthouse on the forty-third floor, his brother the large northern duplex on seventeen and eighteen, and Blankfein the southernmost A-line duplex on the fifteenth and sixteenth floors. Henry Paulson says he doesn't recall being involved, but Will clearly remembers receiving a strong message from him: Lloyd Blankfein was to have his choice of apartment.

Later, Charles Berman, a partner of Victor MacFarlane's; Zeckendorf Development's Judy Kessler, who ran the entire project day to day; and Richard Wallgren would also reserve apartments. "I had an apartment tied up," says MacFarlane, but unsure which coast he wanted to live on, he gave it up. "Worst real estate decision I ever made," he admits. When Wallgren sold his $1.8 million one-bedroom unit in 2013, he would almost double his money.

Those nine individuals appear to have been the only purchasers who received significant discounts, which proved to be as good an investment for the partnership as for those individuals. "People love to see the sponsor buying," says Will Zeckendorf.

None of them wants to discuss their discounts or the negotiations for them in any detail, though. So calculating how they were determined isn't easy. One recipient says each insider got 6 percent off the initial asking price, representing the sum typically paid to brokers, plus an additional 3 percent as a "friends and family" consideration. Another says that regardless of the value of the apartments they chose, each of the three development partners, Goldman, Ofer, and the Zeckendorfs, were given the opportunity to buy two apartments—any two they wished—and receive an equal discount, a specific sum to be apportioned in any manner they chose. But a comparison of the asking prices in the Offering Plan and the prices reported in (sometimes inaccurate) public records doesn't support either formula.

The buying process was almost the same for each of the nine as it would be for other purchasers. Though the sales team did quick background checks on people they'd never heard of and shared the results with the Zeckendorfs, all offers, including those made by insiders, were discussed among the partners in weekly meetings, or in e-mails if there was special urgency, then formalized on a deal sheet signed by the buyer and a representative of each of the three partners. A contract would then be drawn up, though those for outside buyers were given precedence. Typically, buyers of new Manhattan condos get a week to ten days to sign their contracts and pay a deposit. The process is designed to nudge them to sign quickly.

A mere five days after the 15CPW Offering Plan was accepted, the first amendment to it was filed with the state, raising the apartment prices. Thirty such amendments would eventually be recorded before every square foot of the building was sold, and as apartments sold and became more scarce and the developers realized how highly the market valued them, prices soared. So potential buyers had an incentive to make up their minds fast.

The first partnership purchasers didn't have to worry about that. And they clearly had more room for negotiation than those who followed them. Though his duplex was priced at $29 million, Blankfein paid only $25,726,596, a discount of about $3.3 million, or just over 11 percent. The Zeckendorfs each got discounts of $3.5 million, or almost 25 percent on their much less expensive apartments. Eyal Ofer paid a bit more than the original asking price on the one he finally bought after giving up the forty-third floor to an insistent buyer, but his brother, Idan, got about a $4 million discount on his $30 million pad, or 14 percent off. Eyal appears to be the only partner who paid list price, but since his brother got the biggest break of all, perhaps Idan was the fortunate recipient of an elder sibling's generosity. Or maybe, Eyal just chose to show his friend Carl Icahn that hondling wasn't kosher at Fifteen.

Even within the partnership, it is apparent that hard bargaining took place. Because they were among the first to buy, and the appliances and finishes had not yet been ordered, the insiders were able to do what most later buyers could not: negotiate and win additional price breaks for choosing to finish the apartments themselves.

Goldman's Justin Metz called dibs on a three-bedroom unit on the fifth floor. But later, Metz, who had a growing family, decided he wanted a larger apartment. In October 2006, after the tower was topped off, the latest amendment to the Offering Plan noted that apartment 5F had been eliminated and its square footage split between the adjacent 5A and 5B. Though it was late in the game, 5F, which had windows only on the motor court and Sixty-First Street, was still unsold. Metz proposed cutting it up and grafting a 340-square-foot bedroom onto his apartment.

Metz's desire for a larger apartment was galling after Goldman's persistent lobbying for smaller ones. The Zeckendorfs were privately furious when Stuart Rothenberg pressed for Metz to get his extra bedroom. "It wasn't the easiest thing to accomplish," says someone close to the brothers. "It was good for Justin, not for the project." But they gave Metz what he wanted. After deducting brokerage commissions and a little more than $150,000 for the kitchen and finishes he rejected, Metz paid $5.75 million for an apartment that otherwise could have cost almost $6.4 million. According to an internal Zeckendorf sales document provided to another apartment purchaser, Metz got his home for $1,500 per square foot, the lowest price in the building, though that number rises to $1,750 when all the breaks are figured in. Still, it was a pretty good deal, even for an apartment beneath the Central Park view line; in comparison, Lloyd Blankfein paid $4,262 per square foot for his duplex, Idan Ofer $4,023, and Eyal Ofer $4,035. But after all, Metz had been the building's chief cheerleader at Goldman Sachs; Stuart Rothenberg had "never loved this deal," Will says.

All things considered, the loss of the unloved apartment 5F turned out quite well for the sponsors. Unit 5A next door was reconfigured as a floor-through with four additional rear rooms, adding 1,644 square feet to the spread and allowing a big bump in its initial $9 million asking price. Shortly after its layout was changed, Sonny Kalsi, an investment banker specializing in real estate, agreed to pay just under $15 million for it, or $3,200 per square foot. Metz got quite a deal, but the partnership made more, not less, money.

By then, both wings had been topped off, 80 percent of the apartments were in contract, and the development team had turned the far corner into the stretch where every penny was profit. So Metz's desire for a larger apartment finally became an ironic footnote.

Anyway, the Zeckendorfs had a new and bigger problem at Goldman. Someone quite a bit more important than Metz was insisting they change their nearly finished building. And this time, the Zeckendorfs wouldn't, couldn't, give in.

Part Seven

GROUND-RAISING

*A great building must begin with the
unmeasurable, must go through measurable means
when it is being designed, and in the end must be
unmeasurable.*

—LOUIS I. KAHN

Daniel Loeb took a month to sign the contract for his Fifteen Central Park West penthouse, but after shaking hands on the deal that took the thirty-ninth floor away from Carl Icahn, he was one of the three early purchasers who attended the ground-raising celebration. It marked the start of both construction of the concrete superstructure and of the public relations effort to sell the apartments. The party began in the foundation pit on September 27, 2005, and continued at the building's brand-new Stern-designed sales office on the forty-fourth floor of Carnegie Hall Tower, a few blocks away. One sale was even made at the event. After studying the computer simulations of the apartments and walking through the mock-up rooms to the big model of the building, a couple pointed out a particular apartment and said, "We'll take that one."

Also in the room were buyers Jeff Gordon, the NASCAR racing champion, and his then girlfriend, Belgian-born swimsuit model Ingrid Vandebosch, whom he'd marry a year later, and Barry Rosenstein, another activist investor like Loeb and Icahn and the founder and head of JANA Partners, a hedge fund. Rosenstein had signed a contract for an apartment that very day. They'd all joined the Zeckendorfs, their mother, Guri Lie, Eyal Ofer and his wife, Marilyn, Bob Stern, and a handful of local officials to hail the start of construction and sales.

Richard Rubenstein, a son of the city's most powerful PR man and political fixer, Howard Rubenstein, was in the room, too. Richard ran his own PR outfit, specializing in real estate development. He'd worked on both the Trump International and the Time Warner Center. He considered 15CPW a plum account because the Zeckendorfs were targeting the rootless, new global elite, the newest new money, the kind of customers who will pay $10 million or more for a Central Park–view apartment. Rubenstein had joined the team to augment the efforts of Michele de Milly, whose lobbying and PR firm, Geto & de Milly, also has deep ties to city government. She'd handled the project for Avlon for years and continued to consult for the Zeckendorfs. The developers began meeting weekly with Rubenstein's team just as they had with Paul Whalen.

They decided on a publicity campaign focused on Robert A. M. Stern, who is as polished and well-spoken as he is knowledgeable, and he worked the limestone angle hard. There was a message in the stone. "You're thinking about the kind of people who define a building, not bankers, but tastemakers," says Rubenstein. "We wanted it viewed as a luxury proposition. The limestone was the differentiator." It signaled that 15CPW would attain a level of richness and exclusivity unheard of since the Great Depression.

At first, at least, the names of apartment buyers were not to be revealed—especially the names of Goldman Sachs–related buyers. "That was secret secret," says a PR team member.

The marketing team planned a subtle campaign aimed at the ultrawealthy and featuring lavish sales kits, a highly produced DVD of a conversation with the Zeckendorfs and Stern, double-page ads in the *New York Times Magazine*, and even a brochure wrapped around copies of the *Financial Times* distributed at the World Economic Forum in Davos.

The Zeckendorfs "wanted to establish [15CPW] as a building for affluent New Yorkers, so it became a residence," says Bruce Richards, a hedge-fund manager with Goldman Sachs connections who would soon buy an apartment. They wanted global money, too, but not the sort that would be content with empty hallways. "The marketing was deliberate, calculated, and efficient." They "targeted, invited the Fifth and Park buyers," says Corcoran CEO Pamela Liebman. "They pulled the market to Central Park West. They made it feel like Fifth Avenue. It really helped that rich and powerful people were associated with the building early on. It really set a tone. So it became a very cool place to live, an exclusive club, and to be a buyer made you look really smart."

Buying wasn't exactly easy. At first, only a handful of apartments were "released" to the sales team to test the market. If everyone wants A-lines, they're underpriced. So only a few A- and D-line apartments were made available, and in the house, middle apartments at treetop level were held back, too. Nonetheless, once the sales office opened in Carnegie Tower, "you'd have thought they'd let the bulls loose at Pamplona," says salesperson Karen Duncan. "We were deluged. The brokers started beating the drums."

The salespeople made as many as nine presentations a day, and appointments were booked as late as 9:00 p.m. "Elaborate tap dancing" ensued, says another salesperson. "People would say, 'Can I reserve 9B?' And I'd go into the next conference room with a note saying it was gone, and that would cause the next person to buy. When somebody fell out, we had backups. We were targeting people with means, wildly successful professionals, people with busy lives who wanted service and amenities and to be pampered. They wanted a place that reflected their status and taste, but they didn't want small windows, kitchens, or bathrooms or a co-op board prying into their business."

As hoped, many less desirable apartments went fast, relative bargains at around $2,000 per square foot, when the best apartments were marked and selling at $6,000 per. The very first signed deal was with Robby Browne, a broker for Corcoran who'd brought seven clients to the Broadway construction office to see the plans as soon as he could. "I called everyone I could think of," he recalls, "and said, 'You *need* to buy this.' After three weeks, I thought, *I'm* buying. It had everything I want. It's like a country club. I couldn't afford the front, of course." In the days that followed, four B- and C-line apartments in the tower and six more Broadway apartments were sold, only a few to people who planned to live there.

Jacob Gottlieb, the managing partner and chief investment officer of Visium Asset Management, a $4 billion hedge fund, and his wife, Alexandra Lumiere, then a Brown Harris Stevens broker, bought two of the ninth-floor tower units, giving themselves five bedrooms and almost eleven hundred square feet of terrace over Broadway. The son of an economist and a pediatrician, Gottlieb had traded baseball cards as a boy. Torn between business and medicine, he'd studied both but chose full-time investing after an internship at a New York hospital. A health-care analyst, he became the top earner at a Chicago hedge fund and launched his own the year he bought his apartments. He was living in an East Side condo when he heard about 15CPW, which was walking distance from Visium's offices. "I'm always looking for compelling investments, including real estate," he says. "I couldn't pass up the chance."

The owners of Mercedes/Berk, a real estate boutique, commercial broker Noel Berk and her life and work partner, Elizabeth Omedes, bought a small two-bedroom just above on the fourteenth floor. Once they moved in, Berk and Omedes would take advantage of their residence in the building and begin representing other owners who'd decided to sell. Berk was also elected to the condo's managing board, a conflict some co-op boards would find troublesome.

The Zeckendorfs had hoped to keep investors away and sell mostly to people who planned to live there, but there was no way to force buyers to reveal their true intentions, and anyway, the rear units were not trophy apartments. With a partner, Dorothy Somekh, a West Side condo broker who also invests in them, picked up a two-bedroom unit two floors below the Gottliebs. Somekh, once married to an Israeli, is fluent in Hebrew and has many Israeli clients. Three weeks after she bought hers, she sold the C-line apartment on the twenty-fifth floor to Dr. Eli Zahavi, an Israeli energy investor, for about $4.225 million. In the seventies, Zahavi had headed a fuel program for the Israel Defense Forces, then became an international energy expert working in Israel, Puerto Rico, and Texas. He'd just acquired the empty shell of a public company listed on the Tel Aviv stock exchange and formed an American subsidiary, EZ Energy (its first name his initials), to operate gas stations and convenience stores in the United States. He was intrigued by 15CPW and knew of the Ofer family.

Many purchasers preferred to be anonymous and hid behind LLCs, offshore companies, and trusts. Unit 11G, for instance, is held in the name of Tokolosh Holdings LLC of Washington State. A tokolosh is a mysterious beast in Zulu mythology. The owner behind that corporate mask clearly wants to be mysterious, too. Later, as interest in the building grew and public documents recording sales began to be filed, real estate and gossip reporters tried to discover who was behind those semi-anonymous entities. Despite them, in those first sales, 15CPW's social profile began to emerge.

Real estate professionals were the first to catch on to its value, and eventually several dozen developers, brokers, and realty financiers would buy or rent its apartments. Foreigners, whether they planned to be absentee investors or residents, would also emerge as an important cohort. Israelis and Koreans would pick up a half dozen apartments each. Chinese owners would follow closely with five units, and multiple apartments were sold to Russians, Greeks, Indians, and Central and South Americans. Other units would initially sell to an Italian businessman and a Senegalese cell phone tycoon.

Wall Street buyers set the tone, though, thanks mostly to Goldman Sachs's involvement. At Corcoran, brokers were convinced that Goldman executives and favored clients and counterparties were being given the inside track on apartments by the developers—and worried that brokers were being edged out. A letter went out from Goldman, insists a broker who says she saw it. "It was a huge mailing. It went not just to clients but to everyone they did business with. It said clearly they'd be treated preferentially. Clients wouldn't talk to us. We were going nuts. We were furious. Can you imagine?" The Goldman Sachs executives insist that it did not send out any letters or make any organized effort to attract its network to the building. But neither did it keep the building a secret. "Within the culture, we knew," says a longtime Goldman executive.

It doesn't take a Goldman Sachs executive to know that when you have early information you act on it—and many did, both for themselves and their clients. "It's not unusual for clients to call" Goldman's personal-wealth-management division and ask about potential investments, including real estate developments, says Goldman's Alan Kava. "It was hard to get into the sales office," he continues. So he made sure his Goldman colleagues and clients were taken care of. "We weren't shy about that. They called us, we introduced them to the Zeckendorfs, and they bought."

Aside from Lloyd Blankfein and Justin Metz (who has since left Goldman for Steve Ross's Related Companies), seven present and former Goldman bigwigs were among the first class of purchasers at 15CPW. The former partners, especially, had money to burn; significant fortunes were made when Goldman went public in 1999.

Dan Neidich's 0.9 percent stake in the firm, for instance, reportedly yielded him almost $150 million.

In January 2006, Alan Shuch of Goldman signed its first 15CPW contract with his wife, Leslie Wohlman Himmel; the co-owner of a real estate investment company, she's been called "the ranking female landlord" of commercial property in Manhattan. An MBA from Harvard and the daughter of an accountant, she started her career at Integrated Resources, the insurance and real estate company that went bankrupt just before its planned move into Zeckendorf Towers. She cofounded her own company in 1985, shortly after marrying her first investment banker. Shuch, her second husband, had joined Goldman Sachs in the bond division in 1976 after getting an MBA from Wharton. Credited with helping build the bank's corporate and high-yield bond departments, he made partner after ten years, started Goldman's money-management arm in 1988 when he was thirty-nine, and retired as a partner six years later, but remains with the firm as an advisory director and a member of several of its boards of trustees and managers. Shuch and Himmel could obviously afford the $8.6 million asking price of their D-line apartment on the twenty-sixth floor.

A month later, John E. Waldron, a young star in Goldman's investment-banking division, bought an $8.5 million D-line apartment in the house. An unusual investment banker, he was an English major in college who became global head of Goldman's retail sales force. At the same time, Donald C. Opatrny Jr. bought a D-line in the tower for $11.8 million. He'd joined Goldman in 1978, become a partner the same year as Shuch, and had just retired. Opatrny would later sell his unit to Victor Vargas, a Venezuelan banker with six homes, a polo team, and a daughter who married Luis Alfonso de Borbón, a great-grandson of Francisco Franco and relative of the king of Spain. Vargas lives there with his girlfriend, Maria Beatriz Hernandez Rodriguez.

Raj Sethi, a derivatives trader, was the next at Goldman to buy a Fifteen apartment, but his was comparatively modest. Sethi signed a contract for a $4.2 million tower apartment with north and west views in March 2006. Born in India, he'd come to America as a child and grown up in Connecticut, where his father was in charge of manufacturing for American Can. A graduate of Cornell, Sethi joined Goldman Sachs out of school in 1998 and spent the next fourteen years trading commodities while bouncing between New York, Singapore, and London, where he was living when he spotted Fifteen rising while in New York on a vacation and bought his apartment unaware that Goldman had helped finance the building.

Apartment 7A in the house went to Ravi M. Singh, Goldman's cohead of Global Securities Services and another partner, in May 2006, for a little over $16 million. Singh joined the firm right after graduating from Columbia University in 1989 and ran various departments trading derivatives. His brother Dinakar was also a Goldman partner until 2004, when he left to set up his own hedge fund. Ravi remained at Goldman until he retired late in 2008, a year that began tragically when his wife, Elizabeth Yeh, a television journalist and cookbook author, died at age forty-one, leaving him with their daughter. Singh listed his apartment for $32 million that September and fourteen months later sold it to an LLC called CPW Park Views, after his broker had repeatedly dropped the price and then taken it off the market. Behind CPW Park Views were Robert and Suzanne Karr, a persistent couple who finally talked him into selling at $22.5 million. Robert Karr had worked for the legendary hedge-fund manager Julian Robertson before setting up his own firm, Joho Capital, in 1996.

Seven months later, another Goldman partner signed a contract at Fifteen. Ashok Varadhan, Goldman's baby-faced, bespectacled head of currency trading and emerging markets, comes by his facility with numbers naturally. His father, Srinivasa Varadhan, is an award-winning professor of mathematics at New York University, specializing in esoteric fields: probability theory, stochastic processes, partial differential equations, and statistical physics. Raised in Greenwich Village, Ashok and his elder brother, Gopal, both studied math and went into finance.

Ashok attended Duke, where he was manager of the men's basketball team, then enrolled in a PhD program at Stanford, but, instead of finishing his degree, started his career at Merrill Lynch. He joined Goldman in 1998, was named head of interest-rate products in 2001, and became a partner in 2002 when he was only twenty-nine years old. In between those promotions, he lost his brother, who was in his Cantor Fitzgerald office on the 105th floor of the World Trade Center when it was attacked on September 11, 2001.

Varadhan lived in a loft on cobblestoned Bond Street in NoHo before buying his ninth-floor D-line unit at Fifteen for $16.3 million at the end of 2006, shortly before he was named Goldman's global head of currency trading. At the time, finance gossip set his annual income at $10 million a year, and one blogger called him a demigod.

The last of the Goldman Sachs buyers, Thomas Wagner, came on the scene so late, he paid a premium of more than $2 million over the initial asking price for his treetop-view D-line apartment in the house. Wagner had an accounting degree from Villanova and an MBA from Columbia when he joined Credit Suisse in 1998 as an analyst. Two years later, he moved to Goldman Sachs and spent the next seven years there, rising to managing director in 2004. Wagner's wife, Cynthia "Cindy" Brower, also worked at Goldman for nineteen years in a group that handled sales of loans and distressed debt and was made a managing director a year before her husband. The Wagners had lived together in an apartment across the park where they watched Fifteen rise out their windows and moved shortly after they got married.

Wagner left Goldman early in 2008 to launch Knighthead Capital Management, a hedge fund reportedly begun with $750 million.

Brower remained but, like Raj Sethi, left as part of a mass exodus early in 2012, which coincidentally or not, was around the same time that a London-based Goldman staffer announced in an op-ed article in the *New York Times* that he was quitting the firm because of its "toxic and destructive" environment. Brower's next move was neither toxic nor destructive: she competed in a charity Ironman race in Kona, Hawaii. Retirement didn't mean relaxation.

❧

It's impossible to identify every Goldman Sachs–related purchaser at Fifteen, but many others heard about the building through the bank. Joshua S. Friedman, cofounder of Canyon Partners, a Los Angeles–based hedge fund (which ranked number 28 on the 2012 list of the Hedge Fund 100 in *Alpha*, a magazine that covers the industry), bought apartment 6B in December 2006 for about $11 million; its initial price was $7.25 million. A graduate of Harvard, Harvard Law, and Harvard Business School, he'd started his career at Goldman. Friedman's roommate from Harvard, Mitchell R. Julis, graduated from Princeton and Harvard's law and business schools and worked with him at pioneering junk-bond firm Drexel Burnham Lambert before starting Canyon with a third partner in 1990. A month after Friedman signed his contract, Julis bought at 15CPW, too, taking a fourth-floor A-line apartment for $10.335 million.

"Aggressiveness is part of their DNA," an investment consultant once said of Canyon's partners. But Julis and Friedman aren't so simply summed up. After one of their funds had its first down year, Julis began practicing Judaism. "I got shaken," he told Aish.com, a Jerusalem-based humor and culture website he bankrolls. "I knew I needed something beyond my hedge fund to ground me. Torah was the answer."

Michael Alexandre Zaoui agreed to buy apartment 30A for almost $10.4 million in March 2006. Moroccan born, raised in Rome, and educated at the London School of Economics, the Institut d'Études Politiques de Paris, and Harvard Business School, Zaoui started his career with Banque Rothschild in Paris and later joined Morgan Stanley's mergers department in London, where he was a friendly competitor with his brother, Yoel, the head of European investment banking at Goldman. They sometimes worked together, too, on both the same and opposite sides in deals, together advising Elf Aquitaine, a French oil company, when it became the target of a hostile takeover by Total Fina, and Aventis, the French pharmaceutical firm, in a similar attempt by Sanofi. In 2000, they were reportedly the highest-earning bankers in London's City financial district, hauling in £20 million between them. Still a resident of London (where he, his French wife, and their children live just behind the famous Bluebird restaurant on King's Road), Michael retired from Morgan Stanley in 2008 at age fifty to become a freelance consultant. At the time, he'd rented his 15CPW apartment to Frank Newman, the former chairman of Bankers Trust and Shenzhen Development Bank of China, and a onetime deputy secretary of the treasury.

The richest Goldman-related buyers are likely Pan Shiyi and Zhang Xin, the married heads of SOHO China, the third-largest property company in China, known for its stylish, starchitect-designed buildings and for collaborations with artists such as Ai Weiwei, the famously outspoken dissident. Both were born poor. Zhang Xin, who was shunted among relatives and friends after her parents split up during the Cultural Revolution, left mainland China at age fourteen and then departed Hong Kong for England at nineteen with money she'd made working in sweatshops. She studied at Sussex and Cambridge, wrote a thesis on privatization in China, and won a job at a merchant bank. After a move to Goldman Sachs, Zhang ended up on Wall Street in 1993, and a year later became an investment banker at Travelers Group, run by her future neighbor Sandy Weill.

Zhang met Pan Shiyi at a meeting while on a business trip to China. The son of a family considered right-wing outcasts, Pan grew up a farm boy so poor he sometimes begged for food. But as Chinese society loosened up after the Cultural Revolution, he was able to move to Beijing to study and then won a job in China's Ministry of Petroleum in the 1980s. Taking advantage of the country's move toward free enterprise, he got into real estate. Later dubbed China's Naughty Boy for painting an apartment complex in bright colors, he'd demonstrated his headstrong ways by proposing to Zhang four days after meeting her. A year later, they both quit their jobs to found the company that became SOHO.

In China, they were considered an odd couple, she Westernized, he very much Chinese. But they adapted and became media sensations, with Pan often appearing on television and even blogging. In New York, they fit easily into four of the Fifteen tribes, the Goldman, real estate, entrepreneur, and foreign cohorts, after they agreed to buy their New York pied-à-terre, apartment 2A, for about $7.7 million in November 2006. According to *Forbes*, with the $2.65 billion they earned from taking their company public in Hong Kong, they are the twenty-first-richest family in China and rank number 442 on the magazine's list of the world's billionaires. The *Times* of London has dubbed them the It Couple of Beijing.

Another Goldman apartment, 12L in the tower, went into contract in February 2007 for just over $4.4 million. The LLC that bought it was domiciled in Marlboro, New Jersey, at the home of Gary and Tamar Tolchin, philanthropists, thoroughbred breeders, and co-owners of a New Jersey restaurant. Tolchin was a partner at Spear, Leeds & Kellogg, a decades-old "clearing" firm—it served as an intermediary, clearing transactions and holding securities to facilitate trading, which is known as market-making. Spear, Leeds was sold to Goldman Sachs in 2000 for $6.5 billion, including $4.4 billion in Goldman Sachs stock, and Tolchin ended up with thousands of shares. He profited again four-plus years later, when he sold his apartment to Midwest shopping-mall heiress Deborah Simon for $7.5 million and bought a much larger condo on Upper Broadway for just over $10 million. That time, Tamar Tolchin's name appeared on a document filed in public records.

The Ofers and Zeckendorfs brought in buyers, too. Eyal Ofer knew the Laskaridis shipping family from Greece (apartment 27A, which went for $11.7 million), and the Logothetises (apartment 31D, $12.9 million), whose Libra Group has interests in shipping, aviation, real estate, hospitality, and energy. Anathasios Laskaridis, whose family has expanded into hotels and casinos and owns a large share of Aegean Airlines, asked Ofer for a discount. "I said, 'If you want a discount, you better buy one today because tomorrow the price is going up.' For which he was ever thankful. George Logothetis followed him" and sold his unit for $24 million in 2011 to Mac Holdings (America), a subsidiary of a shipping-based conglomerate based in Sri Lanka. Min Sun (apartment 14B, almost $14.5 million), who runs Transfield Asset Management, has been in shipping for twenty years. Transfield's parent ships grains, fertilizers, and minerals, 85 million tons in 2007. Later, when apartments began to be resold, units traded to Elisabeth June Steckmest, whose family owns Viken Shipping of Norway, and Ruth McLoughlin, the daughter of shipowner Gunter Neunhoeffer, who runs Transocean in Monaco.

There were Zeckendorf friends, too, such as James Kohlberg, the son of Kohlberg Kravis Roberts cofounder Jerome Kohlberg, and now his partner in Kohlberg & Co., a private equity boutique. He learned of the building through Will, whom he met through a mutual love of burgundy wines. Kohlberg bought apartment 6C as a pied-à-terre but never moved in, selling for a $5 million profit. But buyers and residents in the building, particularly those not previously identified, are a subject the Zeckendorf brothers are loath to discuss.

The crucial element of the building's success, though, was what might be called the Goldman Effect—not the Zeckendorf or Ofer social networks. Right from the start, a signal seemed to summon financiers from far and wide as effectively as one of those whistles that only dogs can hear. Goldman Sachs executives didn't need to make phone calls or write letters to make its building desirable. The mere fact that Goldman people were buying en masse made it so. "You had people here making a shitload of money, looking to upgrade, and this hit the market at the perfect time," says a resident Morgan Stanley banker. "You knew they wouldn't skimp on anything because Lloyd was going to live here." The Zeckendorfs had figured right. There *was* a pent-up demand for luxury apartments in New York. And moneymen and -women and the sort of entrepreneurs Goldman financed and later invested for were the likeliest candidates to be clamoring for them.

"Remember the time," says Realtor Haidee Granger. "These people were making heinous amounts of money. Obscene funds were floating about. There was lots of construction, but it was mostly glass boxes. This had the Park Avenue accoutrements. And a brilliant location. It had the ethos of a co-op in a state-of-the-art building." So Goldman didn't need to "actively market," says its Stuart Rothenberg. "People heard. People are always worried about the operation of a new building. We could say that the Zeckendorfs were going to live there. That was a great thing. It made the buyers feel good. It had a lot of hype, it's the building this one and that one are in, so it's the place people want to look. All the big names came out of the woodwork. Who wouldn't want to look?"

Though he refers to this as "the flocking effect," Rothenberg doesn't think the early buyers were birds of a feather. Instead, they were birds of the purse. "Where was the wealth?" he asks. "The Goldman Sachs IPO. Hedge funds. It was financial. Where does world-class philanthropy come from? Finance. Who had money and wanted to stay in the city? Finance. They're the ones that could afford it."

"Major wealth was created by those people" between the dot-com crash of 2000 and the opening of the 15CPW sales office, says Arthur Zeckendorf, and it was sitting around waiting to be spent. "You can say negative things about [Wall Street people]," he continues, "but they're brilliant people; they're computers. Manhattan attracts the smartest people in the world. You can't be here and not make money. It took a big brain to pay those prices in advance. But the smart people, by definition, knew they'd get a great product and make money."

The calculation was actually quite simple, says former Whitehall executive Ralph Rosenberg. "The combination of efficiently laid-out, modern apartments in prewar style with tremendous unobstructed views and amenities?" he asks rhetorically. "Those are big things, particularly when you also want privacy. The generation of wealth created between 1995 and 2005 doesn't care where Rockefeller lived. They value the best living space available."

The first penthouse buyer outside the partnership group didn't go through the sales office, and his purchase remained a secret for two years, but he was another Goldman Sachs alumnus who'd become one of the financial world's best-known and most-admired figures. Daniel Saul Och, who'd gone on to head his own hedge fund, Och-Ziff, was the bellwether leading the finance flock to Fifteen. He'd heard about it through friends at Goldman, of course, and immediately asked them if he could buy the top floor of the tower. They made it happen for him. "Dan wanted it, so I said, 'My mistake, I should have taken the one below originally,'" says Eyal Ofer, who agreed to abandon his reserved forty-third-floor aerie and take the penthouse beneath it with the King of the World terrace, instead. "As far as I'm concerned, I'm better off."

Och (pronounced *Ock*) is the middle child of a doctor and his wife, a founder of the Solomon Schechter Day School of New Jersey. Daniel was in its first-ever kindergarten class, then studied Jewish culture and history there, alongside a traditional curriculum before going on to Wharton. Choosing trading over graduate school, he started his career at twenty-one in 1982 as an analyst at Goldman, where he asked to be assigned to the mergers-arbitrage unit run by the future Clinton administration secretary of the treasury Robert Rubin, then one of the more challenging and profitable departments at Goldman. Its specialty was juggling the stocks of merging companies.

Och stayed at Goldman almost a dozen years, and though he never made partner or managing director, he rose to cohead of its US equities trading before leaving in 1994 to form Och-Ziff Capital Management with the Ziff brothers, third-generation heirs to Ziff Davis Media, the publisher of enthusiast magazines such as *Popular Aviation* and *Stereo Review*. He'd met Dirk Ziff when the slightly younger heir worked as an intern at Goldman. In 1994, Dirk and his brothers inherited $1.4 billion from their father after he sold the business and retired on learning his boys did not want to succeed him. Instead, they formed a family investment partnership to manage their money and asked Och to run it for them.

Seeded with $100 million, Och-Ziff grew steadily, produced returns characterized as "spectacular" by *Pensions & Investments*, a newspaper covering money management, and began taking in other investors after a five-year exclusive with the Ziffs expired. According to *Forbes*, Och became a billionaire in 2007 when Och-Ziff went public in an initial public offering run by Goldman Sachs and Lehman Brothers. A year later, *Forbes* estimated his fortune at $3.6 billion when he first made its list of the world's billionaires. Och still owns the majority of the business, and the Ziffs retain a 10 percent stake. In 2012, it managed almost $29 billion (down from a peak of $33.8 billion in 2008) out of its headquarters on Fifty-Seventh Street, a short walk from 15CPW. Proximity to the boss as well as the office likely explains why Och-Ziff's CFO, Joel Frank, also bought a sprawling $9.5 million D-line apartment in the house with treetop views of Central Park early in 2007.

Tall and fit, with tousled brown hair, piercing eyes, and a ready smile, Och is described as driven and disciplined, steely-eyed, but he has an eye for art as well as money. Once he moved into his oversize penthouse designed by Anthony Ingrao, he decorated it with, among other pieces, oversize works by such blue-chip modern masters as Cy Twombly, Mark Rothko, and Henry Moore. "There are at least six of them," says a visitor, "and they're huge." Although surely not as big as his bank balance.

Och and his wife, Jane, are both philanthropists who favor Jewish and Israeli causes, such as the American Jewish Committee and the UJA-Federation. Och has served on both the boards of trustees and governors of the former and chairs the latter's Investment Management Division. In the Westchester suburb of Scarsdale, where the Ochs and their three children still occupy a large house, Jane ran its local women's philanthropy group. Och is also the chairman of the board of the Birthright Israel Foundation, which subsidizes trips to Israel for Jewish young adults; vice chairman of the hedge-fund-heavy Robin Hood Foundation, which, among its many initiatives, sponsored the 12-12-12 concert benefiting victims of Hurricane Sandy; and a trustee of New York Hospital, Lincoln Center, and the University of Pennsylvania.

Och may have the loftiest apartment at 15CPW, but he is a relative shrinking violet. He did have a birthday party before his apartment was finished, filling it with flowers and setting up a stage on his huge terrace where Five For Fighting, the piano-based pop act, played. "You could see it in New Jersey," says a member of the building staff. But visible as it may have been, that party didn't make the newspapers, as the notorious birthday parties of the last generation of financial highfliers such as 740 Park's Saul Steinberg and Steve Schwarzman did. "Och is very nice," says the staffer, "and his wife is down-to-earth." "Page Six" material, they're not.

Och's home in the clouds reflects his standing in the new hierarchy of finance and the super–global elite. The heads of hedge and alternative investment funds emerged from the great bull market of the late twentieth century as the new apotheoses of wealth, the Rockefellers and Morgans of the early twenty-first century. Hedgies, as they're known on Wall Street, occupy a new upper echelon of wealth far less lonely than the one the industrial plutocrats did a century earlier.

The first hedge fund was created in 1949 by Alfred Winslow Jones. The polar opposite of the buttoned-up money managers of the time, Jones, the son of a General Electric executive, followed a traditional education at Harvard with less usual jobs such as the purser on a tramp steamer, an export buyer, and a statistician, before joining the State Department and serving in Germany as the Nazis were beginning their rise to political power. After meeting and falling for a socialite socialist, Jones quit the diplomatic corps and turned sharp left. He attended a Marxist school in Berlin and worked for something called the Leninist Organization. Then, after a divorce, he returned to America, enrolled in a PhD program in sociology at Columbia, remarried, and honeymooned in Spain during its Civil War.

Returning to America, Jones grew interested in finance and joined the staff of the young *Fortune* magazine as a writer. In 1948, *Fortune* published an article he'd written that "anticipated many of the hedge funds that came after him," wrote Sebastian Mallaby in *More Money Than God*, a history of the industry. Mallaby summed up Jones's conclusions succinctly: money was a medium, he wrote, "through which greed and fear and jealousy expressed themselves; it was a barometer of crowd psychology."

Before the article was even published, Jones left *Fortune* to launch what he called a "hedged" fund. Its main characteristics still define how the industry operates. Jones took 20 percent of the profits off the top, structured his fund to avoid regulatory oversight, hedged his bets through short-selling (borrowing stocks he thought would decline in value and selling them before buying them back at a lower price and returning them) to reduce his exposure to market swings, and used borrowed money as well as his fund's capital to increase potential profits. For the next twenty years, he operated in the shadows, raking in previously unheard-of returns. In years to come, those returns would come to be referred to as Alpha, a measure of the return delivered by an investment manager above and beyond the expected, the average, the benchmark that an index investor might receive.

In the late 1960s, defectors from Jones's fund began setting up copycats, and by 1969, Mallaby writes, there were hundreds of them, by then known collectively as hedge funds. Jones thought the truncated term "a grammatical barbarity," John Brooks wrote in his book on finance in that decade, *The Go-Go Years*. It would be another forty years before hedgies were themselves considered barbarians. By then, though, they'd also become Mallaby's "unofficial kings of capitalism."

Hedge funds, mostly run by alpha males in a relentless pursuit of Alpha, attracted new investors with big profits and an aura of exclusivity. Brooks compared them to the pools of the 1920s in which the wealthy came together to manipulate public markets. Many a then-new Park Avenue co-op was purchased with gains derived from swimming in pools. After the stock market crash, their worst excesses were curbed, but the rich will always find ways to get together to gain and exploit their edge. "Like the pools of ill repute a generation earlier, the hedge funds of the sixties were the rich man's stock market blood sport," Brooks wrote. They were also "a highly desirable club" that "certified one's affluence while attesting to one's astuteness. . . . Wall Street's last bastions of secrecy, mystery, exclusivity and privilege."

Though they still cultivate an aura of secrecy, hedge funds came out of the closet in 1968 when *New York* magazine ran a cover story on them. At the time, it said, hedge funds managed about $2 billion. Thirty-five years and many market bumps and jumps later, they were no longer strictly hedged funds; they employed a vast array of strategies from the prosaic to the impenetrable, including arbitrage, futures, options, derivatives, commodities, bonds, credit securities, currency speculation, event-driven trading, and quantitative analysis, as well as focused investments in specific market sectors such as health care, real estate, and technology, often in multistrategy stews. But despite bad publicity (in 1992, George Soros's Quantum investment fund famously bet against the British pound, "broke" the Bank of England, and cost that nation about $6 billion) and the odd disaster (Long-Term Capital Management lost most of its equity in two nightmarish days in 1998), they flourish like mushrooms after a rain. By 2003, the top hundred hedge funds managed $500 billion. Despite the imposition of some regulatory oversight in 2004, the three years that followed saw that sum double, with the money coming mostly from institutional investors such as pension funds, sovereign wealth funds, endowments, and foundations, but also from wealthy individuals and families, and from other money managers who act as feeders to the hedgies.

The lowest-earning hedgie on a list of the top twenty-five published in 2006 made $240 million. Several made more than $1 billion. In comparison, Lloyd Blankfein's take-home pay from Goldman Sachs that year was a chintzy $54 million. That summer, the *New York Times* made it official, noting that "the balance of power is shifting," when it observed hedge fund and private equity moguls suddenly elbowing their way onto the guest list at Allen & Co.'s exclusive annual roundup of business leaders in Sun Valley, Idaho.

By the time of the ground-raising party in September 2005, that dog whistle was blowing, and the hungry pack was circling and baying. Before long, word got out about 15CPW, but at first the ban on leaking buyers' names held. Then Braden Keil at the *New York Post* heard a story that would reshape the marketing plan for 15CPW. It began as an attempt to derail the development.

In the mid-oughts, Keil's Gimme Shelter column in the real estate section of the *Post* was the best "get" there was for property publicity-seekers. Some brokers worked with Keil, feeding him scoops in exchange for prominent column plugs. People in Manhattan real estate circles muttered that one particularly aggressive and publicity-savvy broker had Keil in her pocket. Certainly, she appeared often in his column, and she and the Zeckendorfs had a long history of bad blood between them. "It goes back twenty years," says an intimate of theirs, adding that they believe the broker heard about their conversations with Carl Icahn—and leaked the story that he'd walked away from an apartment, both to give him a measure of revenge and to taint the building.

"She sold no apartments at Fifteen, she was furious, apoplectic," says a Brown Harris Stevens executive, echoing sentiments also heard within Zeckendorf Development. "It was all from her." But regardless of who planted the Icahn item, it backfired. It created a hunger that inspired the 15CPW PR team to turn the sales process into a news peg on steroids, a gift that kept on giving to them, to the newspapers that raced after the stories, and to buyers as well, or at least those whose egos fed on exposure or proximity to the white-hot center of things.

The *New York Times* would eventually discover the rewards of printing celebrity real estate gossip, even if some there still hold their noses at the scent of it. But at the time, the *Times* seemed to have missed the boat, burying David Dunlap's scoop on the building, and then treating 15CPW like a one-night stand. The third paper in town, the *Daily News*, is considered a working- and middle-class paper, not a place to promote luxury real estate, so the PR team's gaze fell on the *Post*, which treated the buying and selling of ritzy real estate as a sport. "It's got the market: us," says a participant in the process. "It's geared to high-net-worth New Yorkers." Nobody's saying exactly how the *Post* started getting story after story about who was buying at Fifteen, but the newspaper turned its edge into a mini-industry, stirring up interest right in the market's sweet spot, the nexus of power, money, information, and consumption.

Will Zeckendorf submits that it was all obvious. "These guys all came to the ground-raising, which is a public event," he says, and reporters were there. "It wouldn't have been very hard for a reporter to figure out who's buying an apartment. Jeff Gordon's not there by accident."

But reporters sometimes miss things. Though Keil ran a story on Dan Loeb's purchase a month after the contract was signed, it would be nine long months before Keil reported that Gordon was a 15CPW buyer. Keil's earlier Carl Icahn item, which said that other billionaires who'd reserved 15CPW apartments were also having second thoughts, was correct. Initially, a surprising number of issued contracts—between a third and half of them—never came back. One went out to Richard Fuld, then the chairman and CEO of Lehman Brothers, the venerable investment bank founded in 1850, which would infamously collapse in 2008. But Fuld backed out. Another was issued to, and never signed by, a top mortgage broker. Some "people concocted wild excuses" instead of signing, says Will Zeckendorf. One said the apartments were too expensive. Another's check was stopped after it was delivered. "There were a lot of naysayers," Arthur says. "A lot of people didn't have faith." But Keil either didn't know or didn't show the whole picture. In fact, apartments had been selling at a steady clip since they were first made available, and those bound by contracts that were not signed were quickly sold again, often for more money.

Och got there first and proved a vital draw, but the Zeckendorfs credit Loeb with stoking the burning desire among the wealthiest for apartments at Fifteen. Loeb isn't the richest hedge fund runner in the world, nor even the richest at Fifteen—Och-Ziff and London's Brevan Howard Asset Management, run by Alan Howard, who bought a 15CPW apartment just a day after Loeb, are both ranked among the top ten hedge funds in the world on *Alpha*'s annual list—but Loeb (whose fund, Third Point LLC, ranked number 53 on the 2012 list) is as visible as the species gets. With his legendary sharp tongue, mighty pen, and $8.6 billion behind him, he's hard to ignore.

Loeb says his path to investing was set early on. "Almost bizarrely, I was interested at five or six," he said in a 2009 speech. His father was a lawyer who ran marathons, wrote poetry, coauthored a textbook on corporate governance, and was lured out of retirement to serve as general counsel of Williams-Sonoma. Loeb's mother is a historian who specialized in Herman Melville. Loeb grew up in their large, art-filled home on the beach in Santa Monica. But a great-aunt, one of the creators of Barbie and founders of Mattel, was his professional inspiration. "I associated success in business with Hot Wheels and Barbie dolls," he said.

The young Loeb loved surfing (Third Point is named for a surf break off the beach at Malibu), skateboarding (he started a skateboard company), *and* investing. He was so enamored of Milo Minderbinder, the wheeling, dealing, black-marketeering soldier in Joseph Heller's World War II novel, *Catch-22*, that one of his teachers pinned the nickname on him. As a teen, he was already putting his money where his mouth was: he hired a junior high classmate, Robert Schwartz, for twenty-five cents a day to be his bodyguard against bullies. "Dan's mouth would get him into trouble," Schwartz told *Bloomberg Markets.*

Loeb spent two years at the University of California–Berkeley and then transferred to Columbia, where he traded his way to a $120,000 bankroll by his senior year in 1983. Already cocky, he took a plunge on a company that made medical respirators. After several people using its products died, Loeb lost his small fortune plus more money he'd borrowed to buy the stock on margin. It took him a decade to pay it back.

He started doing that at Warburg Pincus, thanks to a little old-fashioned nepotism: his father knew a top executive and a godfather helped him engineer his first trading coup, a $20 million score. In 1987, though, he fled Wall Street, hiring on as a financial adviser to Chris Blackwell, the founder of Island Records, home of Bob Marley and U2; he helped sell the company to the Dutch recording giant PolyGram two years later for £272 million and dallied in the nascent East Village music-art fusion scene. He lived in the heart of it on Avenue D.

In 1989, Loeb was out of work for nine months. "Every day was a job, looking for that job," he's said. Two jobs later, in 1991, he landed at Jeffries & Co., which was picking up the pieces of the high-yield bond market after the collapse of Drexel Burnham Lambert. Loeb demonstrated both a demonic work ethic and a talent for networking, earned enough to buy a two-family mews house on MacDougal Alley in Greenwich Village for $850,000 and converted it to a single residence.

Loeb decided he wanted to start his own fund. Comparing himself to a lovesick schoolgirl, he recalled writing its name "over and over on a piece of paper, Third Point Partners, Third Point Partners, Third Point Partners." He even designed a logo. He took one last job trading junk at Citicorp Securities before he finally set up Third Point at age thirty-four in 1995 with $3.3 million, a third of it his own. "The night before I started," he's said, "I absolutely panicked. 'What am I doing? I'm a fraud.' My mom gave me 250 grand. I'd just bought a home. I had a mortgage." But after a month, he was up 8 percent and the fear seeped away.

In the midnineties, Loeb had started expressing his opinions about publicly traded securities on Internet bulletin boards, hiding behind fake names or, in Web lingo, sock puppets: "John_Crimiakis_Stock-Swindler" and "Mr. Pink," the latter the name of one of the crooks in Quentin Tarantino's film *Reservoir Dogs*. Mr. Pink listed his occupation as Minister of Truth and his job title as Lord of All Things. A post by Mr. Pink once led to a lawsuit, later settled, charging Loeb with damaging a Web company called Hitsgalore.com by, among other things, referring to it as sHITT (it's ticker symbol was HITT) and writing of its owners, "These crooks belong in jail." Loeb has told various stories about Mr. Pink's real identity, but in a declaration in the Hitsgalore litigation, he admitted, "I wrote the Internet bulletin board postings . . . under my screen name of Mr. Pink."

One Internet blogger claims that Loeb had another, even snarkier sock puppet, posting under the name Senor_Pinche_Wey (a slur in Spanish slang) during a campaign against a publicly traded drug-development company in Florida. Pinche_Wey called one of its executives a "mega scum bag" and wrote of its chairman, Lisa Krinsky, "I will reciprocate felatoin [*sic*] with Lisa even though she has fat thighs, a fake medical degree, 'queefs' and has poor feminine hygiene." In 2008, an appeals court in California barred Krinsky's attempt to get Yahoo!, which ran that investor board, to reveal the identity of the pseudonymous posters, one of ten who'd written what the court deemed "scathing verbal attacks" on her and others. One had moved to quash her subpoena, but the trial court denied the motion. So the poster appealed, contending that he had a First Amendment right to speak anonymously on the Internet.

In its ruling upholding that right the appeals court quoted a mention of Loeb in one post: "[F]unny and rather sad that the losers who post here are supporting a management consisting of boobs, losers and crooks . . . while criticizing a charitable and successful hedge fund manager, who, unlike his critics and the longs here, has done his homework. . . . No, Loeb earned his $ $ $ and those of you who are whimpering on each other's [sic] shoulders crying to be saved . . . are a bunch of pathetic losers." Though the court called the posts "juvenile name-calling," the poster won the right to protect his identity.

The Pinche_Wey–Pink-Loeb connection was made by Judd Bagley, a self-styled investigative blogger with an open animus toward short-sellers. He says Loeb has never challenged his claim. "I wish he would," Bagley says. "I'd love to depose him."

In 2000, Loeb took a cue from another activist hedge fund runner, who attached an incendiary letter of complaint about a company to a public SEC filing (a 13D, which is required whenever an investor buys or sells shares if he or she owns over 5 percent of a company's stock and is trying to influence how it does business). Loeb stepped out from behind the curtain and began penning 13D letters himself. He later expanded his oeuvre of clever outrage in letters to Third Point investors that, inevitably, went viral.

By then, Loeb had left behind his other reputation as a player. Slight and slope-shouldered, but five feet nine and fit (besides surfing, he runs triathlons and is a devotee of Ashtanga yoga), he has brown hair speckled with gray and the handsome face of a pretty-boy boxer who's never taken one on the nose. He was portrayed as a horny "Mr. Hedge Fund" in a 2001 article on yoga fanatics by Vanessa Grigoriadis in *New York* magazine. Though she won't confirm it, Loeb is said to still be furious over her portrayal of him. "I'm like Rambo in the office, headset on, three computers in front of me, mowing them all down," he proudly told her. "Yoga is all about focus and perfect aim."

Another woman, an ex-employee of Third Point, portrayed Loeb in an even darker light two years later, when she sued him and his hedge fund in federal court in Manhattan after she was fired, describing him as "unstable" and his behavior as "particularly abusive and erratic." In her complaint, the analyst said she'd tried to resign a few months before she was dismissed, but was convinced to stay with a promise of bonuses she never received. (She would ultimately make a confidential settlement.)

The immediate cause of her aborted resignation was a trip Loeb took to Cuba in March 2002 during one of the intermittent thaws in its relations with the American government. Though planned as a long weekend, that trip stretched into a seven-week stay, she said, after Cuban authorities "refused to allow him to leave" and Loeb told his staff "he would be detained there indefinitely." Though "the precise circumstances remain murky," the complaint said, some of Loeb's business associates and friends say he told them he'd been in a car crash in which a child was injured. One reported that he'd spent several days in jail until he was bailed out by another young financier, the designer Diane von Furstenberg's son Alex, who'd been traveling with him on what Loeb had described as a guy's surfing trip.

Robert Chapman Jr., a California hedgie who was then friends with Loeb, told *Vanity Fair* Loeb called from his Cuban hotel room, "curled up in a ball on the floor of his room crying, promising God that he'd do anything if the Almighty got him out of his predicament." For his part, Loeb confirmed to the writer William D. Cohan that he had been involved in a car accident, had a legal hearing, and everything turned out fine.

Remarkably, the incident enhanced his reputation. Though someone who worked at Third Point at the time denies this, two unrelated sources, a longtime friend and a competitor, both say he'd left standing orders that if his Third Point team lost contact with him for any reason, they were to cash out all positions in its funds until further notice. Fortunately for Loeb, both sources say, his absence triggered such a sell-off, which coincided with a steep drop in the stock market. "He made a lot of money as a result," says the competitor, who is often described as a friend of Loeb's but adds, "I don't know what being friends with Dan means."

Loeb's life changed radically after his Cuban misadventure, perhaps due to his vow to God. In 2004, he married Margaret Munzer, a brown-haired beauty with rosy cheeks about a decade his junior. A graduate of Brown and the School of Social Work at New York University, she is said to have worked as a yoga instructor, but now gives her occupation as mother and homemaker.

Loeb developed a spiritual enthusiasm around that time or at least made it a visible part of his life for the first time. The couple was married at his Rafael Viñoly–designed beach house by Rabbi Heshy Blumstein, the leader of an Orthodox Jewish synagogue. Under Blumstein's tutelage, Loeb began studying the holy texts of Judaism. Before that, he said in a 2009 speech made at a venue called the Jewish Enrichment Center, he'd been "much more identified with my day-to-day, moment-to-moment activities." But after beginning religious studies, it was "the first time in my life when I had a framework that I could refer to . . . that's not just bigger than us but kind of lays out for us a set of principles that you could apply to your life." Loeb then segued to describing his bachelor years. "I was having a good time, I thought, but you know what? I've had a much better time being a family guy." Loeb said that, ever since, he'd assumed a "very principled approach" to business.

But Loeb kept making caustic comments about business colleagues, and his words kept stirring up trouble. In 2005, he pulled out his poison pen again when a rival fund manager, Ken Griffin of Citadel Group in Chicago, tried to hire away some of his employees. Loeb's letter accused Griffin of running his "bloated," "over-rated firm" like a gulag, treating his staff like indentured servants, and surrounding himself with sycophants and "people who . . . despise and resent you." That blast makes it particularly intriguing that Griffin briefly considered buying a 15CPW apartment, then rented a pied-à-terre, unit 9B. Building staff knew of the Griffin–Loeb feud but not if they ever crossed paths in the lobby or restaurant.

Public records about the unit Griffin rented give a sense of how well ownership of a New York condo can be hidden by a determined buyer. In 2008, when the purchase of apartment 9B closed, one local newspaper reported that its owner was a New Jersey tech company CEO named Betty Lau, which appeared to be the name scrawled on filed paperwork as the president of Olmsted Holdings, Inc., which had bought the apartment (and is likely named after the designer of Central Park). But a careful check of filings shows Olmsted is a British Virgin Island corporation and a Betty Casazza of Queens, New York, is its president and sole director. She is also chairman and CEO of Kensington Investments, Ltd., formed in Delaware in 1986, apparently to buy a town house at 37 West Seventy-Fourth Street. Tax bills for the apartment at 15 CPW are sent to a Peggy Zalamea at that same address. Zalamea, a graduate of Harvard Business School, is a relative of Cesar Zalamea, the onetime chairman of the Development Bank of the Philippines, and a longtime executive of AIG, the too-big-to-fail insurance company. An internal Zeckendorf sales document read to the author by another apartment purchaser shows that 9B is owned by Suthira Zalamea, Cesar's wife. There are frequent references to Cesar Zalamea, who owned an apartment at the Galleria on East Fifty-Seventh Street for a few years in the 1970s, in accounts of the years-long efforts of the Philippine government to recover the late strongman Ferdinand Marcos's billions.

Around the same time as his blast at Zalamea's tenant Griffin, Loeb responded to a job seeker whose tone annoyed him, jabbing the applicant with insults in an e-mail exchange that, like many of his screeds, was promptly e-mailed around the world. When the job seeker suggested that Loeb's informality and brashness wouldn't play well in Europe, where Third Point was seeking to issue stock on the London exchange, Loeb sneered, "You will have plenty of time to discuss your 'place in society' with the other fellows at the club. I love the idea of a French/English unemployed guy, whose fund just blew up, telling me that I am going to fail. At Third Point, like the financial markets in general, 'one's place in society' does not matter at all. We are a bunch of scrappy guys from diverse backgrounds (Jewish, Muslim, Hindu etc.) who enjoy outwitting pompous asses, like yourself." The exchange got out after Loeb himself forwarded it to friends.

At his Jewish Enrichment Center talk, Loeb described his public-shaming technique as "using social pressure" and said it was "near and dear to my heart." He'd recently reread some of his letters, he said, and "They're actually quite brilliant."

By the time he signed on the dotted line at 15CPW, the press was watching Loeb's every move and carefully chronicled his adventures in real estate. Since 1994, Loeb had lived in his mews house on MacDougal Alley, but in April 2005, he'd bought a twelve-thousand-square-foot, forty-four-foot-wide mansion on a similarly charming, cobblestoned street in the far West Village, for $11.27 million. Before moving in, though, he bought his penthouse and put the mansion back on the market with an asking price of $18.95 million. The next year, he managed to sell it, but only got $12 million. He did better with the mews house, though again he failed to get his asking price. Listed at $7.85 million, it sold in 2009 for $5.5 million, a solid return on his investment.

Meantime, in summer 2006, he'd made the papers again when he and a number of other fund managers were sued by a Canadian insurance company that claimed they'd teamed up to destroy the value of its stock. The most colorful aspects of the conflict emerged a year later in e-mails from Loeb contained in court filings that revealed he was still an edgy, profane character. In one, he suggested that the insurance company's CEO "bend over [because] the hedge funds have something special for you." He also called the CEO, whose ancestry is Indian, a *shwartze*, a Yiddish slur for a black person.

⎯⎯⎯∞⎯⎯⎯

Loeb collects postwar and contemporary paintings and photographs, some feminist and some sexually charged, by artists such as Richard Prince, Jean-Michel Basquiat, Andy Warhol, Jeff Koons,

Lisa Yuskavage, Ed Ruscha, Georg Baselitz, and Cindy Sherman. His own modest artistic talent—and his pride at owning a 15CPW apartment—is displayed in the holiday cards he and Margaret have sent out to friends and associates in recent years. Their 2009 card featured the couple, their two kids, and their dog photoshopped into an image of George and Louise Jefferson from the TV sitcom *The Jeffersons*, accompanied by lyrics from the show's theme song. "Well, we're moving on up, to the West Side / To a deluxe apartment in the sky."

The house-proud theme continues with their 2012 card, inspired by the film *The Wizard of Oz*. The front of the elaborate four-page card shows Daniel's face superimposed on a munchkin and Margaret as Glinda, the Good Witch, under the headline "Somewhere over the rainbow." Inside, their children's faces are superimposed on the faces of Dorothy, the Tin Man, and the Scarecrow, and their dog, Biggie, appears as the Cowardly Lion. On a facing page, those characters stand on a rise, looking across a fantasy landscape toward Loeb's own Emerald City, Fifteen Central Park West. Above them, the legend reads "Way up high . . . There's a land . . . But there's no place like home." When the card is opened, it plays a snippet of the late Hawaiian singer Israel "Iz" Kamakawiwoʻole's ukulele version of "Somewhere Over the Rainbow." Appropriately, the sample ends, "Dreams really do come true."

Alas, Loeb's first political dreams did not. A registered Democrat married to a supporter of reproductive rights, he was one of the many hedge fund managers in America who were big backers of Barack Obama, a classmate of his at Columbia University. That reflected the same generally progressive attitude toward society shown in the donations Loeb made to charitable organizations through his personal foundation. In 2000, most of his giving went to the underprivileged and medical causes, though he also gave small sums to organizations dedicated to wildlife, running, and Jewish identity.

Loeb's giving accelerated after his marriage, quadrupling to almost $2 million in 2005 and including several more Jewish and Israeli causes, among them a Hasidic group and the Jewish Enrichment Center, which got $100,000; he also gave to a pro-choice group and the cause he is most associated with, Prep for Prep, dedicated to educational diversity, which received $1 million.

Loeb's political contributions began to attract attention in 2007. "I offered to do whatever it takes," he told the *Wall Street Journal* of his call to arrange a meeting with Obama. "Obama has electrified and inspired a lot of newcomers, including myself." But 2010 marked a turning point for Loeb, as it did for the new president. The previous year, the Obama administration had been focused on stabilizing an economy that had collapsed into the Great Recession and pushing its health-care plan, but that spring, Obama took to the bully pulpit at New York's Cooper Union a week after the SEC sued Goldman Sachs for defrauding investors through the sale of securities tied to subprime mortgages. Those were risky loans made to unqualified home buyers, often at high interest rates, and Goldman had continued to package and sell them even as the housing markets started to collapse. In his speech, Obama pressed for financial regulatory reform, sternly lecturing the seven hundred business leaders in attendance (prominent among them, Goldman's Blankfein) about the growing divide between Main Street and Wall Street. Loeb's love affair with the president was over.

Though Goldman had just agreed to pay the largest penalty in history for a Wall Street firm, $550 million, and reform its business practices to settle the SEC charges, Loeb sided with the bank. He'd acknowledged their ties at the Jewish Enrichment Center. "I have a good relationship with Goldman Sachs, so I'd like to keep it that way," he'd said to knowing chuckles. Now, he called the SEC action against Goldman "politically laced" and fretted that it had damaged investor confidence already shaken in "an increasingly worrisome landscape of new laws and proposed regulations" that would "promote 'redistribution' rather than growth." He was particularly incensed by a proposal (later abandoned) to tax the proceeds of the sale of hedge funds as normal income, as well as one to eliminate the carried-interest provision that allowed the managers of hedge and private equity funds to pay a low tax rate on much of their income.

Loeb's donation-investment strategy evolved, too. In October 2010, he gave $100,000 to the Emergency Committee for Israel PAC, almost two-thirds of the funds given to the group since its founding earlier that year. ECI's website was registered by political consultant Margaret Hoover, the great-granddaughter of President Herbert Hoover, a TV commentator and a social conservative known for her support of gay rights. But its board consists of neoconservatives and opponents of gay marriage and abortion, and initially, ECI was run out of the consulting firm of a onetime chief foreign policy adviser to failed vice-presidential candidate Sarah Palin. It "appears to be just another partisan astroturf group financed by anti-regulatory interests and advised by Republican strategists hoping to peel away Jewish support" from Obama, reporter Eli Clifton opined on ThinkProgress, a liberal blog. (*Astroturfing* refers to the practice of obscuring a political agenda—in this case opposition to financial-industry reform.)*

By spring 2011, Loeb's political change of heart had made it into the mainstream media when the *Wall Street Journal* revealed that, despite his record of support for Democrats (and continuing support for gay marriage and progressive eleemosynary causes), Loeb had switched allegiance to the Republicans, donating nearly half a million dollars to the party since Obama took office. In 2011 and 2012, Loeb's largesse (more than $500,000) was directed exclusively to Republicans. In those two years, Margaret Loeb demonstrated her po-

---

*"That notion makes no sense," counters Hoover. "ECI has nothing to do with financial interests." In an odd twist, Hoover is married to John Avlon, a writer for the *Daily Beast* and the son of the man who assembled the 15CPW block.

The front entrance of Fifteen Central Park West with its golden-granite base. The Pentagram-designed Fifteen logo, and the spindle-and-lantern metalwork created by the office of architect Robert A. M. Stern, are visual motifs that are repeated throughout the building and were used in its promotional materials. (MIKE TAUBER)

Columbus Circle, looking north, circa 1861, 1903, 1921, and 1931. Originally farmland (*this page*, *top*), the area developed after Central Park was begun just to the east. In 1903 (*bottom*), the Broadway subway was under construction, streetcars ran up the length of the park, Durland's Riding Academy occupied the northern end of the circle, with apartment houses, private homes, and the Century Theater beyond. In the 1920s (*opposite*, *top*), Durland's was replaced by William Randolph Hearst's low Gothic building. He planned, but never built, a skyscraper above it. Automobile Row stretched above the circle. The Coca-Cola sign (*bottom*) later became a local landmark, as did the Mayflower Hotel behind it, and the Century apartment house to the north.

"Big Bill" Zeckendorf, paternal grandfather of Fifteen Central Park West's developers, in his prime, behind his desk in his I. M. Pei–designed cylindrical office. (DICK DEMARSICIO/WORLD TELEGRAM, LIBRARY OF CONGRESS)

Arthur (*left*) and Will Lie Zeckendorf (*right*) flank their maternal grandfather, Trygve Lie, first secretary-general of the United Nations. (COURTESY WILLIAM LIE ZECKENDORF)

Big Bill Zeckendorf (*standing*), William Jr., and Will Zeckendorf. (COURTESY WILLIAM LIE ZECKENDORF)

Big Bill Zeckendorf with grandsons Arthur (*left*) and Will (*right*). (COURTESY WILLIAM LIE ZECKENDORF)

William Zeckendorf Jr. and son Arthur in front of Zeckendorf Towers on Manhattan's Union Square in November 1986. (SHERRIE NICKOL/CRAIN'S NEW YORK, COURTESY ARTHUR ZECKENDORF)

Will Zeckendorf re-creates the moment he tore the "tower" from the model of Fifteen Central Park West created by SLCE Architects and reoriented it parallel to Central Park West. (MICHAEL GROSS)

Robert A. M. Stern Architects designed this never-built glass-and-masonry tower for the Columbus Circle site of the New York Coliseum. Stern would shortly design the all-masonry Fifteen Central Park a block to the north. (ERNEST BURDEN III/ACME DIGITAL)

Architect Robert A. M. Stern and Fifteen Central Park West partner (and future resident) Eyal Ofer at the building's ground-raising ceremony, September 27, 2005. (JIMI CELESTE/ PATRICK MCMULLAN CO.)

In the Fifteen Central Park West sales office a few blocks from the construction site, potential purchasers could light up individual units in this model of the building. (JIMI CELESTE/PATRICK MCMULLAN CO.)

The construction site for Fifteen Central Park West. (JIMI CELESTE/PATRICK MCMULLAN CO.)

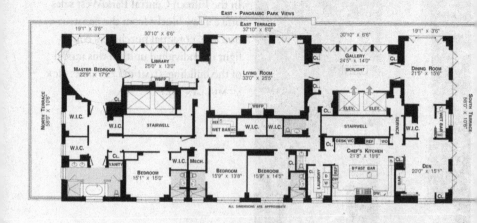

Floor plans of the penthouse trophy apartments bought by Sanford Weill (*this page, top*), Lloyd Blankfein (*below*), Eyal Ofer (*opposite, top*), and Lindsay Rosenwald. Rosenwald's duplex (*opposite, bottom*) would later be quietly offered for sale for $90 million, and Weill's would sell for $88 million to a

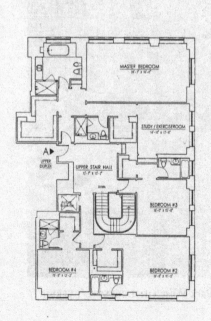

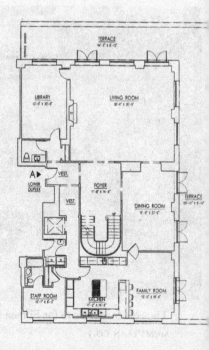

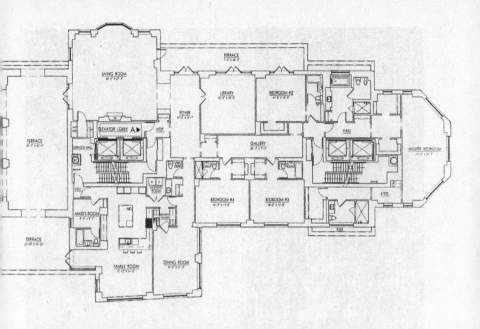

trust controlled by Russian fertilizer oligarch Dmitry Rybolovlev. It is allegedy used by his daughter. Ofer's apartment boasts a "King of the World" terrace beneath the building's swooping roof arches. Blankfein and Sting, the musician, have adjoining terraces.

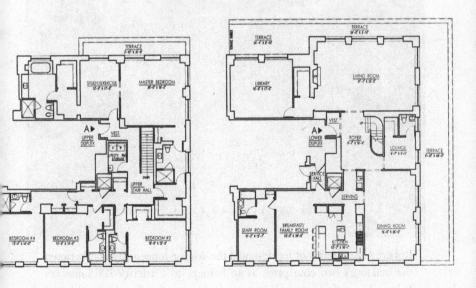

Robert A. M. Stern's office designed the copper-topped pavilion between the building's two courtyards as an homage to Frederick II's Sanssouci Palace. The reflecting pool sits atop the seventy-five-foot lap pool in the health club below. Light passes through the water and a skylight into the pool enclosure. (PETER AARON/OTTO)

Fifteen Central Park West's lobby is decorated with English-oak paneling, red-, pink-, and purple-marble fluted columns, two fireplaces, and a seemingly floating ceiling with a central oval cutout that gives the illusion of sky above. (PETER AARON/OTTO)

The elaborate health club beneath Fifteen Central Park West is reserved for building residents. It boasts a skylit pool, as well as areas devoted to weights, cardiovascular machines, yoga and workouts, private massage rooms, two steam rooms, and a sauna. (PETER AARON/OTTO)

its building includes. It boasts a skin pool, wellness areas devoted to
weight, cardiovascular, stretching, yoga, and workouts, private massage
rooms, two steam rooms, and a sauna. (15220 AA89747770)

Apartment 33D in the tower, originally owned by Duquesne Capital Management managing director Zachary Jared Schreiber and his wife, Lori, was sold for $29 million, almost three times what they paid for it, in July 2013. It boasted a lavish library (*below*), sprawling living room (*opposite page, bottom*), and stunning park and skyline views (*above, and opposite page, top*). (MIKE TAUBER)

Codeveloper Eyal Ofer and his brother, Idan, are two of the world's richest men. Idan's duplex apartment in the front "house" portion of Fifteen Central Park West was built by Stern Projects, and run by Nicholas S. G. Stern, the building architect's son. The starkly modern apartment in the postmodern building features a custom-designed staircase by Legorreta & Legorreta and a bathroom with a dramatic shower view. (PETER AARON/OTTO)

Fifteen Central Park West seen from across Central Park. (MIKE TAUBER)

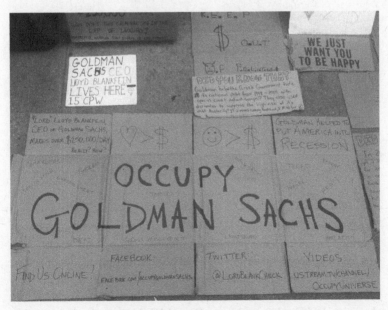

In fall 2012, protesters calling their action Occupy Goldman Sachs set up a vigil across the street from Fifteen Central Park West and camped there for several weeks. (CHRIS PHILLIPS)

The *New York Observer* heralded 15CPW with a story accompanied by an illustration showing some of the most illustrious apartment-buyers (*clockwise from top*), hedge-fund runner Daniel Loeb; Citigroup founder Sanford Weill (in the building's restaurant); sportscaster Bob Costas and his wife, Jill Sutton (swimming in the pool); producer Norman Lear; NASCAR champion Jeff Gordon; and actor Denzel Washington (in the screening room, of course). (GARY HOVLAND)

litical independence with donations to a number of Democrats as well as Planned Parenthood, Women Vote!, and Emily's List.

That fall, Loeb threw his weight behind Mitt Romney's run against Obama, attending a Romney fund-raiser at the 740 Park Avenue home of Steve Schwarzman, cofounder of the private equity group Blackstone, who was forced to apologize after comparing Obama's attempt to close the carried-interest loophole to the Nazi invasion of Poland. After Obama's State of the Union Address the next January, Loeb described it as "class warfare" and said he was "sick and tired" of being criticized for being a capitalist.

"There are some people who think it is fashionable to denigrate success, while others try to stir up class warfare," he said in May 2012, accepting an award for distinguished professional achievement from Columbia. "It is even more upsetting when our leaders tell us that it is their role to make amends for [the poor distribution of wealth] via increased and capricious regulation, excessive entitlements, ill-conceived subsidies, and punitive prosecutions." Loeb's hopes were high on election eve 2012, when he joined his fellow hedgies Paul Singer and Steven A. Cohen, the head of SAC Capital, for a steak dinner overlooking Boston Harbor before heading, or so they assumed, to a Romney victory celebration. "You win some, you lose some," Loeb told the *New York Times* the next day.

Presumably, Loeb says something similar to the neighbors he's had issues with at Fifteen Central Park West. One is Jerry Yang, a cofounder of Yahoo! in 1994. Yang bought apartment 11A in the house for just over $20 million. Gregg Ireland, a fund manager at Capital Research and Management, the largest shareholder in the pioneering Internet search firm, would close on apartment 15C within minutes of Yang's closing. Eight months later, Yang, then forty and CEO of Yahoo!, announced he would leave the company. Yang had refused to sell it to Microsoft for $33 a share, and when his company's stock went into a nosedive, was blamed and replaced, but remained as a board member while a new CEO attempted to right the ship. She failed and in fall 2011 was fired.

Two days later, Loeb disclosed in an SEC filing that Third Point had bought more than 5 percent of the company, making it the third-largest investor. That caused a spike in Yahoo!'s share price. In January 2012, Scott Thompson, who'd run PayPal, was named the company's latest CEO. A few days later, Yang left Yahoo!, and soon four longtime board members said they would leave, too. Loeb was having his desired effect.

Yahoo! announced replacements and prepared for a proxy fight against Loeb while Thompson looked ahead, announcing plans to shrink and reorganize the company. But in May (just a few days after Loeb's father died following a years-long struggle with Alzheimer's disease), Loeb dropped another bombshell: Thompson had lied about his educational credentials, claiming to have a computer-science degree when he'd really studied accounting. Five days later, the board member who'd led the search that found Thompson quit, and then the new CEO did, too. Soon enough, Loeb and two allies joined the Yahoo! board and recruited Marissa Mayer, a highly regarded director of Google, which had long since outflanked Yahoo! and become synonymous with Internet search, to take over as Yahoo!'s CEO.

The *Wall Street Journal* described the three-month-long coup as Loeb's "biggest victory as an activist investor." To *Newsweek*, the Yahoo! "assault" confirmed Loeb's place in the "pantheon of bad-ass investors," where Carl Icahn had reigned supreme. Fortunately, Loeb lives in 15CPW's tower and Yang and Ireland in the house, so the odds of a claustrophobic elevator encounter aren't as high as they might have been.*

---

*Yang could not be reached. A lawyer, responding to questions for Loeb, says there is no animus between them and they've never run into each other. In mid-2013, Loeb left Yahoo!'s board and Third Point sold its shares back to the company. That year, Loeb also picked a fight with Sony, and alongside Carl Icahn, bought stock in Herbalife, a nutritional supplement company often accused—by one of his 15CPW neighbors, among others—of functioning as a pyramid scheme. Those purchases helped support the company against its detractors.

Loeb has brought his pugnacity to 15CPW, however. In 2009, he was sued for nonpayment by a rigging company he'd hired to hoist some of his larger belongings through his thirty-ninth-floor windows after rushing his renovations so he could move in by the end of 2008. During the job, a cable got tangled, delaying the process by three hours, and the Loebs used that and charges for warehousing, storage, and transportation to challenge the bill. Margaret Loeb and several lawyers appeared in court to make their case that their LLC owned the apartment, not them, only to be admonished by the judge and told to resolve the matter. The rigger's claim for almost $99,000 was promptly settled for $82,500.

Loeb has also tangled with his neighbors at Fifteen, or rather, just beneath it. A swimmer, he likes the water cold in the 15CPW pool. Other swimmers, particularly the many mothers with kids in the building, like it warm. Conflict followed and a questionnaire was sent to all the owners, polling them on a number of gym-related issues, including the pool temperature. Again, it seems, Daniel Loeb lost a battle. Shortly after the questionnaires were returned, Loeb quit the building's gym committee.

Loeb is hardly the only bare-knuckle hedgie at Fifteen. It is indicative of the approach of another early buyer, Barry Rosenstein, that one of his funds is called Piranha; he once bragged to the *Wall Street Journal* about making a corporate opponent retch in a meeting. A big man with a receding hairline who alternates between jeans and striped shirts (in the office) and handmade Italian suits (for meetings when, in Gordon Gekko fashion, he seeks to intimidate), Rosenstein is the middle child of a tax accountant from West Orange, New Jersey. He was suspended from high school for spray-painting the basketball coach's garage.

After studying accounting at Lehigh University, Rosenstein got an MBA at Wharton and went to work for Merrill Lynch, where he's said his Armani suits won him another rebuke, so he decided to find a less institutional job. He lacked "the pedigree and patina of those Waspy guys" at Merrill, he's said, so he cold-called Asher Edelman, one of the superstars of eighties finance and talked his way into a job at his firm, which mixed hedging, arbitrage, investment banking, and activism, and became an Edelman protégé. Rosenstein told *Bloomberg* that he'd asked for $1 million in salary and Edelman agreed. Edelman recalls the lunch, but takes issue with Rosenstein's account of it. "He asked for a hundred thousand dollars," Edelman says, "and I said, 'We can't go that far.' Think about it! He was twenty-four years old and he was hired to crunch numbers, nothing else."

Chutzpah is not a negative in finance, though. In 2001, Rosenstein launched JANA Partners—an acronym from the names of his four children—hoping to take advantage of the dot-com stock collapse and the growing skepticism about corporate management after the fall of such companies as Enron, Tyco, and WorldCom. His first big target was Herbalife, the distributor of weight-loss and nutritional supplements that had been (and is still) accused of being a pyramid scheme. Rosenstein doubled his money after forcing Herbalife's sale, then merged JANA with Marathon Advisors, another hedge fund, to increase his war chest. It was run by Gary Claar, a former corporate lawyer, who joined JANA as a co-owner. Claar (who describes himself as U2's the Edge to Rosenstein's Bono) would sign a contract to buy an $8.75 million D-line apartment on the thirtieth floor of the 15CPW tower a week after Rosenstein bought his.

In the interim, JANA had taken part in dozens of activist campaigns, and they'd brought Rosenstein and Claar multiples of the sort of wealth the former had hoped for from Asher Edelman. They also made him controversial. In 2004, when JANA's assets hit $2 billion, the head of a data-processing company accused it of spreading lies about the firm. The next year, Kerr-McGee, an Oklahoma oil company, sued Rosenstein as well as Carl Icahn, who'd joined JANA in a proxy fight. Kerr-McGee accused them of violating a federal law requiring disclosure of an investment. But Rosenstein's pugnacious strategy bore fruit. Between 2003 and 2006, JANA earned annual returns of more than 30 percent.

Rosenstein spent some of his take on his 15CPW apartment. He either refused or ripped out all of Robert A. M. Stern's moldings, baseboards, flooring, and trim, as well as some walls and the legally required rudimentary staircase. His design team opened up the public rooms, dispensing with curtains and doors, aside from the five sets of French doors to the ten-foot-wide, L-shaped terrace. Solar shades that are invisible when retracted are the only window treatments. The walls are covered with limestone-colored Venetian plaster and Japanese tamo paneling and custom-crafted zebrawood floors were added. A heated wood floor went into a yoga studio. LED lighting that mimicked natural light was installed on the ceiling of the switchback staircase to the seventeenth floor. Rosenstein filled the beige, pale gray, and white apartment with modern art including two Warhols, a John Chamberlain car-crash sculpture, a small, early Roy Lichtenstein painting, and a large Gerhard Richter canvas over the ebony-and-rosewood table and leopard-print chairs in the dining room. Above the table hangs a delicate alabaster-and-bronze chandelier. Elsewhere, interior decorator Orlando Diaz-Azcuy placed an Axel Salto vase, Chinese bronze vessels, a Hiroshi Sugimoto photograph, a grand piano, and a mix of midcentury modern antiques and spare modern furniture. The Rosensteins' desire for comfortable, informal furniture and fabrics led their decorator to nickname them Mr. and Mrs. Chenille. Money can buy you more than just stuff: it all took only eight months to complete.

As the renovations were under way in 2008, JANA, by then reportedly an $8 billion fund, set its sights on CNET Networks. Bought after its CEO branded Rosenstein an opportunist, the ma-

neuver reportedly earned JANA about $100 million. This likely
came in handy as JANA had also acquired a large stake in a deriva-
tives-trading service, MF Global, which lost 80 percent of its value in
the first six months of that year.* In a letter to shareholders, that investment was described as "an utter disaster" likely to win a place in
"the JANA hall of shame." Rosenstein had made the *Forbes* list of billionaires in 2007 and 2008 with an estimated net worth of $1.3 bil-
lion, but then fell from that pantheon of plutocrats. Nonetheless, in
2012, JANA was said to have about $3.5 billion under management.

Loeb, Och, and Rosenstein were the first of a herd of hedgies and
alternative-investment managers at Fifteen Central Park West. Many
bought the more expensive and significant apartments in the building, but one of the wealthiest hedgies in the world, Alan Howard,
co-manager of the London-based hedge giant Brevan Howard, and
his wife, Sabine, bought the comparatively small apartment 10C in
October 2005 for $11.5 million. Though he has an MBA in chem-
ical engineering, Howard began his career as a trader at Salomon
Brothers in his hometown, London, and eventually found his way
to Credit Suisse First Boston. There, at age thirty-seven, he was
considered one of the best traders in the world and earned a bonus
estimated at £10 million in 2002, tying with the head of Barclays
Capital, Bob Diamond, for the best-paid banker in London's City
financial district. Howard and five colleagues promptly quit to co-
found their own hedge fund, which floated a public listing on the
London Stock Exchange five years later. A supporter of England's
Conservative Party, he left the country in 2010, establishing residence in Geneva, where he'd long enjoyed skiing holidays with his
French wife (they have four children). He also has a home in Israel.

In 2011, with $32 billion under management, Brevan Howard

---

*It would later be taken over by Jon Corzine, the former head of Goldman Sachs,
and would subsequently collapse.

tied for fourth place with Paulson & Co., the New York fund that famously bet against subprime mortgages, on *Bloomberg Markets'* list of the world's largest hedge funds. Howard can easily afford multiple residences; in 2012, when Brevan Howard's coffers held $39 billion, he topped the *Sunday Times* of London's list of the richest local hedgies with a fortune of £1.4 billion. Like Dan Loeb and Dan Och, he counts his favored causes as Judaism and Israel.

The hedgies just kept on coming. Shortly before Christmas 2005, Anthony Yoseloff, another Ivy League standout with degrees from Princeton and Columbia's law and business schools, bought unit 34D for almost $10.7 million. A managing director of Davidson Kempner Capital Management, he underwrote a dormitory at Princeton that was named for him. His boss, Thomas Kempner, is the son of the late East Side socialite Nan Kempner and is a former Goldman Sachs bond trader.

A few days later, Arnold Snider and his wife, Katherine, bought 12D for just under $16.3 million. Snyder started his career as an analyst at Kidder, Peabody & Co. and joined the famous hedge fund Tiger Management before launching his own, Deerfield Management, which focused on investments in health care. He has since retired. Richard O. Rieger, a portfolio manager at Kingdon Capital Management, apparently bought apartment 31A the following February through an LLC called Mayflower Redux, but insists, "It's not me," even though Mayflower shares an address in Bedford, New York, with his home there and his name appears on public filings concerning the apartment. Rieger "spends most of his time there," says someone who worked with him at Kingdon, adding that he found the place through a friend at Goldman Sachs. Then, perhaps to excuse him, the source goes on, "He never answers a question directly. He's a master of obfuscation." But not a master of using an LLC to hide his real estate purchases.

Ruvim Breydo is a master of mathematics. A managing partner

at D. E. Shaw, one of the computer-driven trading and investment firms known for its quants, the quantitative analysts who drive their businesses, Breydo was a student at Math School #239 in Leningrad before the collapse of the Soviet Union but, by 1991, had emigrated to New York. At Harvard, he was elected to Phi Beta Kappa in the class of 1995. He started at Shaw as a trader and programmer and lived a few blocks from the Long Island Expressway in Queens, but by 2004 was able to buy his first trophy apartment, a $2.9 million three-bedroom condo in Trump Place on the Hudson River. Breydo and his wife, Olga, coauthor of a self-published book on parenting, upgraded to apartment 6A at 15CPW for $14.56 million in April 2006 and sold their Trump apartment three years later after dropping its price from $5 million to $3 million. Sometimes, the math just doesn't work out—even for a genius.

<hr />

In October 2012, angry Occupy Wall Street protesters marched on 15CPW, and a few weeks later, an offshoot calling itself Occupy Goldman Sachs set up a ragtag vigil across the street in the shadow of Trump International. The focus of their protest was Lloyd Blankfein. "What a natural location to occupy, considering how Goldman Sachs engaged in some of the worst financial fraud the world has ever seen in the lead up to the 2008 financial crisis," the group wrote on its blog. "But despite such blatant lawlessness not a single official of Goldman Sachs has been prosecuted. Rather the corporation was rewarded, receiving more taxpayer funded bailouts than any other investment bank. Indeed this is a reminder that, as we close in to the 2012 elections, All Roads Lead to Wall Street. Heads they win, tails we lose."

Had Occupy gathered the press clippings and looked past the LLCs and other shingles that owned 15CPW apartments, it would have found many more targets for its rage. Goldman Sachs wasn't the only bank at Fifteen with connections to the financial crisis. Not by a long shot. Some were associated with multiple apartments there as well.

Take, for instance, the banker for whom Robert A. M. Stern's office prepared those special plans for the twentieth-floor penthouse. It's hardly a stretch to say that Sanford I. Weill, the eighty-year-old founder of Citigroup, was the father of the Great Recession. He's taken credit for tearing down the Depression-era walls between consumer and investment banks, insurance companies and other financial institutions, and celebrated that accomplishment with a plaque in his office that called him the "Shatterer of Glass-Steagall." When he bought his apartment, he'd recently relinquished his post as Citi's CEO and sold more than $250 million of its shares back to the bank, a huge pile of money just aching to be spent. Rumors that Weill was about to exit as the bank's chairman had begun circulating in summer 2005, and the *Wall Street Journal* reported that negotiations over his retirement only faltered due to his demands for unusual retirement benefits such as the use of a corporate jet and a Citigroup-paid security detail.* Finally, Weill announced that he would step down in spring 2006 and, on April 18, handed over the reins of the company to his successor at its annual meeting at Carnegie Hall (where a recital hall had recently been named for him).

Weill's rise from scrappy Wall Street trader to the man who invented the too-big-to-fail bank had long since made him a living legend. The son of Polish Jewish immigrants, he was raised in Bensonhurst, Brooklyn, graduated from Cornell, and started his career on Wall Street in 1955 earning $35 a week at Bear Stearns. In 1960, he and three friends started a brokerage firm that they would build

---

*To this day, the caller ID signature for his personal office reads "Citigroup." A writer who has been there says the large suite in the General Motors Building is paid for by the bank. Weill declined to be interviewed.

through acquisitions of other companies—Weill's forte—into the second biggest in America. In 1981, American Express paid $930 million to acquire what was by then called Shearson Loeb Rhodes and made Weill its president as well as chairman and CEO of an insurance subsidiary.

But American Express was a "white shoe" operation with deep roots in the patrician traditions of Wall Street, and Weill, who had triumphed in the alternate universe of the more recent rough-edged Jewish iteration of finance, never fit in. So in 1985, he quit in frustration over his inability to really run the company and went looking to start again. He got back in the game in 1986 when he took a small Baltimore lending company public and again began acquiring other companies, most notably after the 1987 stock market crash, when he took over Primerica Corp., which owned mutual funds, an insurance company, and the Smith Barney brokerage. In 1993, it acquired Travelers, another insurance company, and took its name. Then in 1997, Travelers bought Salomon, a leading brokerage and merged it with Smith Barney. A year later, after failing to combine with J. P. Morgan, it instead agreed to merge with Citicorp in a $70 billion deal often described as audacious because it could not have survived government review unless the Glass-Steagall Act was repealed.

Beginning in the 1970s, financial firms started nibbling at the edges of the restrictions imposed by that act, and during the Reagan administration, banks got their snouts into the investment trough again. Under Alan Greenspan, a former director of J. P. Morgan, the Federal Reserve Board loosened the rules even further, turning Glass-Steagall into a joke by the late 1990s, when Weill effectively forced the issue with his proposed merger after receiving signals from Washington that it might just be allowed. Indeed, it soon was, thanks to the 1999 passage of the Financial Services Modernization Act. That's when securitization, the practice of packaging loans into

Wall Street–traded securities, which had played a central role in the stock market collapse of 1929, returned with a vengeance.

By 2005, Citigroup's assets had soared to $1.49 trillion, but along with them came an investigation of its investment banking practices by New York's attorney general Eliot Spitzer (resolved with a settlement of $400 million and promises of reform); a Federal Trade Commission lawsuit against a Citigroup subprime-mortgage subsidiary (settled for $215 million); a $120 million settlement with the SEC, which charged that the bank had helped Enron commit fraud; and a $2.65 billion settlement of class action suits over Citigroup's part in the collapse of WorldCom. That pileup led to Weill's departure as CEO, and after his replacement announced an ethics plan to guide Citigroup in the future, Weill started talking about leaving altogether, first proposing that he spin off a private equity fund to manage money for Citi, a plan he abandoned when its board told him he would lose his use of company jets if it went forward. Instead, he decided simply to retire.

He'd already decided on his retirement gift for himself and his wife, Joan. Weill's homes, Judith Ramsey Ehrlich and Barry Rehfeld wrote in *The New Crowd: The Changing of the Jewish Guard on Wall Street*, "marked clear stages in his passage from limited means and obscurity to financial success and a high profile." He and Joan had lived in apartments in East Rockaway on the south shore of Long Island before moving up to an attached house in the working-class suburb of Baldwin, a fancier one in posh Brookville, and a colonial on the water in Great Neck. Then, as Weill turned his brokerage firm into an investment banking powerhouse, he had a Fifth Avenue apartment he was forced to sell during a bear market, and later a home in Greenwich, Connecticut, a Park Avenue penthouse, and an Adirondacks camp.

Though he'd been thinking of buying a new place on Park Avenue and had even consulted an architect, Weill signed a contract twelve days after he left Citi to buy the biggest apartment at Fifteen, the simplex penthouse atop the house. The $43,687,752 price proved that, while he may have stepped down as King of the Citi, he was still a king. He was also being a hero to his wife. Their conversation about buying the apartment had actually begun earlier that year. "He'd always been very conservative and lived modestly," says a member of the Goldman Sachs team. "But Joan loves to swim and he saw an opportunity. He surprised her with the apartment for Valentine's Day."

Like Dan Loeb, Weill paid full price for his penthouse, but at the close of six weeks of direct negotiation with the Zeckendorfs, he won a break, picking up a sixth-floor staff unit in the base of the tower with Broadway views for $978,000; by that time, its official price was $2.3 million. "Storage locker included!" says Arthur. "That's how we would negotiate." A member of the Fifteen sales team says that Weill's broker, Kyle Blackmon (whose mother had worked for Citigroup under Weill, though someone else apparently connected her son to her boss), celebrated by spending his commission on a Fifteen apartment of his own, albeit a small, $2.7 million two-bedroom unit in the rear of the tower.

⸻⸺⸻

One of the last hedgies to buy at 15CPW was Arthur Shepherd Estey, who cofounded Realm Partners, a multistrategy hedge fund, in 2009. But in the early days of 2007, when he and his wife agreed to pay just over $17 million for apartment 7D, he was still a managing director at Lehman Brothers, then the fourth-largest investment bank in America (only Goldman Sachs, Morgan Stanley, and Merrill Lynch were larger). The Lehman cadre at Fifteen was also a significant one: Estey's wife, Evelyne, a former French professor who'd gone on to head the private investors' arm of Merrill, had just left Lehman Brothers Holdings, where she was also a managing director and the chief accounting officer.

Lehman executives were trained to spot and seize profitable opportunities. "At the time, Lehman wasn't bankrupt, but things were getting difficult," says another Lehman buyer. "I'd seen a bunch of buildings going up, and you didn't get the impression the developers were focused on quality in every aspect. I saw a precious asset [at 15CPW], and I thought it would be good to get in early. It was obvious to me it would be a rare opportunity."

David Scott Bizer, another Lehman employee, lived in London but owned an apartment at the Century next door when he paid just under $5.4 million for Fifteen's apartment 24C in October 2006. Raymond C. "Ray" Mikulich was the co-head of the Lehman division that financed real estate (similar to Goldman's Whitehall) when he signed to buy apartment 15D for more than $17.2 million. Annica Cooper van Starrenburg may be better known for her exploits on the tennis court—she was a top player as a teen—than for her later work at Lehman Brothers, but she and her husband, Daniel van Starrenburg, bought a pied-à-terre in the rear of the 15CPW tower for a little over $4 million. Van Starrenburg, an accomplished Dutch-born arborist, heads SavATree, a shrub and tree-care firm operating in nine states, but based in posh Bedford Hills, New York, where they also live. Once Richard Fuld folded his tent and departed the scene, the most significant Lehman player at Fifteen was Erin Callan, Lehman's chief financial officer. She is also one of the few 15CPW purchasers who was symbolically tarred and feathered for her role in the events that set off the Great Recession.

The international economic decline wasn't Callan's fault, of course. Its seeds had been sewn many years before, early in Bill Clinton's presidency, when it became public policy to encourage home ownership, and the financial industry did all it could to make that "dream" come true. As William D. Cohan wrote in *House of Cards*, a book on the death of Bear Stearns, it created in 1997 the first investment products based on subprime mortgages, the risky loans that might not have been made in a more careful era, and the rest of the financial industry followed suit. Focused on their banks' windfall profits and their personal bonuses, the creators and promoters of those securities ignored what with hindsight seems like the distinct possibility that those loans, packaged into securities and hedged with credit default swaps, would lead to an international nightmare.

Loans of all types had become significantly easier to get in the early twenty-first century. That was mostly thanks to derivatives, which are contracts—though some would call them wagers—between parties that are used to hedge risk and have fluctuating value based on underlying assets (which can be anything from stocks, bonds, and currencies to intangibles such as interest rates). They are "unregulated contracts . . . agreements between two parties to exchange payments based on such things as interest rates, currencies or changes in credit quality," *Businessweek* has explained. "The most notorious of these instruments are credit default swaps, which provide protection against a borrower failing to pay its debts." They created "a huge unseen web of financial obligations" that would soon catch the world in a sticky mess.

Mortgage-backed securities, complex bundles of loans packaged as investment vehicles called CDOs, collateralized debt obligations, became wildly popular—even as they inspired concern. In 2003, Warren Buffett warned that they were "financial weapons of mass destruction" that posed a "mega-catastrophic risk" for the economy. Nonetheless, throughout 2004, the Department of Housing and Urban Development continued to encourage low-income borrowers to take on what would prove to be unaffordable loans; over the next two years, Fannie Mae and Freddie Mac, the government-sponsored companies that supported the secondary mortgage market, would buy more than $400 billion in subprime-backed securities. At that point, the risky underlying mortgages made up about a fifth of the US housing market. Mortgage fraud had become an epidemic, but with homeownership rates and home prices reaching record highs, few were willing to entertain the notion that the bubble could burst.

In 2004, warning bells finally started to ring as the value of the market for subprime-mortgage-backed securities crept over $500 billion. Former Federal Reserve Bank chairman Paul Volcker warned of "disturbing trends: huge imbalances, disequilibria, risks" in a speech at Stanford University in February 2005. "I think we are skating on increasingly thin ice." That August, Yale economist Robert Schiller warned that a "dangerous housing bubble" had led to "irrational exuberance." Yet one month later, just after the 15CPW sales office opened, the incoming chairman of the Federal Reserve Bank, Ben Bernanke, told Congress that he did "not think the national housing boom is a bubble that is about to burst" because "US house prices have risen by nearly 25 percent over the past two years," reflecting "strong economic fundamentals." He couldn't have been more wrong. It was the beginning of the end, as predicted by the financial analyst Meredith Whitney that October, when she warned that the credit quality of the underlying assets in mortgage-backed CDOs and other derivatives were deteriorating. After a decade characterized by the lowering of both borrowing standards and required down payments, interest rates in America rose substantially between 2004 and 2006, slowing the overheated housing market and triggering the first defaults of the loans tucked inside all those securities.

Erin Callan's main responsibility as Lehman's CFO was to assure its partners, customers, and investors that even though Lehman held mortgage-backed securities worth billions, the investment bank was not in trouble. In retrospect, her primary qualifications for that job appear to have been her preternatural self-confidence, poise, presence, and, most of all, ambition. Callan's fierce need to achieve was visible even in childhood. The youngest of three daughters of a policeman growing up in a lower-middle-class community on the border of urban Queens and the Long Island suburbs, she was a top gymnast at thirteen, basking in the admiration of her school's football players, who would crowd the gym to watch her practice until her hands bled. "She would think nothing of it," her coach told Patricia Sellers of *Fortune*.

After graduating magna cum laude from Harvard, Callan earned a law degree and got a job as a tax lawyer assigned to Lehman. In 1995, she called her top contact at the investment bank and asked if she could work there, instead. Lehman had just been spun off from Sandy Weill's first financial "supermarket"; it had gone public as Lehman Brothers Holdings the year before.

Callan was a "woman to watch" in more than one sense long before she was named one by *Fortune* toward the end of her dozen-year climb to the top of Lehman. She favored high heels and sexy, expensive designer clothes from Chloé and Chanel, and with her blond hair and good looks attracted both attention and a husband from inside the firm; she'd married a Lehman vice president in 2001. Her looks were matched by her talent for explaining complex transactions to Lehman clients, and she was named head of Global Finance Solutions, an in-house think tank.

In 2004, Callan was "noticed by all the senior management" of Lehman Brothers when she gave a keynote speech at its annual dinner for women executives, Vicky Ward wrote in *The Devil's Casino*, a book on the firm's collapse. A top Lehman executive saw her as a telegenic poster girl who could send strong signals to the outside world about Lehman's vigor and diversity. Callan became, Ward continued, a particularly well-compensated teacher's pet. Other Lehman executives noted that her pay surpassed those of her peers in the company.

Callan lived in the south tower of Time Warner, but was also ambitious when it came to status signifiers and decided to move up in the world. Apartment 31B at Fifteen fit the bill, and at the end of

2005, she agreed to pay almost $6.6 million for it. Though it was not one of the trophy apartments, 15CPW was already *the* trophy building.

Shortly after signing her 15CPW contract, Callan was named head of Global Hedge Fund Coverage, a new business for Lehman. Then, in September 2007, she was named Lehman's new CFO. Her husband, who'd left Lehman, left her the same year and sued for divorce. Colleagues, outraged by her rapid rise into a job for which they deemed her unqualified, complained openly about her utter lack of an accounting background and about her wardrobe—which had grown more provocative, as her hair had gotten blonder, since her promotion.

A year earlier, Nouriel Roubini, an NYU economist, had given a speech to the International Monetary Fund predicting "homeowners defaulting on mortgages, trillions of dollars of mortgage-backed securities unraveling worldwide, and the global financial system shuddering to a halt." Late in 2006, some investment firms, including Goldman Sachs, began betting against the same mortgage-backed securities they were selling to investors, secretly positioning themselves to profit when (for it no longer seemed like an if) the housing market crashed.

In the months before Callan started her new job, that had begun to happen. In March 2007, the New York Stock Exchange suspended New Century Financial, a big subprime mortgage lender. A month later, it filed for bankruptcy protection. By June, the bond-rating agencies were downgrading instruments backed by subprime mortgages. By summer's end, the mortgage market was melting down. Investment banks such as Bear Stearns were frantically trying to dump their subprime positions.

Late in 2007, the Commerce Department reported a 28 percent drop in new home permits. Experts predicted millions of foreclosures as the subprime mortgage market, then valued at $1.3 trillion, withered. Freddie Mac stopped buying mortgage-backed securities. Citigroup became the first bank to admit defeat and write off the value of those it was still holding. The International Monetary Fund would shortly estimate that the final cost of the collapse of the subprime market would approach $1 trillion. Many of the largest financial institutions on Wall Street began selling preferred stock in a frenzy of bargain-basement dealmaking to attract new capital and stay afloat.

Some couldn't survive. That January, Bank of America took over Countrywide, another subprime lender. In February, President Bush signed the Economic Stimulus Act. In March, Bear Stearns, the smallest of Wall Street's big investment banks, faced imminent collapse and agreed to sell itself to JPMorgan Chase for $2 a share. "You didn't see it as a life-or-death event," Callan would later observe. "You just saw it as something that was going to be problematic." But initially, Lehman benefited. Hedge funds were fleeing Bear, she continued, and "we were the beneficiary of some of those pullbacks."

Though the Bear sale price inched up to $10 a share before the deal was completed a week later, it was about a tenth of Bear's book value just a few months earlier. The word on the street was that Lehman Brothers, the runt of the litter of the four big banks still standing, but with a whopping $85 billion portfolio of mortgage-backed securities, was going down next. Lehman would soon complain to the SEC that hedgies and short sellers were doing their worst to bring down the bank.

Callan spent the weekend after Bear collapsed on the telephone, insisting Lehman was still solvent and had sufficient liquidity to survive, even though it had billions in toxic debt on its books and she had neither the skill nor the power to do anything about that. Monday, as Lehman's shares declined by 19 percent, Callan kept at it. She was well-suited for this high-wire act; the teenage gymnast had been a performer all her life.

The next day, she presided over an earnings conference call with analysts. Just before it started, Fuld backslapped her and wished her good luck. "I was like, 'Oh, my God,'" she told William D. Cohan. "Like it just hit me at that point. There's a *lot* of pressure here. There's a *lot* at stake, a *lot* at stake." She spent an hour parsing Lehman's numbers, then another taking questions. Lehman's stock rose steadily throughout the call, and afterward she got high fives, hugs, and an ovation from Lehman's bond traders and its executive committee. "Dick [Fuld] said, 'The only complaint I have is that you shouldn't have hung up the call, because as long as you were on there, the stock kept coming up,'" she recalled.

Callan kept beating the transparency drum while raising her own profile. "Her seeming candor and confident turns on CNBC briefly fueled positive publicity," *Fortune* later observed. That May, the *Wall Street Journal* even dubbed her "Lehman's Straight Shooter" in the headline over a story that closed with the image of her personal shopper from posh Bergdorf Goodman delivering racks of new clothes to her apartment. Inside Lehman, the piece was perceived as part and parcel of the same hubris that saw her keep a model of a private jet on her office desk and a framed photo of herself debarking from a limousine on its wall. It had appeared in a glossy business magazine story headlined "Wall Street's Most Powerful Woman," which called her "the only female now in line to run a major financial institution." She was likely also one of the best-paid women on Wall Street. Though her salary was never reported, a 2007 list of Lehman's fifty best-paid employees *below* her corporate rank shows its three top earners making between $30 million and $51 million a year, and eleven more hauling in $15 million to $20 million.

With press and pay like that, Callan should have been feeling on top of the world when she closed on her new apartment on April 24, 2008, but two days later, she put it on the market asking $14 million. It's tempting to think she was worried she was on shaky ground because, just a few weeks later, a hedgie named David Einhorn, who had serious doubts about Lehman's stability, turned her world upside down. Within days of her closing, Callan had spent an hour on the phone with Einhorn, who felt the bank was overvaluing its assets and wasn't impressed by the CFO's responses. That call was followed by an acrimonious e-mail exchange. Then, on May 21, Einhorn gave a speech and explained why he was shorting Lehman's stock. His argument was a frontal assault on Callan's credibility. Lehman's stock dropped sharply the next morning.

Einhorn was right. A few weeks later, Callan announced Lehman's first quarterly loss since its spin-off from American Express— almost $3 billion—and a $6 billion share sale to bolster its bottom line. Heads had to roll. "I was the public face of the firm and we had to show the world we were making changes," she would soon tell *Fortune*. In only three more days, Callan was demoted (her corporate mentor, the bank's chief operating officer, was as well). But instead of her getting a new job, "they ignored me," Callan said, so a month later she quit to join Credit Suisse as head of its hedge fund business, the same job she'd excelled at before. Credit Suisse even bought her Lehman stock from her. "I was lucky to get out, but I was so sad," she said.

Callan's ritual sacrifice didn't help Lehman. It filed for Chapter 11 bankruptcy protection on September 15, setting off shock waves in markets around the world that would still be recovering five years on. Callan's troubles weren't over, either, though her tenure as a 15CPW owner would end two weeks later, when she sold her never-occupied unit for $11.8 million to a neuropsychologist who'd founded ComPsych, which provides mental health programs for employees of corporations and governments, and union members. Two weeks later, CNBC revealed Callan was one of a dozen Lehman executives subpoenaed by federal prosecutors investigating Lehman's collapse.

"I think I was personally naïve," she admitted at that time. "Any kind of positive exposure runs the risk of negative exposure. It becomes celebrity, and you get a persona. Not only does it get away from you personally, it gets away from the firm, and they can't control it." But Callan did find a way to control it—one that had the added benefit of confounding most of those who'd been riveted by her rise and fall. In February 2009, she quit Credit Suisse, though the move was described as a leave of absence until a year later, when she officially retired on the last day of 2009. CNBC then revealed that she'd left Manhattan behind, too, moving to a home in East Hampton she'd bought with her ex-husband in 2005 for $3.93 million. He'd transferred it to her two weeks before her closing at 15CPW, likely as part of their divorce settlement. She was living there with a New York fireman she'd known since grade school. He'd called after seeing her on CNBC and they'd started dating.

Callan was still not free and clear of the Lehman mess. Lawsuits for misleading investors followed her for years and were the likely reason for her departure from Credit Suisse, and for the sporadic listing and unlisting of the East Hampton house. Finally, though, late in 2011, she married her fireman and the couple bought a second home on the west coast of Florida. The *New York Times* hit the right note when it dubbed her Wall Street's Greta Garbo. By staying silent and avoiding the limelight, Callan, like the film star, ensured her status as a fascinating enigma.

Callan's story also reveals the astonishing rise in the value of a Fifteen Central Park West apartment in the two and a half years between her contract and her sale. For the truth is, Callan's apartment wasn't, isn't, that special. Yet it was immediately clear as the building opened and closings began in November 2007 that the appreciation of its apartments was unusual, even unprecedented.

The Zeckendorfs had orchestrated something extraordinary. Whether Fifteen units are worth the prices paid for them then and since is and will likely remain a matter of argument. Many people believe it is the best and best-situated apartment house to be built in Manhattan since the Depression. Some, especially those paying huge sums to buy there subsequently, clearly believe the units are the best in New York, worth more per square foot than any others. Another school of thought, however, casts 15CPW as the naked emperor of buildings—more about image than realty reality. Regardless, the rise in prices there—as real estate just about everywhere else sank in value—boggled the mind.

Behind the fireworks of those big prices, something else just as fascinating was going on. While Callan, the brainy blonde who created the means of her own destruction, had to check out of Manhattan and sell her place at Fifteen to find some privacy, other less visible, but no less wealthy and powerful, types were hiding in plain sight there. Three were employees of Morgan Stanley, another too-big-to-fail bank. Emil Costa, recently named a managing director, bought 25A for $6 million. Guy Metcalfe, just appointed cohead of the real estate banking division, bought 2C with his wife for $9.5 million, though he immediately listed it and flipped it for $11 million. ("He was nervous," says a Morgan Stanley colleague at 15CPW. "His whole net worth was in Morgan Stanley stock. In my mind, this was a safer place for my money than the financial markets.")

The last Morgan man among the initial buyers was Sonny Kalsi, the real estate specialist who bought the A-line apartment next door to Goldman's Justin Metz. Born in London, the son of a nuclear physicist of Indian descent, he was raised in Tennessee and joined Morgan Stanley in 1991. By 2006, Kalsi was global head of the firm's real estate, running a division rather like Goldman's Whitehall funds, and bought his apartment when he moved back to New York from a stint overseas. A real estate banker who knows Kalsi well says he bought at Fifteen after being turned down when he tried to buy a co-op from an ailing, elderly man. "The notion that a board of knuckleheads could keep a guy in a nursing home from selling his apartment?" the banker says. "I'd go postal."

A number of other so-called too-big-to-fail institutions—among them JPMorgan Chase and the insurance giant AIG—are also represented at Fifteen. After three decades in the insurance business, Rodney O. "Rod" Martin was the COO of AIG's worldwide life insurance business and chairman and CEO of its American Life Insurance Co. unit in 2006 when he and his wife bought apartment 3B for just over $8 million. American International Group sold billions of dollars of credit default swaps, another form of collateralized debt obligation, which allowed investor-gamblers to bet on the probability that borrowers might default. They brought the insurer to its knees just days after the collapse of Lehman Brothers, leading to a $182 billion government bailout of AIG. Just before the US government arranged for AIG to pay $13 billion in taxpayer money to Goldman Sachs to settle derivative contracts at the height of the mortgage mess, Martin and his wife got a $4 million loan from Goldman, with interest-only payments due for the first decade, at two percentage points below the prevailing mortgage rate, the blog Gawker revealed. It noted that "as evidence of how important Martin was to Goldman's business, the mortgage was executed by William Yarbenet, the firm's chief credit officer, himself." A Goldman spokesman subsequently identified Martin as a private client of the banks. Martin was clearly a good credit risk: he earned more than $10 million in 2009. After the government limited compensation at companies taking its bailouts and Martin's 2010 take-home was cut from $7.26 million to $3.6 million, he left AIG; he is now CEO of ING Insurance.

The last big banker at 15CPW owns two apartments there. Jeffrey C. Walker retired as chairman and CEO of CCMP Capital, the $12 billion successor to JPMorgan Chase's global private equity fund, ten months after signing his contracts at Fifteen. Walker, who was also a vice chairman of both JPMorgan Chase and of the JPMorgan Foundation, uses 2B, which has three rooms and an open kitchen and cost $3.7 million, as an office and lives upstairs in 14D with his wife, a former fashion designer, and their children. It set him back another $21 million–plus.

A graduate of the University of Virginia with an MBA from Harvard, Walker began his career as an accountant before moving into investment banking at Chemical Bank, where he ended up running a venture-capital and leveraged-buyout subsidiary and founded its private equity fund. In 1996, when Chemical acquired Chase Manhattan Bank in a merger (and took the name Chase), Walker kept his job, and in the last quarter of 1999, his group accounted for a fifth of the bank's $6.27 billion in revenues—and he became a public figure, his investments in tech and telecommunications watched and sometimes copied.

A year later, when the bank changed its name again after merging with J. P. Morgan & Co., Walker joined a new executive committee while also keeping his job running their combined private equity businesses. Perhaps in celebration, he gave $1 million to the Thomas Jefferson Foundation, which operates the former president's home in Monticello, and another $500,000 to his alma mater, the University of Virginia, to upgrade its library's technology. Walker would continue to spread his wealth widely in an active philanthropic sideline.

"When the Limelight Turns Harsh" was the *New York Times* headline on a story in summer 2001 tracking a change in Walker's fortunes when his unit's assets were written down by $1 billion and the larger bank suffered a 63 percent drop in quarterly profits. But in an interview with the paper, Walker expressed confidence despite the pain caused by the bursting of the dot-com bubble—and time would prove him right.

Late in 2006, Walker and his wife decided to return to New York after raising their children in his hometown of Wilton, Connecticut.

"I was definitely tired of nineteen years of commuting," Walker says, adding that 15CPW "was the only place we looked at when we decided to make the move. Once we saw it, we fell in love with it."

Ironically, Walker ended up commuting again immediately after retiring from JPMorgan Chase, when he accepted a position as a lecturer at Harvard's Kennedy School in 2008 and as an executive-in-residence at Harvard Business School, his other alma mater, from 2009 to 2010. Since then, he's devoted himself mostly to good works. But he is also an unpaid advocate for Fifteen Central Park West and has served as head of its condominium board ever since control of it passed to its resident owners. His one brief comment on the building demonstrates that his determination to make it different from its models mirrors that of the Zeckendorfs and Bob Stern.

The real-property embodiment of Hegel's dialectic, 15CPW grafted the thesis of the impenetrable limestone-clad Park Avenue co-op with the antithesis of the amenity-rich glass-tower condo to forge a synthesis, a new kind of club for the newly enriched and those who aspire to join them. The cost of entry aside, Fifteen's location, where the West Side meets Midtown, symbolizes its aspiration to be an open club, one that anyone might be able to join. It's a limestone, steel, and concrete embodiment of the persistence of the American Dream. "We've designed the culture here so it's open, friendly, efficient, and family-like," Walker says. "My fourteen-year-old comes in and everyone high fives. That's not what I'd call an East Side building."

Part Eight
_____

SEEKING ALPHA

I worked and I saved
and I was sharper than all Adam
and here I sit, by golly, by golly!

—F. SCOTT FITZGERALD, *THE BEAUTIFUL*
AND DAMNED

Anathema. That's the only word to describe how traditional Manhattan luxury co-ops look on celebrities. It's how they view the leading tribes in the taxonomy at Fifteen Central Park West, too: hedgies, foreigners of all sorts, proud Jews. So it stands to reason that more of the famous would soon join Jeff Gordon in the celebrity cohort at 15CPW, attracted to the same thing the too-big-to-fail bankers want: comfort, escape, privacy, security, and status. From its website to its hushed salesroom, 15CPW used understatement to attract the overstated and the overexposed.

Understatement only goes so far, though. So alongside the restrained promotional campaign—"trying to set a quiet tone," as PR man Richard Rubenstein puts it—he and the Zeckendorfs kept up a steady drumbeat of unsubtle publicity. "It snowballs and there's a shift," says Rubenstein, who noticed and carefully nurtured the growing frenzy. "People want to be associated with the building. It was running on its own."

The second member of the celebrity-fashion-infotainment nexus to arrive at Fifteen never actually lived there. The press would say Joseph Betesh, the Syrian-born founder of the Dr. Jay's fashion label, which began as a surplus store in the South Bronx in 1975 and grew into a fashion empire with the neighborhood's hip-hop scene, agreed to buy apartment 28B for $5.7 million late in September 2005 and closed on it in April 2008. In fact, it was the founder's son, also a Joseph, and a condo investor. He co-owned a sixty-sixth-floor apartment at Time Warner, and broker Joanna Cutler, who co-owned another, had convinced him they should buy at 15CPW together, "to rent out and one day sell," she says.

They rented it almost immediately to another celebrity of sorts: Robert Stephan Cohen, one of New York's leading divorce lawyers. He'd been living at J. E. R. Carpenter's 920 Fifth with his wife, Stephanie Stiefel, a managing director at the money-management firm Neuberger Berman, when they got a call out of the blue offering to buy their apartment. They decided to buy a new one on Beekman Place, in a co-op where renovation rules were quite strict, and work could only be performed in summer. So Stiefel suggested trying to rent at 15CPW. Cohen, who hadn't lived on the West Side since the mid-1960s, was dubious. "It will be an adventure," Stiefel promised him.

"Our apartment was perfectly nice, but a lot smaller than we were used to," he says. He was also used to a different ambience. "We were always in prewars where it was quiet, we knew everybody, they knew us. This was like a glitzy hotel with lots going on, people from all over the world we never got to know, little kids running around. I couldn't wait to get back to a small, quiet building." After two years as renters, Cohen and Stiefel left for Beekman Place and the apartment was sold to Gina Lin Chu, the estranged, philanthropist wife of another fashion label founder, Nautica's David Chu. She already owned 6N, a large two-bedroom in the base of the tower, which they'd picked up for just under $3 million. Their second purchase gave them more space and Betesh and Cutler a $5.5 million profit. Cutler would later broker the sales of several more apartments in the building, including two to Russian buyers, and would rent apartments to Keith Barish, the financier-turned-producer, and Todd Cohen, a real estate heir, and his wife, a *Cosmopolitan* editor.

The penthouse that shared the forty-first floor with Will Zeckendorf's went to the first member of the media to join the 15CPW flock, but he'd come out of the finance world and his wife remains in it, so they fit right in. Marvin Shanken, the publisher of *Wine Spectator* and *Cigar Aficionado* magazines, is fond of recalling that he finished last in his class at the University of Miami in the midsixties. The son of a New Haven jeweler, he had to go to night school to qualify for an MBA program. In 1969, he went to Wall Street, eventually making partner at an investment firm, and fell for the wine business while doing deals to finance vineyards. He bought a small newsletter covering the international "drinks," or liquor, market and, after two years, decided to turn his new business into a full-fledged publishing company. He began publishing research reports on the wine, liquor, and beer businesses, trends in drinking, and even wine coolers, and organized seminars and tastings for his subscribers out of a $330-a-month, one-bedroom Manhattan apartment. In 1979, he added the biweekly *Wine Spectator* to his stable.

By the end of the eighties, Shanken had accumulated an East Side apartment, a home at the beach in Quogue, and a San Francisco condo and built a new office with a steam bath, a humidor room for his cigars, and a nine-thousand-bottle wine cellar. By then, he was married to his second wife, Hazel, a vice president with Drexel Burnham Lambert, now a senior vice president at Morgan Stanley.

In 1992, Shanken launched *Cigar Aficionado*. "The same nut who loves wine, that same emotional interest and passion exists with cigar smokers," he told *USA Today*. "We are a beleaguered group of men who have been treated in the last ten years as lepers." A year later, the

Washington Times pegged the cost of his personal cigar consumption at $10,000-plus a year. His wife wouldn't let him smoke at home, so he turned his office humidor into a walk-in with an exhaust system so he could smoke with impunity.

A noisy advocate for his expensive habits, he conducted his magazine's 1994 interview with Fidel Castro himself, praising the dictator for creating the world's best cigar. Round and fuzzy, with a thick mustache, Shanken favored clear nail polish and eye-catching ties and suspenders. But in his politics, he was conservative. In the 2012 election cycle, he and his wife gave generously to Republicans. In 2005, Shanken also bundled about $25,000 from cigar manufacturers for a New York mayoral candidate running against the incumbent, Michael Bloomberg, who'd banned smoking indoors in public places in New York City.

That wasn't enough to drive Shanken from New York, though. Early in October 2005, he paid $19.754 million for his half-floor penthouse at 15CPW, which represented a small discount from the $19.9 million asking price. As an earlier buyer, he may have saved money by rejecting finishes.

Shanken moved to Fifteen from the Belaire, a Frank Williams–designed, Bill Zeckendorf Jr.–developed condominium, where he'd cobbled together an empire on the thirty-third floor, buying and combining three apartments and owning a fourth, too. A year later in 2006, while Fifteen was still rising, a small plane piloted by New York Yankees pitcher Cory Lidle flew into the building seven floors above Shanken's apartment, killing Lidle and a flight instructor. At the time, Arthur Zeckendorf lived on the forty-second floor of the Belaire, just above the highest apartment damaged in the crash. Arthur moved out that night due to smoke, as Shanken likely did, too, if he was home. But both were soon able to return and await the completion of their new apartments.

Bob Costas was far more famous, so while the NBC sportscaster was revealed as the purchaser of the $11 million apartment 8C, Shanken was never mentioned. Big as Shanken's apartment was, for the Zeckendorfs, Costas's purchase mattered more. "It was a validation," Will says. "He left Time Warner, which felt pretty good because obviously he perceived something. I've never met the man, by the way."

Divorced in 2001 from the mother of his two children (both now in their twenties), Bob Costas lives with his second wife, Jill Sutton, whom he married the year before paying his Fifteen deposit. Often described as a "marketing guru," Sutton was from El Paso, Illinois, went to Illinois State, was named a 1987 Illinois Junior Miss, started out as a weekend broadcaster and segued into TV production jobs at Fox and NBC. She met Costas at the Super Bowl in 1998 and is said to have reconnected with him several years later. Despite his fame, they live quietly. And despite his profession reporting on others, Costas shows no inclination to have others report on him. "It's a nice building," he says through an NBC spokesman. "We enjoy living there. That sums up everything I'd like to say."

Also living quietly at 15CPW is a fashion-world figure whose very life has been something of a mystery ever since she was born. Tyler Alexandra Gallagher Ellis lives alone in tower apartment 33A, which is owned by the Perry Ellis Management Company LLC, named for the late American fashion designer, who was her father, though she never knew him. Tyler was only a year and a half old when her father died of AIDS on May 30, 1986.

At the time, the cause of Ellis's death was a deep, dark secret, at least to the public. His longtime companion, Laughlin Barker, the president of his company, had died that January at age thirty-seven, allegedly of lung cancer. The fashion world had known for months, if not more, that Ellis was dying, too, but AIDS was still a dark and dirty secret, the disease that dared not be named. In months to come, as Ellis visibly declined, his PR person would bristle if the acronym was so much as whispered in her presence.

Ellis was already infected when Tyler was conceived by artificial insemination. Her mother, Barbara Gallagher, was an old friend of the designer's. Though it's been widely speculated that Ellis knew of his condition and fathered the child anyway, Gallagher says that's not true. "Perry didn't know," she says. "He found out right afterward—and he was afraid to tell me. He told me when Tyler was eight months old. He was in denial until the day he died."

Gallagher first met Ellis in 1968 through another of his lovers, Robert MacDonald. They'd met at Expo 67 in Montreal, where MacDonald was a media coordinator and she a young assistant working for television's *Ed Sullivan Show*. After he nursed her when she came down with measles and she returned the favor by helping him get a US green card, she and MacDonald became close friends. He introduced her to Ellis just before she moved to Los Angeles for a a new job as a television writer for first Carl Reiner, and then Dick Van Dyke, Mary Tyler Moore, Bob Newhart, and Norman Lear, who would, in a complete coincidence, end up her daughter's neighbor at 15CPW. After a brief stint as a producer on the then-new *Saturday Night Live*, Gallagher became a network executive.

Gallagher had long said she'd like a child even if she never found Mr. Right. "You're not getting any younger," MacDonald told her one day. "What about you and Perry?" He proposed that, if she raised a child, Ellis would provide for it. Though Tyler inherited a third of Ellis's estate, she was raised comfortably but not grandly in LA. "I dressed her in Target her whole life," Gallagher says. When Tyler went to Boston University, Barbara bought a pied-à-terre at the Mayfair on Park Avenue. Around the time she decided to refurbish it, another friend of MacDonald's, a Realtor who lived two blocks north of the Mayflower block, called and told her "the biggest, best apartment building in Manhattan forever" was going up and took her to the sales office. Might as well buy new, Barbara thought, and returned with the officer of Tyler's trust, which agreed to pay $10.997 million for apartment 30A in February 2006. Barbara sold the Mayfair apartment, moved to the Trump International, and watched 15CPW go up. As it rose, the trust spurned an offer of $20 million—all cash—for the apartment. Barbara and Tyler's broker nudged the offer to $25 million. "Real estate is great," says Tyler.

When it was time to move in, Tyler didn't want to live in New York. "Mom, you live there," she said. Then Tyler took another look, said, "I kind of like this," and Barbara moved out. Decorating took a year. Tyler had to pay for it and went through her budget, so "it's still not done," says Barbara. But Tyler earns her own money; she has started Tyler Alexandra, a luxury handbag line. "She's getting even" for those Target clothes, says Barbara.

Though she has no direct memory of her father, Perry Ellis is alive to Tyler and she has kept him alive: her handbag line's handwritten logo is from an envelope he addressed to her on her first birthday. "I grew up in Los Angeles, and my mom kept me away from the fashion scene—his world," Tyler says. "But I spoke weekly with his mother and stepfather and visited them in Virginia a couple times a year throughout my childhood. Obviously my mom told me stories about him and saved some of his designs for me, but it wasn't until I began Tyler Alexandra that I really felt his presence. I have been contacted by many of his peers, who have shared their personal stories about my father with me. . . . These stories have given me a real sense of who he was and what a typical day in the life of Perry Ellis was. And we are *very* similar! Put it this way: he would not have had me dressed in Target."

Ellis often travels for work, "and also, I'm younger than most people who live here," she says, so she doesn't know her neighbors. But she uses the gym and loves the restaurant "and room service doesn't hurt." Only once has she been discomfited by living in what she calls "a closed community" of the rich and powerful, the night plainclothes security men "freaked out" when she showed up at the restaurant with friends wearing backpacks. Israel's minister of defense was inside, dining with one of her neighbors. "I had no idea who he was," she says. Ellis has recognized some of the better-known faces, such as Denzel Washington, whose wife, Pauletta, an actress and concert pianist, is often in the gym when Ellis exercises. "She's the nicest," Ellis says.

Washington's arrival on the 15CPW scene was another crucial moment in the creation of the building's image. He signed his contract to buy 14C for just over $13 million on April 27, 2006—becoming the first world-class entertainer in the building. It didn't hurt Fifteen's image that he was also a prominent African-American (who would thus have had two strikes against him had he tried to buy a home in a typical co-op). This time, there was no delay in the news getting out. Within a week, the *Wall Street Journal*'s Private Properties column led with the story, which was sourced to "people familiar with the deal."

Washington, a workaholic actor whose primary residence is in the foothills above Beverly Hills, bought his New York apartment through an LLC called 14C Park. "He'd been looking," says Michael Bolla, his Realtor. "We walked into the showroom and within five minutes, he said, 'This is it.'" Several people in the Zeckendorf camp say that Bolla was a tough negotiator who insisted that Washington not pay full price, so in exchange for a small discount, the developers were given permission to publicize his purchase. "We never authorized that," Bolla insists, but he adds that Washington didn't mind. "He's accustomed to it. He didn't care." The actor's request to move some plumbing lines was granted, and public records indicate that he did get a small discount.

Washington's easygoing nature is evident in his modesty about his accomplished three-plus-decades-long career. "I'm just a working actor," he told the *Hollywood Reporter* in 2012. "I'm still not famous, as far as I'm concerned. The fame part, other than getting a reservation at a restaurant . . . I'm just a regular guy." Asked what he does when people recognize him in restaurants, he joked, "I just slap the shit out of them." Later in the same interview, he hinted that proximity to Broadway might have inspired his purchase of a New York apartment. "I love the stage," he said. "In the last ten years, I've gone back to Broadway twice now. I'm going back next year. I'd go off-Broadway in a minute, and fortunately I'm independently wealthy. I mean, I got enough money is what I'm saying. I got a couple of dollars!"

The Denzel moment gave the Zeckendorfs the chance to brag about more than bagging an Oscar winner. The *Journal*'s item on Washington included a tidbit aimed at competing developers: after nine months of selling, two-thirds of the 15CPW apartments were in contract, a hurdle the paper noted had taken far longer to achieve at Time Warner. Sales had passed the billion-dollar mark, and that magic number—which the hype machine claimed was a North American record—was deemed worthy of celebration, so late in June, the Zeckendorfs took over the Allen Room at Jazz at Lincoln Center for what they called their Billion Dollar Bash, with a guest list limited to purchasers with signed contracts, brokers, and press. Prospective buyers were pointedly left on the outside looking in.

The big-name apartment buyers didn't show that time, but it hardly mattered. Though the party celebrated a monetary milestone, 15CPW was no longer just a money building; now it had celebrity cachet. Two days later, it got even more, when Braden Keil at the *New York Post* let the world know that, three weeks earlier, Gordon Sumner, the musician also known as Sting, had agreed to pay just under $27 million for apartment 16B, the duplex next door to Lloyd Blankfein's, adding it to a collection of homes that has included a Tudor manor house in Wiltshire, a farmhouse once owned by the family of the poet William Wordsworth, a two-hundred-acre estate in Tuscany, and a Malibu mansion purchased from the former star of

Dallas, Larry Hagman. Sting's latest purchase was no less impressive. He got the last 15CPW penthouse.

Keil pointed out that Sting, the teacher-turned-rock-star with the Police, his wife, Trudie Styler, and their four children wouldn't have far to move, since they already owned a duplex co-op a few blocks north at 88 Central Park West. Purchased from fellow song-smith Billy Joel and his then-wife Christie Brinkley for $4.8 million in 1989, that sixteen-room apartment was on the far less desirable second and third floors, but did boast twenty-eight windows and twenty-three closets. Listed for almost $25 million right after the couple first bought their new duplex, it finally sold for $17.75 million in summer 2010.

Truth be told, 15CPW attracted far more glamour-industry executives than glamorous celebrities. Many of them are based elsewhere but can afford luxurious second homes. In rapid succession in fall 2006, Los Angeles–based Norman Lear, the legendary television producer, bought the sky-high 38B for $10.2 million; one of Lear's closest friends, Alan Horn, the president of Warner Bros. (he'd later become chairman of Walt Disney Studios) and husband of the eighties fashion model and actress Cindy Harrell, bought the unit just below for $9.7 million; Leslie Wexner, founder and chairman of the Columbus, Ohio–based Limited stores, who has kept a foothold in New York since opening a store there in the late 1980s, bought 10B for $13.339 million; and Ed Snider, the chairman of Comcast Spectacor, which owns the Philadelphia Flyers, that city's Wells Fargo Center, and a regional sports network, dropped about $7.5 million for the apartment directly below Horn's on the thirty-sixth floor.

"My wife is totally responsible for our being here," says Lear, "but everything I care about seems to be over here" on the West Side. "Theater, theater, theater. One of the great joys of New York." So when his third wife, Lyn, heard about Fifteen from friends she won't name, she brought him to see the building, just blocks away from the homes of two of Lear's daughters, who both live on Central Park West, and proposed it be their second home.

"The only decision I made," says Lear, came after the then-eighty-four-year-old rode the construction hoist to the top of the unfinished tower. "We looked at the floor below," he says, "but its ceilings were a foot lower. I said let's do the higher ceilings."

They ended up doing more than that. "We changed almost everything," turning their foyer, dining room, and living room into a single open space, Lyn Lear says, "and were disturbed that we had to [buy] the apartment as Stern designed it and then tear it down and redo it to our liking, but that was the way it was." Then, in February 2009, before the Lears moved in, there was a leak from Daniel and Margaret Loeb's penthouse above, which was also still under renovation. A pipe in an exterior wall froze and burst.

American International, Rod Martin's insurance company, which had issued policies covering both the Lear and the Loeb apartments, paid $375,000 to the Lears and more than $779,000 to the Loebs' LLC, Panorama on the Park, to settle damage claims, then filed suit against several of the Loebs' renovation contractors, the condo partnership, the builder, and Brown Harris Stevens, which had taken over management of the building when it opened—attempting to affix blame for the leak.

By fall 2006, a year after 15CPW first went on sale, it was three-quarters sold, and *Forbes* reported the building had broken a North American record with $1.4 billion in signed contracts. Prices then ranged from $2,000 to $6,000 per square foot, with an average of $3,300. Despite (or perhaps because of) those record-setting numbers, there were still eager buyers as the Zeckendorfs began releasing the last trophies, having raised their prices substantially. By February 2007, all that remained were "a few leftovers," says a sales team member. "But people were still flying in, so we put them on a list and said we'd be in touch."

That was when gossip about who planned to live there was overtaken by even more titillating chatter, the astonishing sums the apartments would trade for in the days and years to come. For the truth was that Fifteen's biggest celebrity names, Gordon, Washington, Costas, and Sting, were as understated as the building they'd chosen to share. They were tasteful, one might even say boring, celebrities. And something was brewing at 15CPW that wasn't boring at all.

Flipping, or selling an apartment for a profit without ever occupying it and sometimes before actually owning it, became a defining Fifteen phenomenon. The world economy was reeling, banks and insurance companies teetering on the edge of insolvency, corporations declaring bankruptcy at unprecedented rates, jobs disappearing, the stock market plunging, retirement funds vaporizing, and home values plummeting, but Fifteen Central Park West would prove to be the exception to all those rules. Armed with their investment savvy and their stockpiles of cash, those fortunate to buy the Fifteen dream before it was an obvious sure thing won big, again proving the wisdom of the old cliché that the rich get richer.

In most new condominiums, purchasers are barred from listing or advertising their apartments before closing because the developers don't want buyers competing with them and speculating with their product. They want a velvet rope outside their club—at least until they've cashed out. The Zeckendorfs went further to discourage investors: their offering included a rule limiting rentals to one year; renters then have to get a new approval from the condo board. They also tried to limit purchasers to a single apartment (though they were welcome to buy staff and guest suites), succeeding in all but a few cases.

Behind the scenes, though, a gray market for Fifteen apartments blossomed, says real estate investment banker John Fowler. Another third-generation member of a real estate family, Fowler had a fascination with the Zeckendorfs that dated back to his reading Big Bill's autobiography at the beginning of his career. Late in 2005, while renting an apartment at Time Warner, he made an appointment to visit the 15CPW sales office. "One thing led to another," he says, and he put down a deposit on apartment 32B, but almost immediately "I wanted a better unit." In January 2006 Fowler was allowed to transfer his deposit to the larger 32A. "I had every intention of moving in," he continues. He hired an architect and even bought furniture, but grew frustrated, early in 2008, because gaining access to the apartment before he closed was "a pain in the ass," he says.

His 15CPW salesperson had already tried to tempt him to sell. She says, "Prices kept going up and up and up, and I'd see him or call him and say, 'Y'know, I could sell it for twelve million dollars.' 'No, not interested.' Two months later, fourteen. 'Yeah, tell me when it's sixteen or seventeen.' I called back: 'Sixteen.' He said, 'Why not eighteen?' There's always that greed factor, and I sold it for eighteen and he didn't move in."

Meantime, Arthur and Edward Falcone, two of three brothers who co-own a multibillion-dollar real estate company in Boca Raton, Florida, had decided to flip 35A above him—apparently without the Zeckendorfs' knowledge—and a bidding war for it had broken out. Peter Simon, a British fashion tycoon "came in second," Fowler says, and "was desperate" to get into Fifteen. The founder of Monsoon, a store chain, Simon was fortunate. "They'd told me no flips," but decided to allow a few, for reasons unknown, Fowler continues, though he had to pay "several hundred thousand dollars" for the privilege. Flying under the radar as Corolana Property Holdings of the British Virgin Islands and Liechtenstein, Simon signed a contract agreeing that, on closing, he'd pay the Zeckendorfs their $10 million–plus and Fowler another $7 million–plus for his place. Fowler used some of his profit of about $4 million to rent 25F in the rear of the tower because "I still wanted to live there," he says. What surprised him the most was "that the über-rich would want to live with the not-so-rich. I've been blessed, but these people just make my head spin."

Though his company had gone public in 1998, Peter Simon tightly controlled it through a family trust set up to benefit his four children. A onetime hippie who'd lived in a nudist colony on the Spanish island of Ibiza and started his business selling hand-crocheted coats out of a stall in London's Portobello Market, he'd made about $100 million when Monsoon (so named because Simon was born during a rainstorm in Sri Lanka) went public.

Just before he bought at Fifteen, Simon was the subject of a brief but spicy column in London's *Sunday Express*, detailing what it deemed his eventful year. After pegging his fortune at £600 million, columnist Adam Helliker reviewed Simon's romantic entanglements, beginning with the twenty-year marriage that produced his four children before ending in divorce in 2000. His ex-wife had then had a two-year fling with James Hewitt, who'd first famously bedded Diana, the Princess of Wales. Simon went on to have a son with a girlfriend named Svetlana Astakhova before segueing to a Belarussian model named Liudmilla Bakhmat, "who is at least two decades his junior," Helliker wrote, and was "still married with two small daughters."

Simon was apparently generous with his women. A member of the "Simon clan" told the columnist that while Bakhmat was partying in Simon's "palatial villa" on Ibiza, Astakhova was living next door to his home in London, subsidized by "a huge monthly cheque." That family member was likely pleased when Peter installed Bakhmat across the Atlantic Ocean at 15CPW, considering the last words of the column. "Liudmilla is ghastly," the relative said. "Svetlana's an angel compared to her."

The first closings took place in August 2007, beginning with the buyers of the white-box apartments in the house such as Jeff Gordon, Barry Rosenstein, and Sandy Weill, who had the most work to do. By November, apartments in the lower floors of the tower were finished and began to be transferred to buyers. The Weills were the first to move into the building, albeit into their little one-bedroom in the bottom of the tower. A month later, closings began on the upper floors of the tower, too. Daniel Loeb took possession of his penthouse in February 2008. That July, Daniel Och was the last to close on a penthouse. A handful of apartments on the second and third floors of the house and on the twenty-third floor of the tower closed last, after the construction crews, who finished a floor at a time, "backed out" of the building.

By then, the flipping had accelerated. The next apartment to be resold belonged to Michael Holtz, the founder of a boutique luxury-travel agency, Smartflyer. Holtz and a friend had each bought a three-bedroom in the tower with views of Broadway, Sixty-Second Street, the reflecting pool, and a bit of the park and planned to combine them. Holtz had rented in the Park Millennium when he first came to New York, bought his first apartment, and "got hooked" on luxury real estate, he says. He owned an apartment in one of the Richard Meier glass towers on Perry Street and had just sold another in the Park Imperial to Sean Combs, the rap impresario, when he bought at Fifteen on impulse. "In 2005, there was only one way the investment could go and that was up," he says.

His partner was Evan Cole, who'd cofounded ABC Home in the early 1980s with his wife, whose family had owned ABC Carpet, a huge rug emporium, for more than a century. After their 1999 separation, he'd taken over the company, but the year before buying at 15CPW, he'd sold his share to his ex and gone to California, where he opened a home-furnishing company of his own. He also kept an apartment around the corner from Fifteen on Central Park South, loved the neighborhood, and was fascinated by the Mayflower property. "I wanted to be in that location and park there for the rest of my life," Cole says. "It just beckoned to me." When he heard about 15CPW from a friend at Madison Capital, which had bought half the retail condo, he went to the sales office with his friend Holtz, and they bought apartments together. Cole didn't care that they were in the back of the bus. "My whole apartment on Central Park South faced the park," he says, "and it's a static picture. Central Park views are the most overrated thing ever."

Cole was planning to move to New York and had just sold his home in Los Angeles. But at a good-bye party, he met the woman of his dreams, and when she asked him why on earth he would sell his house, "I ripped up the contract," he says. "She's my wife now and we have a beautiful son. I'm staying in California." He'd already planned the design of the 15CPW duplex, but she found the building pretentious and announced she'd never live there. "So I stopped the whole thing," Cole says. "If she'd said jump out the window, I would've. I was going with the love juice."

When he and Holtz closed, the building was still unfinished. Holtz liked living downtown and Cole had recommitted to Los Angeles ("the nicest place on earth as long as you don't talk to anybody," he says). "I had no idea how successful it would be," adds Holtz, who put his unit on the market for $8.5 million three days after buying it. Three months later, he got his price. Cole sold his a month after that for $9.15 million to an investment manager in Chicago, whose son would eventually occupy the apartment. Cole thought they were "Goldman Sachs people," he says, "but I didn't look. They're probably smarter than me. I'm sure it's worth millions more than they paid."

Holtz's buyers clearly knew what his place was worth; they already owned two apartments in the building. Under the name Lovebirds LLC, Jesse Itzler and Sara Blakely had bought 37A, a three-bedroom stunner with park, river, and downtown views, for $12 million two years earlier and had added 14J, next door to Holtz, eight months later for another $2.7 million.

Jesse Itzler's father was a plumber and his mother, the president of the Board of Education in the New York suburb of Roslyn. After graduating from American University in 1990, Itzler had a brief career as a self-styled frat-rapper under the name Jesse Jaymes. He also staged $50-a-head parties for Manhattan singles at which guests played the part of bride, groom, and guests at a mock wedding and reception. Then, at twenty-two, the tall, athletic, curly-blond-haired Itzler and a rapper partner named Mozie penned a theme song for the New York Knicks and wrote more music for sports franchises, then started and sold a record label to SFX Entertainment in 1998 and went to work for its owner, an entrepreneur who told them to think big. Flying around the country in private jets for SFX, they had a lightbulb moment. "*This* is the drug," Itzler's partner declared.

After researching the private-jet industry, they identified a vacuum, decided to broker flight time in jets owned by others to the young and wealthy, and cofounded Marquis Jets just before the 9/11 attacks turned commercial flying into a nightmare for passengers. Financed by the partners, who put up $1 million each, and hedge funds and investors who put in another $4 million, they bought aircraft hours from NetJets and resold them in twenty-five-hour blocks. By 2003, they had seven hundred clients, including sports stars and celebrities such as Madonna, Michael Jordan, and LeBron James. "We target the hip-hop guys who have made their first $2 million and don't want to take their shoes off before getting on a flight," Itzler said. By 2007, Marquis had $700 million in annual revenues.

Itzler met Sara Blakely when she became a Marquis client. The daughter of a lawyer from Clearwater, Florida, and granddaughter of the owner of clothing stores, Blakely started dreaming up money-making schemes as a child and became a champion high school debater at sixteen, right around the time her parents divorced. In one version of a story that's been told several ways, her father gave her a set of motivational tapes as a parting gift. She listened to them so often, she knew them by heart by the time she became a Tri Delta sorority girl at Florida State University. After disappointing LSAT results that dashed her childhood hopes of following her father into the law, she started her adult life as, depending on which version of the story you're reading, a chipmunk at Disney World (she was too short for the Goofy costume) or wearing Mickey Mouse ears while buckling visitors into rides, and then spent seven years selling photocopy and fax machines door-to-door, rising to the post of national sales manager for an office-supply company.

Several versions of how she got the idea for her Spanx line of underwear and hosiery have also circulated. Both involve a pair of white pants with a visible panty line and her desire to wear them with open-toed shoes. In one, she was going to wear them to a party, in another it was while moonlighting as a stand-up comic in Atlanta in 1998. Regardless, she cut the feet off her panty hose, and a legend was born.

One of her sorority sisters later told a reporter that the Tri Delts had actually discovered that if they cut the legs off control-top panty hose, they were left with a perfect body-shaping undergarment. No matter. Armed with that idea, her skills as a public speaker and saleswoman, and $5,000 (alternately described as a loan from her grandmother and her fax-selling savings), the sprightly blonde researched and improved her product so they wouldn't roll up her legs, applied for a patent for her invention, and launched Spanx the next year, with its slightly sassy name (ending with an easily remembered K sound inspired by brands like *Kodak* and *Coca-Cola*) and slogan ("We've got your butt covered"), after finding a hosiery-mill owner whose daughters liked her idea, and talking her way into a Neiman Marcus order by changing clothes in a bathroom stall to show a store buyer how well Spanx hid panty lines.

Abjuring advertising, she used her Tri Delta sisters as a word-of-mouth marketing force and cleverly sent prototypes to Oprah Winfrey's stylist with a note thanking the talk-show host for inspiring her. "I love Spanx, I've given up panties," Oprah declared on air in 2000. That was either three weeks after or two weeks before Blakely quit her job to sell Spanx full-time. Sales took off, rising from $4 million the first year to $10 million the second. Pitching herself as a model entrepreneur, she became a women's-page favorite. By the time Blakely turned thirty-five, a year later, Spanx had annual global sales of $250 million.

Blakely met Itzler in Las Vegas. Urged by her Marquis salesperson, she asked for a seat at a poker tournament he sponsored. It was sold out, but when Itzler saw her photos, he agreed to make room for her. Soon Blakely broke her engagement to a photographer and put on a new ring from Itzler. "Jesse was the first person I had ever really dated where I didn't feel like I was carrying the load," she later told *Worth*. "We were old enough to know that how we felt about each other was really rare." So both put their businesses on hold for six months of whirlwind romance.

A thoroughly modern couple, they bought their home first and got married later. In the interim, Blakely did some reality TV and Itzler formed a brand-development and marketing company and invested in coconut water, a vodka, and a racehorse syndicate, bringing in Marquis customers such as Jay-Z and quarterback Tom Brady. (He would sell Marquis to NetJets owner Berkshire Hathaway in 2010.) The invitations to their wedding, a twelve-page bound booklet, informed the invited that Itzler and Blakely had rented out the entire Gasparilla Inn resort near Boca Grande, Florida, for a long weekend for the October 2008 nuptials. "We had very successful people and, like, thugs," says Itzler. Olivia Newton-John performed. Sara promptly got pregnant and gave them a son to share their home in the sky.

That's where she sat for an interview with the *New Yorker* early in 2011, during which she claimed to have a fear of heights, as well as a fear of flying and stage fright, despite her years spent on private planes and appearing in public. "When we first got this apartment, I thought I might have to sell it as soon as we moved in," she said. To calm her fears, the couple hired a former Navy SEAL to suggest emergency escape plans.

Their apartment "is decorated in a modern rococo style," Alexandra Jacobs wrote. "Hidden behind the bar are jet packs and an inflatable motorboat." Blakely confided that in the event of an emergency, they'd jump out the window and, presumably, jet-pack their way to the Hudson River, where they'd float their boat and escape, leaving behind the books noted by Jacobs, which included a Wayne Dyer library, *Living Gluten-Free for Dummies*, and works by the New Age advice author Eckhart Tolle, as well as by Henry Miller, Milan Kundera, and Phyllis Diller.

That was a banner year for the Blakely-Itzler household. In May, a company founded by Itzler and LeBron James, among others, launched a controversial product called Sheets, caffeinated strips that dissolve on the tongue and give users a burst of energy. In July, Blakely spent $8.8 million on two lots and a mansion surrounded by hedges on a thin isthmus of land between the Gulf of Mexico and St. Joseph Sound in her hometown of Clearwater, Florida. They'd just sold the second of their two small units at Fifteen for a $1 million profit. They'd already unloaded the one they'd bought from Holtz but, according to Florida's *St. Petersburg Times*, still had homes in La Jolla, California; New Fairfield, Connecticut; and Atlanta, where Spanx is still based.

In 2012, Blakely made the cover of *Forbes*'s twenty-fifth annual billionaires issue, billed as its "youngest self-made woman." She was one of seventy-four people tied for last place on the 1,226-person-long list; *Forbes* deemed the value of Spanx at $1 billion. In the flurry of press that followed, Itzler revealed that he'd hired another Navy SEAL to move in with them and give them cardio workouts. "Money makes you more of who you are already," Blakely told the *Times* of London. "It holds a magnifying glass up to you. So if you're an asshole, you become a bigger asshole; if you are insecure, you become more insecure; if you are nice, you become nicer; and if you're generous, you become more generous." It's a tribute to Itzler and Blakely that they are singled out for both admiration and praise by a member of the building staff. "They're very approachable," he says. Itzler often entertains associates, inviting LeBron James and Jay-Z to poker games and Tom Brady and Gisele Bündchen to use the gym. "He's the coolest guy in the building," says the staffer, who adds that Itzler is referred to downstairs as Mr. Cool. "But he belongs in California surfing, not at Fifteen Central Park West."

⠶

It was hard for some to resist the chance to double what they'd paid for a Fifteen apartment. As the building rose, Realtor Dorothy Somekh's partner worried that the real estate market was peaking, so they put 7J on the market right after closing late in 2007. Thanks to Barry Salzberg, who'd just been named the CEO of Deloitte and Touche, the Big Four accounting firm, and his wife, Evelyn, who bought it, Somekh and partner walked away with a profit of more than $2 million on a $2.5 million investment.

Arie and Doreen Liebeskind's investment did even better, but their story, which includes a cameo appearance by Itzler and Blakely, was anything but happy at the end. The Liebeskinds had met as medical students in the mid-1960s. Arie was from Haifa, Israel; Doreen was the daughter of a fabric manufacturer in New York's garment district. They worked together for years as radiologists, eventually opening clinics near their home in Great Neck and later on Park Avenue. Shortly after they sold 255 acres to New York State for a state park, the Liebeskinds, who also owned a hotel suite in the Trump International, were taken to the Fifteen construction office to meet Robert A. M. Stern and found themselves among the first half dozen buyers in the building.

Music lovers, they'd decided to move into Manhattan full-time, but only if they could find a new home near Carnegie Hall and Lincoln Center. "I took them to lunch and said, 'This is what you should buy,'" says broker Douglas Russell. "I got them in quick and they got a little discount because they were in the first tranche." Through an LLC named Amanda for their dog, a rescued cockapoo, they paid $6.9 million for apartment 29C in the tower after Doreen was assured she could bring in a piano with a crane if it wouldn't fit in the elevator. When they left their clinic on Park Avenue, they could look across town and see the building going up. But in May 2006, eight months after they signed their contract, Arie, then sixty-eight, got sick and was diagnosed with cancer. A few months later, Doreen was stricken, too. She died first, early in 2007, and never saw her dream apartment. The ailing, grieving Arie did get to see it, but then put it on the market the day he closed.

"The question was how to price it," says one of their children, Marc, also a radiologist. "The value kept going up by the week—ten and a half million, no, eleven million dollars." It was finally listed for $12.5 million, and within a week there were two offers. Trying to break the deadlock, the brokers announced a deadline for final sealed bids. That's when Itzler flew Blakely in on a Marquis jet to see it—and submitted a winning bid of $14.1 million. Unfortunately, Josh Barbanel of the *New York Times*, who'd recently begun writing its Big Deal realty gossip column, had realized that 15CPW was making news, chose that week to write about it, and learned of the bidding

war for the apartment. Though he didn't print their names and some
of the numbers were off, Barbanel disclosed Itzler and Blakely's bid,
and when Itzler saw the item, "he pulled out," says Marc Liebeskind.
The runner-up, an LLC called Fifteen Timber Trail, won the apartment for $13.8 million. Behind it was Parag Saxena, CEO of a pri-
vate equity firm, who lived on Timber Trail in Rye, New York. The
Liebeskinds "doubled their money to the penny," says Russell, but
Arie didn't live to enjoy it. He died two days before Saxena signed
his contract.

Unlike the Liebeskinds, lots of buyers flipped quietly—and the
profits they made were a clear indication that Fifteen was amazingly
unaffected by the economic turmoil that had turned other cities, and
other buildings, into real estate sinkholes. The building was also so
immediately desirable that its co-op–like thirty-two-page package
of transfer requirements didn't prove a deterrent to resales. Buyers had to jump through twenty-three hoops and offer up personal
and financial references, bank and brokerage account numbers, the
names of schools they'd attended and clubs they belonged to, fill out
a financial-disclosure form and back it up with monthly bank and
brokerage statements, *and* acknowledge they'd read and agreed to
seven pages of single-spaced house rules. They also had to pay two
months' common charges as a transfer fee, a $1,000 nonrefundable
move-in fee, an additional $2,500 move-in deposit, $1,400 to Brown
Harris Stevens for a credit report and application processing, and a
deposit to ensure that all closing documents would be completed.
The only difference from the co-op admission process is the absence
of a board interview. But even though one top-tier broker calls the
process "brutal, ludicrous, anal," there is no indication that a buyer
has ever balked over 15CPW's requirements.

Brian France, the CEO and chairman of NASCAR, who'd signed
a $10.8 million deal for 34A in the tower five months after his star
driver Jeff Gordon bought in the house, sold for $12.5 million to

India-born, Nebraska-raised Gotham Makker, a onetime port-folio manager for Ken Griffin's Citadel hedge fund, and his wife, Vicky, a gynecological-cancer doctor at Memorial Sloan-Kettering. They'd moved to 15CPW from Time Warner, where they'd bought an apartment from Fifteen's Joseph Betesh and Joanna Cutler. First, they bought a small rear apartment, selling it when they moved upstairs. Makker soon joined the 15CPW condo board.

Richard Fields, a casino and hotel developer, flipped 38A, which he'd bought for $13.6 million, for $27 million, to a faceless corpo-ration. A year into the Great Recession, the Israeli energy entrepre-neur Eliahu Zahavi sold his $4 million unit for $7.35 million in cash to Larry Ruskin, a retired businessman from Calgary, Canada.

Though Ruskin was upset when a brief bidding war forced him to up his offer for the place by thousands, his distress soon faded. "You keep seeing the prices going up," he says with a satisfied smile. The biggest negative about the building, he adds, is the letters from real estate brokers urging him to sell. "A day doesn't go by you don't get two or three," he says.

The desire that motivated those letters and at least some of the flips was surely stirred by the owners of three trophy units who tried to sell early and cash out big. The noise their listings made was am-plified in the echo chamber of Manhattan real estate—and sealed Fifteen's reputation as the world's richest new building. In May 2008, still playing catch-up with the *New York Post*, Josh Barbanel caused a sensation when he led his *New York Times* column with the scoop that a $100 million offer had been made for a Fifteen pent-house. Appropriately, perhaps, the story came from the apartment owner himself, a biotech hedgie who has seen more than his share of bad publicity.

Lindsay Rosenwald comes from Abington, a suburb of Philadel-phia, attended Penn State, where he studied economics, then spent two years in health care before enrolling in medical school at Temple. But even there, he kept a hand in finance. "I put my student-loan money in a brokerage account," he says, "and started investing in health care and biotech. I made a lot of money." Nonetheless, he pursued medicine, interning in his hometown and then setting up a suburban practice. "The two and a half worst years of my life," he says. In 1985, he quit and got a job at an investment bank as a junior analyst of pharmaceutical and biotechnology companies. A fellow analyst who knew that the diminutive, curly-haired, and sharp-eyed Rosenwald wanted a wife and family pressed him to meet Rivki Davis. She was one of four daughters of J. Morton "Morty" Davis, né Davidowitz, the son of a pushcart peddler.

A Harvard Business School graduate, Morty Davis joined D. H. Blair, an investment bank, in 1961. Blair, which had its roots in the garment business, was known as an aggressive firm, and Davis fit right in. By 1966, he'd made himself into a brand of sorts, soliciting clients for Blair by advertising the *Davis Letter*, which that year discussed "inflation . . . the Viet Nam War . . . the economy . . . the stock market . . . Elizabeth Taylor . . . the New York Yankees . . . and what you as an investor should do right now!" By 1968, he was Blair's president, quoted in the *Wall Street Journal* predicting market trends.

Rosenwald and Rivki Davis went out on a few dates. He thought her stunning. But as an Orthodox Jew, she feared a romance with someone less religious. Still, impressed with his professional skills (he'd found a promising diet drug in Europe and created a company to try to bring it to market in America), in 1986 she recruited Rosenwald to Blair, where she was her father's in-house lawyer. "They were big in biotech and wanted a medical doctor who understood medical technologies," Lindsay says. "We worked there together for a while and then we became involved romantically."

By the end of 1988, they were married and had a child when Rosenwald was named a managing director of the firm, heading a team charged with finding more medical advances worthy of investment.

"To make money honestly on Wall Street, you have to find legitimate inefficiencies in a business" and exploit them, he says. When
he decided to bet on unproven drugs that couldn't gain strong pat-
ent protection in America (meaning the companies that marketed
them would have only short exclusivity periods), "some companies
laughed at me," he recalls, but he bet that even without those protec-
tions, a good new drug could quickly make a fortune, and after Blair
took his first company, Interneuron, public, its stock leapt from fifty
cents to $50 a share, the company was worth $2 billion, and Rosenwald was briefly considered the richest man in biotechnology, worth
about $675 million.

Rosenwald says he'd "always wanted my own shop" and, in July
1995, left Blair to found Paramount BioCapital, a venture capital
business. He says his departure was unrelated to issues like those
reported in a front-page article in the *Wall Street Journal* in 1991,
which revealed an SEC (and National Association of Securities
Dealers) investigation of Morty Davis and D. H. Blair for what the
paper called a "churn and burn" scheme to pump up the value of
newly issued stocks, then dump them for big profits before they fell
in value. The *Journal* also revealed that NASD had fined the firm
two years earlier for unfair pricing of stock; that a year before that,
two Blair clients had brought a $3 million civil-racketeering suit
against it; and that in 1986 a Blair customer had charged Davis with
breach of contract and won a $3 million jury verdict. Davis's trou-
bles with regulators went back even further. In 1973, the Securities
and Exchange Commission had charged that he and Blair had illegally used insider information while trading in a biomedical stock.
"What's the secret of his success?" *Forbes* asked in the mid-1980s.
"Better you shouldn't ask."

Separated from Blair, if not his father-in-law, Rosenwald won
both fervent admirers and detractors as he built Paramount into a
merchant and investment bank and asset management firm. The

crash of Interneuron after a similar drug to its Redux was found to be dangerous and Redux was abruptly pulled from the market has often been used as a stick to beat him. So while several websites of unclear origins hail him as a great leader in biotech, thanks to his investments in clinical research and drug development, others have charged that his investment success stories are balanced by "evident abysmal failures," as the *Seeking Alpha* stock-market-opinion website put it late in 2012; the stories of some of those companies, the "enticing smoke screens" used to promote them, and the subsequent "dilution" of their value "through stock issuance and bad financing deals" harken back to the pump-and-dump charges leveled against Rosenwald's father-in-law.

"It's easy to take potshots at people on Wall Street, unfortunately," says Rosenwald, who proved the *Seeking Alpha* story to be false and had it removed from the site. Attacks on him continue all over the Internet, as well as in several books, that reach a finding of guilt by association with his father-in-law. "What am I going to do? Divorce my wife?" he asks. "Morty's a wonderful guy, a wonderful father-in-law, a wonderful business associate." Rosenwald admits he hired "reputation management" professionals to create those websites that extol him on the Internet. But he clearly prefers to defend his own record, first in venture capital with Paramount and then, since 2009, as the cofounder of OpusPoint Partners, a biotech-focused hedge fund.

Rosenwald was among the first twenty buyers at 15CPW, picking up the A-line duplex on the eighteenth and nineteenth floors of the house for $30 million on the day of the September 2005 groundraising after watching the block for years. He decided against one of the tower penthouses and chose his duplex despite its $30 million price because "it's more a painting than an apartment," he says. "It's a very limited asset. You can never put a price on it. I didn't know if I was overpaying at the time. But I was one hundred percent certain that over the long run the rate of return would be fabulous."

As major donors to Republicans, to medical and homeless charities, yeshivas, and a Torah-study website, the Rosenwalds would fit right in with their neighbors at 15CPW, but they live in Lawrence, a Long Island suburb favored by religious Jews, near Rivki's father. Lindsay never planned to flip; he had the apartment decorated even though he only used it "very occasionally," he says, usually on the nights he played with an Orthodox Jewish ice hockey team at a rink in Manhattan. Then he was injured and stopped playing, and "my wife wasn't rushing to move back into the city."

Meantime, a broker had called and asked what he'd sell the apartment for. In a second call, she offered $95 million, but then she never called back. "So I didn't think it was real," Rosenwald said. Nonetheless, word of the call made it into broker gossip, and Barbanel of the *Times* heard about it, called Rosenwald, and reported that he'd said he'd actually gotten five or six calls offering as much as $100 million, but turned them all down. He also told the reporter that he'd heard of a $125 million offer on another apartment.

Two weeks later, Barbanel published a follow-up report that two Fifteen apartments were "quietly" on the market as so-called whisper or pocket listings, unadvertised and unofficial. One was Rosenwald's. Barbanel said he was looking for $90 million. The other was penthouse 40B, which was being offered for $80 million by its owner, who, the reporter speculated, was Amit Ben-Haim, a London investor who'd sold an Israeli biomedical company to Johnson & Johnson some years earlier for $400 million.

Speculation about those apartments rose even higher a few days later when Dolly Lenz, a broker with a taste for publicity, said in a price-inflating speech that she knew of four 15CPW whisper listings, with one asking $150 million. If there were such listings, they never surfaced, but Lenz got her name in lights by stoking the frenzy.

Rosenwald never did list his apartment. "I didn't buy it as an investment," he says, though he adds that if someone made him a "ridiculous" offer, "I'd probably take it." Instead, about nine months after the $90 million flurry, he rented it out for $75,000 a month to a quiet businessman he won't identify. But the tenant, Peter Fine, a real estate developer, should know that Rosenwald still hopes to convince his wife to move in and keeps close watch on his investment through binoculars mounted in his office a few blocks away, focused on his penthouse.

A few days after Lenz gave her provocative speech, penthouse 40B came out of the shadows, when it was officially listed for $80 million. But the owner wasn't Amit Ben-Haim, even though the deed was in the name of a Geneva company that lists him as chairman; the apartment actually belonged to his brother Shlomo, an Israeli scientist who, likely not coincidentally, is a friend of Eyal Ofer's.

Born in Haifa, Shlomo Ben-Haim studied nuclear physics at Technion, the oldest and most renowned university in Israel, and continued his education with a medical degree with a cardiology specialty and several doctorates. After his mandatory service in the Israel Defense Forces, he would teach medicine at both Technion and Harvard. At the former he met his wife, now a professor of nuclear medicine in London. They have four children and split their time between London and Caesarea, an Israeli coastal town named by King Herod for the Roman emperor Caesar Augustus, where Ben-Haim owns a $30 million villa.

He first worked as a heart doctor in Haifa, where, in concert with an American investment banker named Lewis Pell, he began founding companies such as InStent, which marketed his invention, one of the first stents, the mesh tubes that keep blood flowing through vessels constricted by disease. After selling that company for $200 million in 1996, Ben-Haim and Pell became serial entrepreneurs. Their biggest success was Biosense, based on another invention of Ben-

Haim's, a catheter-like device that is inserted into the groin and sent to the heart through veins to give doctors a three-dimensional view of electrical activity within that organ and guide diagnosis and cardiovascular surgery.

When a subsidiary of Johnson & Johnson bought Biosense for a reported $500 million in 1998, Shlomo got J&J shares worth $75 million, and brother Amit, who'd invested with him, walked away with another $88 million. Another investor in Biosense was a fund controlled by the Ofer brothers. Pell and Ben-Haim's subsequent ventures created $1.33 billion in equity, with Ben-Haim's share estimated at $200 million.

Inevitably, perhaps, with that kind of money in play, he found himself entangled in litigation. "He has been sued twice by entrepreneurs of companies he founded, who accused him of stealing their assets," Gail Weinreb wrote in *Globes*, an Israeli business newspaper, and "once by his former partner and friend, Lewis Pell, for alleged unfair distribution of assets between them." In a 2004 suit, Ben-Haim was accused of making false accusations of sexual harassment. More recently, the founders of RF Dynamics, whom he'd removed from their posts, accused him of calling them thieves, and behaving in "an extremely deceitful and fraudulent way." In 2012, the Israeli government sued him and another partner for stealing from a government-run research center technology that allowed cells, tissues, and organs to be frozen. Ben-Haim denied the claims in the RF Dynamics suit, and a spokesman for the company involved in the latter case described the charges as "scandalous" and Kafkaesque.

Fellow entrepreneurs defended Ben-Haim, albeit anonymously. "Shlomo is a man of black and white," one said. "So you're either with him or not with him, in which case you're out." Ben-Haim himself is notoriously press shy. Asked once if he was harsh in business dealings, he responded with a modest smile and only said, "I have four children to support."

Ben-Haim agreed to buy penthouse 40B at Fifteen for $21.5 million three weeks after sales began, closed in April 2008, and listed it early that June. It stayed on the market until November, when it was suddenly delisted. In the interim, Ben-Haim had found a willing buyer. Dmitry Rybolovlev, the Russian oligarch who would eventually buy Sandy Weill's penthouse, ostensibly for his daughter, had been in New York and Florida with his wife, looking for real estate. He wasn't fond of winters in their home city of Geneva and was hoping to find a warm place to spend the season, as well as a pied-à-terre in New York, or so he said. He checked out the Plaza but really wanted to buy in 15CPW, even making an unsolicited offer for Sandy Weill's penthouse. "That guy was running all around the building, trying to buy people's apartments," says another penthouse owner.

Born in Perm, an industrial city in the Ural Mountains, Rybolovlev planned to follow his parents, both doctors, into medicine, studying to become a cardiologist like Ben-Haim while working as a cardiac-unit orderly and nurse, and marrying a fellow medical student, who quickly gave birth to their first child, a daughter named Ekaterina. Dmitry became a local doctor and prepared to join the Communist Party, but with the advent of perestroika, or restructuring, under Soviet leader Mikhail Gorbachev, some dormant capitalist instinct arose, and instead, he went into business with his father, setting up a company to sell alternative medical treatments using magnets.

With the Soviet economy teetering on ruin, Rybolovlev found himself bartering treatments for goods instead of money and became a middleman for whatever was on hand—bringing beer from Moscow to Perm, for instance. A natural strategist, he realized he needed working capital to grow his accidental business career and "began to search for a new, lucrative niche," a colleague told the Russian magazine *Ogonyok*.

In 1992, Rybolovlev became one of the first graduates of a Finance Ministry–sanctioned broker course in Moscow, earning gov-

ernment certification as a securities dealer. In the Wild West days
after the dissolution of the Soviet Union, with Boris Yeltsin as the
new leader of the smaller Russian Federation, the shares of what had
been state-owned industrial enterprises were distributed to workers. Returning to Perm, Rybolovlev opened an investment company,
offered local businesses his services to keep track of all their new
co-owners, and like other oligarchs-in-training around the country
started buying up their shares on the cheap. By 1994, he had his own
bank, Credit FH, and soon became its chairman; under its auspices,
he made an agreement with the local committee that managed state
property to keep an inventory of the shares of Uralkali, a former
state-run enterprise that mined potassium and manufactured potash
for fertilizer. In partnership with the deputy chairman of that local
committee, he located the shareholders and began to buy their Uralkali shares. Foreigners were trying to do the same thing, but Rybolovlev had an edge. He knew the local mentality and would pull
semitrucks filled with the Russian cars called Ladas up to the gates
of Uralkali and other factories and offer them to workers for their
shares. In exchange for their acquiescence, he would buy apartments
for factory bosses.

In 1996, after Yeltsin was reelected over a Communist opponent, Rybolovlev became Uralkali's chairman and began to turn the
company into a potash powerhouse, combining it with a competitor from Belarus before offering its stock back to the public in 2007.
Rybolovlev sold 12.75 percent of his Uralkali holdings, cashing out
about $1 billion.

His ascent to the ranks of billionaires wasn't smooth, though.
In the mad-bad Russian 1990s, enemies lurked in both the criminal
shadows and the corrupt bureaucracy. In 1993, he moved his family
to Odessa, Florida, and later that year (or in 1995—reports differ),
he deposited them and presumably some of his money in Switzerland, hired security guards to protect his parents and all the direc-

tors of his businesses, and began forcing criminal elements out of his companies. "He himself left the bank only behind a live shield of bodyguards," said a friend. "Identical cars with identical license plates" registered to him roamed the city to foil ambushes.

He was right to worry. One of those cars was attacked, and in May 1996 he and his partner at Uralkali were arrested as the masterminds of a murder. Evgeny Panteleymonov, the only one of Rybolovlev's executives to refuse bodyguards, had been shot in the doorway of his own apartment building. Oleg Lomakin, arrested for the shooting, won a promise of reduced charges for saying Rybolovlev put him up to it. This murky murder plot was allegedly hatched because Rybolovlev felt Panteleymonov had threatened his income stream by telling him that a joint venture had been taken over by criminals.

The potash prince was jailed on charges of conspiracy to murder and spent eleven months in prison. For the first month and a half, he was moved to a new cell every week in what he considered an effort to break him. In response, he announced his medical credentials and started treating his fellow inmates, winning a position of respect in each cell. The day he turned thirty, all the local radio stations played his favorite song, "Hotel California" by the Eagles. Offered his freedom if he would sell his shares in Uralkali, he refused. He later told the Russian edition of *Forbes* that he was ready to spend ten years in jail and wouldn't give up what he'd worked for. Finally, Rybolovlev was released on bail of a billion rubles, and at the end of 1997, Russia's Supreme Court dismissed the charges against both executives and found Lomakin guilty of organizing the murder; his puppeteers, assuming they ever existed, were never identified.

"I prefer to regard this as a mistake of the law enforcement agencies," Rybolovlev said in a rare interview. He added that his attitude never wavered. "When you're afraid, that's the beginning of the end. Business and fear are two incompatible things, so you must know how to control this feeling. As soon as this becomes impossible, anyone can come to a proprietor and take everything away from him. This means that you must be absolutely confident: no matter what happens, you won't give away what's yours."

In a profile of Rybolovlev in *Kommersant*, a Russian newspaper, he is described as "a totally lonely person," who'd by then cut ties with all his old associates, spent most of his time on airplanes, and a week or less a month with his family (they'd had a second daughter, Anna, in 2001). He was "a sea of charisma but with steel teeth and the cold gaze of a professional appraiser. . . . a matchless and most rare intellect of a strategist and at the same time blindness to people and their human qualities."

Rybolovlev's interest in American real estate emerged in the summer of 2008 with his purchase of a mansion in Palm Beach, Florida, from Donald Trump for $95 million. He bought the property through an LLC and called it an investment. Around the same time, he offered Shlomo Ben-Haim's brokers $75 million for his 15CPW penthouse and his offer was accepted. He even transferred a deposit and contracts were drawn up. But Ben-Haim got cold feet. It was, a real estate lawyer speculates, most likely after he learned of the serious tax implications of a short-term capital gain by certain types of corporations owned by foreign nationals. Several months later, in March 2009, Prominence Acquisition LLC was formed as the successor by merger of Prominence Corp., which owned the apartment. Three weeks after that, it changed its name to Prominence LLC. Simultaneously, the penthouse reappeared in the database of listings used by New York City brokers. But economic reality had by then come even to Fifteen; the most insane phase of the flipping frenzy ended and Ben-Haim's new price was more realistic: $47.5 million.

Dmitry Rybolovlev was no longer interested, but he'd be back at Fifteen before long. Not that Ben-Haim cared. It took next to no time to sell the penthouse for $37 million to a limited liability company named after the Russian city Novgorod. So it was easy to assume, as the real estate blog *Curbed* did, that the "mysterious buyer" had "Russian overtones."

Though Rybolovlev's interest in the building was still a secret shared only by insiders, Fifteen was no secret among the newly enriched Russians who'd been bringing their money to Manhattan for years already. Like many of the world's new rootless, wealthy nomads, they were buying houses all over, traveling between them at a moment's notice, and sometimes using them to avoid taxes or other claims on their purses. Before long, Rybolovlev's wife would accuse him of buying US real estate to hide money from her.

⌘

"New York City has always been a port town," says Will Zeckendorf. "Foreigners always felt welcome here." Between a third and half of the "Russians" who bought from the 15CPW sponsor are, more accurately, Eastern European Jews who'd left the Soviet Union years, even decades, earlier, fleeing a society they deemed anti-Semitic. But others who kicked Fifteen's tires came from the post-Soviet era and were closely scrutinized, say members of the 15CPW team. Was their money real? And where did it come from? "We definitely turned some down," a development team source says carefully.

Eyal Ofer is more candid: "I don't think we allowed Russians to be first." They did what they could to ensure that early buyers would be "an inducement and not a deterrent. Since we were all intending to live there, we wanted to make sure that at least the first round [would be] people whom we'd like to be with. We wanted to have the right group of people, a base of quality, not of pure money. We weren't just selling square footage. We created a community." They were able to use the frenzied desire for apartments as an excuse to fend off some buyers. "They were told that there's competition on the apartment," says Global Holdings executive Samuel Kellner. "The hype was on, so it was very believable that there [were] competing bids. So people of certain disqualifications were told that their apartment was sold to others. There was an attempt to keep the building American, the buying group distinctive."

Among the real estate lawyers watching this process with interest was Edward Mermelstein, who'd left his native Ukraine in 1974 to get an education in New York. In the last decade, he'd built a thriving practice advising what he calls "high-net-worth" individuals, mostly Eastern Europeans, but also Germans, Italians, Koreans, and Chinese, on the purchase of "second to fifth homes" in New York City. In 2001, several of his clients had contracts at Time Warner, but after September 11, "everybody took off," he says. "They were very scared the New York market would collapse" and moved their money to Cyprus, Switzerland, London, and even Miami, instead.

But a counterbalancing force was at work, particularly for Russians. "They understood that Russia was a very unstable place, and as quick as they made money, they could lose it," so by 2003, they were eyeing Manhattan again. Mermelstein advised them to avoid cooperatives. "They have no way of showing credit history," he says. "There was no history. Why start the process and subject clients to an impossibility?" So Eastern Europeans focused like lasers on high-end condos, and their wealth changed the market. "Pricing has skyrocketed because they were willing to pay whatever it took," says Mermelstein. "They go to developers and say, 'You're asking fifty million dollars? Here's sixty, but we close next week.'" Like so many others, Mermelstein had watched the Mayflower lot and alerted clients as soon as it was in play. "The clients that missed out on Time Warner understood it would not be good to make the same mistake twice." But he understood that the 15CPW developers weren't exactly eager to sell to them. "It was definitely kept quiet," he says. "You had the titans grab the top apartments."

Still, some Russians did manage to infiltrate the ranks of early buyers. Natalia Pirogova, a real estate investment-fund manager and developer who was then building a hotel-condo on Madison Avenue, was the first buyer of 16M, a small two-bedroom overlooking Broadway, which she rented out, and later she bought 27C, a much larger unit, from Rosita and Ricardo Leong, two ethnic Chinese based in the Philippines, where the seventy-seven-year-old Leong, a graduate of Fordham University, is a director of several companies. Pirogova rented it out to Andrew Roberts and Susan Gilchrist. Roberts, an author, historian, and broadcast personality, is a self-described "reactionary," a noted neoconservative and supporter of Israel. The *New Republic* once described him as "a caricature of a caricature of the old imperial historians." He is also the heir to a British dairy and a Kentucky Fried Chicken franchise fortune. He followed his wife to America when the former journalist was named the CEO of Brunswick Group, an international corporate public relations firm. A business associate of Pirogova's, Luiza Dubrovsky, bought and occupies an adjacent unit, and Marina Martyslane and Z. Richard Mecik, who run an airport-equipment supplier, own a small two-bedroom unit over Broadway, which they rent out for $16,500 a month.

The most important Russian in the building—at least until Dmitry Rybolovlev came along—doesn't live there, either, but apparently his son does. With an estimated $1.6 billion fortune, Valery Mikhailovich Kogan ranked number 804 on the 2012 *Forbes* list of the world's billionaires, and number 61 among its Russian members, thanks to his co-ownership of a company that holds a seventy-five-year contract to run Moscow Domodedovo Airport.

Born in Ukraine, Kogan is a former Soviet navy man who'd studied economics and worked as a diplomat. In the 1990s, he and a partner, whose father reportedly had ties to the failing Soviet government, formed a company called East Line and, like Rybolovlev, grew wealthy, in their case by moving merchandise between Russia and China and dealing in real estate, a business that first brought them to the attention of authorities, who accused them of deceitful practices when they built homes on a former chicken farm near Moscow.

Kogan moved to America after Russian authorities disputed the airport lease with East Line in 2005 and threatened to nationalize it. Ever since, it's been unclear if East Line owns, leases, or merely operates the airport. After a terrorist attack there early in 2011, Kogan and his partner refused to confirm that they owned the airport, apparently out of fear they might be held accountable for the breach in its security. Later that year, East Line said Kogan's partner owned the airport through a company based in Cyprus. Making matters even murkier, *Haaretz*, an Israeli newspaper, alleges that Kogan is connected to the secret services in Russia and repeats vague claims from the Russian press that he is a close but "secret" friend and skiing buddy of Russian president Vladimir Putin, while an investigative TV show in Russia claimed its government is persecuting East Line.

What is sure is that Kogan collects luxury real estate. Public records indicate he owns a large villa near a golf course in the wealthy Silicon Valley suburb of Atherton, California, and a smaller home in Fairfax, Virginia. He also owns a $30 million apartment near Tel Aviv; five beachfront villas in Caesarea (which he razed and is replacing with a fifty-four-thousand-square-foot complex), just down the road from Israeli prime minister Benjamin Netanyahu's vacation place; and an $18.5 million estate in Greenwich, Connecticut, which the Kogans also hoped to raze and replace with a home so massive, even by the loose local standards, that it set off protests ("It's not a residence, it's an industrial project," said one neighbor). Kogan's plans in Greenwich were subsequently scaled back considerably.

More relevant to 15CPW is Kogan's ownership of a $10 million duplex apartment on the thirty-fourth and thirty-fifth floors of the Zeckendorfs' 515 Park, likely the reason he was able to get around the quiet ban on Russians and buy both penthouse 40A next door to Ben-Haim's, for which Kogan agreed to pay almost $23 million, and a $2 million one-bedroom unit in the base of the tower, early in 2006. According to a member of the building staff, neither Kogan nor his wife is in residence. Instead, the staffer says, the sprawling penthouse is used by one of their two sons, Alex, an aspiring singer-songwriter who, *New York*'s Michael Idov wrote, has "been trying and failing to launch an awesomely bad rock career with Dad's millions."

Neither Kogan père nor fils attracts much attention at 15CPW. But another Russian, this one a renter, got the staff's attention when his father-in-law came to visit with a large security detail. Nikita Shashkin rented apartment 8B from Gerald Ross, a litigator who specializes in suing law firms on behalf of other lawyers. Ross invests in condos on the side and also owns unit 8A (for a total expenditure of $28 million). Shashkin, who was Ross's tenant in 2012, worked for a Russian bank in Manhattan. In 2010, he'd married Luvov Khloponina at a lavish event where Joe Cocker sang, and among the guests were oligarch Mikhail Prokhorov, owner of the Brooklyn Nets, and Yuri Luzhkov, then the mayor of Moscow, attracted, no doubt, by the father of the bride, Aleksandr Khloponin, a former employee of both Prokhorov's Norilsk Nickel company and the same bank where his son-in-law works. Presumably, Khloponin needs bodyguards because he's a deputy prime minister of the Russian Federation.

It was natural to assume that Novgorod LLC hid a Russian, too, but the man behind it isn't Russian; he's an American-born, London-based banker—and was once one of the best paid in the world. According to the *Guardian*'s annual survey of executive compensation at top public companies, he made £70 million between 2006 and 2008. He also scored a £10 million profit selling his seven-bedroom London town house in 2007, when he decided to move his family to New York. There, outside of banking circles, he was a relative unknown. Which may explain why his name never appeared on the oft-published lists of 15CPW's wealthiest tenants.

Only after he entered the rogues' gallery of international finance was the face behind Novgorod LLC unmasked: Robert Edward "Bob" Diamond III. When Diamond bought Ben-Haim's penthouse for $37 million, he was the CEO of Barclays Capital, the investment arm of the global bank. Three years and one month later, in summer 2012, he was CEO of all of Barclays when he quit his job after becoming the poster child of the LIBOR interest-rate-fixing scandal. By then, he'd moved into his apartment. But first, he'd stalked the building like a cat, visiting Goldman partner Ravi Singh's apartment multiple times before making a lowball bid Singh rejected. Diamond also rented 9G with his wife, Jennifer. But finally, he became an owner and embarked on a renovation. His applications to the city estimated its cost at just under $1.8 million. A small price to pay (especially compared to Rybolovlev's) for an alpha dwelling in which to lick one's wounds and, perhaps, plot a comeback.

The last of the spectacular but failed flip-outs at 15CPW crept onto the market just after Ben-Haim sent Rybolovlev packing. In November 2008, one of the duplexes in the house was said to be available via a whisper listing for between $75 and $90 million. Richard Ullman had bought the smallest of the three duplexes atop the house, apartment 18B, between Lindsay Rosenwald and Idan Ofer's larger units, for $23.5 million, early during sales. A onetime pharmacist, he'd designed one of America's first prescription benefit plans in the 1970s, then made a fortune as a founder of two companies that managed those programs. He sold the first of those for more than $500 million in 2002 and was running the second when he bought at 15CPW.

Though he would later be described as a devoted family man, Ullman bought the apartment after getting a divorce from the mother of his three children and marrying a younger woman he'd been dating since 2001. His new wife, Barbara Marcin, was a Harvard MBA who worked as an investment fund portfolio manager and lived in a condo of her own at Broadway and Sixty-Second Street. By the time of their marriage, Ullman owned a home and an apartment in New Jersey, a home in the country club community of Windermere, Florida, and a condo in the Trump International. The Ullman Family Partnership, which included his two sons and a daughter, had bought its first apartment at the Trump in 2001 and sold it after buying a second on the forty-fourth floor for $8 million in 2003. Two and half years later, the same family entity bought the 15CPW duplex, apparently as an investment.

In 2008, the Ullmans moved to Florida and the next spring made their Fifteen listing official. Though the apartment appeared on a broker's website at an undisclosed price, the *New York Times* reported Ullman wanted $55 million. Some speculated that Ullman was selling due to financial reversals, but that seems unlikely; a financial statement he'd prepared in 2006 showed he was then worth almost $460 million. (The recession barely affected Fifteen, but its effects were briefly felt; Ullman's price drop, like Ben-Haim's, likely reflected the new reality.) Multiple offers followed, but only one reached his magic number of $50 million. Unfortunately, that buyer, Merryl Tisch, a New York heiress, backed out for reasons unknown.

The Trump aerie remained the Ullmans' New York residence until October 2009, when they sold it for $16 million to a trust associated with Linda Mirels, the daughter of Nathan Kirsh, a property tycoon from South Africa and Swaziland, and then the wife of Hilton Mirels, an orthopedic surgeon in Westchester. The Mirelses already owned an apartment, 8D, at 15CPW, for which they'd paid just over $14 million.

In June 2011, Ullman was diagnosed with cancer, began chemotherapy at a New York hospital, and occupied his 15CPW apartment on a sustained basis for the first time. In the interim, it had gone on and off the market, says a source close to the Ullmans. Unfortunately, that September he learned his treatments had failed and his cancer had spread; he was soon admitted to a hospital and spent his last five days there.

Six months later, some of what followed was revealed when Barbara Ullman filed suit against her husband's children, claiming that she was entitled to his share of his last business, and $3 million he'd promised to her in writing, and that his sons had broken his promise to give her the Florida home outright as well as lifetime use of the duplex. In her complaint, she claimed that, at the time Ullman learned he was ill, he had not written a will since 1993 and was only reminded of that fact when an attorney representing one of his sons showed up at his home with a new one Ullman had no hand in drafting. Though he was too ill to read it, Barbara continued, he signed it anyway, albeit with a visibly shaky hand, and only read it the next day, when he decided it would have to be redrafted because it didn't give her enough.

That same day, Barbara charged, he told his two sons he wanted her to get more, and in response one of them uncovered the eighteen-page prenuptial agreement the couple had signed before they married and demanded she read it again. "That's all you're getting," the son allegedly said. According to Barbara, neither she nor Ullman had even bothered to keep a copy, and so, to ensure she got her due, Ullman had his will revised, increasing the sum he'd agreed to leave to her in a trust from $25 million to $40 million. Though he signed that revision six days before he died, his widow also claimed he'd promised to redraft it entirely once he recovered, as he was sure he would. After their father died, her complaint continued, Ullman's two sons invaded her Florida home, changed the locks, and refused to give Barbara access to it or any of her belongings within. Not only did they refuse to let her stay there, they hired security guards to keep her out when they thought she might show up.

In an answer to the lawsuit, Kenneth Ullman denied most of the claims it contained, but, besides swearing that his father had, in fact, begun writing a new will prior to the cancer diagnosis, did not offer an alternate version of the events around his death. The lawsuit, which was filed in a Florida state court, apparently hinged on Barbara's proving she was a permanent resident of Florida, a notion the children rejected. Soon, the case was moved to a federal court, where a document indicating that the matter had been settled via mediation was filed two months after Barbara Ullman first sued her stepchildren.

Early in 2013, Barbara still occupied the Ullman Family Partnership's duplex at Fifteen, but someone close to the Ullman children predicted that her tenure there would be limited. By August, she was indeed gone, according to a building employee. When the duplex was listed in mid-October by Sandy Weill's broker, Kyle Blachmon, for $62.5 million, the first resale of one of its crowning duplexes began to feel imminent as well as inevitable.

Part Nine

TOP OF THE WORLD

For whosoever hath, to him shall be given,
and he shall have more abundance.

—MATTHEW 13:12

When Larry Ruskin, the retired Canadian oil and gas executive, bought his apartment at Fifteen Central Park West, Gregg Carlovich, the building's resident manager, told him that 168 of its 201 apartments had already been or were being renovated. In the end, most of the apartments were altered somehow, with the work ranging from mere decoration to gut renovation, and at any given moment a hundred separate jobs were in the pipeline between request and completion. Practically, that meant that normal life at 15CPW wouldn't begin for a year or two past the day the first buyers put keys into their doors. As with their planning, bidding, and building, the Zeckendorf brothers put a skilled team in place to deal with the transition from transactions to the takeover of the building by its residents. But they are understandably unwilling to discuss anything that happened after closings began.

Some hints can be found, however. "I facilitated the goals of the most exacting and demanding residential purchasers in the world along with their design and construction teams," Thor Thors, an independent project manager for developers, explains on his website. Her job as sponsor representative, says Margaret McAdams on her LinkedIn résumé, "required intensive and direct communication with a formidable cadre of Unit Owners, and with the project's governing entities, to establish a superior quality of life for those who chose to purchase a home in this premiere property."

Like Fifteen's architecture, its transition from a business deal to an apartment house worthy of its "formidable cadre" of "exacting and demanding" owners was a collaborative effort involving architects, engineers, interior designers, contractors, and Brown Harris Stevens, which has managed Fifteen since it opened. That effort actually began in the sales office, where some buyers wanted contractual "adjustments" to the design of their apartments. "If they wanted the world's biggest shower directly over someone else's living room, we tried to figure out how to make it work" ahead of time, since new buildings full of demanding, wealthy people can have "huge problems if you give them too much freedom," says a hand-over team member. "Our job was to prevent that from happening," usually by convincing the owner he didn't really want that bathroom after all.

Formal, detailed alteration requests weren't reviewed until after closings, and the first big requests were from the first owners who closed, and the rest of what the team member calls "the penthouse people—all these billionaires living on top of one another." They and their designers "make demands and we had to both keep the last construction on track and not be unduly influenced by powerful people wanting to do things their way. There were two things the Zeckendorfs wanted: first, that what they'd agreed to in the sales process was adhered to, and second, that personal influence, the who-is-more-important game, would not unduly influence what was going on." Each owner expected a dream apartment, and their hired hands were determined to give them what they wanted. The more alterations, the higher the fees they earned.

Negotiating the shoals of those relationships was a delicate art. "It's a very different type of clientele, and a certain decorum is expected," says Patricia Garza, a former girl Friday at Zeckendorf Development who was recruited to help with punch-list issues—the little details purchasers feel haven't been properly completed by the developers. Before closings, she "brought in a majority of the clients to see what needed attention, riding in the construction hoist a majority of the time," she says, then returning again to ensure "the work was done to their specifications."

Garza singles out Sandy Weill and his wife, Joan, as the nicest people she dealt with. "I have to say the people who were the most genuine and who you loved were the people like them that just have all they need and then some. I can see where I got that impression. I met them when they were staying in their chef's apartment, living in servants' quarters!" Garza is less forthcoming about those she didn't like. "It tended to be people who came by their millions all at once who were a little entitled," she says.

The team had to deal with everything from cracked marble and misaligned corners to the owner of a terraced apartment whose architect had decided "to put a forest on the roof," as one of the closers puts it. That architect came away horrified and wasn't alone in claiming that the Emperor of Condos wore shabby clothes. In the ranks of general contractors, there was lots of talk of Fifteen's growing pains. Bovis, the giant multinational construction contractor now called Lend Lease, was still in the building "fixing things that got mangled in construction," says a contractor on one of the early gut renovations. He thinks that where the Zeckendorfs abjured value engineering—the art of cutting corners—their builder's work was "junk" because "they had to come up with a way to hit their numbers." He saw three apartments, each of them finished "up to union and legal standards," he says, "but union residential work is generally garbage and the high end doesn't care about legal requirements. It wants perfect. Nothing was quite right. Entire apartments went into Dumpsters. The bathrooms weren't top tier. Nobody wanted base-level junk stone, mediocre Carrara, Calacatta gold." He felt the bathrooms had been designed to be demolished.

"It looks nice to someone who doesn't know better," says the contractor, citing a long list of immediate issues: floors off level, too-small pipes in heating and air-conditioning systems, inadequate subfloors, cheap hinges and levers, shoddy doors, and windows he compares unfavorably to the brass ones at 740 Park, where he has also worked. There, windows are heavy as guillotines, he says, in a bit of unintended irony. At 15CPW, "they're not great. They're certainly not the best in New York. They're acceptable. But they're a cheap tie on a good suit."

A member of the development team scoffs at these complaints. "Contractors complain so they can pull everything out and charge two thousand dollars per square foot to replace it," he says. "No developer spends that much. It's an unfair comparison."

The renovation teams were more justified in being frustrated by the gridlock caused by dozens of contractors. Everyone was renovating simultaneously. Freight came from the street, down to the basement, which seemed like a cholesterol-filled artery. Then, it had to go upstairs to apartments, but the elevator configuration—two cores per building, two elevators per core (the apartments in the base of the Broadway building had an elevator of their own), with only one per core equipped for service use—proved woefully inadequate to the task at hand. "Deliveries took four hours," says the contractor. "You had a rush of a hundred guys at once. You had guys on lockdown, collecting dust in the basement. Everyone was on the same schedule." Construction hours were limited: 9:00 a.m. to 4:30 p.m., with no loud noise before 10:00 a.m. Tempers flared because many construction crews are subject to penalties for delays.

As the ranks of high-profile owner-occupants swelled, things got rougher. One morning, Bob Costas came home off an overnight flight and wanted to get some sleep. Contractors working in apartments around his were asked to stop making noise. "It's not uncommon," the contractor sighs, "but you get nothing done in a two-and-a-half-hour workday." There were issues outside, too, particularly with the Century, which overlooked Fifteen's loading dock and service entrance. "The street was jammed with moving vehicles and tradespeople," says Penny Ryan, chairman of the local community board. "But street closures are pretty routine and the two buildings worked it out."

Those "daily inconveniences" were "nothing outstanding," agrees Roberta Gratz, the neighborhood activist who watched from the Century as sofas, artwork, and pianos that wouldn't fit in the elevators were hoisted up to apartments by cranes. Which doesn't mean that she considers 15CPW's occupants good neighbors. "What struck me was the excess," she says. She's also irked that many of them encourage their drivers to park illegally in the fire lane directly in front of Fifteen, which is clearly marked a no-standing zone. "They triple-park!" she complains. "It is nothing short of an outrage that both Trump International and Fifteen get unmatched parking privileges. Some days, there are a dozen limousines. They don't own the sidewalk and the streets, but they act as if they do." That limos do the same thing all over Manhattan gives Gratz no comfort. "It's the arrogance of wealth that gets too much respect in this city. It's symbolic of the divide that we live with. They don't play by the same rules and that offends me. It's an affront to urban democracy."

— ∞ —

In December 2009, fifty-four people were on the Fifteen payroll, led by the resident manager, his assistant, a chief engineer, a security manager, and a handyman. There were seven concierges, six doormen, eight white-gloved lobby attendants, three package-room attendants, eight porters, a maintenance man, four security guards, twelve part-time engineers, and an administrative assistant. Six people man Fifteen's lobbies by day, two each for the doors, concierge desks, and lobbies. Three more work the package room, and four porters and one or two engineers are always on duty. Another man is always stationed at the security entrance on Sixty-Second Street. The day shift runs from 7:00 a.m. to 3:00 p.m., the afternoon shift until 11:00 p.m. At night, the visible staff is cut in half and the pavilion off the motor courtyard closes and residents must enter on Central Park West. One employee predicted how a resident would react to the limited access: *I just bought an eighty-million-dollar condo and I want to drive into the courtyard. You gonna tell me no?*

The staff was hired and began assembling before the first closings, studying the building. First, they learned "the geography, so you know where you're going," says a former staffer. "Figuring out how to get people in and out without being seen. They want to come home and relax without any problems." That wasn't really a problem until spring 2008, when people first started to move in en masse. The elevators were "a nightmare," the ex-staffer says. "A lot of kinks had to be taken care of."

There were kinks both inside and outside: those complaints about the chauffeured cars stacked up out front, for instance. The former staffer doesn't think anyone cared about Roberta Gratz and her ilk. "There's an underground NYPD precinct across the street in the subway," he says. "*They* didn't want cars out front. They were ticketed, towed." Then, the powers-that-be at 15CPW "started greasing the wheels," he continues. "It became a corruption thing." The chauffeured cars still wait there.

The NYPD might just be outgunned at Fifteen. Security is tight—and for good reason. Members of the staff believe that terrorists have threatened, if not targeted, the building. Several of the high-profile in-house bankers have been threatened, too. One of them, Bob Diamond of Barclays, "had his private security team train us about what to watch out for," says the staffer. "Badly taped boxes, misspelled names. It was a bit ridiculous. I think Al Qaeda is a little more sophisticated than that."

But no one was taking any chances. Renter Alex "A-Rod" Rodriguez of the New York Yankees and owner Denzel Washington both used pseudonyms, the former for guests, the latter for deliveries. At New York's Department of Buildings, a clerk says 15CPW is classified as a "sensitive building," and unlike the files on most residential buildings in New York, its records and building plans can't be shown to just anybody who walks in and asks to see them.*

One absentee owner, a New Jersey pain doctor who rents out her rear tower apartment, worries the building has become so high-profile, its address alone makes her a target. Some who actually live there might really be targets. So private security men, many of them former NYPD cops, are everywhere, not just accompanying visiting Russian officials and the politicians who breeze through for fund-raisers.

Paparazzi are often outside, but they're not waiting for the bankers. Rather they are hoping for a week like the one in October 2011 when Alec Baldwin, Al Gore, and Bill Clinton came to 15CPW for a fund-raiser, Rick Perry visited a resident, and Robert Downey Jr., Robert De Niro, Lady Gaga, Tom Hanks and Rita Wilson, Bruce Springsteen, and Jake Gyllenhaal all passed through, en route to a sixtieth birthday party for Sting, who'd finally moved in after massive renovations in his duplex.

The photographers come by "twenty-four/seven," says an ex-staffer, often waiting "in cars across the street with superzooms. I've seen myself on *TMZ*." But they mostly focused on the building's handful of high-profile renters such as Rodriguez, and the actors

---

*New York City's Department of Law did not respond to repeated requests for confirmation that a "sensitive" designation exists.

Kelsey Grammer and Mark Wahlberg, and not on its less famous if far more powerful owner-occupants. The stars may take a different view. "For celebrities, the money people are celebrities," says the staff member. "You see it when they come for dinner. They're nervous." Who wouldn't be when, as once happened, Sandy Weill hosted Bill Gates and Warren Buffett?

Aside from its resident music and film stars, Lloyd Blankfein of Goldman Sachs is the highest-profile person in the building, usually named, alongside Sting, Denzel Washington, and his fellow banker Sandy Weill, among its marquee names. Born in the South Bronx, the child of a bakery truck driver who reinvented himself as a postal clerk after getting fired and a receptionist at a burglar-alarm company, Blankfein is one of 15CPW's notable self-made men.

He was raised in a housing project in Brooklyn, where he shared a bedroom with his grandmother and earned spending money working as a lifeguard and as a hot dog vendor at Yankee Stadium. He attended a public high school once renowned for its accomplished Jewish graduates, where he was a teacher's pet, as witty as he was smart. Though his school and the neighborhood around it were deteriorating (Thomas Jefferson High would later be shut down due to its low graduation rate), Blankfein skipped a grade and graduated at the top of his class at age sixteen. Then came Harvard and Harvard Law where he was a scholarship student. He "had to work in the cafeteria and was shunned by the social clubs," William D. Cohan wrote in *Money and Power*, a book on Goldman Sachs. Blankfein's friends were other lower-caste outcasts shunned by Harvard's privileged preppies and clubs. After graduating in 1978, he spent four years as a tax lawyer, then joined a commodities-trading subsidiary of Goldman. His fiancée, also a lawyer, cried when she heard that, afraid he was throwing his future away.

Blankfein first got attention when he designed a $100 million trade for an Islamic client who needed a way around Islam's rule against receiving interest payments. By 1984, he'd been put in charge of the bank's team trading foreign currencies. Propelled by his strength at managing others, he began to rise, making partner in 1988, taking over his division in 1994, and in 1999, when Goldman went public, gaining new recognition as the head of its most profitable unit, which traded with the firm's own capital. By 2004, when he was named Goldman's president and COO, the right-hand man of chairman Henry "Hank" Paulson, effectively running the firm while Paulson played Mr. Outside, Blankfein owned Goldman stock worth almost $200 million. The boss was sure he deserved it. "He ate, slept, drank the business and the markets," Paulson told Cohan. In 2006, as a Goldman vice chairman, Blankfein joined the ranks of Wall Street's best-paid executives when he took home $54.4 million and topped that the next year, earning about $68 million.

During the financial crisis, Blankfein's reputation took a series of hits, most notably in summer 2009, when *Rolling Stone* writer Matt Taibbi wrote an exposé of Goldman Sachs, famously damning the bank as "a great vampire squid wrapped around the face of humanity, relentlessly jamming its blood funnel into anything that smells like money.

"In fact," Taibbi continued, "the history of the recent financial crisis, which doubles as a history of the rapid decline and fall of the suddenly swindled dry American empire, reads like a Who's Who of Goldman Sachs graduates." Goldman alumni populated the Department of the Treasury, the Federal Reserve Bank, the White House, the State Department, the New York Stock Exchange, and the SEC. Taibbi also pointed out that, in 2008, Goldman had paid $14 million in taxes, an effective rate of 1 percent, and one-third the $42.9 million Blankfein made that first year of the Great Recession as Wall Street's highest-paid executive.

In the months that followed, the vilification of Goldman and of Blankfein continued. He was repeatedly summoned to Washington to testify before Congress and the Financial Crisis Inquiry Commission and was the investment bank's face when it was sued for fraud that April by the SEC. Goldman initially dismissed the claims (related to CDOs it packaged) as unfounded, but later that year it paid $550 million, one of the largest such settlements on record, though the sum represented only about two weeks' worth of profits for the firm. At the press conference in April 2011 where the Senate Subcommittee on Investigations released its report on the mortgage mess, Senator Carl Levin, its chairman, called Goldman a "financial snake-pit rife with greed, conflicts of interest, and wrongdoing."

Goldman and Blankfein began fighting back with a press blitz at the end of 2009. "People are pissed off, mad, and bent out of shape," Blankfein told London's *Sunday Times*. "I know I could slit my wrists and people would cheer." But he went on to defend Goldman, ending with what he later characterized as a joke that went a step too far. Goldman, he said, was doing "God's work."

Afterward, it was reported, he was inundated with as many as a hundred pieces of hate mail a day—and that brought security at 15CPW to a whole new level. Suddenly, says the ex-staffer, "he'd get whisked away, a split-second thing, in and out of the building, usually through the garage, but sometimes out the front. He'd have a bodyguard with him, another one outside, a driver-bodyguard waiting in the lobby. He also had security for his wife." The staff was ordered not to address him by name in the lobby. Yet despite the wall of security, and his somewhat fearsome position in the financial world, Blankfein is one of the best-liked people in the building, "the nicest guy around," says a member of Fifteen's Morgan Stanley tribe, "humble, sweet, always says hello." Laura Blankfein, the former lawyer? Not so much. "She can bite your head off," says the current employee. "She's a tough nut to crack, hot and cold."

"The boss's wife is tough," a banker and 15CPW neighbor agrees. "She's tough."

Like Blankfein, Sandy Weill had a security detail and an intricate security system in his apartment, which was lavish, customized to his specifications for an extra $10 million or so by Robert A. M. Stern and designed by Mica Ertegun. When it appeared in *Architectural Digest*, identified only as the home of "major philanthropists," the magazine called it "about as glamorous a pad as can be imagined." It was the product of two years of weekly Monday meetings. Weill was "going for broke," as he put it in describing the decor, and let Ertegun execute an art deco theme echoing 15CPW's lobby in precious materials such as rosewood and ebony.

Stern raised the ceilings as much as he could and redesigned the master bedroom as an oval to maximize the full views of skyline and park from the bed. Weill, who watched over the work through binoculars from his office across the park, was a micromanager. He insisted on extra closets for his wife; book-matched onyx walls for his bathroom (because mismatched stone made him dizzy); a living room designed to accommodate a suite of paintings by Thomas Hart Benton that he'd bought from American Express; and a particular narrow antique brick from France to line his fireplace. He also specified the size of the fireboxes to fit the precise length of wood he liked to burn. He designed the sconces and Murano glass chandeliers himself and personally chose every piece of china.

The electronics installation was particularly elaborate, with moisture sensors that e-mail the resident manager in case of leaks, temperature sensors on water pipes, and an anemometer on the roof to measure wind speeds and retract the canvas awnings over the terrace. All the technology was "stealth," said *Architectural Digest*. "You don't see a thing." Yet malfunctions still occurred. One night a Weill alarm went off and security men darted through the lobby. "It was a false alarm," says a renter who watched. "He'd left a window open."

Unlike the Blankfeins, both Weill and his wife are disliked by some staffers. Weill, says a former 15CPW employee, "is a very controlling man, and very cheap." The current employee says much the same. "Everyone ran for him and no one liked him," he said shortly after the "very demanding" Weill sold the penthouse and again began using their tiny staff apartment as their city pied-à-terre. "An automatic call is made to the manager if a letter or a magazine doesn't arrive when it's supposed to. But you get used to them and you just don't screw up. He's a pain in the butt but he's rarely there. They're either on their yacht or in their place in Florida."

Working at a building like 15CPW can be lucrative. At first, the staff had had high hopes for Weill. In 2008, he was "very generous," says a former staffer, "but the second year they cut their tips in half." Weill's alleged cheapness should be seen in context. Another former staffer thinks Weill handed out about $90,000 the first year. An ex-staffer recalls another early move-in, a former Goldman Sachs partner. It was December 2007 and he arrived bearing gifts, Christmas tips for everyone on the staff, even though he'd just met them. The typical resident gives $100 to $500 to every employee, says a staffer still employed in the building. Jesse Itzler tipped $650 a head. Fashion executive Elie Tahari, who rented, gave $300 and a $200 shirt. In 2011, the typical employee's holiday take was about $22,500. The concierges and anyone who does special favors "get more," up to $100,000. One employee thinks the resident manager, poached from Time Warner, is the highest paid in the city, estimating he is paid $600,000 before tips, making him a truly *super*-intendent.

To facilitate tipping, a two-page list headed "Happy Holidays" is distributed to all residents, with captioned, color thumbnail photos to help them remember employees, their job titles, and when they joined the staff. The list shows that the resident manager arrived in January 2007, followed by four concierges and a security man and doorman that summer. The slow, steady accretion of staff is indicative of the slow pace of renovations and move-ins. One concierge was added that September, two more the following spring. A second doorman arrived in fall 2007, a third the next January, a fourth that April, and a fifth a year later. The other jobs were filled at a similar pace. The building wasn't fully staffed until spring 2009.

The staff is paid to serve the needs of the owners and residents. But some tenants need more. "Billionaires don't worry about anything," says an employee. "They don't want to be bothered. Sting has a private chef, three or four assistants all day long. They handle everything. You can tell how demanding [the owners] are by how their household staff acts."

The most annoying tenants, though, are those "in lesser apartments," who deal with Fifteen's staff themselves. "People who have to get taxis are like, 'Get me a taxi!'" They're the ones who need to tell the world they live at 15CPW.

<hr />

"Where I live, I know my neighbors," observes a 15CPW employee. "It's very rare [Fifteen occupants] have conversations. It's only their kids that get them together." But it's the families with children who, most of all, have made the apartment house a home. "There's definitely a sense of family, which you wouldn't expect," says Lindsay Boutros-Ghali, an architect who rented broker Robby Browne's apartment. "Everyone has children. It's surprising to see so many small kids. It may look like a cross between a Four Seasons and a gentleman's club, but there's a huge caring about the kids. They're not just appendages." When she and her husband, Adam Klein, a South African–born academic, strategic consultant, and former executive of companies such as Ask Jeeves and Hasbro, moved out in 2012, so they could live closer to their daughter's school, she was sad, but adds hopefully, "That doesn't mean we won't come back."

One of the Goldman Sachs buyers didn't know a soul in the building when he bought, but has gotten to know lots of his neighbors since moving in, thanks to their children. "It's very family friendly," he says. "Lots of kids have been born in the building, and that's a big shared theme. It's nothing superdeep, but just living lives. I don't think we're linked because of the area or industry where we work. But the people are all very accomplished and, through various avenues, arrived here." Asked if he feels the building symbolizes anything, he pauses to think. "Yes, I think it does," he says, "but I don't want to say that. I don't want to sound boastful."

Benjamin Cohen, an actor, lives in a 1,658-square-foot, two-bedroom tower apartment overlooking Broadway, thanks to his father, Michael, a managing director of JPMorgan Securities in Chicago, who decided to save the money he was spending on hotels for his son when Benjamin was appearing in a revival of *Gypsy* on Broadway. "My mother and I forced my father to buy. I had to wait years for it to be built, of course," says Benjamin, who would sometimes visit the construction site just to watch. "It's depressing to be an unemployed actor."

When they took possession, Benjamin moved in, even though the bathroom marble and cabinets were damaged. "They said they'd fix it right up and they did," he says. "And it turned out to be a great place to live. My dad used a treadmill in the gym next to Bob Costas. One time, I walked out and Lloyd Blankfein looked at me like, *Do I know you? Should we share a car?* I looked at him like, *No, we shouldn't.* It's funny for us, who are not those people. There's not a lot of camaraderie, but there are a lot of New Yorkers, a lot of families. It's a lot of people who've done well for themselves. But you can actually live in New York in this building." He laughs at himself. "That's a Midwesterner talking."

Sobhi el-Debs, a Lebanese Muslim born in Japan and educated in San Diego, whose wife, Wafaa, was born in Lebanon and raised in Austin, Texas, agrees. The couple decided to move from Japan to New York "for our kids' sake," he says. El-Debs, whose grandfather founded a textile business and sent his siblings to England, Africa, and the Far East in search of cheap sources of cotton and manufacturing and new markets, calls himself "a third-culture kid," with New York as that third culture. "I don't have a home," he continues. "I didn't want my kids to go through the same identity crisis. I wanted them to be in an international atmosphere, so the choice was London or New York. For me, New York was easier because I have acquaintances and business opportunities here."

He started looking for an East Side rental in 2002 and was shocked by how high rents were and how little value he could get for his money. "Then I started to understand," he says. "You could smell it from the brokers." The message appeared to be that his family wouldn't fit in. "My wife liked way downtown, but it wasn't suitable for families, so we started looking on the West Side" and began to think about buying. Money obviously wasn't an issue: they moved into the posh Mandarin Oriental Hotel while they searched. Looking at another apartment, they overheard someone talking about 15CPW and went straight to its sales office at Carnegie Tower. "I asked for a discount," el-Debs admits. "You know, our people have to get a little break. The response was, give us a deposit within seventy-two hours or that's it."

They signed the building's eightieth contract in December 2005, buying unit 7B for just over $9.5 million. Two years later, almost to the day, they took possession of their apartment. Though el-Debs often travels, "my family is here full-time," he says. "Our kids are basically New Yorkers." He loves his building. "It has East Side glamour and a West Side heart. Everyone is friendly with each other. Everything on the other side of town feels like a façade."

Bruce and Avis Richards moved to Fifteen when their kids left home, but still managed to bring a family feeling with them from the suburbs. Richards, the cofounder of Marathon Asset Management, a $10 billion hedge fund that manages money for the US Treasury, and more typical investors, read about 15CPW and called a friend at Goldman Sachs, who was "very helpful with the transaction," he says. It was a complicated one because they originally bought 9D, just under Arthur Zeckendorf, when no A-lines were available. "It was like pulling teeth," says Bruce, when he tried to find out what would be available and when. "They wouldn't tell you." Months later, they were given permission to flip their contract to 12A, when Goldman's Ashok Varadhan decided he wanted 9D.

Like Lloyd Blankfein, Richards grew up in Brooklyn. Though his parents were both college educated, his father had a construction job from eight to four and then drove a *Daily News* delivery truck every night from midnight to 5:00 a.m., "until he could finally move to Maryland and open a hardware store," says Richards, who worked there after school. His future wife shopped in their store when she was a student at the University of Maryland and thinks she may have met her future husband cutting keys there. "Bruce grew up on the wrong side of the tracks," Avis says, and was bused from his working-class suburb to middle school in inner-city Washington, DC. He went on to Tulane, graduated summa cum laude in economics and math, and in 1982 headed to New York.

"I barely had two shekels," says Bruce, who slept on a cousin's floor on arrival. "Just my bar mitzvah money. No job. I knew nobody. But I'd read the *Wall Street Journal* every day from high school on, and I knew I wanted to work there because it was a system of meritocracy, hard work, and competency as opposed to a Fortune 500 company, where you have to climb the ladder. I was always first in, last out, falling asleep with textbooks on my chest. I was hell-bent and driven to never go back to where I came from."

Avis and Bruce, both new to New York, met again in a West Side bar and dated for seven years before marrying in 1989. She developed health clubs and he got jobs at Paine Webber, Lehman Brothers, and Donaldson, Lufkin, & Jenrette, where he headed the mortgage-backed securities desk. Avis rarely saw him; he was always working or studying. "He's still the same, up at five-fifteen a.m.," she says, "though he may not be the first in the office anymore."

Their first apartment together was a co-op on Central Park West, but they moved to a tower condo at the Century with a three-thousand-square-foot terrace in 1989. "We watched the Mayflower for years," Avis says. "We always knew something would happen there, and we kept our ears open." They moved to the Westchester suburbs in 1993 when their daughter was two and a half and stayed almost sixteen years. In the interim, Richards moved to Smith Barney. After he took classes to learn to curb his demanding intensity, he and a colleague formed the predecessor to Marathon, named for themselves. They started investing with $17 million, more than half of it their own, and were faced almost immediately with the shocking collapse of Long Term Capital Management, which caused sharp drops in the values of many similar funds—though not theirs. Though it's been suggested that concerns about the general economic situation caused them to change the name of their management firm to one that didn't contain their own names, Richards says he was just moving the focus to his "world-class team." By fall 2001, they were managing more than $400 million. Today, Marathon has offices in London and Singapore and about 130 employees.

When their eldest child approached college age, Avis started Birds Nest Productions, a nonprofit that produces multimedia materials and films for charities (she's won Emmy nominations for her work), and the couple began to think about buying another place in Manhattan. "We were thinking of a pied-à-terre and someplace to move to later," she says, but then they decided, "Let's get [our son] into school in New York and get a different life." A visit to Time Warner proved a disappointment. "I asked why it was so quiet," says Avis. "There was nobody there. I didn't want that." Then Bruce heard about Fifteen.

The apartment they ended up with is over 4,000 square feet with a 355-square-foot terrace that gives them river as well as park views.

"When we saw those, it was like, 'Wow!'" says Avis. "You couldn't tell that from the model." As the building rose, they enrolled their son in a Manhattan prep school and drove him in every morning. While Bruce went to work, Avis went to a restaurant in Time Warner for breakfast "to watch the building being built for a year," she says. "I could see straight across Broadway to my apartment. It got taller and taller, the limestone went on. It was exciting to watch." After breakfast, she took a local spin class, meeting others from the neighborhood. At day's end, she would pick up her son and drive back to Westchester. "I created a whole new life," she says. "It made moving back so much easier."

After they closed on Valentine's Day in 2008, the Richardses took a table, two chairs, and candles into the apartment and had a romantic dinner. Then they moved in without renovating because they'd just lived through a renovation in the suburbs. They didn't even decorate. "We wanted to really take our time and plan." Three years later, in 2012, they moved out and began turning their public rooms into "one big loft space," says Avis. "We're going very modern." She professes to love "old, traditional buildings, but to have services and amenities makes a world of difference." She also moved her company into 15CPW, buying a ground-floor suite.

Though they knew none of their future neighbors beforehand, "we all moved in at the same time," Avis continues, "and when that happens, people are open to meeting. It created a real community. I go to dinner in the restaurant now and I know almost everybody." The restaurant is "a huge plus," she says. "They try to be farm-to-table and use organic meat and poultry. There are very educated palates in the building and they listen to the residents."

The restaurant (which is so accommodating, it keeps a separate set of kosher pots for one family) caters Bruce's partner dinners and provides a venue for parties such as the one they held for a child's graduation. "I invited all the neighbors," Avis says. Not that she needs excuses to see them. "The building has a real sense of community. Six or seven hundred people come to a Thanksgiving brunch before the parade," which passes right by Fifteen's front door. "It's become an instant tradition." The restaurant also offers wine classes and such events as a Super Bowl party, a Mother's Day brunch with unlimited buffets ($55 for adults, $25 for kids, with a special drink included for Mom), Sunday dinners with a family focus, Wednesday grill nights in the garden in summer from 5:30 p.m. until dusk, and women's lunches every two weeks with speakers on such subjects as yoga, art collecting, and surgery-free "facial rejuvenation." "Forty or fifty women come," says Richards, who takes issue with the staffer who thinks residents rarely mingle. "I see Sting with his bicycle and working out in the gym. Lloyd is a sweetheart. We all ride the elevators together. There's no class difference, no separation between the front of the building and the back. Everyone is just so happy to live here."

Not everyone agrees. Such as the divorce lawyer Robert Stephan Cohen, who thought 15CPW felt a little too much like a hotel, with its long, beige corridors and transient renters. Another renter, a twenty-eight-year-old who'd grown up in a prominent business family on the East Side, was also put off by Fifteen, but for different reasons. "It was a little too much," he says. "To stand out for not standing out was not enjoyable. In my parents' building, nobody is a big shot. This was too fast-paced."

Quotidian life at Fifteen keeps to a steady rhythm. Its men are early risers and hard workers. The lobbies and elevators are busy from 7:00 to 8:00 a.m., then dead until lunchtime. Family activities, nannies, and dogs rule the day, then the men come home and the place drops dead by 9:00 p.m. At least, in the public spaces. Jesse Itzler's poker games aren't the only late-night diversion. A few of the younger residents, such as Bob Diamond's daughter, are partyers, says a staff member. In her early days at Fifteen, Tyler Ellis drew a *Gossip Girl* crowd and complaints about loud music.

Residents also fill the rust-colored leather loungers in the screening room all the time. Avis Richards loves it when neighbor Caroline Lieberman, an aspiring producer, invites her to see a documentary. Lieberman is described as a socialite when she makes the papers, but she's another of Fifteen's heiresses, and like Tyler Ellis, she comes from the fashion business. Caroline Lewkowitz's family fled the Holocaust in Eastern Europe for Australia, where her father got into the dress business. His children inherited a small fortune and Caroline formerly had a penthouse overlooking Sydney Harbour.

Married briefly (to a Lieberman), she lived on the East Side, but was on her own when she bought a $3.38 million rear apartment at Fifteen in fall 2005. She was looking at Time Warner, saw the hole in the ground, and dived in. Soon, a 15CPW doorman greeted her: "Welcome home, Miss Socialite." That annoyed her. "To me, a socialite is a lady who lunches, spends the husband's money, and goes to charity balls. I was in fashion," says Lieberman, who designed bodywear and accessories in Australia. "I have more substance. I'm an executive producer." She has a musical version of *Dr. Zhivago* that's "going to be very big," she continues. (Fifteen producers are listed on its website, and ten associate producers. She is one of the latter.) She's also writing a book about her Havanese, Mumbai, whose adventures she chronicles in e-mails to her friends. "He's a little boy in a dog's body," she says, then sounds distracted. "Yes, we're talking about you, Bubby." Back to the subject at hand. "Make me look like the most incredibly beloved person in the building."

Another heiress is Rebecka Belldegrun, who has a rich husband, too. One of Lindsay Rosenwald's bigger successes was a company that Arie Belldegrun, an Israeli-born urologist and medical school professor, founded and chaired called Cougar Biotechnology, which develops cancer drugs and was sold to Johnson & Johnson in 2009 for about $1 billion. His wife is one of two children of Shlomo Zabludowicz, a Polish rabbi's son who survived the Nazi death camp at Auschwitz and moved to Finland. There, in the 1950s, he became an industrialist specializing in heavy machinery and arms. An Israel-based subsidiary manufactured advanced artillery systems, mortars, and ammunition for the Israel Defense Forces and had annual sales of as much as $100 million; it also supplied weapons to Iran and Far Eastern countries. After the Iranian revolution in 1979, Zabludowicz sold out and diversified into real estate, hotels, and high tech, doing business with the Ofer family, among others, and putting his fortune into trusts in Liechtenstein and Gibraltar. After his death, his daughter and son fought over their inheritance. A friend of hers says they settled in 2004 with Rebecka getting less than half. Her brother is one of the richest men in Britain, with a fortune of about £2 billion.

In 2008, through an LLC called BMRD Properties, the Belldegruns, whose primary residence is a sprawling Charles Gwathmey–designed estate in the Bel Air district of Los Angeles, bought apartment 36B for $12.4 million. Their connections at 15CPW run deep. Aside from their link to the Ofers, they are close friends of Norman and Lyn Lear's and fund a directorship in a life sciences program at the University of Pennsylvania named for Roy Vagelos, the former CEO of Merck, the pharmaceutical company, who owns the $21 million–plus apartment 14A.

Another LLC, Tatacis, would have hidden the heiress owner of the $6 million apartment 3C if she had not chosen to rent it out, but she ended up in court with her tenant. Marisa Chearavanont's father-in-law, Dhanin, is the richest man in Thailand, with a fortune estimated by *Forbes* at $9 billion. Her husband, Soopakij, one of three sons, is the CEO of the family's CP Lotus Corporation, a subsidiary of their agricultural business, Thailand's largest. The family fortune sprang from a seed, fertilizer, and insecticide company opened in 1921 by two migrant Chinese brothers. Dhanin took over in 1964; CP's revenues exploded as it went into livestock and feed and, in the late 1970s, entered China. It became the world's largest producer of prawn feed, its second-largest producer of poultry, and the third-largest producer of animal feed. It invested in everything from China's CP Lotus supermarkets and Kentucky Fried Chicken and 7-Eleven franchises to telecommunications. Its revenues in 2009 were $25 billion.

Five months after closing on her apartment, the Hong Kong–based Chearavanont, who is Korean by birth, rented it for $20,000 a month to Russell Abrams, who'd founded the Titan Capital hedge fund, in 2001, and needed a place to live while renovating a nearby brownstone. Abrams was yet another Goldman Sachs alumnus, though he only worked there two years before moving on to positions at Swiss and French banks and Merrill Lynch.

Abrams sued Chearvanont's LLC and her real estate broker in 2010, alleging that he'd been promised a two-year rental and then been asked to vacate (along with his wife, their ten-month-old daughter, and two puppies) due to the broker's "unbridled greed," and her "transparently desperate" desire for a five-figure commission from a new renter, fashion's Elie Tahari, who'd already signed a $30,000-a-month lease. Though Abrams knew he would have to reapply to the condo board for a second year, he claimed he'd depended upon the broker's assurance that an extension would not be an issue.

At the time that suit was filed, Abrams was knee-deep in litigation, beginning with a suit brought by his wife, Sandra, right after they moved into 15CPW. She sued two former administrative assistants at Titan who were pursuing a sexual harassment claim against her husband and Titan through the US Equal Employment Opportunity Commission. They claimed that late in 2008, Abrams had asked one of them to get some film from his honeymoon developed, which included topless photos of his wife, and that he "smirked callously, taking pleasure in [her] obvious embarrassment and discomfort" when she handed the pictures over. "You liked them, didn't you?" he allegedly demanded.

Abrams's wife sued to get back copies of the photos her husband somehow managed to leave with the employee and asked for damages of $1 million, in what the employees' lawyers would later describe as Abrams's retaliation against them through his wife. The dispute went public, complete with accounts of messages left on one of the employees' answering machines by Abrams's brother Marc, another target of the complaint, who had dated her. He supposedly called her "a hooker," a "cheap, piece-of-shit stripper" and a "fucking rotten piece of dirt." Another message left on her boyfriend's answering machine described how she'd given Marc Abrams "the longest blow job in my life." The two former employees filed and withdrew a federal case and then sued in a New York court instead. Their suit recounted other litigation involving Abrams. A fresh matter was added to the stack at the end of 2010 when one of Titan's investors sued for fraudulent misrepresentation after losing most of its money.

Abrams's suit against Chearavanont's LLC was thrown out of court, he says, and after reaching a cash settlement with the broker, he and his family moved out of Fifteen in August 2010, making way for Tahari. Chearavanont's lawyer told the *Wall Street Journal* it was a case of "a wealthy guy not being used to being told no." Sandra Abrams's suit against her husband's former employees was thrown out of court, too, and though their claim was dismissed by the Equal Opportunity Commission, their suit against Abrams, his brother, and Titan is ongoing as this is written. Fortunately for 15CPW, the whiff of *that* scandal left the building with Abrams. But he was hardly the only tenant who attracted unwanted attention.

In November 2010, in an episode of television's *The Real Housewives of Beverly Hills*, Camille Grammer is shown in apartment 14K, which her husband, the actor Kelsey, had rented from Jesse Itzler and Sara Blakely that April for just under $29,000 a month. It was his crash pad while he appeared on Broadway in a revival of *La Cage aux Folles*. The reality TV crew taped his then wife and children as they checked the place out, and Camille griped on camera about the thirty-five-hundred-square-foot apartment. "For us, it's small," she said. "That seems pretty obnoxious [but] I'm used to living in a substantial-sized house."

Between the taping of that show and the time it aired, Camille Grammer filed for divorce after thirteen years, citing irreconcilable differences. Her husband immediately married a former flight attendant, Kayte Walsh, twenty-seven years his junior. Another renter at Fifteen at the time thinks he knows what triggered the divorce. "Kelsey Grammer's wife called from California before she knew about his girlfriend," he says. "They told her his wife was already in the building. They genuinely didn't know. Incidents followed."

Writing about Grammer's rental, Jennifer Gould Keil, a reporter who'd taken over her husband's *New York Post* column after his 2009 death, wrote that Grammer was joining a cast of prominent renters that included two "noted philanderers." One of them was Alex "A-Rod" Rodriguez, the highest-paid player in professional baseball, who'd been in Manhattan since joining the New York Yankees in 2004. A-Rod was looking for a rental at Fifteen even before it opened. He saw one owned by Warren Estis and Gary Rosenberg, real estate law partners who have a sideline in condos. That twenty-sixth-floor, C-line unit was later rented to Mark Wahlberg, the actor, and when it sold three years later to a Monte Carlo–based shipping heiress, Ruth McLoughlin, for more than twice what the partners had paid for it, Jason Sheftell of the *Daily News* wrote, "There are so many bold-faced names involved with this unit, we wonder if any apartment in this building doesn't have a celebrity attached to it."

A-Rod then turned to the larger and higher 35A, offering slightly below the asking rental price, but a local financier named Henry Silverman, Jennifer Gould Keil's other philanderer, swooped in and took it away. A-Rod tried to match the higher offer, but was told no and rented the smaller 35B next door, instead. A year later, his lease up, he would try to dislodge the latest renter to take 26C by offering more money for it. Again, his offer proved insufficient. "It was bottom of the ninth, bases loaded, and A-Rod struck out," says broker Ken Deutsch, who had that listing. "But how many people could have even stepped up to the plate?"

Silverman and A-Rod both rented from Leroy Schecter, a steel manufacturer from New Jersey. Born in Brooklyn, Schecter was "a very poor kid who worked for his father's floor-finishing business and moved back home after serving in the navy," says his second cousin and real estate broker Emily Beare. Schecter made his fortune from a company he bought in 1975 that cut and shaped steel.

Schecter was another who'd heard about 15CPW while considering an apartment at the Plaza. He wanted a view and agreed to buy 35B for $8.5 million in February 2006 because it was the highest unit then available, but he really wanted something bigger, so after he closed, he slipped a note under the door of the next-door A-line unit, offering to buy it. When its owners, Florida's Falcone brothers, decided to flip, they sold it to Schecter for $18 million (sorely frustrating Monsoon's Peter Simon, who would immediately make the offer for 32A that John Fowler couldn't refuse).*

Schecter decided to keep both, furnished them, and moved into the A-line unit. A year later, he decided to combine them, but the

---

*The public records of Schecter's two 15CPW purchases in New York City's online database are erroneous, he says through his broker, Emily Beare. They indicate that Schecter bought his A-line apartment first—and directly from the sponsors—for $10.5 million, and the B-line second for $8.5 million. In fact, all the principals in the transactions say Schecter bought the A-line unit second, from the Falcone brothers of Florida, after they closed on it. Schecter adds that he paid $18 million for that unit alone. None of the parties involved can explain the discrepancies.

condo board had decided that combinations would have to wait until owners of single units had finished their renovations. On learning that, Schecter decided to move to a $22.5 million, 16,228-square-foot house he'd bought in 2006 in a gated community with a golf course on a private island near Miami Beach and rent out both apartments. It was late 2009 "and the [sales] market was funny, but rentals were still pretty good," says Beare. "He got immediate offers."

The first was from Silverman, who already lived downstairs in a unit on the sixteenth floor of the tower, owned by Saurabh K. Mittal, cofounder of Indiabulls Financial Services Ltd., a New Delhi–based $10 billion holding company. The sixty-eight-year-old Silverman had moved there in October 2008 after leaving his wife of three decades, Nancy, for Karen Hader, a Pilates instructor forty years his junior. They'd met after Silverman's hip surgery when Hader was his physical therapist.

A onetime tax lawyer, Silverman had moved to Wall Street in the 1960s and learned the takeover game while running a leveraged-buyout fund for Saul Steinberg, the famous corporate raider; its principal investor and adviser was Michael Milken, the head of Drexel Burnham Lambert, the junk bond brokerage that was forced into bankruptcy in 1990. After that, Silverman moved to Steve Schwarzman's Blackstone, using the private equity group's capital to found Hospitality Franchise Systems, an umbrella company for hotel brands. After taking it public, Silverman became its CEO.

Over the next five years, Silverman acquired Avis, Coldwell Banker, Century 21, and more hotel companies, too, making HFS the largest hotel company in the world, and in 1997 he merged it with a direct-marketing goliath to form Cendant, a $38 billion company, which agreed to pay him $258 million the next year, but almost immediately announced the discovery of accounting irregularities at the marketing firm. That caused Cendant's stock price to drop by almost half. A raft of class-action lawsuits and an SEC investigation followed.

Silverman was furious, some say humbled, but not defeated. He and wife number two, Nancy, stopped going out. He saw a psychiatrist, became a gym rat, replaced the company's executives (many of whom would later be convicted and jailed for their part in the fraud), sued its accountants, stabilized the company and made it profitable again, and spun off subsidiaries, earning more millions for himself. By mid-2006, when Cendant ceased to exist, he was out the door, running one of the spin-offs. Having announced he'd retire at the beginning of 2008, he sold that company to the parent of the real estate investment company AREA and went to work there. His severance package totaled $110 million.

Silverman seemed set for a relaxed last act. But still, he was vilified. "If they were building a Mount Rushmore for overpaid CEOs, they'd reserve several spaces on that edifice for Henry Silverman's likeness," said an executive of a proxy advisory firm. No longer a CEO, he dropped from the public radar—at least until he left his wife and moved to Fifteen. In 2009, Karen Hader got pregnant, and Silverman gave her an upgrade, Fifteen-style, renting Leroy Schecter's A-line apartment for $40,000 a month. A-Rod immediately settled for a one-year rental next door for $30,000 a month.

A-Rod turned out to be "the best tenant," says Emily Beare. "He decorated the apartment beautifully. It was impeccable. He paid on time." In spring 2010, Schecter put the two units—still separated—on the market for $55 million. "No one wants people walking through," says Beare, but A-Rod "was fantastic" about letting the apartment be shown and then, when he moved out a few months later, "returned it in better condition than he got it. He removed the paneling, the wallpaper. You'd have never known anyone had lived there." And he never once complained about the paparazzi outside.

Henry Silverman turned out to be a different story, or rather his girlfriend did. "Henry was great" is all Beare will say when asked about a story that went around the building. His lease had a show clause, too, allowing potential tenants and purchasers to see it, but the flu was going around, Karen Hader, a new mother, became quite germophobic, and random visits from strangers didn't sit well with her. She often got upset over last-minute showings and, once, demanded building security accompany the broker and a sneezing client, yelling at them to take off their shoes, use hand sanitizer, and limit their visit to five minutes. The potential renter turned and walked out.

In spring 2010, Silverman bought a town house off Central Park on West Seventy-Sixth Street and began renovating it. He and Hader got engaged as his bitter divorce from Nancy slowly played out; they'd never signed a prenuptial agreement, and Nancy was determined to exit the marriage a wealthy woman. A year later, Silverman and Hader left Fifteen for their new home. Shortly afterward, a judge rejected Silverman's attempt to introduce "scientific" evidence in court to prove that his and his wife's joint property should all be his because his genius, his "innate intellectual talents," and his "unique personal traits" disqualified her from sharing in his $450 million fortune. The judge decided that Nancy had managed their lives, raised their daughter, and provided introductions that had to be taken into account in distributing their property.

Silverman remained capable of infuriating his soon-to-be-ex-wife, even introducing Hader as his spouse at parties. He blamed conflict between Nancy and his two daughters from his first marriage for precipitating their divorce. Finally, though, just before they were set to battle it out in court, the couple settled. Hader and Silverman married and have since had a second child together. Nancy is said to have walked away with $150 million, their Manhattan apartment, and their beach house in Southampton and is described by friends as radiant and restarting her life, too.

Despite all they see and all the fortunes housed above them, the 15CPW staff are still dazzled by celebrity, taking note when supermodels such as Naomi Campbell and Gisele Bündchen visited, respectively, Andrea Kerzner or Jesse Itzler, or when Cameron Diaz left her boyfriend Alex Rodriguez's apartment, sailed out the front door, and hailed her own cab. "But sometimes you had to get a cab and bring it down to the garage to wait for her," says a staffer. "I got hassles from the drivers, but I'd just say, 'You'll be happy when you see who you're waiting for.'" But fame alone was not enough to win the praise of Fifteen's staff or its residents. Diaz "was way too nice for A-Rod," the staffer continues. "He was a douche. No one liked him." An owner from the Morgan Stanley tribe agrees, describing A-Rod as "the exact opposite" of Lloyd Blankfein, "not a nice guy, an unfriendly narcissist."

That is likely why staff members tell tales they probably shouldn't about the Yankee slugger, who was still married when he got to the building. One day, his wife showed up—and said she was Mrs. Smith. "We didn't know who she was so we wouldn't let her in," says a former staffer. "Why didn't she say who she was? She was uptight, nonresponsive, and belligerent. When Alex came in ten minutes later, we knew. He was with Goldie Hawn's daughter."

Fifteen became A-Rod's home plate as he segued from dating Madonna (who lived a few blocks north at Harperley Hall), to Kate Hudson (whose mother, Hawn, lived a few blocks to the south at Bill Zeckendorf's Central Park Place), and then to Diaz. But apparently, they weren't enough for A-Rod. "He got hookers all the time," says the building staff member. "Usually two at a time, two times a week. One time he had two go up, they came down and left, and ten minutes later, Cameron Diaz walks in. He doesn't care. I hate the guy. He thought he was God."*

The staffer adds that ill-behaved celebrities should generally be wary of building staff. "We're here twenty-four/seven. We know ev-

---

*Several years after leaving 15CPW, Rodriguez would be taken down a notch when he was suspended by Major League Baseball over his use of performance-enhancing drugs.

erything you do. We know your secrets." Any other secrets? "Some crazy parties. Illegal things for sure. Dealers come weekly. It's usually for the kids. A couple of them smoke weed. The engineers get complaints." A former engineer, Pasco Cornejo, says he was often called to one apartment to stop floods and faced another sort of crazy. "I was told don't worry what I saw," he recalls. What did he see? "Paraphernalia. Sexual toys." The resident was, "let's say, walking around with very sexy see-through. We'd see her diddling herself."

<hr>

Sandy and Joan Weill's first year at 15CPW was likely not perfectly happy. Citigroup crumbled and Weill's successor as CEO was disposed of in the autumn of 2007 after the bank revealed subprime-mortgage losses of $11 billion and was forced to raise billions in new capital from Abu Dhabi's investment authority; sovereign wealth funds from Singapore and Kuwait; an arm of the New Jersey government; 15CPW neighbor Gregg Ireland's Capital World Investors; and Saudi prince al-Waleed bin Talal. Weill even put some money where his pride was, investing $20 million of his own. Citi also cut its dividends to shareholders, saving another $4.4 billion.

Then, early in 2009, just after Citigroup borrowed $45 billion more in bailout funds from taxpayers, the *New York Post* ran a front-page photo of Weill with the headline "Pigs Fly; Citi Jets Ex-CEO to Cabo." Weill had taken a corporate jet full of relatives to Mexico on vacation. And at the end of that year, Weill was the subject of a profile in the *New York Times* with the poignant headline "Citi's Creator, Alone with His Regrets." Reporter Katrina Brooker noted that Weill's vast office in the General Motors Building across the park from Fifteen "feels empty. Other than a few assistants, he is alone." The scene, she decided, was "incongruous."

Weill told Brooker he was horrified by his bad press, and declared that he would never take Air Citi again. "The most important thing to my husband was his reputation," Joan Weill said. "There are a few people I want to kill, but I am not going to name names." Brooker ended her piece with the nugget that Weill had been dropped from the Forbes 400 list of the richest Americans, even though he still had three homes and his yacht, named *April Fool* for the day he met his wife, and would shortly buy a 362-acre Sonoma County vineyard for $31 million.

A year later, in November 2011, Weill abruptly began, as he put it, "downsizing a little bit," offering both his Fifteen penthouse and his yacht for sale, explaining to Josh Barbanel, who'd moved to the *Wall Street Journal*, that it was "a pretty good time" for the American rich "to be quiet," and that his intention was to give "the proceeds of what we get" to charity. In August 2010, he and his wife had signed Warren Buffett and Bill Gates's Giving Pledge, promising to give away most of their wealth before they died.* Within weeks, their penthouse was reported sold, and just before Christmas, the buyer revealed himself—sort of.

First, word leaked that Dmitry Rybolovlev, the same Russian who'd tried to buy Shlomo Ben-Haim's penthouse, had finally gotten a foothold at Fifteen, buying Weill's penthouse for the asking price. When Barbanel sought confirmation, a spokesman for the Russian oligarch was ready with a statement: it wasn't Rybolovlev but his elder daughter, Ekaterina, a twenty-two-year-old student at an unnamed American college, doing the buying. That assertion set off one of the looniest episodes in 15CPW's short history.

That fall, father and daughter had repeatedly visited another brand-new condo, starchitect Jean Nouvel's 100 Eleventh Avenue, to look at one of its penthouses. After a bidding war, six weeks of ne-

---

*Weill appears to have experienced a slow-motion Damascene conversion. In July 2012, he even went on CNBC to advocate the reinstatement of the very same Glass-Steagall-style restrictions on banks he'd once so proudly dismantled. And having done that, he disappeared from sight, making it clear that statement was a comment, not a crusade. In another downsizing twist, he sold his yacht to neighbor Dan Loeb for just over $50 million early in 2013.

gotiations, and an engineering inspection, they flew into New York late in November to sign a contract to buy it for about $20 million. They'd set up the appropriately named Property NY 100–11 LLC to do that a few weeks earlier. The apartment was to be Ekaterina's to use while she went to school in America. But that day, Dmitry's lawyer called, asking for one more site visit—and appeared with the pair, who spoke only in Russian until Ekaterina turned and coolly told the broker, "We'll let you know." It later emerged that on the spur of the moment, she or they had decided to buy Weill's penthouse instead. They used that same LLC to do it.

Back in Russia, Rybolovlev had an issue: the Kremlin was trying to take Uralkali away from him, opening a fresh investigation of the mine collapse two years earlier, which drove its stock down 60 percent. More of the backstory had emerged after December 22, 2008, when his wife, Elena Rybolovleva, filed for divorce in Geneva and sought both immediate financial relief and a freeze on his assets, alleging that he'd been hiding their money for at least six months.

Elena's divorce petition explained that they lived in Cologny, Switzerland, where they'd bought properties and received permission to demolish existing structures and build a new "sumptuous" estate, including a concert hall with a stage big enough for thirty-five musicians. Elena said that she'd stopped working as a doctor after moving to Switzerland in the 1990s; she'd later studied cosmetic surgery in Paris, but turned down a job there because their second daughter, Anna, had just been born. Instead, she returned home, where she raised their daughters, managed their staff (a butler, a cook, a gardener, two chauffeurs, a nanny, and a maid), and created "a vast social network" to support Dmitry's endeavors. But soon she concluded that her husband had lived a double life since they'd moved to Switzerland. In 2000, when she was four months pregnant, she'd received an anonymous package containing a photo of her husband and another woman.

Five years later, she alleged, Rybolovlev had asked her to sign a postnuptial contract that would have given her $100 million in the event they split up. But he was worth $1 billion then, so she saw a lawyer and refused. Ever since, she continued, he'd kept having affairs, and spending lavishly on his girlfriends. Early in 2008, she'd mentioned divorce but then backtracked, hoping for a reconciliation. That spring, she alleged, he booked a trip to the ski resort of Courchevel and shuffled his mistress out of his hotel a mere four hours before she and Anna, then seven, arrived. By June, he was on his yacht in Croatia, where he first entertained multiple young women and then, again, the mistress. More trips and more assignations followed in Venice, Monaco, and Dubai. When she confronted him, she said he boasted of his conquests of girls Elena suspected were younger than Ekaterina. She even alleged that he shared his women with other oligarchs and said he'd bragged he'd organized everything "in an industrial way": the girls were all virgins and submitted to VD tests before boarding his yacht. Ekaterina, Elena believed, knew all about his exploits and Elena charged that he'd bought his daughter's silence with gifts: a $1 million horse and a $500,000 car.

In December 2008, while the couple were looking at American real estate together, he again asked Elena to sign a document—a surety bond for €45 million; he claimed he was under financial pressure and would have to fire their staff and cut their living expenses if she didn't sign. Again, a lawyer warned her not to, and Rybolovlev left for a weekend in Paris with his mistress at the posh Hotel George V. So, was he going broke or not? That's when Elena sued.

Elena then quantified the family's fortune, which fluctuated between $7 billion and $13 billion, and provided a list of their assets, which included more real estate in Gstaad, Moscow, Perm, and Cyprus; four private jets; two yachts; three Mercedeses, a Bentley, and a Rolls-Royce; art and furniture worth $670 million; bank accounts and billions in stock, tucked away in banks and anonymous shell companies in Cyprus, the British Virgin Islands, Panama, and Jersey, all tax havens known and loved by the rich for their loose financial regulation.

She listed multiple paintings by Modigliani, Monet, and Picasso, and more by van Gogh, Gauguin, Degas, and Rothko, and a vast collection of museum-quality, eighteenth-century French and German furniture originally intended for their Swiss estate. The art and furniture had recently been moved to London and Singapore. Though she'd known of the shipments, she worried Dmitry had "the intention of moving them out from her reach." She asked for custody of Anna, and a limit on his visits, as she feared he would try to kidnap her. "Love and trust has completely disappeared from the life of the couple," the filing concluded. "Madame can no longer put up with his infidelities, his egotism and contempt."

In spring 2009, Dmitry agreed to pay family support, the mortgage on her home in Cologny, and her share of their taxes while they battled it out over their fortune. But he also informed Elena that in 2005, just after she refused to sign the postnuptial agreement, he'd transferred most of his assets to two irrevocable trusts on Cyprus, and now, even though he was the protector of those trusts, as well as a beneficiary (the others were his daughters, but *not* his wife), under Cypriot law the trustees were refusing to tell him what they contained or what they earned, and he insisted that, anyway, he didn't own any of the companies she'd listed in her divorce papers. He also pointed out that she was the co-owner of their Swiss properties, another in Paris (reportedly bought from the fashion designer Pierre Cardin), and that in 2008 he'd given her jewelry worth almost €29 million.

Back and forth the charges flew. Court filings show that two of his Panamanian companies bought a €100 million apartment in Monaco and rented it to him for €600,000 a year, and that though he'd paid the Russian government $71.8 million in damages for the Uralkali mine collapse in 2009, he was still in jeopardy of being dunned for more. The following June, the war of the Rybolovlevs became an international affair when the *Palm Beach Post* uncovered documents showing Elena had sought a court order there to freeze the former Trump mansion. Her husband suddenly changed his tune, saying he didn't own it after all.

As the sparring continued, a process server claimed he'd twice served legal papers on Rybolovlev in Maui, Hawaii, slapping them onto the windshields of two different Cadillac Escalades as their drivers sought to evade him. By then, Elena had hired a New York law firm to quarterback her multifront battle with Dmitry; she'd also sought asset freezes in the BVIs, London, Singapore, and Cyprus. In March 2012, after the Swiss divorce court ordered all his assets frozen, she filed suit in New York, too, seeking to freeze his new Fifteen apartment—and all hell broke loose. The suit contended that the apartment wasn't Ekaterina's at all, but rather that the LLC was a sham created "with the specific intent of hiding and diverting" Dmitry's assets. The story was an irresistible feast for the city's feisty tabloid press.

The New York suit claimed that, in the preceding eighteen months, Rybolovlev had liquidated his potash interests, which had been in the hands of that Cypriot holding company (controlled by Dmitry through a Cypriot trust), and had gone on a spending spree, buying a $295 million stake in a Cyprus bank, a majority interest in AS Monaco, a soccer team, and the Weill apartment. Simultaneously, Elena's lawyer gave a series of interviews to press her case. "Mrs. R [as he called her] wants to be sure there are sufficient assets" to cover an eventual divorce settlement, said David Newman of Day Pitney. He added that any settlement would have to include a number "with a *b*," for billions. He was talking to the press, he said, because "litigation is leverage to ultimately negotiate something. If people think he's doing things in a questionable manner, it gets attention. People don't like you looking in their underwear." Finally, he scoffed at the notion that Rybolovlev deserved privacy: "Private people don't buy trophy properties."

After months of silence, Rybolovlev finally shot back at his wife and chose the *New York Times* to give his side of the story. Less than a month after Elena sued in New York, one of his Swiss lawyers, Tetiana Bersheda, gave an interview to Alexei Barrionuevo, the *Times*'s latest real estate columnist, for a story on Russians trying to get money out of their homeland by buying trophy real estate. She told the reporter Rybolovlev's story, spinning it to show that his asset machinations were set in motion by a desire to keep them out of reach of the Russian authorities—not his wife.

Though the *Times* didn't attribute its statement on the ownership of the penthouse, which came at the conclusion of a long page-one story, the source seemed to be Bersheda. Ekaterina had "bought the condominium with cash" from "a trust set up to benefit her and future children," the paper reported. Then it quoted Bersheda: "She hopes to be able to stay in the apartment between September and December, when she expects to be finishing a liberal arts degree from Harvard University Extension School. She has been attending most of her classes online."

The next day, Barrionuevo had another story on Rybolovlev, this one headlined "Divorce, Oligarch-Style." It repeated the claim that Ekaterina would use the apartment, while noting that changes to the house in Palm Beach had been put on hold until the litigation was settled. Now, Bersheda maintained Rybolovlev was engaged in "succession planning," not trying to hide assets. "He was not a model husband," allowed Sergey Chernitsyn, a Rybolovlev spokesman who'd previously done PR for another oligarch, Mikhail Prokhorov, at his Norilsk Nickel company. "Mr. Rybolovlev never denied his infidelities, but the wife knew about it for many years and passively accepted it."

After that, silence suddenly descended. "Unfortunately, because of the state of current litigation, the lawyers are advising us not to answer questions at this particular moment," B. J. Cooper, another spokesman, said by e-mail in August 2012. (Cooper works for APCO Worldwide, a damage-control PR firm best known for defending the tobacco industry in the 1990s.) No further news of the Rybolovlev divorce surfaced for many months thereafter, though in Russian circles in Manhattan, it was whispered that Elena Rybolovleva might be a pawn of her husband's powerful Russian enemies. Regardless, between September and December 2012, when Bersheda had said Ekaterina Rybolovleva would use her apartment, the lights in the disputed penthouse rarely came on. But then, as her father's lawyer had told the *Times*, she preferred spending time in Monaco, where she could be close to her horses. Finally, Christmas week 2012, the whole place blazed with light for several evenings.

Then it went dark again.

———

Rybolovlev's purchase of Sandy Weill's penthouse caught Leroy Schecter's attention. Safely tucked away in Miami Beach, Schecter had almost sold out in 2010 to a Russian composer named Igor Krutoy, who offered about $45 million but ultimately decided he wanted a finished space and went to the Plaza, instead, where he paid $48 million, setting a new condo price record in Manhattan. "Nobody wanted two apartments," says broker Emily Beare. "They wanted the work done or they wanted the A-line." But Schecter insisted the units be sold together or not at all. "He finally realized he had to combine them, took them off the market, and waited for the [combination] moratorium to end." He would file plans in February 2012 and start work that June. In the meantime, Schecter monitored the Manhattan real estate market, waiting for the perfect moment to relist the apartments. It didn't take long to come.

"Suddenly," says Beare, "you started seeing more foreign money looking for a safe place. It wasn't real estate as real estate. It was real estate as a commodity." Europe seemed on the brink of economic collapse, and elections in Greece and France threw a harsh light on divisions within the Euro zone. The London real estate market was "on fire," says Beare, and New York's suddenly looked "like it's for free in comparison." So shortly after his renovation began, Schecter decided it was time to list his 15CPW apartments again—this time at a price calculated to attract attention, $95 million.

"It was just a number, not a value," Realtor Beare says vaguely. It bore little relationship to what real estate pros call comps, sales of comparable apartments in the same or similar neighborhoods. In truth, the comps were two in number, Weill's sale, which "validated everything," says Beare, and a $100 million listing that came on the market two days before Schecter's of an octagonal-shaped, eight-thousand-square-foot penthouse at the long-troubled CitySpire, a few blocks south. Though that price was clearly a publicity ploy, unlikely to be attained, Fifteen's aura likely convinced Schecter that he could, in fact, make a 258 percent gain on his initial $26.5 million investment in his two apartments. "That's the number he wanted, so we put it on the market to see what happens," says Beare. Cleverly, the eighty-five-year-old Schecter linked the sale to his plan to give 90 percent of his wealth away to charity in an interview with Barbanel of the *Wall Street Journal*, saying he wanted the proceeds to be used to alleviate poverty in the New York area. "He has an eye for property and always focused on buying the best so his foundation could do a lot of good," Beare says. He was following Sandy Weill's lead again.

Weill and Rybolovlev, Schecter's apartments, their tenants, and the outlandish price he hoped to sell them for* all kept the eyes of the world on Fifteen Central Park West, but some stories remained

---

*Schecter's apartment would continue to bounce on and off the sales and rental market.

below the radar. Someone was once led from the building in hand-cuffs by the FBI, claims a member of the building staff. Who that was isn't known, but it wasn't the perp who robbed Bob Diamond's apartment. That crime occurred while Diamond still had his big job at Barclays, which had just taken over Lehman Brothers' investment bank and capital-markets units for the distress price of $250 million. Diamond hadn't moved in yet, but some of his possessions were al-ready there. Presumably, his security detail was watching him and not his stuff when the theft occurred.

Residents of Fifteen carry electronic fobs that allow them to take the elevators from floor to floor. But those movements can be tracked by the security staff and its cameras. The only way to avoid being seen was to take one of the staircases that run behind the el-evator cores. It's not known why the son of a neighbor in the tower decided to climb those stairs one day, only that he was on a break from a good school, and his parents were away when he did. "He takes the back stairs up a few flights to Diamond's apartment, it's open, there are no locks," says one of several people who tell the story. "He takes a painting and leaves it in his parents' apartment. Diamond discovers the painting is missing."

Diamond's security team was called, but it was the building's se-curity staff that figured out what had happened and who'd done it from electronic records of fire doors opening; there were then no cameras on the back stairs. The thief "was confronted and he fessed up," says a onetime building employee. "Diamond was a real sport about it," adds someone at Brown Harris Stevens. It should proba-bly come as no surprise that no charges were filed and the story of the incident has heretofore not left the building. "That kid got *very* lucky," says a renter who heard what happened.

A high potential for scandal exists wherever money, power, and ego collide, so even if some stories get hushed up, Fifteen Central Park West will likely be a petri dish, incubating unseemly activities, for years to come. So far, though, it has mostly served its function as a fortress protecting its owner-inhabitants, even when infamy has knocked on their doors.

"Misfortune has stalked New Silk Route Partners from birth," *Businessworld*, an Indian publication, wrote late in 2011, before cataloging the series of mishaps that plagued the Mumbai-based private equity firm since its founding, four years earlier, with plans to invest $1.4 billion in India and Asia. The worst of those mishaps came when one of its cofounders, Rajat Gupta, the former CEO of McKinsey & Co., and a member of the boards of Goldman Sachs and Procter & Gamble, was charged by the SEC with insider trading and later found guilty of four counts of securities fraud for sharing confidential information with Raj Rajaratnam, founder of the Galleon Group hedge fund. Rajaratnam received a sentence of eleven years in prison. In October 2012, Gupta, too, would be ordered to jail, in his case for two years with another year on supervised release, and fined $5 million. One of his cofounders at New Silk Route was Parag Saxena, who bought Fifteen's apartment 29C from the tragic radiologists Arie and Doreen Liebeskind.

After earning an MBA from Wharton, the Indian-born Saxena joined Citicorp in 1983; he ran a division that later evolved into a venture capital firm that invested in biotechnology as well as such companies as Costco, Starbucks, and Staples. Suddenly, with Gupta's arrest, Saxena found himself calling his investors and partners, assuring them that Gupta wasn't actually active at New Silk Route and that ten other partners would ensure business continued as usual. "This had nothing to do with Silk Route," Saxena told anyone who would listen. He also predicted his friend would be exonerated.

He wasn't and, even before Gupta's conviction, his arrest raked up muck from Saxena's and New Silk Route's past. The *Washington Post* reminded its readers of the payment, in 1994, of a $250,000 fine to settle civil claims that Saxena bought discounted stock in companies before they went public and improperly touted them to clients of his investment firm, that another of New Silk Route's investors was fined $2.7 million and forfeited profits to settle charges that he'd sold shares in Citigroup in advance of an announcement of a subsidiary's losses, and that Rajaratnam himself was a New Silk Route investor. "You're an eagle," a friend of Gupta's had told him, warning him away from the New Silk Route team, "so why do you want to be with these chickens who can't fly? You'll get the chicken flu."

Parag Saxena isn't the only financier at 15CPW whose firm is associated with bad behavior. Though he still lives cheek by jowl with several Goldman partners, Raj Sethi no longer works there. He quit in spring 2012, when about twenty Goldman commodities traders exited the firm within a few months. Their departures were blamed on tightened regulations; many went to less regulated hedge funds. Sethi chose to join SAC Capital, where another Fifteen owner, Derek Cribbs, already worked. Soon, eight former SAC traders would be charged with criminal insider trading, and after a six-year investigation of the hedge fund, SAC was indicted on criminal charges in the summer of 2013, when it was described by the federal government as a "veritable magnet of market cheaters." That November, it agreed to plead guilty, pay a record total of $1.8 billion penalty, and stop managing money for outside investors. Its assets under management had already shrunk from $14 billion to $9 billion as investors fled.

Jay Glenn Goldman, who occupies the $6.6 million apartment 5C, has also seen his hedge fund, J. Goldman & Co., linked to the investigation of SAC, in its case regarding Cougar Biotechnology, run by his neighbor Dr. Arie Belldegrun and backed by Lindsay Rosenwald. But those vague accusations, denied by the trader involved, and Jay Goldman's own links to SAC's founder and namesake, Steven A. Cohen, who has spoken of their friendship in a sworn deposition, may be the least of Jay Goldman's troubles. Early in 2013, he was sued for giving his sixteen-year-old son the keys to his Land Rover just after Hurricane Sandy; the teen crashed into a tree near their weekend home on Long Island, leaving a passenger a quadriplegic. News stories on the lawsuit noted that Goldman had also recently been hit with a $21,000 tax lien.

And then there's Piofrancesco Borghetti, owner of both an Italian cosmetics company and Fifteen's $10 million apartment 32C. After he was charged with fraudulent bankruptcy and embezzling €19 million from his company, he listed his apartment for $27.7 million in 2012. When it failed to sell after more than six months, he took it off the market and listed it as a rental, asking $45,000 a month. Maybe he needed the cash to pay his lawyers.

Clearly, both Fifteen and its owners will remain in the news. All might do well, then, to look at the story of another renter at Fifteen, its only resident convicted felon, Adam Weitsman, whose life thus far offers up the promise of redemption, even though Weitsman would never be allowed to live in a stuffy co-op.

Weitsman was the renter in apartment 26C whom Alex Rodriguez was unable to dislodge. "Hopefully, I'm a good tenant," he says sheepishly. "I pay my rent on time." But the stocky, muscular young man with a beard, short hair, gravel voice, a tattoo of his daughter's name in Hebrew running up his left arm, and a face with some wear on it, also has a story unlike any other at 15CPW.

Weitsman comes from Owego, New York, where his grandfather and his father ran a scrap-metal business. A self-described "nerdy, comic-book kid," he left college without graduating and moved to Greenwich Village, sharing a two-bedroom apartment on lower Fifth Avenue with five roommates and working at an art gallery. He'd been fond of American stoneware, which was made near Owego, since he'd been a youngster. He was thrilled to have "an unimportant job I pretended was important," he says, working in the art world.

A few years later, when his gallery decided to off-load some of its lesser holdings, Weitsman offered to sell them and opened a gallery of his own in a storefront in Manhattan's West Village. But when his father fell ill and asked for help, he dutifully returned to Owego and "ended up staying," he says. His father soon sold the family firm, but Adam started a new one, this time shredding metal, with loans and a job-creation grant. "I got destroyed," he says. "I couldn't get the equipment to work. I used up my credit lines. Then I got into trouble."

Out of money, he began kiting checks, running them through two banks for a year before he got caught when one of the banks was sold and the buyer, conducting due diligence, "saw unusual activity and called the FBI," he recalls. Neither bank actually lost any money, and both wrote the judge on his behalf, but when he refused to snitch on the bankers, he continues, he faced a jail sentence. "I was guilty," he says. "I was totally stupid. It wasn't the banks' fault so I took the jail [time]. It was in every paper and it was the age of the Internet, so it doesn't stay local. I lost my reputation." He also lost nine months of his life, spent in the Federal Correctional Facility at Otisville. "All my swagger got taken away."

Fortunately, in the six years between the crime and his imprisonment, he'd fallen in love with an aspiring fashion model and gotten married (after he told her his situation), so she ran the business until he won early release for good behavior. By the end of 2006, he was back at work and making enough money to buy back his father's company. By then, too, he'd started cruising real estate websites, looking at Manhattan apartments again, "and I started reading about Fifteen," he says. First, he rented a rear-facing, sixth-floor apartment from a St. Louis doctor who'd bought it as an investment. Two years later, he rented 26C and was allowed to remain when the shipping heiress Ruth McLoughlin bought it.

"The rent has gone up dramatically," Weitsman says. "It's just astronomical. But we have no debt. I never wanted to go back to a bank." He hasn't left Owego, where he still owns a small house in town and a large lake house for weekends. But he wants to stay at Fifteen, too. "The staff treats you really special," he says. "They're friendly and not fake friendly. I expected something different. I love it here." But if his fortunes take another turn, he says, he'll still be fine. "When I was younger, stuff was important," Weitsman says. "Now, we're content, the three of us. Stuff is just props. The core is us. If I can't afford this tomorrow, it won't change anything."

Though atypical, Weitsman's fall and rise is quintessentially American. So, too, is the tale told by Gillian Sorensen, widow of Theodore, who was John Fitzgerald Kennedy's special counsel, adviser, and speechwriter, although, when asked which of the late president's words he'd written, he would sometimes reply, "Ask not."

Sorensen spent the rest of his working life as an international lawyer and, for most of that time, lived with Gillian at the Century, "with Lincoln Center out the back door and Central Park out the front," she says. In 2001, though, Sorensen suffered a stroke and lost most of his eyesight, some of his mobility, "but thank God not speech or memory." An ongoing conversation about moving to a new home— Ted longed to live in a building with a swimming pool—went on hold at that point "and we stayed where we were," Gillian says.

A few years later, though, she "heard something was happening" next door at the Mayflower and the Zeckendorfs were involved. "That was interesting to me," she continues, because she works as a senior adviser at the United Nations Foundation and knew the boys' mother, Guri Lie, who lived nearby. "One day I ran into her and said, 'Is it true?' She connected me to them." Gillian was invited to visit the Broadway office and see the plans. "They mentioned Stern, and I have a great interest in design and note and remember good buildings. It was very important to me that [Fifteen] was being built in harmony with Central Park West, so I spent several hours studying the floor plans and began to zero in on what would work for us." The pool was vital, but she also noted that the building had no steps, "which was very important so Ted would be safe."

She still had to talk her husband into moving. The $10.75 million apartment 9C "was a reach for us," she admits, "and a leap of faith. We bought when it was a hole in the ground. But it was not accidental. I'd studied. I knew. And he began to feel comfortable and eventually agreed it was the best investment we ever made."

Once they were able to move, Ted would swim five days a week, thirty laps in an hour, almost until his death at eighty-two in fall 2010, after another stroke. A plaque on the wall of Fifteen's gym honors him as the pool's most loyal swimmer. And his widow plans to stay. "They thought of everything here, they really did," she says. "I love the space and especially the light. It really is home."

<hr />

Fifteen is home to people of all kinds, all creeds, colors, and nationalities, all coexisting in a world where conflict is sadly the norm. Sobhi and Wafaa el-Debs aren't the only Middle Easterners sharing Fifteen's paradise with its many Israelis and Jews. Adam Weitsman's first landlord was the Pakistani-born doctor Shakeel Ahmed. "It completely makes sense," thinks Dr. Ahmed. "Money brings us together. Common interests bring us together. Everyone wants the same level of affluence and comfort." Even a member of an Arab ruling family is in residence. As a son of Sheikh Sultan bin Mohammed Al-Qasimi III, the ruler of Sharjah, Sheikh Sultan bin Ahmed al-Qasimi is a crown prince of the United Arab Emirates. He and his wife are "the nicest people," says a building employee. Though they only visit for a month a year, they make an impression, wandering in and out in jeans and sweaters. "When you think of a prince, you think bodyguards," says the staffer. "Nope. None." Their two children, though also nice, are spoiled, the staffer adds. "They pull up to FAO Schwarz and say, 'Fill up the car.'"

Though political cartoonist Ranan Lurie is a seventh-generation Israeli and claims membership in the oldest family in the world, the royal house of King David, he also has a family history of living in peace with Arabs; his grandfather spent most of his life in Egypt and was a leader of its Ashkenazi Jews, he says, "because he came with money." Lurie sits on a white leather chair. His living room is decorated with white orchids. He has neat white hair, a white beard, white jeans, white sneakers.

No doubt, some Islamists would be uneasy living under the same roof as Lurie. He grew up in Tel Aviv and dropped out of private school to join the Irgun, the Jewish paramilitary organization, in what was then still Palestine at age fourteen. Wounded fighting for Israel's independence in the 1948 Battle of Haifa, he drew his first cartoon with a bandaged hand while recovering, emerged to train as a fighter pilot, but washed out for low flying. Three days later, he was made an intelligence officer. Years later, Major Lurie commanded five hundred men in the Six-Day War pitting Israel against Egypt, Jordan, and Syria.

He continued cartooning all along. Ten years after his debut in *Life*, the magazine offered him a month at the Waldorf-Astoria in exchange for two drawings a week—and he became a full-time cartoonist. There was no family money; it had vanished when his grandfather died. "But I can promise you one thing, we had a tremendous name," he says. He got a newspaper syndication deal. "It's a lot of money," he says, which he invested in real estate. He first rented in the Westchester suburb Scarsdale, then bought in Stamford, Connecticut, and traded up to Greenwich. He, wife, Tamar, and their three kids all became US citizens in 1974 "at *Life*'s encouragement," he continues. Tamar became a real estate broker in 1985.

The day their youngest was accepted at Stanford, the Luries decided to return to Manhattan, but instead, he spent the next few years traveling and drawing for publications around the world. Finally, he returned to New York as an animation cartoonist for a PBS news show—and bought an apartment at Trump Tower. "A clever move investment-wise," he says. "Big apartments appeal to people who don't count dimes." Then he bought another and combined them. He spent a little over $2 million and eventually sold them for $6.3 million. Then he bought two more and only recently sold those for $9 million. In the meantime, he bought a unit at Time Warner in 2005, a $2.9 million two-bedroom apartment he uses as an office and archive. Leaving the building, he saw trucks across the street and, without a pause, ended up in Fifteen's sales office. The three-dimensional model of the building and its environs caught his eye, he thinks, because he'd been a skydiver and saw "the huge area this building commanded."

Prospective buyers could ask the sales staff to illuminate an apartment. Lurie asked to see the highest one available in the D-line. "I felt like a wolf circling where I was going to eat. I said, 'How much?'" It was $11.3 million. "I am ready to buy it on condition that a handshake will be sufficient," Lurie said. "I don't want to wait." Arthur Zeckendorf was standing nearby "and gave the nod." Lurie knew exactly what he wanted to do with the apartment; as soon he took possession, he knocked out all the walls in the public rooms, replaced them with glass, and widened the foyer. Now, anyone walking through his front door is hit in the face with a 290-degree view of Manhattan.

"My biggest problem was to call my wife," Lurie says, returning to that moment in the sales office. "I didn't intend to buy it, but when I saw, I knew, it had to be a wonderful investment." Tamara said he was out of his mind for spending $14.2 million on real estate in a few hours. "I'd stormed Arab legionnaires. I'd trained Idi Amin. My parachute burned in midair. I'm used to living dangerously. But this was such a good cause, I knew I couldn't go wrong." Time has borne out his wisdom, as the apartments have soared in value. "It has a momentum all its own." But he has no interest in selling. "Today, never!" he says emphatically. "Tomorrow? Maybe. The time to sell will be dictated by circumstance. But right now, I can think of nothing better than this."

Fifteen's Israeli, Arab, and Muslim population is fascinating, but what's more noteworthy is how many Jewish households the building contains. It marks a significant moment in New York's social history—the first time a self-selected Jewish building has become the city's most desirable. That more than anything else makes Fifteen Central Park West a symbol of America at its most inclusive, even if it's been half a century since "polite" anti-Semitism fell beyond the nation's pale.

At this writing, in fall 2013, several new buildings are rising in Manhattan, some containing apartments that have reportedly gone into contract at $95 million. But none is likely to surpass another of Fifteen's achievements, its masterful conjuring of the illusion of a perfect convergence of international wealth leading to ever-increasing resale value. "It is what it is," says the émigrés' lawyer Edward Mermelstein. "New York is an anomaly. Fifteen is an anomaly." As opposed to an anathema.

Within those Jewish 15CPW households, there is the Israeli cluster, a neocon cluster, a hedgie cluster. There is also a cluster of initial purchasers who left the Soviet Union in the 1970s and came to America in flight from religious discrimination, long before oligarchs such as Dmitry Rybolovlev and Valery Kogan flew in for the sake of their capital. Hedgies may be Fifteen's most powerful tribe, but that first wave of Russians may be its most admirable.

"We all came with nothing, with zero," says Dr. Alex Mikhailov, owner of a chain of dental clinics, who paid $7.9 million for the most expensive of the Russian Jewish apartments, unit 34C. "This is the land of opportunity." Refugees from Soviet Russia—a spectacularly crumbling, bumbling, oppressive country—choose condos because co-op boards "are like party leaders," says Alexander Rabey, a retired manufacturer of complex computer controllers, who left Moscow in 1973 and bought unit 15G for $4.725 million. "If you want to learn what socialism is, buy a co-op."

They can laugh now, but their stories aren't funny. "It's not easy when you come with nothing," says Faina Bitelman, who bought 27B with her husband, Leon, for $5.7 million. "We were running away." Owners of an online diamond retailer that grew out of a jewelry shop they opened in 1980, soon after arriving, they had to rent the apartment out to afford it, but Faina was determined to own it. She's wanted to live on Central Park since the day she arrived in Manhattan.

"What I do, I do the math," she says. "I have researched real estate all my life. I knew that when we closed, the value would double. It's an American dream and I pray to God every day for this country, honestly. People think people got lucky, but we didn't have days off for years and years to come to the point we were able to buy stuff for ourselves. Looking back, I don't know how it happened. It's a miracle. I understand we are not like everyone else in the building. Some people make much more money. I didn't buy there to pretend to be wealthy. It was my dream, to come to that place. And I made it, yeah." In 2013, she and Leon even started renovating, preparatory to finally moving in themselves.

Mike Tsinberg, who lives with his wife, Faina, in the $2.5 million apartment 7L, was born in Ukraine and studied electrical engineering in a Moscow suburb. He filed for an exit visa ("the only way out if you were Jewish") while still in college, but since he'd been exposed to military technology, it was denied. "Which meant my career was finished," he says, because he could no longer be trusted. "There's only one company—the government." Still, he reapplied every six months, nine times in all.

Unable to secure legitimate employment, fearing the draft (military service would have set the immigration hurdle even higher), and without income, he formed a construction crew and went village to village seeking jobs for cash. "I had to learn quickly how to build gas stations." In the cold Russian winter, when construction ceased, Tsinberg repaired TV sets.

Mike describes his Moscow-born wife as a socialite, but like him Faina "didn't know anything about life in the US, in civilization," she says. But a friend, a Bolshoi ballerina, "knew a little bit" and "always wanted to get out. So I thought about my children." Mike had been lucky to go to school at all. "I got amazing results in physics," he says. "You had to be many levels above average compared to non-Jews. I felt gifted but I knew I could not use it. I was set for mediocrity." Their Soviet passports made their status clear. "They said nationality: Jewish."

Semyon Friedman, who bought apartment 6G for almost $3.5 million, can still remember his evacuation to Kazakhstan in a cattle car during World War II. German planes attacked it. Afterward, he moved to Kiev, where Semyon's extended family lived in a damp, two-chamber basement with holes cut in its wall for air, sleeping on the floor together.

In 1948, Friedman's father was sent to the gulag, a Siberian labor camp, "for nothing," as best as his son could tell, and his mother, a seamstress, supported the family, in part by doing "what was considered a crime," he says, "buying kilos of black pepper, packaging it in the evenings, and selling it at a Sunday market." That won her ten years in the gulag in southern Ukraine for the crime of speculation. So at age fourteen, Semyon had to get a job in an electrical shop by day, but he spent his nights in school. "Then, thank God, Stalin died," he says. His parents returned, and miraculously, Semyon was allowed to enroll in a technical institute near Rostov-on-Don, where he studied chemical engineering. Graduating fourth in his class, he should have gone on to a PhD program, but as a Jew he was denied entry. Instead, he had to take a three-year job wherever the government sent him. He was glad to get an assignment to a chemical plant making synthetic fiber in a Moscow suburb.

His second year at the factory saw him elected chief of a group of young engineers, infuriating their boss, who expelled him, allowing a return to Kiev, where a friend arranged a similar job at another chemical factory, but the KGB man who ran its personnel department refused to hire him until the chief of engineers insisted—and then made him a manager. He met his wife, Janna, a professor of biology and chemistry, worked for his PhD at night, wrote a thesis on chemical filtration, was promoted to chief of the factory's research lab, and finally, through Janna's father, who had an influential job at a political institute, was appointed a professor at Kiev Polytechnic. "It was the time of the '67 war [between Israel and its Arab neighbors], a bad time for Jews," he says, "but I was accepted because I was a worker."

Janna's mother had been a music teacher in Kiev until 1953, when "the Jews were all fired from the school," Janna says. Nonetheless, Janna followed in her mother's footsteps. Only one Jew was allowed to study music each year at their local high school, and Janna won that slot, then another for the one Jew allowed into the best music conservatory in Ukraine. "I was very lucky," she says. "A great Jewish conductor lived in Kiev and he got to choose one student."

They know that under the circumstances, they had a charmed life. "We had respect," says Janna, "we had a car." But still, she wanted to leave. "We are good parents and everywhere it was 'No Jews.'" Semyon disagreed, but Janna kept arguing they had to go. They had friends in Israel and arranged to be invited there, a necessary condition for an exit visa. But that invitation, though repeatedly sent to them, never arrived. Finally, a friend managed to slip it into a diplomatic envelope. "We hid it until we started to breathe again," Semyon recalls. "A couple of months." His department head begged him to stay. "Guarantee my son can study here and I will," Semyon replied. "Go," his boss answered glumly.

Finally, the Friedmans got permission to leave—and followed a well-worn path. Semyon went first and Janna followed with their children. They took a train to the Ukraine border with what was then Czechoslovakia, where it was known that the midnight stop would last only fifteen minutes. So before reaching the border, the passengers organized teams to pull luggage out windows. Then, the departniks queued up in lines that lasted three days as all were carefully searched. "They were looking for gold," says Semyon. From Bratislava they went to Vienna, where they were meant to continue to Israel, but that was only a pretense for many, who dreamed only of America. For the Freidmans, that meant a turn to Rome and then on to Baltimore, where they had relatives.

Mike and Faina Tsinberg followed a similar path, despite his fear that his scientific background would cause the Soviets to keep them imprisoned. Fortunately, Soviet computer systems were rudimentary at best and couldn't talk to each other, or so Mike suspects. "Our file surfaced on some bureaucrat's desk, and my wife has a lovely smile and she smiled and it worked," he says. Next stop, Vienna, allegedly en route to Israel, but instead they spent a few weeks in Rome and arrived in New York with their ten-year-old and "not a word of English," Mike says. "A Jewish agency supported us, but wanted us to work," so he got a minimum-wage job repairing security cameras while learning English, commuting from Washington Heights atop Manhattan to far-off Princeton, New Jersey, and repairing TVs on the side. Their daughter's first American birthday was celebrated on a table made of a door laid across two suitcases and covered with a bedsheet. But once he learned enough English to write a résumé, he got an $18,000-a-year engineering job. "I thought I was the richest man in the world!"

Janna and Semyon Friedman learned English, too; she opened a music school for the growing Russian Jewish community in Baltimore, and Semyon became the first Russian to teach at Johns Hopkins University. But just as the local Russian community had helped them, he felt drawn to help those who followed. "At the time, only one hospital in Baltimore would accept immigrants," he says, "and nobody spoke Russian." A Russian doctor who'd won a license to practice begged him to help her set up a clinic. A lawyer whose children studied music with Janna did the paperwork. The Friedmans' children handled billing. By 1995, the clinic was so busy, Semyon quit teaching to run it and then opened more. Today, he owns a chain of fifty clinics in Maryland and Virginia.

After several years in the Connecticut suburbs, Mike and Faina Tsinberg set two new goals in 1983: to move to New York City and to find Mike a job with better opportunities. Philips Research offered him the latter, and they managed the former, barely, when they rented a house on the northernmost street in the Bronx neighborhood of Riverdale. Philips, the Dutch electronics company, was running scared; Japanese manufacturers dominated their field. Mike's group was charged with inventing a new standard for better television. His suggestions led to a job as senior research manager, and for six years "I invented like no tomorrow," he says, winning more than thirty patents as he, effectively, invented high-definition digital TV.

In 1990, he was poached by Toshiba, which had a joint venture with Warner Bros. and "had to invent something," Tsinberg says, "to justify the investment." A researcher in his new lab had found a replacement for the videotape, recording a two-hour movie on a CD-size disc. "It wasn't totally my idea," says Tsinberg. "I was part-engineer, part-businessman," but he created and ran the research group that invented the DVD and DVD players, helped broker a deal with Sony and Philips to ensure a single standard, and launched what became the most successful new electronic format in history in 1993.

"I was forty-four, and I asked myself, 'What next?'" says Tsinberg. "I'd made economic success for others. Maybe I could do it for myself. If I'd been born here, maybe I would have thought of that earlier." While still working at Toshiba, he founded a new company, Key Digital, to create theatrical equipment for retailers, restaurants, and bars, digital signs for public spaces, home theaters, and, most recently, digital home-appliance-control centers.

Their successes led both the Tsinbergs and the Friedmans to the "open door" of Fifteen Central Park West, Mike says of his move to the heart of Manhattan. "We belong here, in this atmosphere," says Faina, sitting in the lobby library one afternoon. "We adapted to this very quickly. Everyone says hello. You never see snobs. The people are very, very rich, but you never feel it. A lot of rich people don't understand other people. Some Russians, they're like princes, like gods. We came here with three hundred and fifty dollars, five suitcases, and a daughter, so I appreciate everything."

"It's difficult not to lose your humanity, especially in Russia, where you can go from zero to billions in a short time," says Mike, "and not always based on talent. We have an advantage. We understand every detail of what we have. We built it, brick by brick. We went from the Soviet Union to the most prominent building in New York, and it was all created by ourselves. Yes, we have talent. But America accepted us."

Janna and Semyon Friedman improved their living standard, too, over their years in Baltimore, moving twice to better homes as their children went to college. After getting degrees in law and business, their son even went to work for Goldman Sachs and began to agitate for his parents to move to New York City. He sent them condo marketing brochures, but not until they walked by the 15CPW lot and saw the sign on the fence did they find what they were looking for. "It was the only two-bedroom with a terrace," says Semyon. "We had no time to consider" and paid a deposit. Though they still commute to Baltimore for work, they began to split their time between the two cities.

Semyon enjoys the fact that, since they sold their penthouse, Sandy and Joan Weill often sleep next door in what had been their staff apartment. "I meet Lloyd Blankfein in the gym all the time," he adds. After Blankfein's appearance before a Senate committee, Friedman told the Goldman Sachs boss he worried for him. "Don't worry," Blankfein said, laughing.

Janna used to worry, but no longer. "I suffered here," she says. "I couldn't understand. I couldn't drive. It made no sense for us but I thought differently for my children, and step by step, life changed. In the Soviet Union, I thought I had a life. Here is a richer life. I enjoy life more. When I left, I thought it was only for the children, but that wasn't correct. I did it for myself, also. I was never religious, but when I see what happened, I think, there is a God."

Some people think that at the right address confers prestige. Some would say Fifteen Central Park West is different, that it's an address made by names—Sting and Denzel, Weill and Blankfein, Och and Loeb, Kogan and Rybolovlev—and the fame and giant bank accounts attached to them. But the Friedmans and the Tsinbergs, despite their patrimony, their relative anonymity, and the location of their apartments in the lower rear of Fifteen's tower, may be the soul of the building. They are proof that you need neither billions nor a big name to make an apartment house a home. Proof, too, that New York remains America's melting pot. And that America, for all its flaws, is still big enough to embrace the world.

Epilogue

A Place of One's Own

*Money can't buy happiness, but it can make you awfully
comfortable while you're being miserable.*

—CLARE BOOTHE LUCE

Eyal Ofer and the Zeckendorf brothers announced their next project together late in 2012, a forty-four-story condo tower near the United Nations designed by Sir Norman Foster. The trio had recently begun selling condos on Gramercy Park and were proceeding with plans to build on the East Sixtieth Street property that drew them together. Goldman Sachs was no longer their partner.

Goldman's Whitehall real estate funds hit a wall in the financial crisis of 2008, leading to billion-dollar losses—and their closure. But the long-simmering tension between the 15CPW partners came to a head two years earlier, just after Lloyd Blankfein took the top job at Goldman Sachs in spring 2006 and the house building, where he'd reserved a duplex, was topped off that summer. That's when Lloyd and Laura Blankfein's architect made a series of requests that led the Zeckendorfs to worry they might all end up in court.

"I think her architect set it off," says someone inside Goldman Sachs. Alex Antonelli, that architect, rejected Robert A. M. Stern's floor plan. "I was able to show the Blankfeins how much better it could be by rearranging the staircase, the dining room, and the living room," he says. Blankfein didn't like the idea, "but Laura agreed and she was the saving grace. I think she respected me for standing my ground." So Antonelli met with the developers, who were "clearly giving my client more attention than they would have any other purchaser," he says, but though the Zeckendorfs agreed to most of his requests, they said he couldn't move a structural wall that separated the apartment entrance from the kitchen.

"I don't know that the Blankfeins expected that," says the Goldman insider, "but when they were told the building wouldn't let them do something, they probably asked why and said, 'Push it.' The Zeckendorfs got their backs up because the architect, in his zeal to get what he and the client wanted, played every card he could. Very early on, the Zeckendorfs got a chip on their shoulders with respect to that. They're quirky little guys who want to feel like equals, and when they don't feel they are, even if they are, it caused not a butting of heads, but a less-than-friendly demeanor."

The conversation around the partnership table took a bad turn. "They were all pains in the ass, between their wives and their lawyers," says a Zeckendorf insider. "Every deal was tough. A lot of jockeying went on. But Lloyd's apartment was a big to-do, a series of requests, each petty on its own, but cumulatively, they were enormous in number and scope." Moving that wall "couldn't be done without impacting other units and causing delays and possibly extra charges from the general contractor. They would have said 'Screw you' to anyone else but they tried to accommodate them." Finally, the Zeckendorfs tried to contact the Blankfeins directly, but they were "walled off. It was frustrating, difficult, and driven by the wife." Blankfein appeared to do nothing to curb her.

Laura Blankfein's sense of entitlement would soon get unwanted public exposure. In 2009, the day after Blankfein asked Goldman's employees to "avoid making big-ticket, high-profile purchases" in a bad economy, Laura tried to scream her way into a charity event ahead of other ticket holders. Page Six quoted her complaining that she shouldn't have to wait with "people who spend less money than me." Blankfein would later defend her. "Even the Mafia leaves wives alone," he said. But the Mafia doesn't let wives negotiate, either.

"Whatever we did from then on was never enough for her," says the Zeckendorf insider. "It was not a good situation." A conciliatory letter to Lloyd and Laura was drafted, but never sent. Instead, the Zeckendorfs appealed to the city's best-wired real estate lawyer, Jonathan Mechanic, whose firm represented the Blankfeins. Mechanic calmed things down, but ill feelings persist, at least in the Zeckendorf camp.

The Blankfeins won't comment, but someone who knows their thinking says they blame their architect for being pushy. They knew nothing about it then and recall even less now. Which is the sort of nonanswer one expects from someone with experience testifying before Congress.

It's convenient that the apartment that Goldman Sachs's first family chose is in the building's A-line, a block away from Arthur Zeckendorf. Arthur considers the building "a life achievement," he says. "It'll be hard to achieve that again. I take great enjoyment and pride living in a property we built."

His brother, it would soon emerge, wanted something quite opposite: a classic Park Avenue cooperative. "I did not want to live in a building I codeveloped," he says. "If a doorman is not at his post, I get angry. I take it personally. I kept going back" to the half-floor penthouse he'd reserved "after it opened and I could just never relax."

After a decade in his father's Park Belvedere, Will and his family had moved to the Majestic, a co-op since 1955, where he lived while building 15CPW. But he'd always wanted to live at 740 Park, the building his grandfather had owned for an eye-blink back in the 1950s. In spring 2010, he heard of a whisper listing (an informal listing not recorded in shared broker databases) for the very apartment once owned by the Hearst lawyer Clarence Shearn and then the fashionable heiress Thelma Chrysler Foy, which his grandfather had tried to buy after he had helped John D. Rockefeller Jr. turn 740 into a co-op. But just after Will went to see it, the owner pulled it off the market and "I didn't want to wait around forever," he says, so Will put his Fifteen penthouse on the market, and sold it to Min Kao, the Taiwanese billionaire cofounder of Garmin, the GPS navigation system, who paid $40 million for the empty forty-first-floor aerie, setting a record of $10,259 per square foot, by that measure the most expensive property ever sold. Will's profit was $29 million. But attaining that astonishing price per square foot might have been even more satisfying.

"You can't go to another new condo, a building you *haven't* built, from Fifteen," he continues. "That leaves you in the prewar category." At the end of 2010, Will managed to snare a prewar trophy, an eleventh-floor duplex at 927 Fifth Avenue, paying the estate of the investment banker Bruce Wasserstein, who'd owned it, just over $29 million for it. But the next summer, he flipped it—after only a week on the market—for more than $34 million. Real estate gossips asked why. It turned out the Shearn-Foy apartment was back on the market. "I had a tumultuous weekend," Will says. "I had to decide." Why did he want 740? "I just knew it. Leaving Fifteen wasn't easy, but 740 is special in another way. And three terraces are hard to beat." He bought it in November 2011 for $27 million.

Will had not only renounced his own building and his brother's life achievement, he'd chosen to live in one of the originals upon which 15CPW was modeled. And he'd chosen a co-op and was moving east, back to the old ways. He'd gotten a good deal, too, thanks to the rise of the luxury condo: a huge trophy apartment at a great address for far less per square foot than Fifteen then commanded. And he still had plenty of pocket change left to decorate.

Like any smart co-op owner, Will politely resists discussing his new apartment or any connection it might have to his grandfather and the rest of his tangled family history. He's bucking the tide "a little bit," he admits, a boat against the current he created himself, but he refuses the notion he's backsliding into the past.

"Arthur and I are both pretty good at looking forward, not back," he says. "Fifteen bucked the tide, too."

ACKNOWLEDGMENTS

In 2006, I was deep into writing a book about the Metropolitan Museum of Art when I got a phone call from Richard Rubenstein, a public relations man for Will and Arthur Zeckendorf, the brothers who built Fifteen Central Park West. He asked if I'd be interested in writing an authorized book about the building, which was then beginning to rise. With my plate full, and a disinclination to write an "authorized" book I wouldn't control, I declined. A few months later, though, Peter Kaplan, then editor of the *New York Observer*, asked me to profile the building and its developers, and I accepted. I already had a working connection to the Zeckendorfs: their grandfather is a vital character in my first book on a luxury apartment house in New York, *740 Park*, and would also pop up in a later book about Los Angeles. I'd also moved just around the corner from 15CPW, albeit into a century-old cooperative apartment house. Then, in 2011, Dan Strone, my agent at Trident Media Group, suggested I write about Fifteen, and the stars had aligned. Dan brought the idea to Leslie Meredith, my editor at Atria Books. I'm indebted to Richard and Dan for the idea, to Peter for my ride up the hoist at Fifteen, and to Leslie, for whom I am grateful every day. Thanks, too, to Leslie's associate Donna Loffredo, to Martha Levin, and at Atria, to the president and publisher Judith Curr; jacket director Jeanne Lee; the unbelievably patient Lisa Keim, VP director of subsidiary rights; production editor Laura Wise; Dan Strone's assistant, Kseniya Zaslavskaya; Paul Olewski and Bobbilyn Jones on Atria's publicity team; and

Diane Mancher at One Potato Productions. I feel blessed to have worked with each of you.

I am also deeply grateful to Will and Arthur, who agreed to cooperate with an independent book. They not only gave me their trust but countless hours of their time, stayed out of the way when I was researching the parts of the book they felt unable to help with, and reacted with good humor when I came to them with matters they likely wished I hadn't discovered and questions they wished I hadn't asked. They also introduced me to their partner Eyal Ofer, the principal and chairman of Global Holdings, a private, US-based real estate holding company specializing in large-scale commercial development, and the president of its New York subsidiary, Samuel Kellner, who were equally open and accommodating. None of them asked to approve what I wrote about them, and the opportunity to tell this story with complete access to its principals and without obstruction when enterprise reporting was called for was unique in my experience. The Zeckendorfs' decision to not only allow but encourage this book still boggles me as much as it has delighted me. It would not, could not, exist as it is without them. Thanks also to Will and Arthur's father, William Zeckendorf Jr.; his wife, Nancy; and his sister, Susan.

It wasn't strictly necessary to gain the cooperation of the executives at Goldman Sachs who were also key characters in the story, but it was desirable. What was necessary was patience. I especially recall the day I peppered Goldman Sachs with phone calls unaware (as I'd gone to work without reading the newspaper that morning) that one of its employees had resigned from the bank using an op-ed piece in the *New York Times* as his kiss-off. Many months went by before Andrea Raphael, a managing director of the investment bank, got me the interviews I'd hoped for, but eventually she did. So thanks to her, and to Stuart Rothenberg, Alan Kava, and Jerry Karr, and also to their predecessors at Goldman, Dan Neidich and Ralph

Rosenberg (and Tina Buyea in Ralph's office). All were (or seemed) open and candid in describing the usually secretive bank's vital role in the story—and like the Zeckendorfs were sophisticated enough to understand that my account would not be hagiography. Thanks also to the major Manhattan real estate players who helped me, especially John Avlon and Bob Konopka, but also Earle and Bill Mack, Ben and Henry Lambert, Joanna Rose of the Related Company, Phil Aarons at Millennium Partners, Miki Naftali, and Donald Trump (and Rhona Graff in his office).

Architecture is as vital to this story as finance. At Robert A. M. Stern, thanks to Stern himself, to Paul Whalen, Peter Morris Dixon, and Christian Rizzo. At SLCE, thanks to Jim Davidson and Peter Claman. Thanks also to Costas Kondylis and Margaret Clare Norton, Rafael Pelli, and Jim Polshek.

For twenty years, my books have occupied the intersection of public and private lives, a delicate position, to be sure, so it was with considerable trepidation that I picked up the phone to call the supporting cast in this story, the owners and residents of 15CPW apartments. But many of them understood and supported what I hoped to do, and some were even willing to help. Some of those allowed me to quote them by name; others agreed to speak to me only if I didn't acknowledge that I had. I interviewed several dozen residents of the building and visited more than half a dozen apartments. I thank all those who are quoted by name in the preceding pages, the anonymous others, and also those who didn't contribute but agreed to check facts. And I apologize to the residents of the building who do not appear in the text, though some no doubt prefer it that way.

As I interviewed one resident, an envelope appeared under his door. Later, he called to tell me it was from Fifteen's condo board—warning residents that I was prowling the building, seeking information. But instead of asking them not to cooperate, the board merely noted that scrutiny came with the territory and left it up to residents to decide for themselves how to deal with me. Some did and some didn't, some were nice, a few were not, and only one sicced a lawyer on me. So I thank Jeffrey Walker, the condo's president, for that measured missive, and for his good humor when I called him. And I thank those who were kind, even if they chose caution over cooperation. But just in case there is any lingering unhappiness, I will not name the other residents who invited me into their homes, took me on tours of Fifteen, and even treated me to lunch in the restaurant, but I am grateful to them, too. To those few who snarled and snapped, all I can say is, if you don't like attention, you probably shouldn't buy or rent a trophy apartment in the media capital of the world.

The building staff, on the other hand, was warned not to speak to me, yet several employees, both current and former, did. So thanks to Pasco Cornejo, who didn't care if I quoted him by name, and to the others who asked to remain anonymous for the sake of their present and future employment. Your perspective on the building and its occupants was invaluable. I also thank the other staff members, who were invariably gracious to me when I visited Fifteen, even as I wondered if my picture was posted behind the concierge desks.

I'm often asked how I identify and find the people who live in buildings like Fifteen (and "How did you get my phone number? It's unlisted!"). My jocular answer is, invariably, that's why I get paid the medium-size bucks. But the truth is, it's a matter of good sources, hard work, and some luck, digging through press reports, deeds, mortgages, voter registrations, and other public records, cross-referencing names and addresses, and then picking up the phone in hope of gaining confirmation. I do that myself, but I also depend on researchers, most of them present or former journalism students. They may not know it, but they inspire me as well as help me do my job. So thanks to Alex Cacioppo, Alessia Pirolo, and Makkadah Saleh, who did most of the grunt work, and to Ann Ellwood, Yuyu

Chen, Kristi Goldade, Chantel Tattoli, Katy Olsen, Marusca Niccolini, Dayna Clark, and Bilal Khan. Also, thanks to Dasha Boudnik, who translated Russian for me, and to David Hyun Kim, who helped me understand the romanization of Asian names.

Thanks also to journalists Stefanie Cohen, Jennifer Gould Keil, Max Gross, and Andy Wang at the *New York Post*; Lockhart Steele and Sara Polsky at *Curbed*; Christopher Gray of the Office of Metropolitan History; Roberta Gratz; Dana Thomas; the late Ada Louise Huxtable; David Patrick Columbia of *New York Social Diary*; Laura Gatea at *PropertyShark*; Taki Theodoracopulos; John Avlon of the *Daily Beast*; Amanda Cantrell at *Absolute Return*; and Joey Arak, the founding editor of *Curbed*, for their help and kindness. I am particularly grateful to William D. Cohan, both for his financial oversight and for his unpublished interview with Erin Callan. Anyone interested in more on Goldman Sachs should read his book *Money and Power*.

A number of attorneys also gave advice and assistance. Thanks to Elliot Meisel, my consigliere for all things real estate related, Judd Burstein, Jeffrey Horwitz, Patricia Cardi, Edward Mermelstein, J. Joseph Jacobsen, Michael Grabow, Jeffrey Mutterperl, David Newman, and Steven Singer.

Thanks also to Kathryn Hanes and Ajay Kapur at Deutsche Bank; Alan Segan and Gabrielle Berman of Rubenstein Public Relations; Steven Rubenstein of Howard Rubenstein PR; Todd Alhart at GE Global Research; Anna Kadysheva; Annalise Carol and B. Jay Cooper at APCO; Asher Edelman; Dr. Octo Barnett; Katie Marquedant; Bill Hooper at Time Inc.; Fredrika Low at Cornell University; Adam Friefield at NBC Sports; Ian Smith in Lyn Lear's office; Tiffany Haynes in Norman Lear's office; Jeffrey Sventek at ASMA; John Bickford and Debbie Hunsucker at Jeff Gordon, Inc.; Kate Wood and Arlene Simon at Landmarks West; Ken Frydman; Doug Blonsky; Lisa Castro; Michele Davis; Paul Gunther; Ellen West at Google; Rena Resnick; Steven Sandoval at Los Alamos;

Kate O'Brien Ahlers in New York's Department of Law and Cheryl Leon in its Department of Buildings; Nurit Gal Reches; Margaret Hoover; Duffe Elkins at the Indiana Limestone Company; and Mary Hedge at the MTA, for helping me find information I needed.

Also from the real estate community, thanks to Karen Duncan and Marlene Marcus of the 15CPW sales office, Judith Kessler, Patricia Garza, Carol Lamberg, Martha Kramer, Robby Browne, John Burger, Elizabeth Stribling, Pamela Liebman, Felicé Donatiello, Emily Beare, Haidee Granger, Howard Morrell, Suzanne Howard, Richard Wagman, Victor MacFarlane, Susan de França, Joanna Cutler, Maria Pashby, Ken Deutsch, Nora Arrifin, John Dyson and Meghan Haskins at Millbrook Capital Management, Donna Olshan, Larry Kaiser, Jonathan Miller, and Alice Mason.

Several of my professional colleagues were understanding about my need to sometimes put this book ahead of other work: thanks to Xana Antunes and Glenn Coleman of *Crain's New York Business*; Richard Burns, Daisy Prince, William Pecover, Randi Schatz, Haley Friedlich, and Tom and Janet Allon at *Avenue* magazine; and Gabe Doppelt, Lucas Wittmann, and Justine Rosenthal at *Newsweek/Daily Beast*. I'm also grateful to Linda Buckley at Tiffany & Co., even if the good ship *Charles* never managed to set sail, and to John Benditt, Laurie Kratochvil, Robb Rice, and Susan Murcko, who all know why.

And thanks most of all to my wonderful friends Lavinia Snyder, Roy Kean, Barry Kieselstein-Cord, David Netto, Andrew Alpern, Michael and Patricia Jean, Pierre Crosby, Sheila Weller, and Kee Tan, and to my wife, Barbara Hodes, all of whom have always been there when I needed them and understood when I said, "Can't talk to you now."

SELECTED BIBLIOGRAPHY

Ahuja, Maneet. *The Alpha Masters*. Hoboken, NJ: John Wiley, 2012.

Alpern, Andrew. *New York's Fabulous Luxury Apartments*. New York: Dover Publications, 1987.

———. *Luxury Apartment Houses of Manhattan*. New York: Dover Publications, 1992.

———. *Historic Manhattan Apartment Houses*. New York: Dover Publications, 1996.

———. *The New York Apartment Houses of Rosario Candela and James Carpenter*. New York: Acanthus, 2002.

Alpern, Andrew, and Seymour Durst. *Holdouts! The Buildings That Got in the Way*. New York: David R. Godine, 2011.

Birmingham, Stephen. *Life at the Dakota: New York's Most Unusual Address*. New York: Random House, 1979.

Brooks, John. *The Go-Go Years*. New York: John Wiley, 1973.

Burnham, Alan, ed. *New York Landmarks*. Middletown, CT: Wesleyan University, 1963.

Cohan, William D. *House of Cards: A Tale of Hubris and Wretched Excess on Wall Street*. New York: Doubleday, 2009.

———. *Money and Power: How Goldman Sachs Came to Rule the World*. New York: Doubleday, 2011.

Ehrlich, Judith Ramsey, and Barry J. Rehfeld. *The New Crowd: The Changing of the Jewish Guard on Wall Street*. New York: Little, Brown, 1989.

Fitzgerald, F. Scott. *The Short Stories*. New York: Scribner Classics, 1989.

The Guilds Committee for Federal Writers' Project. *The WPA Guide to New York City*. New York: Pantheon, 1982.

Heckscher, Morrison H. *Creating Central Park*. New York: Metropolitan Museum of Art Bulletin, 2008.

Homberger, Eric. *Mrs. Astor's New York: Money and Social Power in a Gilded Age*. New Haven, CT: Yale University, 2002.

Jackson, Kenneth T., ed. *The Encyclopedia of New York*. New Haven, CT: Yale University, 1995.

King, Moses. *King's Views of New York and Brooklyn: 1896–1915*. New York: Benjamin Blom, 1974.

Lockwood, Charles. *Bricks and Brownstone: The New York Row House, 1783–1929*. New York: Abbeville Press, 1972.

Lurie, Ranan R. *The Cartoonist's Double Mask*. Manuscript in preparation.

Lyons, Bettina O'Neil. *Zeckendorfs and Steinfelds: Merchant Princes of the American Southwest*. Tucson: Arizona Historical Society, 2008.

Mallaby, Sebastian. *More Money Than God*. New York: Penguin, 2010.

Morr, Jonathan. *Perry Ellis*. New York: St. Martin's, 1988.

Morris, Lloyd. *Incredible New York: High Life and Low Life of the Last Hundred Years*. New York: Random House, 1951.

Mott, Hopper Stryker. *The New York of Yesterday: A Descriptive Narrative of Old Bloomingdale*. New York: G. P. Putnam's and Sons, 1908.

Phillips, Kevin. *Wealth and Democracy: A Political History of the American Rich*. New York: Broadway Books, 2002.

Reich, Cary. *Rockefeller: The Life of Nelson A. Rockefeller: Worlds to Conquer, 1908–1958*. New York: Doubleday, 1996.

Rochlin, Harriet, and Fred Rochlin. *Pioneer Jews: A New Life in the Far West*. Boston: Houghton Mifflin, 1984.

Rosenzweig, Roy, and Elizabeth Blackmar. *The Park and the People: A History of Central Park*. Ithaca: Cornell University, 1992.

Ruttenbaum, Steven. *Mansions in the Clouds: The Skyscraper Palazzi of Emery Roth*. New York: Balsam Press, 1986.

Sabbagh, Karl. *Skyscraper: The Making of a Building*. New York: Viking, 1989.

Salwen, Peter. *Upper West Side Story: A History and Guide*. New York: Abbeville, 1989.

Shachtman, Tom. *Skyscraper Dreams: The Great Real Estate Dynasties of New York*. New York: Little, Brown, 1991.

Sorkin, Andrew Ross. *Too Big to Fail*. New York: Penguin, 2009.

Stern, Robert A. M., Gregory Gilmartin, and John Massengale. *New York 1900: Metropolitan Architecture and Urbanism, 1890–1915*. New York: Monacelli Press, 1983.

Stern, Robert A. M., Gregory Gilmartin, and Thomas Mellins. *New York 1930: Architecture and Urbanism Between the Two World Wars*. New York: Monacelli Press, 1987.

Stern, Robert A. M., Thomas Mellins, and David Fishman. *New York 1880: Architecture and Urbanism in the Gilded Age*. New York: Monacelli Press, 1999.

Trager, James. *West of Fifth: The Rise and Fall and Rise of Manhattan's West Side*. New York: Atheneum, 1987.

Trump, Donald J., with Tony Schwartz. *Trump: The Art of the Deal*. New York: Random House, 1987.

Ward, Vicky. *The Devil's Casino*. Hoboken, NJ: John Wiley & Sons, 2010.

Wharton, Edith. *Custom of the Country*. London: Everyman's Library, 1994.

Wiseman, Carter. *The Architecture of I. M. Pei*. London: Thames & Hudson, 2001.

Zeckendorf, William, with Edward McCreary. *Zeckendorf*. Chicago: Plaza Press, 1987.

INDEX

ABOUT THE AUTHOR

Michael Gross is America's "foremost chronicler of the upper crust" (*Curbed*) and author of the *New York Times* bestsellers *740 Park* and *Model: The Ugly Business of Beautiful Women*; *Unreal Estate*, the *Los Angeles Times'* bestselling social history of that city's estate district; *Rogues' Gallery*, the controversial exposé of New York's Metropolitan Museum of Art; and *Genuine Authentic: The Real Life of Ralph Lauren*. The real estate editor of *Avenue*, he's written for *Vanity Fair*, the *New York Times*, *New York*, *Departures*, *Esquire*, *GQ*, *Town & Country*, and *Newsweek*. Online, Mr. Gross writes his own blog, *Gripepad*, and has contributed to *Gawker*, *Curbed*, the *Huffington Post* and the *Daily Beast*.